MULTICULTURAL TEACHING IN THE UNIVERSITY

Multicultural Teaching in the University

Edited by
DAVID SCHOEM, LINDA FRANKEL,
XIMENA ZÚÑIGA, & EDITH A. LEWIS

 PRAEGER

Westport, Connecticut
London

Library of Congress Cataloging-in-Publication Data

Multicultural teaching in the university / edited by David Schoem . . .
  [et al.].
     p.   cm.
  Includes bibliographical references and index.
  ISBN 0–275–93852–2
  1. Intercultural education—United States.   2. Education, Higher—
United States.   I. Schoem, David Louis.
  LC1099.3.M86   1993
  370.19′341—dc20   92–16141

British Library Cataloguing in Publication Data is available.

Library of Congress Catalog Card Number: 92–16141
ISBN: 0–275–93852–2

First published in 1993

Praeger Publishers, 88 Post Road West, Westport, CT 06881
An imprint of Greenwood Publishing Group, Inc.

Printed in the United States of America

The paper used in this book complies with the
Permanent Paper Standard issued by the National
Information Standards Organization (Z39.48–1984).

10 9 8 7 6 5 4 3 2

To Our Children:

Adina

Bakari

Diego

Gregory

Javiera

Kamilah

Rachel

Shana

We wish you a life of happiness and
learning filled with the riches
of a multicultural community.

Contents

x   Contents

Acknowledgments

We wish to thank all the authors of this book for their intellectual and personal contributions to this book and to our thinking about multicultural teaching.

We would also like to thank Diana Campbell for her outstanding editorial assistance. T. Alexander Aleinikoff, Mark Chesler, and Sharon E. Sutton read an earlier draft of our introduction and offered valuable insights and suggestions for which we are most thankful. Also, we thank Biren A. (Ratnesh) Nagda for his help with the chapter on exercises and special assistance with other chapters and Gretchen Martens for her editing, indexing, and bibliographic work. John Diamond, Andy Echt, Lauren Hirsch, and Monica Johnson provided very able assistance with a wide range of tasks. We also wish to thank Anne Kiefer, Lynn Flint, and Bill Neenan of Praeger Publishers for their support of this project.

The Program on Conflict Management Alternatives of the University of Michigan gave intellectual and financial support to this project. Elizabeth Douvan was the first to suggest that we consider this project. Her conviction of its importance to university faculty and to teachers at all educational levels ultimately convinced us to carry it forward.

Finally, we wish to thank our families. The collaborative effort that is this book, with over twenty-five authors and four editors, was enormously stimulating and rewarding; it was also time-consuming. We look forward now to return to our families, friends, and community life and ease the burden that this project has placed on those around us. We thank all of you for your steadfast support.

Part I

The Meaning of Multicultural Teaching: An Introduction

David Schoem, Linda Frankel, Ximena Zúñiga, and Edith A. Lewis

This book represents part of an ongoing process among university faculty to enhance teaching and learning in an increasingly interconnected multicultural society. We view this text as a dialogue with both our authors and readers, offering possibilities and opportunities more often than answers and solutions. Our desire is to explore the meaning and practice of multicultural teaching. In doing so, we attempt to integrate new scholarship that reflects a more expansive notion of knowledge, find new ways to communicate with diverse populations of students, and join together in a new vision of the scholarly community built upon the equitable sharing of power with all members of our multicultural society.

To organize our thinking about multicultural teaching we have focused on three interconnected dimensions of multicultural teaching: content, process and discourse, and diversity of faculty and students. Implicit in our thinking about each dimension are issues of power, conflict, and change. The dimension of content refers to a broadening of the curriculum so that students and scholars are exposed to a much wider range of topics, theory, and data than would be the case in monocultural teaching. The dimension of process and discourse speaks to different ways of knowing, or ''a quality of mind,'' and it calls attention to communication, classroom dynamics, and bringing different perspectives to bear on content. The third dimension, diversity of faculty and students, refers to the representativeness of the backgrounds of those present in the classroom and the institution. We broadly characterize multiculturalism to be inclusive of groups organized according to race, ethnicity, culture, gender, sexual orientation, religion, and socioeconomic class.

Our authors bring a spirit of inclusiveness to each of these dimensions of multicultural teaching. No one, for instance, devalues Western civilization or seeks its elimination from the curriculum (despite the fears of some critics, such as Ravitch 1990); rather, our authors attempt to make students aware of Western civilization in a context that includes exploration of other sources of thought, culture, history, political and social organization, music, and art. Similarly, our authors desire students to develop thinking and communication skills that extend beyond a single perspective, point of view, or manner of discourse. Finally, our authors build upon the distinctive contributions and backgrounds, as well as the shared characteristics, of students and faculty from different cultural groups. They envision diverse representation and a diversity of ideas both in the classroom and on college curriculum committees and other policy-making bodies. Elizabeth Kamarack Minnich (1991: 6) writes: "We can find guidance in the wisdom of many individuals, cultures, traditions, bodies of knowledge, and forms of practice. It need not be us versus them, old versus new, or one versus many—not if we can exercise some of the most basic of our human capacities fully and courageously."

CURRICULAR TRANSFORMATION

The pedagogical components of multicultural teaching have been woven from many different strands—ethnic studies, feminist pedagogy, liberatory education, and interactive and experiential learning methods (Sleeter and Grant 1987). Johnella Butler (1989) stresses the importance of recognizing the connectedness of racism, sexism, classism, and ethnocentrism and also acknowledges the necessary role of implementation of the transformed curriculum through new pedagogy, texts, and administrative practice. In so doing, she joins the call for a holistic approach to multicultural transformation—reshaping content, teaching methods, and institutional practices—that many involved in similar efforts share (Minnich, O'Barr, and Rosenfeld 1988; Spanier, Bloom, and Boroviak 1984). Marilyn Schuster and Susan Van Dyne (1985) point to four elements that distinguish teaching that puts gender, race, and class at the center of attention: incorporation of students' experience, attention to the learning process, recognition of how the culture is reproduced in the classroom, and the creative use of conflict as a basis for change. Nancy Schneidewind (1990) takes the position that students learn as much from classroom process, the hidden curriculum, as they do from the overt content of the course.

Not surprisingly, there has been ongoing debate about teaching approaches since instructors began to acknowledge the importance of including content on multicultural perspectives into course curricula. Approaches have differed both across and within disciplines. For example, the accrediting organization for schools of social work, the Council on Social Work Education (CSWE), since 1972 has maintained CSWE Standard 1234A, which states (1979) that each social work course must contain content on people of color. The ways in which this standard is operationalized in teaching methods, however, differ radically from one instructor to another, even when controlling for the content of the course.

How, then, is multicultural content handled within particular courses? Transformation of the curriculum often proceeds through a series of stages, or inclusion patterns, variously described. These stages sometimes overlap and are part of an ongoing, open-ended process. Although these stages are not meant to be ranked hierarchically, nor do they necessarily follow a linear progression, they do reflect greater degrees of inclusiveness.

In the preparation of this book, we have identified different inclusion patterns that reflect the experience of our authors' multicultural teaching in their different departments. In some ways these patterns parallel the stages of curricular transformation discussed by other scholars (McIntosh 1991; Schuster and Van Dyne 1985). In the first of four stages, faculty restrict the discussion to one part of the course. In the second stage, faculty may include additional information throughout the course, but only for the reason of comparison to the dominant norm. The third stage of inclusion behavior integrates broader-based materials and critical analysis throughout the course. In the fourth stage, there is a synergy of the course content, classroom process, and diversity among faculty and students that elevates understanding to a new level of depth and complexity.

The first stage, as noted above, limits discussion of ethnic, racial, and gender differences to one lecture or section of the course, thereby "ghettoizing" the information. Although representing some degree of inclusion, this strategy is problematic. If the discussion of multicultural issues is relegated to the end of the semester, an instructor faced with time constraints may be tempted to eliminate it altogether or substitute more central course content if the class is behind. In worst cases, this allows faculty members to include topics and readings on their syllabi and draw attention to their work at the time of peer review, but sidestep the sometimes difficult task of handling the material in the classroom. In any event, even if well-intentioned, professors must be careful of the consequences of appending one article or one week's discussion to their courses without helping students to understand that work in some broader context.

Historically, there is another first-stage strategy. Most Women's Studies, African American Studies, and other ethnic studies programs and departments in universities in the United States emerged because of the lack of this content in other arenas of the university. The nurturance of scholarship and learning fostered in these autonomous departments continues to provide an important grounding for integration efforts across the curriculum.

We believe that both first-stage strategies—the lone course and the separate department—are often necessary starting points but are not in and of themselves sufficient. The first course strategy, in particular, must be viewed as a time-limited initial effort, which will be expanded within the unit. The concern of this book, however, is with "traditional" content within generalized courses in universities, not specialized courses as in this historical first wave. However, we acknowledge that women's studies and ethnic studies programs must not be undercut as we work to transform the curriculum as a whole. The strong presence of these programs provides a much-needed core of scholarship and personnel for curriculum integration on many campuses.

In the second stage, cross-cultural comparisons are made at several junctures in a course. However, these comparisons often take the theoretical or empirical perspective that the dominant group's behavior or tradition is the "norm" or the "truth," while the different behavior of women, the poor, or communities of color is contrasted as "the culturally deviant" (Allen 1978). This style of comparison is common among faculty grounded in theories not conceived or tested for their applicability to different racial, ethnic, or gender groups. In such cases, if the people do not "fit" the category, the people, not the category, are questioned.

Nevertheless, there are several possible positive consequences of comparative analysis in the classroom. For example, we can discover different notions about "what is good" by making comparisons within various cultural contexts. Some also argue for a second strategy that attempts to make equal comparisons in a cultural vacuum. A third strategy for making comparisons is to do so, acknowledging their social and political implications.

In the third stage, teachers integrate information about different cultures throughout the term by questioning the standard theories or practices as they relate to different groups within the national or international perspective guiding the overall course. In the integration stage, theories emerging from the study of women or populations of color are presented and discussed alongside others generally included in the departmental guidelines for the course. Students are encouraged to think about the political, social, and economic implications for all people and the inclusion or exclusion of this material. There is in this stage a shift away from "norms" and "truth" toward "alternatives" and "probabilities" or "truths" as the course content explores ways in which theories are differentially applicable to human behavior.

In the third stage, too, race and gender often become core organizing concepts for material processed within the classroom. Through the integration of these concepts, the works being studied reconverge into different and new modes of meaning. This new picture provides a multicultural experience that students can use as a building block for their own intellectual growth and transformation in other areas.

In the fourth stage, all the components of multicultural teaching are in place: content, process and discourse, and diversity of faculty and students. Together, they allow classroom learning to rise to a new level of understanding, one that transcends particularistic knowing (see, e.g., Chapters 1, 2, 13, and 20). These components of multicultural teaching provide for a dynamic learning environment that permits a new synthesis of understanding and analysis that is deeper and more complex.

While there is potential for department or unit recognition for each of these stages, the implications for student and faculty learning differ. Students obviously learn nothing from material that is listed on a syllabus but not taught. Teaching "ghettoized" material is a limited step forward, but one that still sends a telling message about marginality. Cross-cultural comparisons can be instructive and informative, but the danger is that too often they misinform because comparisons are made in an unequal balance, either contrasting less powerful groups with culturally bound norms based on the dominant group or holding onto theoretical "truths" for which empirical support declines as they are tested for ethnic and gender sensitivity. We believe that integration of content, together with changes in instructional processes and discourse in a classroom composed of faculty and students from diverse backgrounds, has the greatest potential for achieving a new synthesis of understanding that will inform and enrich the learning experience for both faculty and students.

ON ACADEMIC FREEDOM

Today a constructive process of reflection, debate, and exploration is occurring on many campuses; faculty members across the nation are, in a serious and scholarly manner, struggling to reshape the content and practice of their classroom teaching to expand the horizons of knowledge for all students in a way that reflects the diversity among us.

Those skeptical of innovation, however, are becoming more strident and vocal in their attacks on what they characterize as a movement for "political correctness" (p.c.). The accusation of coercion and bias contained in the "p.c." label, a rhetorical umbrella for criticism of curricular transformation and related change, is used for political gain at the highest levels of government. The national media have further exacerbated tensions by inaccurately reporting that faculty on many campuses are polarized into two antagonistic groups: those engaged in "ideologically based" multicultural efforts and those determined to defend the "neutral," traditional, Western-oriented curriculum and teaching methods.

Attempts to establish a more inclusive curriculum and teaching environment in the university do push against the barriers and limitations of the traditional academic environment and are considered a threat to historic notions of academic excellence. The idea of a multicultural university is threatening to many faculty because it forces them to acknowledge that their insights and knowledge are limited, that they have studied the world from a narrow perspective, and that even they, the supposed experts, must retool, go back to study, review their life's work, and face difficult challenges in content and pedagogy in their classrooms. It will likely mean, too, that they must share some fraction of power. It is far easier for those who feel threatened to proclaim that multiculturalism is wrong-headed, politically driven, anti-intellectual, relativistic, and counter to principles of academic freedom.

Academic freedom and freedom of speech are among the most strongly held and expressed values of the university. Today, however, they are used defensively and inaccurately by opponents of multicultural teaching to buttress the prevailing cultural norms. They are defined in such a way as to perpetuate narrow curricular and moral content in the learning environment. The rhetoric of objectivity and value-free standards of knowledge and excellence is used unfairly to attempt to make multiculturalism appear partisan, ideological, biased, and subjective.

Yet the multicultural discussion is precisely in keeping with academic freedom, academic excellence, and critical inquiry. It represents freedom to learn more and also more broadly than we have previously been permitted. It requires open questioning and speaking up in classrooms and in faculty meetings. In fact, it would be surprising to learn that most university scholars were not delighted with the possibility of revisiting existing theories, data, and ideas with broadened horizons, varied perspectives, and new insights. The editors of this collection hold strongly that the argument for academic freedom and also the best defense of academic freedom are to be found within multicultural teaching and the multicultural university.

POWER, CONFLICT, JUSTICE, AND CHANGE

As we reach beyond our separate racial and ethnic worlds to join a multicultural world, we will surely face conflict on both personal and organizational levels. We believe that we must learn to utilize conflicts with an eye toward justice, so that we move not only toward what others describe with various meanings as a multicultural society but toward a multicultural society defined and built upon a foundation of social justice.

We know that we will face conflict in a multicultural society because as individuals we have little experience with difference and as a society we are fearful of difference. Our society has led us to believe that difference is dangerous and evil and is a threat to established knowledge and status. Incidents of such conflict from universities across the country abound, as illustrated by the following examples:

- A student does "A" work on papers and exams in a class on race and gender but knowingly and intentionally makes racist comments in class discussion. The student recognizes that our academies resist any linkage between knowledge and practice.

- A class is disrupted by students not enrolled in the course who have heard through the grapevine that their own political perspective is not sufficiently represented in the course syllabus. Issues of curricular exclusion, academic freedom, and political pressure from "outsiders" uncomfortably collide.

- New programs on intergroup relations and diversity are funded on soft money. These programs endure a tenuous and marginal existence, with their staff constantly wondering what will happen when budget tightening is required.

- Harassment of gay and lesbian students increases at the same time a campus celebrates its multicultural diversity. Sexual orientation is not considered part of the discussion of multiculturalism on that campus.

- Senior white faculty object when funds for salary increases are rumored to have been diverted to hire new minority faculty. These senior faculty view such conduct as discriminatory and portray themselves as victims of reverse discrimination.

- Advocates of courses on diversity are labeled as thought-police, and instructors of those courses find themselves isolated within their departments. They are caught in the tension between the multicultural classroom and the monocultural institution.

How can we interpret these and other individual and organizational conflicts in a meaningful way? There are at least three perspectives on the meaning of multiculturalism that play a part in how we interpret and understand the conflicts.

The first perspective—and depending upon one's view, this perspective may be either the most realistic or the most cynical—argues that multiculturalism represents nothing new at all, that it is merely an attempt by the existing power structure to maintain its power. By learning about, and more fully involving itself in, subordinate groups, the dominant group is better able to manage those who are subordinate; that is, multiculturalism serves to maintain the status quo. For example, although a university hires new faculty and admits students from underrepresented groups, the traditionally dominant group remains in power, there is no change in the curriculum or reward structure, and the budget and the campus culture remain the same. In effect, there are new faces at the university, but there is no real change except at the margins. Those who subscribe to this analysis question, Why now, and only now, when groups that have been sub-ordinate for so long are increasing in numbers and power, does the existing white establishment develop a sudden interest in multiculturalism?

The second perspective states that the interest in multiculturalism represents, in fact, a new cultural particularism or balkanization—an attempt merely to shift the existing hierarchy of power from one group to another. From this perspective, the value or the danger of multiculturalism, depending on one's point of view, is that white males could be replaced by other competing groups as the dominant power brokers and decision makers; for example, an Afrocentric curriculum could replace the traditional Eurocentric curriculum. There is distrust, for ex-ample, of attempts to integrate the traditional curriculum with new ''diversity'' courses; one group fears an eventual co-opting of such courses and a delegitim-ization of Ethnic Studies and Women's Studies departments, and another group worries about the elimination of Western thought from the curriculum.

A third perspective, which the editors of this volume share, is that multicul-turalism represents an opportunity to develop and implement a new vision of society in which power and participation are shared equally and broadly and in which there is appreciation for other perspectives and respect for groups different from one's own in terms of membership, practice, process, and values. There is a commitment to ensure that institutional transformation from a monocultural university to a multicultural one will take place; that changing demographics will result in real change in the makeup of the student body, the faculty, and the administration; and that research, teaching, and the curriculum will reflect many different cultures, perspectives, and ways of knowing. It is anticipated that the "campus culture" of the scholarly community will be far more broadly representative, inclusive, and integrative; that decision making will be a shared process rather than one conducted by any elite group; and that the permanent budget will be redistributed to reflect broadened priorities and perspectives.

We recognize, too, that we cannot ignore issues of power in our attempt to define multiculturalism and understand its meaning (Chesler and Crowfoot 1990; McLeod 1984; Troyna 1987). Indeed, one of the primary challenges of multicultural education is the need to recognize that the power of the dominant culture permeates our analytic frameworks and personal expectations, diminishes our critical awareness to examine the ways people of all cultures view one another and themselves, and narrows our ability to think broadly and imaginatively. As such, we believe that the success of efforts in multicultural teaching that take place in the classroom will be measured, ultimately and necessarily, by the ability of educational institutions to change from monocultural to multicultural organizations.

MULTICULTURAL AWARENESS AND PERSONAL AND INSTITUTIONAL RESPONSIBILITY

What are the appropriate linkages between knowledge and behavior, between understanding and action? As we begin to broaden our intellectual perspectives and learn to examine our disciplines and the social world through a multicultural awareness, we are challenged to think as students, faculty, and institutions about the intellectual and personal responsibilities arising from our new insights.

The traditional approach in the academy is to separate practice from knowing. The most common case is that of a faculty member who, for instance, conducts research and teaches in the area of race relations but is not necessarily sensitive to students from different racial backgrounds. In a similar fashion, the university may make an institutional commitment to recruit faculty from historically underrepresented groups but make no other attempt to become a multicultural institution in terms of culture, values, and ideology.

In the case of the faculty member, one might well argue that no one would expect faculty in clinical psychology to be automatically exempt from mental health problems or expect all faculty in economics to have their personal finances in order. Similarly, there is little institutional concern that faculty members in natural resources might not recycle or that professors who teach about the family will necessarily maintain close family relations. In fact, institutional concern or interest in these situations would be considered an intrusion on personal freedom.

But we do not think that the implications of these kinds of inconsistency or lack of congruence are directly equivalent to a disjuncture between knowledge and action in a multicultural context. This is so because our concern is with behavior in the classroom and other campus settings where interpersonal dynamics have a deep impact on educational outcomes.

Interestingly, such standards are sometimes applied differentially with regard to students, so that a student who studies stereotyping in class and performs well on papers and exams on the topic, thus indicating an understanding of such, is likely to be considered insensitive if he stereotypes his peers in the classroom according to racial or gender categories during class discussions. But judging the behavior of students means less if those in authority are not held to the same standards of behavior.

In proposing the linkage between knowledge and behavior, we do not suggest specific patterns of behavior or actions that should automatically follow particular understandings. What we do argue, however, is that the linkage should be considered—that personal and institutional reflection about personal, social, and organizational knowledge and action is a part of multicultural teaching.

We believe that faculty members should reflect upon their personal actions and speech in their classes in light of their awareness of race relations; that the university, in particular, should reflect upon its own organizational culture as it recruits people of different cultures to populate it; and that students should reconsider personal behavior on campus in light of their academic studies.

WHAT TO EXPECT FROM THIS BOOK

The writing of this book has served as a catalyst for bringing faculty and staff members together to share their successes and frustrations in multicultural teaching. The contributors to this volume see themselves as part of an emergent community in which strategies and questions can be openly shared and creatively addressed. The strategies discussed reflect both individual initiatives and attempts to form broader-based support networks for the institutionalization of multicultural teaching.

At a roundtable discussion attended by several of the contributors (see Part Six), our authors discussed their own approaches to thinking about the meaning of multiculturalism, both sharing and questioning assumptions, emphases, overarching goals, and priorities. In this discussion our authors (1) stress an inclusive definition for the meaning of ''culture'' within multiculturalism, (2) explore transformation of content, issues of process, discourse and thinking, (3) insist upon the foundation of multiculturalism within issues of justice and equity, (4) try to locate the relationship between knowledge and practice, and (5) manifest a stirring commitment to teaching.

The chapters in this book articulate multiple dimensions and components of multicultural teaching. Rather than representing a homogeneous view of multicultural teaching, these chapters reflect the debate and dialogue that surround this endeavor. However, we believe that they help us to assemble a more nuanced portrait of what faculty members who do this kind of teaching feel is significant about their efforts.

Our authors were guided by a set of orienting questions about who teaches what, to whom, and how, in a multicultural context.[1] In response, the contributors discuss in their chapters the aims, strategies, hopes, risks, and rewards that underlie their classroom experiences.

As illustrated by our authors, choice of content and organization of materials can include a number of orienting strategies or goals. Some are related to issues of power and empowerment, such as putting the excluded at the center (Edwards, Myers, and Toy; Larimore; Moya-Raggio; Myers; Story; Wong), offering a critique of white cultural hegemony (Bryant), and educating students about the struggle for basic human rights regardless of gender, race, or class (Sutton). Others emphasize the importance for student learning of diversity in the curriculum and the classroom (Aleinikoff; Butter and Siefert; Douvan and Veroff; Frankel; Gerschick; Lewis; Schoem; Zúñiga and Nagda).

There are authors who structure the learning environment to address issues of conflict (Aleinikoff; Frankel; Gerschick; Lewis; Myers; Schoem; Sfeir-Younis; Zúñiga and Chesler). Still others focus on different ways of knowing and individual and group learning styles (Aliaga; Bryant; Butter and Siefert; Douvan and Veroff; Edwards, Myers, and Toy; Kleinsmith; Lewis; Myers; Schoem; Sfeir-Younis; Sutton; Wong; Zúñiga and Nagda; Ortega et al.). Finally, some of the authors discuss institutional, departmental, and individual faculty and student resistance to their efforts to do multicultural teaching (Aleinikoff; Bryant; Butter and Siefert; Edwards, Myers, and Toy; Larimore; Lewis; Moya-Raggio; Myers; Schoem; Sfeir-Younis; Story; Sutton, Wong).

Our primary focus, clearly, is on teaching, not theory, yet we have tried to provide a context in which to think about multicultural teaching. We have tried, too, in this chapter, to clarify for readers our own thinking on some issues about multicultural teaching. In addition, we have attempted in a variety of ways to reflect in the presentation of this book our thinking about multiculturalism. We offer different approaches to multicultural teaching in the many classroom chapters of our authors. We have organized those chapters into separate sections that emphasize (1) an intergroup framework, (2) particularistic issues and the interplay of various "isms," (3) transformation and integration of the traditional curriculum, and (4) education outside the classroom and preparation of teachers for multicultural teaching. We also attempt to make the discussion accessible via different paths to understanding, including the roundtable discussion, the questions and responses, and the chapter on classroom and workshop exercises. In doing so, we recognize that the contributions do not represent all of the various ethnic groups of color present even in our university setting. We have attempted to add a dimension of self-criticism and ongoing exploration throughout, noting in this chapter, the chapter of questions and responses, and particularly the roundtable discussion, our openness to the multiplicity of new and opposing ideas and approaches to this topic.

We emphasize again that we view this book as a form of dialogue with our authors and readers. It is a completed book, yet still in progress, offering models, ideas, and issues that we expect to be helpful, insightful, and enlightening as well as debated and improved upon. We ourselves have learned enormously and continuously as we have read our authors' chapters, talked and consulted with them, and discussed issues among ourselves.

In closing, we wish you, our readers, great success in your own efforts at multicultural teaching and hope that this book provides useful assistance. We welcome you to join us in this dialogue. We invite you to write us with your own thoughts on the meaning of multicultural teaching and with examples from your own teaching. We look forward to the continuing dialogue.

NOTE

1. Questions for Our Authors

Background

The term *multicultural* is in itself problematic, encompassing a whole range of differing interpretations. What, in fact, do we mean by multicultural teaching? How do we understand, confront, and relate the various sources of cultural differentiation—race, gender, class, sexual orientation, ethnicity, religion—without either collapsing or ranking them?

1. How do you define multiculturalism in your teaching? What controversies in the definition of race, ethnicity, gender do you deal with in your class? How do these definitions shape your design and content?

2. Briefly describe the history and purpose of your course—course format, course requirements, and so on. What is your rationale in setting it up this way?

Pedagogy

There are many issues that involve who we are and what we teach to whom. For example, what are the dynamics and problems of teaching material about African Americans or women to a homogeneous group or one that has only minimal representation from the group under discussion? What problems or strategies arise from white faculty teaching about people of color, men teaching about women, and so on? How does who we are and whom we teach affect content and classroom dynamics? How can we deal sensitively with emotionally charged issues?

1. What is your role in the classroom? Is your primary purpose that students learn about themselves, themselves in relation to others, or themselves in relation to the material? How do you hope that discussion, exercises, assignments, activities, and readings help students meet your purposes?

2. Is your course content affected by the composition of the class? In what way? How do you approach different audiences with your material? How do you integrate people's experiences into the discussion? How do you use group dynamics in the classroom as learning events?

3. What is the rationale behind the organization and sequence of the course? What do you hope to accomplish with each assignment? Describe. How do you approach discussion of readings? What do you use?

Assessment and Evaluation

Why is it important to you to incorporate a multicultural perspective (however you define it) in your teaching? In other words, why do you do this kind of teaching and how does this situate you within your department and/or discipline?

1. How do you gather feedback about how the class is going? What do student evaluations tell you? What is the relationship between the design and the actual experience? What are some of the major struggles/dilemmas you face teaching this class? What are your major successes and failures? Looking back on previous teaching experiences, what would you have done differently?

2. Some instructors note that teaching about race and gender in the university affects their perceptions of themselves, their role in the university, and their research. What, if anything, has teaching your multicultural course done to you in terms of personal and professional risks and rewards?

Part II

Courses on Intergroup Relations

As we noted in the introductory chapter, it is seldom possible simply to "teach" a course in intergroup relations to a heterogeneous group. Introducing the concept of difference into the classroom must be done in a thoughtful and careful manner as many are being exposed to the concept for the first time. The process of engaging students in thinking about various groups challenges both the learner and the presenter. The following chapters address the impact of this reciprocal learning arrangement on the authors and their classes.

With the exception of Lewis's chapter, all of the courses discussed were taught as part of the Program on Intergroup Relations and Conflict at the University of Michigan. The Schoem and Lewis chapters present the authors' experiences with teaching about intergroup relationships on an undergraduate and graduate level. In both chapters, the authors present pedagogical and personal reflections in addition to the issues of content regarding these courses. The Zúñiga and Chesler chapter also provides information on "teachable moments"—unexpected experiences of teachers that greatly inform their subsequent teaching. In this case, a class assignment impacted not only the students, but others on the campus as well, which expanded the learning laboratory for all concerned. In both the Ortega et al. and Sfeir-Younis chapters, specific components of courses on intergroup relations are presented. In the former case, the focus is on teaching about diversity with diverse, Latino populations. The Sfeir-Younis chapter provides reflections on the impact of this type of teaching on all participants, with particular recommendations for teachers themselves.

In all of the selections, the emphasis is on teaching about diversity within a diverse setting. When done well, this can result in the transformation of all classroom participants, as is evident in the chapters.

I

Teaching About Ethnic Identity and Intergroup Relations

David Schoem

THE COMPLEXITY OF A MULTICULTURAL CLASSROOM

The courses I teach on ethnic identity and intergroup relations offer the opportunity to bring together in a single time and place the many facets and meanings of multicultural teaching. Given the circumstances of our courses, as teachers we often take only individual pieces of this broad theme for examination and practice. For instance, given a diverse representation of students in the classroom, we may focus only on classroom dynamics or revise course content to reflect a broader range of intellectual perspectives or reconsider pedagogical techniques to reflect different student learning styles. But given the circumstances of my courses, it is the case that my students are representative of various racial and ethnic groups, they think and study together about their own ethnic/racial identity and about intergroup relations, and I attempt to introduce a variety of teaching and learning strategies.

Managing the complexity that constitutes the class roster and course syllabus is not easy, but I believe that we find ourselves in these courses facing some of the very issues that face a multicultural society.

The results of this teaching are at once exhilarating and frustrating. Imagine the most satisfying teaching experience, the most enlightening, analytic discussion. Imagine provocation, challenge, tears, anger, joy, transformation, insight. Imagine deeply hidden life stories and uncensored honesty suddenly bursting forth.

But picture, too, intimidation, posturing, denial, fragility. Picture students who can ''see'' only one perspective, who don't listen or read carefully except when their own group is being discussed, who are so anxious to talk about themselves and their individual ethnic/racial experience that they are ready to dismiss research findings and scholarly debate as interfering with their learning.

Picture students being intellectually passive for weeks for fear of offending their classmates from different backgrounds.

I think and plan and worry about teaching my courses on ethnic identity and intergroup relations for months beforehand. Can I effectively balance scholarly material and personal experience? Can I possibly cover all the reading, the discussions, and the writing that I think are absolutely necessary to these courses? Am I up to the mediation of conflicts—personal and group as well as intellectual? I know that I don't worry about other courses I teach except to hope that my students will be intellectually engaged and active rather than passive learners. But in these courses my students and I take a personal and intellectual journey at ninety miles an hour—I have no choice but to be prepared; the active learning never takes a rest.

I first taught Blacks and Jews: Dialogue on Ethnic Identity about ten years ago. Five years ago I revised and expanded this course to include Latinos. Most recently I broadened the course even more, focusing on themes and patterns in intergroup relations inclusive of many ethnic/racial groups in U.S. society. I usually limit enrollment to about twenty students.

While it may be easier pedagogically to examine two, rather than three or more, groups in a course on intergroup relations because the focus can then remain clearer and more pointed, I view the classroom setting as a first-rate learning laboratory for the study of society's most difficult challenges and in-tractable problems. Clearly there is a semester's worth of study or more for a course on Blacks and Jews (my students repeatedly ask that I extend the course to two semesters), but even that focus limits to some extent the much more complex forces at work in a multiethnic, multiracial society.

When I introduce in my courses topics such as ethnic identity, racism, pluralism, assimilation, gender, education, coalition building, and socioeconomic status, students find that they can't hide behind clichés and simplistic explanations in front of their classmates, who represent a multiplicity of backgrounds. When Black and Jewish students sit together and discuss what it means to be a minority or confront issues such as affirmative action or when African Americans, Asian Americans, European Americans, and Latinos watch Spike Lee's *Do the Right Thing* or examine college admissions policies, the discussion jumps off the pages of the books and into the mouths of the students and then back again.

ORGANIZATION OF THE COURSE AND
STUDENT EXPECTATIONS

I organize these courses to begin with the study of ethnic identity before looking at issues of intergroup relations. We begin the study of ethnic identity with some background on personal identity. I emphasize that for any individual student the importance of ethnic identity to his or her broader construction of self may vary widely. I want students to recognize and feel comfortable with the notion that as much as this class will focus on ethnicity and will ask students to reflect on personal experience about ethnicity/race, at any given time ethnic and racial identity will not and need not be at the center of who they are.

By beginning with the study of ethnic identity, all students are reassured that their own group is part of the syllabus and that issues either particular to their group or common to many groups will be discussed in class. Some semesters I have organized my courses so that each group is studied individually for at least a few weeks, but other times I have organized the course around thematic concerns related to ethnic identity and group experience, such as racism, group naming, ethnic transformation and adaptation, native and immigrant experiences, authentic and symbolic identity, socioeconomic issues, forms of domination, pluralism, and coalition building, using the experience of particular groups as well as case studies to illustrate those themes by comparison and contrast (Alba 1988; Brown 1984; Bulkin, Pratt, and Smith 1984; DeVos and Romanucci-Ross 1975; Ogbu 1978; Schoem 1991; Simonson and Walker 1988; Steinberg 1981; Takaki 1987).

As a result of these discussions, students invariably realize that they know very little about their own group, let alone about others, and many go on to take additional courses about their own group's history and experience. I, too, continue to be struck by how little students know about one another. Students also are surprised at what they learn about other groups and gain an appreciation for both the diversity and commonality of experience.

My students express some disappointment, particularly early in the semester, that I do not provide them with ''answers'' to the questions of intergroup relations. Students frequently come to my course with a dualistic worldview, looking for just two sides to every issue—a right side and a wrong. They come ready to argue and defend what they view as right and attack and ridicule what is wrong, or they feel guilty if they might be perceived as being in the wrong. But whereas I don't wish to dissuade students from their points of view, I do challenge all of them to consider more than two sides of any issue and to confront the much deeper complexity of the topics we study. It takes a considerable amount of time as well as personal and intellectual work for students to accept the absence of answers and to bring an intellectual perspective that incorporates many competing and complementary views of individual issues. For those students who make this intellectual and personal leap, the new insights and level of analysis they bring to class discussion are remarkable.

LEARNING TO SPEAK TO ONE ANOTHER

My students are strangers. As much as they have a compelling desire and need to learn about intergroup relations, my students are frightened by the prospect of discussing this topic face-to-face with members of other groups. Some of my students have no experience talking with members of other racial/ethnic groups about any topic; among others there is a wide range of contact, but very little straight talk with one another about issues that frequently divide their groups.

I take class time to help students learn about talking to one another. I require students to become reflective of group processes and attentive to the initially unspoken strain that is present regarding how the discussions will proceed. One by one, students talk about their individual learning styles and styles of inter-action. I have students read about different groups' interactive styles (Basso 1979; Belenky et al. 1986; Kochman 1981). Although these readings make some students uneasy about being stereotyped, the accompanying in-class critique advances students' awareness of group process and intergroup relations enor-mously. Students now feel much more prepared to begin confronting issues because, without knowing it, they have already done so in exploring their own group processes. I have found that the limited time I spend on this topic actually increases the amount of time I have in each class session because my students are able to engage one another in issues that much more quickly.

Usually by the third week of class, when I feel an initial degree of trust exists among students, I make use of the fishbowl exercise. The fishbowl helps students confront issues more openly and critically by requiring students to listen carefully to one another without interruption. Sitting in concentric circles by ethnic group, students in the inner circle get to speak individually about what it means to be a member of their ethnic group. This is followed by further group discussions until the circles are reversed. Although I devote only two or three sessions of the entire course to the fishbowl exercise, the issues raised are almost always so revealing and profound that they inform class discussion for the remainder of the semester. I am always astounded at the impact and meaning that this simple exercise has for students.

Most recently I asked students to participate in a fishbowl organized by gender after we had completed a series of fishbowl discussions by ethnic/racial groups. At once the issues of gender cross-cutting ethnic/racial lines came to the fore. The women formed a powerful, tight bond, with issues emerging that were far too numerous and deep to be covered in a single class period. The men, who occupied the inner circle first, groped to make conversation, thinking they had little to say to one another as a group of men. The impetus for the gender fishbowl—to demonstrate how gender issues cut across groups in complex yet powerful ways—was clearly demonstrated with a force that no articles assigned in the course could ever do. Importantly, students recognized that there was not to be any clear consensus of views or perspectives among women or men across groups, but that was no different from what we had discovered about the racial/ethnic fishbowls.

The presence in the classroom of students from various backgrounds—one aspect of multiculturalism—has a direct influence on what is and is not said in class and how issues are discussed. My experience is that the quality and intensity of the discussion far exceed the quality and intensity of discussion of the same topic in a classroom comprised exclusively of students from the same background. In the multicultural classroom, whether the topic is affirmative action, assimilation, Black-Jewish relations, and so on, there exists a level of personal interest and immediacy in the topic that is simply not present to the same extent in a monocultural classroom.

Finally, I have little doubt that for many of the students my identity as a Jewish White male has an important influence on their participation and approach to the course. Students of various backgrounds tell me that my own identity does not have any impact on their experience in class, but I remain skeptical. For instance, my impression is that at the outset and perhaps unconsciously, White students, males, and Jewish students, in particular, feel safer, more protected, and more empowered in my classroom. Personally, I think it would be useful to offer these kinds of courses in a team-teaching approach as well as to study the various dynamics that result from using instructors of different backgrounds. However, team teaching is an expensive proposition, and only twice has it been possible for my courses. In those classes, once with a participant-observer researcher and once with teaching assistants—not true team-teaching situations— it was my impression that Black and Latino students and females felt empowered and protected to speak up and participate fully at a much earlier point in the semester because they were from the same background as the other teachers.

I now always raise the issue of my own group identity in class, usually at the time we discuss communication styles; I at least want the question to be raised and students to know that I am sensitive to it and intend to be accessible beyond traditional boundaries to the extent they might wish and to the degree that it is possible.

Becoming aware of learning and participatory styles of students from different groups is part of multicultural teaching. In fact, students learn that they have a great deal in common across groups and that there is considerable individual difference within and across groups. But to their great advantage, they discover that there are alternative ways of talking, interacting, debating, and befriending one another that differ from those to which they are accustomed. One small example is that students in my class discover how much more they can learn by becoming active listeners in class discussions.

LEARNING TO WRITE WITH ONE ANOTHER

Just as I emphasize class participation as a multicultural learning tool, I find writing to be equally important. Some students are outstanding writers and express themselves far better in writing than in discussion. Other students come to class more comfortable with their verbal skills and abilities than their writing, but too often that is a result of having been offered very limited opportunities for different kinds of writing assignments. In addition to requiring essay exams, usually with some choice among exam questions, I have required students to complete one of the following writing assignments.

Ethnic Autobiographies

Students are assigned a thirty- to fifty-page paper to reflect on their own life as a member of an ethnic/racial group (Schoem 1991). I ask students to write five pages per week for the first half of the semester and to use the second half of the semester for revising and editing. Students meet weekly in writing groups in which they discuss the content of their writing and critique the writing itself.

These papers and the collaboration associated with completing them provide many opportunities for student learning. First, students are required to delve into their personal history to reflect on the meaning of their ethnicity in relationship to their identity and life experience. Second, students learn from each other as they share ethnic/racial group issues from a very personal perspective. Although students are advised to write and discuss only what they are comfortable revealing to others, the autobiographies are invariably open, honest, and powerful. My impression is that students are motivated both by the opportunity to be intro-spective and reflective and also by the interest and attention of their peers to each individual's life story. Finally, students spend hours as author, critic, editor, and friend working on these papers—usually far in excess of any other writing assignment they have ever tackled.

Collaborative Research Papers

Admittedly, my first use of collaborative research papers was not successful. I required students to work collaboratively for the first time in the semester on a task—the final paper—that carried some considerable weight for their grade and, therefore, constituted greater risk in the assignment than I intended at that point. That placed an unfair burden on students and was not good pedagogical judgment on my part.

On the other hand, I have required collaborative research papers under less threatening circumstances that have proven enormously successful to students. Students, of course, have little experience with this kind of academic work and find it difficult to negotiate division of responsibility and assume sufficient levels of trust for all group members. But we walk through the process and the obstacles of the project with the entire class so they know what is ahead of them. I assign one grade to all students collaborating on a given paper. In the successful project, students realize how much more they can accomplish as a group of two or four than as an individual, and from the input of their peers, they gain broader insights into their work, insights often reflecting multicultural perspectives. Finally, as a result of this project, students now have had one positive experience working closely on a project with a member of a different racial/ethnic group.

But be forewarned. Collaborative projects can take considerably more of the teacher's time than individual research assignments, unless students have had prior experience with this process, an unlikely possibility. And one needs to make sure that collaborative partnerships that are not successful are not so negative for those involved that students resort to stereotypes and group generalizations based on one unsuccessful experience.

Analytic Journals

The only drawback to the analytic journal is the time it takes a teacher to read student journals on a regular basis—at least every two weeks is recommended, and every three weeks is a bare minimum. But the value of the analytic journal is enormous. First of all, it provides teacher and student with another opportunity for one-to-one dialogue. The student should be given freedom to reflect on both the substantive discussion as well as the group process of class discussions. On numerous occasions, and with students' permission, I have brought to the entire class comments in journals that I realized required further clarity and explanation. I have also sometimes developed an anonymous list of questions and issues that students have raised in journals but that they were reticent to bring to the class in person.

Students, in time, also begin to incorporate numerous experiences from outside the classroom that bear on the topic. This freewriting opportunity quickly leads to students' independently learning to integrate life experience with class discussion and scholarly readings.

The analytic journal should also be used in a more structured way. It allows the teacher to assign specific questions based on readings that require students to think critically and write in essay form about readings and course themes in advance of class discussion or subsequent to them. Once students make the distinction between this analytic journal and a personal diary, which usually happens for everyone by the second or third week of class, it is a good learning tool that students very much enjoy using.

GAINING PERSPECTIVE: LEARNING FROM AND ABOUT OTHERS

My greatest frustration comes from my students' impatience to learn and talk about themselves at the exclusion of consideration of other groups and related theoretical issues. For their part, early in the semester, students sometimes see me as having misrepresented the course to them. Because this is most often their first opportunity to explore group identity and intergroup relations, they want immediately to start discussing their identity and their group's relations with others. While my purpose is to establish a context for productive discussions in future weeks by looking at the experience of groups not likely to be represented in the classroom, such as the Amish or South Africans or the Cambodians under the rule of the Khmer Rouge, students wonder if they will actually have this one chance to talk about themselves with one another. Over the years I have relented somewhat from introducing the broader context and comparative perspective so early in the course but have not given up altogether, even in the face of some remaining tension. Happily, and often surprisingly, students from prior years return to tell me excitedly about the memorable impression one aspect of the course or another has had upon them. For instance, a student from a class of four or five years ago recently commented to me about the strong impression the film *The Killing Fields* had made upon her. She told me that it had helped her understand that the tragedies of slavery and the Holocaust, for instance, although unique, were not exclusive and that the history of other groups also included tragic (as well as celebratory) events of monumental proportions.

The sense of urgency and immediacy that students feel about their own group is often played out on an individual level as well. Because I give students permission to talk from personal experience as one path to learning, some students take license to use their individual experience exclusively to draw broad generalizations and, at the same time, to deny social patterns. One of the worst classroom dynamics is to allow one or more students to operate as if it is their right to tell and retell their personal, often idiosyncratic story, as a metaphor of their group's social experience, for example: "Well, my parents are poor [or rich, educated or self-made, fully employed or laid off—fill in the blank] so that proves such and such" or "I once encountered a Taiwanese [or White or Cuban or German or Peruvian—fill in the blank] and he or she did such and such, therefore I know for a fact that everyone in that group acts that way." For those students who seemingly want to use this classroom opportunity as a form of group therapy, limiting or contesting this inclination can be yet another point of tension.

My goal is for students to reflect personally as well as intellectually on the theoretical and empirical findings of the sociological literature in order to explore and understand deeply the issues of ethnic identity and intergroup relations. In time, most students are able to do this and do so effectively. But along the way, some students who don't want to do the careful reading and inquiry or are too focused on the opportunity to reflect in a personal way have great difficulty with this approach. The integration of the theoretical with the personal, which is what I find makes the class most stimulating, for them becomes an obstacle to learning because they have such difficulty accomplishing that integration.

Finally, my approach to the course creates tension in one other way. I work hard to help students develop a critical perspective that goes beyond their often one-dimensional or dualistic approach to understanding. We read Orwell's "Shooting an Elephant" (1953) and try to rewrite the essay from the point of view of the different players in the story. It's a very difficult assignment for most, because it requires analytic skills they have rarely used, but it does help students see other perspectives. After we have focused exclusively on ethnic groups for some time, I introduce gender issues into the discussion, and students (usually men) rebel at the intrusion of this complicating or, to use their term, "external" factor. But the disruption and debate again force students to go beyond the simplistic paradigms that they have brought to class and through which they have previously viewed their social world.

Taking steps forward in learning, such as making comparisons across groups or transferring understandings across contexts is very difficult, as perhaps illustrated best in my class focusing on Blacks, Jews, and Latinos. In the course of discussing coalition building on campus, students had given careful attention to the perspectives that several different racial/ethnic groups brought to campus issues. We had discussed with great intensity the perception of Latinos as "people of color," but also as a multifaceted group with a distinct identity apart from Whites and Blacks, and also of American Jews as a group who are part of, yet separate from, other Whites. Immediately thereafter, Black students, who had participated actively and listened closely to the discussion of Jews and Latinos, automatically framed the discussion of Black coalition building as being between Blacks and Whites, that is, everyone else who was not Black. Latino and Jewish students interrupted in protest that the Black students had not listened to the careful distinctions that had just been made in class—that both groups were presenting themselves as distinct entities, wanting recognition for who they were, and not as part of some all-encompassing monolithic whiteness. The Black students deferred, acknowledging that they had indeed spoken as if they had not heard, although they had in fact listened carefully. They explained that this was how they had always previously divided the social world—Blacks and Whites (meaning non-Blacks), without distinction. The class then paused to think about how very complicated these issues really were, even for groups of people such as themselves who were trying to move beyond the limitations of the rigid frameworks within which they had been raised and educated.

Central to this discussion is the notion that in teaching intergroup relations, one should recognize that students pass through distinct learning stages (Schoem and Stevenson 1990). First they are defensive, claim to hold no prejudices, and look for simplistic "answers" to the questions of intergroup relations. Slowly they become more critical, open, and honest, and class discussion becomes more analytic, contested, and vigorous.

THIS LEARNING TAKES TIME AND COMMITMENT

One of the most important factors working on the side of studying intergroup relations in a classroom setting is students' commitment to the length of the semester. In many non-classroom settings, participants in intergroup discussions volunteer their time for a limited period or may feel a considerable degree of freedom to leave the group as discussion gets tense, challenging, and uncomfortable. The classroom setting imposes a commitment on students to stay with such discussions in order to receive credit and a good grade. This gives the teacher an unusual advantage for a number of reasons. In my case, it allows me to pace the class educationally—the most difficult issues and discussions don't have to take place until the class dynamics are such that these issues can be handled constructively. It also allows me to persist through the tensions I have described earlier, knowing full well that students are not about to drop out if they are not immediately satisfied with the choice of topics or pace of discussion. Finally, when discussions do become contentious and students leave angry or in tears, I know and they know that everyone will be back at the next class session to continue the discussion after some cooling off and further reflection.

Interestingly and predictably, the greater the number of groups represented in the course content and in the classroom, the more time is needed. In my latest formulation of this course, whose focus was on American Indians, Asian Americans, African Americans, European Americans, Jews, and Latinos, it took students much longer to move through each of the identified stages. As a result, students were unwilling to fully confront and critically challenge issues until well into the semester. What my students learn from this and what I relearn each year is just how much time is required to understand long-standing issues of intergroup relations.

What represents multicultural teaching here is the recognition and facilitation of group dynamics and processes, even conflicts, to make discussion and understanding of substantive material most productive and meaningful. Attempting to separate content from the context and dynamics of the learning environment or attempting entirely to detach deeply rooted personal associations from intellectual and theoretical material simply limits the richness and depth of understanding and interest.

LIBERAL LEARNING OR COALITION BUILDING

I view my courses as a way of educating students about the complexity of intergroup relations and of helping them begin thinking seriously about what a multicultural society can be. I also ask that they consider what their part in shaping that society will be. I hope that my courses help raise the level of discourse for addressing ongoing conflicts and the challenges of intergroup relations.

One of my students who subsequently became a facilitator of dialogue groups asked whether I approach these kinds of discussions as part of a liberal arts education or as an opportunity for coalition building. He had found himself in the midst of a conflict with a cofacilitator of a Black-Jewish dialogue in which it seemed they had come to the discussion with very different goals in mind.

Although many of the learning formats I use in the classroom could be used in other settings for coalition-building purposes, that is not my goal here. In fact, many of my students do subsequently pursue a coalition-building and integrationist strategy with regard to intergroup relations. At the same time, others choose a strategy of self-reliance or follow a separatist strategy; still others become frustrated and disillusioned to the point that they wish to have nothing to do with ethnicity, race, or intergroup relations. I view those choices as individual ones that students make apart from the demands or purposes of the course, though very likely influenced by their interpretation and understanding of the readings and discussions in which they have participated.

LESSONS FROM THE MULTICULTURAL CLASSROOM

I like to think that both my students and I have learned important lessons from our confronting the issues of multiculturalism in this course. The good that we envision in multiculturalism often brings moments of great insight, even transforming experiences—some students use terms like "breakthrough," "eye-opening," or "light bulbs turning on." But more often than not, we also face on a daily basis society's barriers, structurally imposed and personally ingrained, so that with students present in the classroom representing any number of different groups and perspectives, every discussion is difficult, beginning with good feelings but accompanied by mistrust. Perhaps most important is that we realize there is a long road ahead and each student can decide whether to stick with the issues for the duration.

As much as students attempt to overcome their own stereotypes and prejudices toward others within the class, it is not infrequent that they revert to those same practices for those not in the classroom or for those in the room perceived to be most vulnerable. I recall Black and Jewish students together falling back on gross stereotypes of Chaldeans, and I recall European Americans, African Americans, and Latino students joining together to attack homosexuals based on uninformed generalizations. The influence of racism and intergroup hatred is deeply and powerfully embedded in our society and is not easily overcome.

Neither is the path to understanding ever as straightforward as one might hope. Just as students begin to learn about commonalities and differences among groups, they discover not only that no group is monolithic but that each individual within groups is struggling with confusion, ambivalence, and strong emotions of pride and often anger about his or her individual and subgroupings within broader ethnic/racial divisions. Finally, answers do not come easily or quickly, even though persuasive societal critiques of various intellectual and political perspectives may abound. A student may conclude that she or he has carefully and cogently analyzed "the problem," but where does this student turn to begin to think about making constructive and practical changes?

I say to students that they must take it upon themselves to search for answers or at least directions that society has not provided for them. They must begin to see themselves as active players and policymakers and leaders, whether on an individual or family or institutional level, and disabuse themselves of any notion that the "experts" know all and understand completely.

Students take this message with strength and inspiration. They redouble their efforts to become better informed, offer critiques, and respond effectively to challenges from their classmates. There is an awareness that the problems are enormous, the challenges daunting, and yet for most, the vision of a just multicultural society is uplifting and motivating. The opportunity for change is theirs to seize.

2

Continuing the Legacy: On the Importance of Praxis in the Education of Social Work Students and Teachers

Edith A. Lewis

Interest in the inclusion of content on individuals and families of color is not new to social work education. Since 1972, the Council on Social Work Education (CSWE), the accrediting body for social work programs, departments, and schools in the United States, has had an accreditation standard mandating these materials' inclusion in each course in each school. During the last two decades, scholars of color and others interested in issues of ethnicity and biculturalism in culturally competent social work practice, theory, and research have written many helpful articles and texts that can be incorporated into nearly any social work course.[1]

In spite of the availability of written material on populations of color and the CSWE mandate, many courses in accredited programs and schools continue to omit this information. In many cases, this is due to the limited training of social work educators, most of whom completed their own formal training in advanced degree programs that did not emphasize this content. The lack of content in classes is also due to social work educators' discomfort about their ability to teach this content.

Increasingly, social work students training for B.S.W. and M.S.W. degrees will, nevertheless, find that their first work experiences include people of color in their caseloads. Our ability as social work educators effectively to teach new professionals to work with the client populations with whom they will have contact mandates the inclusion of culturally competent practice content in our teaching.

This chapter focuses on one effort to provide such content in teaching M.S.W. students. The course described here, American Cultures, is part of the Human Behavior in the Social Environment (HBSE) course offerings available to students within the University of Michigan School of Social Work. The chapter outlines the scope of the course, the experiences of the African American woman teacher and students from several of her six classes during the last six years, how these experiences have shaped the praxis of all involved, and the implications of the experiences for the teaching of other courses with similar content in the social sciences and social work.

SCOPE OF THE COURSE

On the first day of each class, I explain to those assembled that this course is a gift we will give each other. Of the four courses I have taught within the School of Social Work, this is my favorite because it has taken a different shape with each group of participants and continues to enrich my own process of critical reflection and action, also known as praxis.

Indeed, I consider this process of praxis essential to an understanding of multicultural teaching. In my opinion, a multicultural teacher not only strives to encourage the development of a critical consciousness in students in terms of issues of race, class, sexual orientation, and ethnicity, but remains open to ongoing personal transformation as a result of this interaction. This is accomplished by actively participating in the learning experience, by continually reflecting on what students are learning as evidenced by their ongoing feedback, and by constantly seeking alternative methods of presenting material so that everyone begins to think creatively about ways to approach interpersonal communication. Because of its long-term commitment to work with disfranchised people, I believe that social work education has developed a wealth of information on multicultural teaching, and I attempt to access this information in designing and facilitating future practitioners' learning experiences.

At one time in the history of the School of Social Work, American Cultures was required of all students. During the last ten years, however, with a change in our curriculum, it has become an elective course, fulfilling part of the Human Behavior in the Social Environment (HBSE) sequence. An HBSE sequence, required in all M.S.W. programs, presents theory-based content derived from the social sciences, enabling students to understand how individuals, families, and groups operate within their social environments.

As it fulfills only an elective HBSE requirement, students voluntarily select to participate in the course. Generally, the course has been small during the last six years, with as few as eight students and as many as twenty-three electing it in the semesters I have taught it. The ethnic backgrounds and gender of class participants have varied widely during the six years. One semester, the class was composed exclusively of women, during other semesters it has been heavily composed of students from European American backgrounds, and most recently almost half of the twenty-three students were students of color representing African American, Arab American, South American, Latina, and Asian American backgrounds. It is usually taught only once an academic year, and students who have participated in the course have noted that they chose it as a result of either interest in the topics or their belief that it would be useful in their future practice.

I have chosen to teach American Cultures using family and ethnicity as units of analyses for exploring concepts such as race, class, sexual orientation, religion, rituals, values, poverty, and discrimination. The course is divided into three sections: European American families' experiences in the United States; the intersection of poverty, racism, and discrimination; and families of color.

In the first section, the objective outlined for the class is to identify the ways in which family and ethnicity have been addressed in this nation. This is done by introducing the intra- and inter-ethnic conflicts experienced by early European American immigrants. Specifically, in the first four weeks of class, we read and discuss interactions between British and German settlers, between Irish and Italian immigrants, and the conflict of adding the dimension of religion to culture, as in the case of Jewish Americans. Through these discussions, we begin to come to terms with the systematic restriction of ethnicity in the lives of early immigrants to the United States. Looking at intergroup relations, we are also able to tie in the history of social work practice in the United States and examine the ways in which the field contributed to the denigration of a critical ethnic consciousness on the part of those new immigrants.

Course readings in this section include papers that help class participants understand the fears of the early British immigrants that the Germans would take over their land and, as a result, force everyone to speak German (see Takaki 1987), the conflicts between the Irish and Italians over ownership of the community parishes, and the participation of civic and industrial leaders in the propagation of theories about the "Jewish conspiracy" in our state and nation. Class discussions also attempt to identify differences between values and behaviors thought to be universal in the nation (and particularly among class members) and those based in the experiences of particular ethnic groups. In this latter area, we focus on the creation and maintenance of family and ethnic rituals, the role of ethnic humor in maintaining boundaries, and the concept of family itself.

The second section of the course, focusing on the intersection of racism, poverty, and discrimination, seeks to provide class participants with ways of thinking about why the experiences of the populations we will study in the last section of the course might differ from those of the early immigrants. While the concept of inter-ethnic conflict is introduced in the first section, the systematic manifestations of discrimination based on ethnicity, class, race, gender, and sexual orientation are the framework of the second class section. This section outlines the demographics of poverty, racism, sexism, and discrimination, how these are confounded by social class, the "double" or "triple whammy" experienced by individuals who fall into several of these categories (e.g., poor lesbian women of color), and the possible outcomes for these individuals given the realities of their current existence.

In order to present a range of views to the class participants, readings assigned include, for example, the various aspects of the debate about affirmative action. I make a conscious effort as a class facilitator to present the concept that science is not value-free and that all critical information consumers must think carefully about the assumptions underlying the material they are reviewing. As course readings are incorporated into exercises and discussions, we often stop to review what assumptions underlie the author's argument. Class participants have remarked that they have become far more critical in their examination of content from the media and other scholarly publications as a result of this practice in class.

The last section of the course focuses primarily on the lives and experiences of populations of color in the United States. One of the objectives for this section of the course is that class participants not only be able to describe aspects of the experiences of the four "umbrella groups" considered by the Council on Social Work Education (i.e., African Americans, Asian Americans, Latinos, and Native Americans), but have an understanding of how diverse these groups are. Toward that end, I find it critical to introduce material about Cuban American, Mexican American, Puerto Rican, and South and Central American populations in the section on Latino families, to discuss the differences in historical, political, and social contexts for these families based on the time of entrance into the United States. This need for disaggregation must also be addressed in discussions of class and geographic differences among African Americans, the vast differences in their interactions with the United States governments resulting in devastating consequences for their individual groups among the over four hundred Native American populations in the United States, and the impact of differential governmental intervention for the Chinese as opposed to Japanese, Southeast Asian refugee, or Pacific Islander populations represented in the United States.

In addition to the four umbrella groups outlined above, so many other populations of color experience their "difference" in terms of access to resources in the United States that many of these are also included in the course experience. Our university, for example, is located near one of the largest urban Arab American and Chaldean communities in the country, and class participants are exposed to the complexities of life for these populations as well. Participants are also able to unravel differences between West Indian and African American populations.

The choice of the two organizing themes of family and ethnicity reflects my own experiences as a clinical supervisor with new social work professionals who came to the agencies in which I worked with two basic misconceptions about social work practice. The first misconception was that ethnicity was analogous to race and was something that only populations of color experienced. The second misconception was that the concept of family was fixed, and the goal of practice was to help clients understand their own dysfunctional family and individuate from it. New professionals had little experience working within a dynamic context that viewed individuals as parts of extended families (including fictive as well as biological kin) and communities of color (with histories of corresponding formal and informal institutions), as well as the wider society. Moreover, they had seldom engaged in a process of praxis that allowed them to examine the strengths and biases they brought to their own practice as a result of their socialization within their own families, ethnic communities, and the wider society.

The American Cultures course is designed to address these two misconceptions. Exercises, readings, assignments, speakers, and class discussions have been aimed at introducing the process of praxis and encouraging participants to engage in it as they being working with human service consumers.

PRAXIS IN ACTION: PEDAGOGICAL CHOICES

To assist participants in beginning this process, the first class always includes a review of the "multicultural ground rules" (Cannon 1990a) used by many other authors included in this book. The ground rules set the tone for our interaction throughout the semester. We acknowledge, in particular, the probability of conflict, as disparate theories, beliefs, and values are shared in the class. We also discuss the possibilities for growth as a result of the conflicts aired in class.

An example from a recent class highlights this potential for personal and collective transformation. During an exercise designed to heighten participants' awareness of their own and others' ethnicity (usually undertaken only after trust has been established in the group), students of color lined up on one side of the room, White students on the other, and all completed the statements "One thing I like most about being from the ethnic group(s) I am a part of is" and "One thing I never want to hear again from people who look like the people on the other side of the room is." Usually the structured feedback round after this exercise generates a great deal of discussion about the ability of students of color to respond easily to the first question and the relative difficulty White students have with it. During the last semester the course was taught, two students, who identified themselves as bicultural and biracial, positioned themselves in the center of the room and addressed their remarks to students on either side of themselves. In the ensuing feedback round, students from each side spoke of the new information they had received from the students in the center and their own new insights on the ways they had perceived bicultural or biracial students.

I realize that I am the first African American that many of the class participants, particularly those from smaller colleges in this state and others, have ever had as an instructor. Given this, I have made a conscious decision over time to use the tool of self-disclosure both to model risk-taking behavior among the participants and to broaden participants' knowledge base on the impact of race, ethnicity, and gender on the lives of persons of color across class strata. I understand that when there are racial, class, gender, or sexual orientation differences among class participants, these can influence interaction patterns among those in the group (see Chau 1991; Davis 1981b, Reed and Garvin 1983). I share that information, gathered from research, with the class participants in our first session and how I have experienced my own gender, ethnic, racial, and class difference in classes as a student and professor. It is particularly important to recognize that my direct and open style of interaction is sometimes perceived as different but that I am committed to the development of a ''safe space'' for each participant and the creation of an environment in which all contributions are welcome. In doing so, I feel freer to note that I do not know the answers to some of the questions raised in class when I do not. When students struggle to understand a behavior foreign to the ordering of values with which they were socialized, I may provide a similar example from my own background and share the process I went through in attempting to come to terms with a decision about it. I also acknowledge that I am not the ''expert'' on the course material, but learn something new each semester from my interaction with class participants. This practice of periodic self-disclosure, further, limits the extent to which I am perceived as a ''voyeur'' or non-participant-observer to the interactions between and within class participants.

As a person who believes that the process of building a multicultural society cannot be left solely to those from populations considered ''disfranchised'' in the general social science literature, I realize the importance of showcasing the competence of European Americans doing this kind of practice. Toward that end, I include the work of colleagues from this institution and others in the course readings and attempt to have guest lecturers—both other persons of color and European Americans—present and/or be available to confer with students on their questions or group assignments. This is not always warmly received, however, as in cases where a person from one ethnic background presents material about a different population. In processing these occasions (and corresponding concerns raised by class members), I attempt to remind class members that in many ways they are going to attempt to break through the stereotype that only people from the specific ethnic background can work effectively or know about the experiences of that background. If we are intolerant of those working toward their own increasing multicultural perspective, how can we expect others to be tolerant of our own attempts to do so in working with them?

Most importantly, I have been deeply influenced by the work of Paulo Freire and continually attempt to communicate to students in my classes that I do not subscribe to the ''banking concept of education,'' whereby students are empty vessels awaiting my filling words of wisdom. In validating participants' experiences, I commit myself to working with them to put these experiences into their historical, social, and political contexts and to look at the resultant implications of those experiences for the way participants interact with others in their social environments. In other words, instead of merely presenting new information, we explore together the importance of their current levels of knowledge. Questions that may be raised in this regard are ''What are the benefits and consequences of thinking in this fashion?'' ''What will it mean for the significant and proximal others in your environment for you to hold this view?'' and ''What

will be the costs of altering the view for all concerned?'' In this way, we all
become each other's teachers.

STIMULATING THE DEVELOPMENT OF PRAXIS IN OTHERS: ASSIGNMENTS

The early exercises and assignments in the course are designed to help students
think about the ways in which their own backgrounds influence the choices they
make about interpreting another's behavior and the practice interventions they
select. Three tools used in class are particularly important in this regard.

During the first class session, the group brainstorms a list of American values.
This list is recorded, distributed among class participants, and reviewed periodically throughout the semester. While specific content has varied according to
the particular class, several themes emerge consistently. The first is individualism, which many students view as a core value in the society. Another is
freedom, which is broadly determined to be available in its many forms to all
citizens.

We return to these lists often in discussing the appropriateness of each concept
for extended families, for freedom of non-Christian religions, and for traditional
sex-role division of labor in households. We also review these as they may be
differentially operationalized among particular ethnic groups, devising new op-
erational definitions as we encounter them through our readings and class discussions.

A second exercise designed to stimulate the development of critical consciousness uses a variation of the genogram in two parts (see McGoldrick and
Gerson, 1985 for a description of genograms and their use; also see Part Eight
of this text, in which the classroom exercise is reproduced). At an early point
in the semester (usually within the first six weeks), class participants are asked
to diagram at least three generations of their family (as they define the term).
The diagram must use themselves as the base generation, although they are free
to include any children or grandchildren, and must also include at least parental
and grandparental generations. The assignment requires a listing of all relevant
people and their ethnic group backgrounds, a description or diagram of their
migrational patterns either within the United States or abroad, and a listing of
a minimum of fifteen core values, five for one person in each of the three
generations included in the genogram. Students identify at least three individuals,
including themselves, who were influential in shaping their lives. They have the
option of expanding this part of the assignment to include as many ''family''
members as they wish.

The allowance of any individual considered family in the diagram has led to
some very interesting results. While many students include only biological relatives in their diagrams, some have included a number of fictive kin members.
One student, for example, listed his biological family from an Eastern European
background, but included as his most significant ''family'' members the parents

and siblings of his best friend, an Italian, whom he considered to be his greatest supports during childhood and after whom he modeled his own behavior. Adopted students often find that this exercise allows them to gather information about both biological and adoptive families. Moreover, many students note that they learned information long buried by family members but actively influencing their current behaviors, such that students gained new insights about how these behavioral patterns had been established. One student spoke of the shame the family experienced during the end of the Second World War as a result of its German background and revealed how she had learned "not to be German" outside her home community.

The last part of the assignment is done toward the end of the semester. Class participants return to their modified genograms and reflect on how alike or different their values are from those of their own families and of a particular population of color studied during the semester. For this assignment, students who are from one population of color must choose another population not a part of their umbrella group. Participants must report on how these values influence the choices they have made about selecting a profession and the intervention strategies they have grown more comfortable with in their practice. The implications of these choices on their work with particular populations of color are also addressed. The last part of the assignment allows students to think about their future in practice, given the demographic trends of the twenty-first century, and the impact that the new millennium will have on their personal and professional lives and those of others in their ethnic groups.

Sometimes it is a difficult task to assist participants who have been reinforced for thinking in fixed patterns to expand their horizons and consider other views of the world. One class participant, for example, had come to her radical feminist consciousness some twenty years before and staunchly held that "if patriarchy were eliminated in the country, all other problems would be resolved." Fortunately, she was in the classroom with seven other women, four of whom were women of color. With the assistance of readings from course texts by Monica McGoldrick, Joseph Pearce, and John Giordano (1982), Paula Giddings (1984), and Ronald Takaki (1987), among others, we collectively raised the unique experiences of women of color and those from working-class backgrounds, outlined some of the documented examples of racism in the feminist movement, and attempted to envision a world in which patriarchy did not exist and to think about the impact of that world on the lives of women of color. These exercises took place over a period of five weeks and were built into the existing session objectives. In opening and closing rounds, each class participant was asked to share any new perspective gained as a result of readings or discussions. The class participant identifying herself as holding a radical feminist perspective noted toward the end of the semester that she had shared her own new information (gained through the class) with others in her organizations. While she maintained her idea that patriarchy was a major impediment to the rights of women in the United States, by the end of the semester she was more open to the idea that the demise of racism and classism could not be guaranteed even if a patriarchal structure were eliminated tomorrow in this country.

The last assignment given each class is to work in randomly assigned small groups to prepare a class presentation on a population of color not addressed in other course requirements. Many different ethnic groups have been assigned in this portion of the class, from the Hmong to Caribbean Americans from the island of Nevis. The objectives for this group work are twofold. First, participants are exposed to thinking about the uniqueness of groups that might ordinarily be lumped together with others in census tracking and identify the implications of this uniqueness for the groups' interaction within the wider society.

The second objective for the group assignment is that these new professionals, who will be working primarily in group settings (as parts of multidisciplinary teams, if clinicians, or task groups, if administrators, policy analysts, or community organizers), understand their own behavior and that of others in a group project. This assignment is probably the most difficult for many of the students who have enrolled in the American Cultures course. Class participants, like other students in major universities, are often socialized to individual, competitive work. The task of identifying their own strengths and finding complementary ways of working with others' strengths is a task unfamiliar to most. Most resistance is experienced during the early weeks of the class, when participants are attempting to juggle their schedules so that they can find the time to work in the small groups. For this reason, I devote approximately thirty minutes at the end of each three-hour class session to allow for the small groups to meet during the first month. There is also occasional resistance as groups not accustomed to interaction with each other are thrust into working relationships in a task group. Some of the women have expressed difficulty in working with men, some of the students of color experience discomfort working with students from European American backgrounds, and the like. It is critical for the instructor to acknowledge these difficulties as a part of the dilemma of working in a multicultural society and to attempt to assist each group in exposing, rather than burying, these interactional problems. In this way, the small groups can negotiate ways to avoid subgrouping or scapegoating individuals within the group.

Some of the group experiences have been very successful. One of the first groups, assigned to report on the Arab American and Chaldean groups in the area, was composed of six students. Through working together, the three Jewish American group participants were able to think with the group about their initial reluctance to pursue the topic assigned them. The practice of self-disclosure modeled and practiced among these group participants led to other members' increased openness about their personal life experiences. An adopted member of the subgroup found that the group served as a support for her as she retraced her early life to a settlement house in the eastern United States and the conflicting messages received about her natural and adoptive ethnic backgrounds. The Polish American group member gathered and shared information about the rituals that would be a part of her impending wedding celebration. All group members found that they had a mutual affection for cooking and singing communally and a need to talk about their practicum experiences. Although the last of the student members graduated in 1987 and many have moved away, the core group continues to meet monthly for food and music and to consult with each other on work-related issues. New members have joined the original group, and those who have left the region occasionally return for the monthly activities.

THE GOAL OF PRAXIS: INTEGRATION AND ACTION

This course would be incomplete if participants did not view its end as a beginning of new behavior and critical thinking. In the use of the "How Ethnic Am I?" exercise (see Part Eight), among other tools, the task is to reflect readily on how the historical, social, and political contexts of class participants' lives have influenced their own behavior and how that behavior, in turn, influences others around them. Participants are asked to add a basic question to their thinking on topics: How do race, ethnicity, gender, sexual orientation, and class affect my perceptions as well as the person with whom I am interacting on this issue? If this question is inserted to one's thinking about any topic, it provides a method of breaking clear of the idea that there is only one way to think about an issue and/or one way to behave based on one's thoughts on the topic. In other words, it is a way of breaking free from ethnocentrism and a necessary step if one's goal is working effectively in a multicultural environment.

The goal of the course, then, is to work with participants to identify and acknowledge their own backgrounds, and critically and routinely to look both backward and forward on their interactions with others based on these backgrounds. While there are many opportunities for this type of reflection in the course, I am most excited by the continuation of that growth after the individuals leave the class and the university. Sometimes I receive communications from former participants who are now living in different parts of the world and using the material they were first exposed to in the American Cultures class. Other communications are from former participants who made a commitment to alter their extended family or friend networks' acceptance of racist humor and had succeeded. In one case, a student who is now an administrator of a social service agency has helped the agency in radically restructuring its procedures for the recruitment and retention of persons of color.

In 1969, when I had my own first opportunities to work in the social service field, I was convinced that poverty and discrimination could be eliminated in ten years by a few well-chosen pieces of legislation and even fewer warm and able bodies. While I no longer hold this view, my experiences with the American Cultures course have enabled me to keep faith with the idea that just multicultural environments are possible within the social work profession and the United States. During the last six years, I have met many of the shapers of that environment and hope that they have been able to continue to integrate the concept of praxis into their own lives.

NOTE

1. Among these texts are James Green, *Cultural Awareness in the Human Services* (Englewood Cliffs, N.J.: Prentice Hall, 1982); Devore and Schlesinger, 1987; Kenneth Chau, *Ethnicity and Biculturalism: Emerging Perspectives in Social Group Work* (New York: Haworth, 1991); Nancy Boyd-Franklin, *Black Families in Therapy: A Multisystem Approach* (New York: Guilford, 1990); Chunn et al., *Mental Health and People of Color: Curriculum Development and Change*. (Washington, D.C.: Howard University Press, 1983); Ho, 1987; McGoldrick, Pearce, and Giordano, 1982. Special issues of *Social Work*, *Family Relations*, and *Social Work with Groups* have been devoted exclusively to the topic of practice with people of color.

3

Teaching With and About Conflict in the Classroom

Ximena Zúñiga and Mark A. Chesler

The course described here was offered as an undergraduate seminar in Intergroup Conflict and Social Change. It was undertaken as part of a University of Michigan Presidential Initiatives Program in Undergraduate Education in Intergroup Relations and Conflict. Other parts of this program included two additional undergraduate courses, several minicourses, and dialogue groups aimed at linking academic work to the living and social experiences of students (see Chapters 1, 4, 5, and 20). This program reflects a growing emphasis at the university level on the study of social and intergroup conflict and discrimination. While such curricular efforts have long-standing roots (Kriesberg 1973; Wehr 1979), interest in them has been spurred recently by numerous incidents of campus racism, sexism, and homophobia, and in many colleges these issues have become the focus of substantial faculty debate and innovation and public criticism and support (Bennett 1984; Bloom 1987; Collins and Anderson 1987; D'Souza 1991; Takaki 1989).

This practicum course focused on analytic frameworks and practical skills to help students understand and deal with conflict in ways that could facilitate social change outcomes. Our self-conscious and publicly stated assumption was that the experience of injustice and the quest for justice are key ingredients in many protracted and heated social conflicts. Thus, we elected to pay special attention to those conflicts that overtly or covertly centered on issues of injustice and to examine conflict resolution mechanisms that might spur the movement toward more just social arrangements. Such resolutions often involve not only the settlement of conflicts, but the construction and implementation of agreements that can create long-term change in social structures and institutional arrangements. Thus, the joint focus of the course was on social conflict and social change.

The major topics dealt with throughout the course included:

Kinds and sources of conflict
    Conflict and interdependence
    Conflict at various social system levels
    Destructive and constructive outcomes of conflict
    Social conflicts versus disputes
Interest groups in society
    Objective versus subjective interests
    Organizing and mobilizing around different interests
    Institutionalized discrimination
    Criteria for social justice
Responses to conflict
    Regulation of conflict
    Personal and organizational responses
    The role of conflict in social change
    Intervention in social conflicts
Intrapsychic conflict
    Socialization and learned styles
    Internalization of oppression and denial of oppression
    Resocialization and other forms of personal change
Interpersonal process in conflict
    The interaction of learned personal styles and situational demands
    Communication, influence, and interaction
    Race and gender differences
Small groups and family systems in conflict
    Family roles and disputes
    Small group structures and processes
    Skills in group leadership and facilitation
Race and gender issues in conflict
    Identity
    Interrelationships
    Institutional racism and sexism
Personal challenges to injustice/oppression
    Using conflict to achieve goals
    Challenging injustice
    Intervention skills and assumptions
    Dealing with resistance and counterattack
Organizational and community change

Analyzing and intervening in organizational conflict

Interest groups in organizations and communities

Community mobilization and social movements

Coalitions

Bargaining and negotiating conflicts

Settling disputes versus creating change

Interest versus position bargaining

Getting to the table—problems of escalation and de-escalation

Arbitration

Cases of mediation and arbitration of race and gender disputes

Cases of organizational and community disputes

Litigation and judicial settlement of disputes

Courts as a last resort?

Just courts and unjust courts

Comparisons of formal and informal forms of dispute resolution

Dispute settlement, conflict resolution, and social justice

Definitions of justice (procedural versus allocative, equity versus equality versus need)

Necessary personal and social conditions for justice

Twenty-four undergraduate students who had completed an introductory course in Intergroup Relations and Conflict enrolled in this seminar-practicum (see Chapter 5). As a result of a deliberate recruitment and screening process, approximately one-half the class was composed of students of color, and one-half was Caucasian; one-half, male and one-half, female; one-half, upperclass persons and one-half, freshpersons and sophomores. The course was team-taught by a male, Caucasian faculty member (Chesler) and a female, Latina advanced doctoral candidate (Zúñiga). Throughout the semester, readings, assignments, and class discussions promoted an atmosphere that rewarded self-disclosure and honest exploration of controversial issues (Davis 1990; Stanford 1977). Many activities reorganized the class into race-alike and gender-alike groupings and then generated exchange across these categories; others organized students into heterogeneous learning groups, exploring various forms of interpersonal and social conflict, sometimes within the group itself. Students were advised that if any activities or assignments were offensive or inappropriate for them, they were to make their reactions known to the instructors and to find roles other than direct involvement that might satisfy alternative learning goals. Our view was that any effort to deal seriously with students' (and our own) deeply held views and feelings needed to provide safety for students not to participate, as well as a safe environment in which students might participate.

Students often suggested and made alterations in course content and process, creating some measure of an interactive teaching and learning pedagogy. However, the course was graded, was substantially guided by instructor initiative, and operated within the norms and structures of undergraduate education at a major research-oriented university. In addition to reading assignments and class participation, students were required to fulfill four other criteria: (1) a series of brief weekly papers involving reflection and commentary on the connections between classroom or reading material and their own lives (e.g., describe a conflict incident in your family; discover and challenge an instance of race or gender discrimination); these papers were not graded, but were read and commented upon by the instructors and in general utilized as a form of constant feedback; (2) a personal inquiry paper, in which students were asked to discuss aspects of their own social identity (especially race, gender, ethnicity, class, and so on), the ways in which they learned the meaning of these identities, and their impact on students' current educational and social outlooks; (3) a joint research paper conducted in teams of three or four students, focusing upon their analysis of a situation of injustice and conflict, the nature of the conflict and conflict stakeholders involved, and their suggestions for resolution; and (4) an end-of-the-semester evaluation of their learning, with commentary from two other students. The students' grades in the class were determined by fulfillment of these latter three requirements.

Many classroom activities and assignments were designed to provide students with experiential opportunities to explore several dimensions of the sociology and social psychology of conflict and conflict resolution, and discrimination and oppression. One of our concerns was to complement classroom intellectual work (oral and written) with real world experiences that exposed students to social conflict and discrimination—their own and others' (Andersen 1988b; Berkeide and Segal 1985; Crumpacker and Vander Haegen 1987). As a result, we had several opportunities to explore conflict as a social phenomenon, because students experienced it intrapersonally, interpersonally, and in intergroup and social contexts. Then we were able to examine various mechanisms for the reduction and/or utilization of conflict as a learning tool and as an instrument for social change in concrete and realistic terms and to help students develop specific skills in conflict analysis, intervention, and resolution.

Detailed descriptions of such classroom activities are important, because all of us who undertake instruction about systems of social oppression, conflict, and change need to learn more about how to manage such teaching-learning events. As we deal with real oppression and discrimination and open our classrooms to real encounters with conflict, we begin to work with deeply held psychological and political concerns of our students and of ourselves. Under these circumstances, classroom conflict (whether covert or overt) should be expected (McKinney 1985). In many exercises, including the one described below, we do not know at the outset precisely where our teaching-learning commitments will take us. Both we and students often enter into an uncharted territory where there is great potential for real and immediate teaching and learning and also the potential for risk and danger. We all must learn how to manage better both the potential and the risk, both the substantive and the processual learning opportunities (Gondolf 1985; Berkeide and Segal 1985).

THE PINK TRIANGLE EXERCISE

The pink triangle was the insignia lesbian and gay people were required to wear as they were interned in concentration camps in Europe during the Nazi Holocaust (Heger 1980; Lautmann 1981; Plant 1986).[1] Today this symbol has been claimed by the lesbian and gay movement as a symbol of its resistance to oppression. Students were asked, on a voluntary basis, to wear a button with a pink triangle on it prominently for one full day and to write a short (two- or three-page) paper describing the nature of their decision making regarding wearing the button, their own feelings as they progressed through the day, the reactions of others around them, and the ways in which they responded to others. As this activity was planned, a short discussion ensued regarding some places on or near campus where it might be relatively dangerous to wear the button prominently, and students were encouraged to consider avoiding such risk-laden settings.

Students approached this activity with a variety of attitudes. The decision to wear the button at all, and if so how, was a focus of much serious reflection. The great majority of students eagerly and seriously undertook to wear the pink triangle as a means to explore their own feelings and the reactions of others. Some even saw their participation as a welcome opportunity to express solidarity with a victimized population. As two students commented in their papers and in subsequent classroom discussion:

While I had accepted this notion intellectually, I had never personally experienced what it was like to take a stand and take that risk of being a "suspect." I made a pledge that if I was asked why I was wearing a pin and what the pin signified that I would say only that I was wearing it to show my solidarity with the Gay Rights Movement. I felt that if I stated that I was wearing the pin as part of a class assignment that I would really be copping out.

I confidently put my pink triangle on my sweater and was ready for any comments that my peers had to give me. I think that not too far back in my mind, I was hoping that no one would notice the pin or that those who did notice, wouldn't know what it stood for and wouldn't bother to ask. Why didn't I want them to ask? After all I am not gay and everyone who knew me knows this.

Some students were not eager to engage in the exercise, but decided to wear the button anyway. They clarified their decision to go ahead, despite some personal ideological objections or concerns, primarily on the basis of support for the individual liberty and civil rights of gay and lesbian people.

A few students decided not to wear the button. For some, this was a principled decision based upon their opposition to homosexuality. For others, it was a product of unresolvable confusion or anxiety:

I felt the need to take the button off and hide the pink triangle. I was afraid that certain people would think I was gay.

Many students reported that they were concerned ahead of time about the reactions of others—roommates, friends, classmates, and acquaintances. But several students reported that their friends or peers did not know the meaning of the button and thus did not react. Some were relieved, while others were disappointed at such "non-attention":

Throughout the entire day I wore this pin. No one understood the symbolism associated with the pink triangle. In all instances of discussion, I found myself in the role of initiator. Without exception everyone I talked to stated that they were unfamiliar with the association of the pink triangle to homosexuals and/or how the pink triangle became associated with homosexuals.

Because their friends or peers didn't know the meaning of the button, these students had to initiate conversation; they thus had to "come out" in order to elicit responses from others. This coming-out process elicited varied responses, ranging from hostility to silence to support, and in turn exposed students to some of the forms of discrimination experienced by gays and lesbians.

Almost all the students anticipated and planned strategies for managing the interpersonal conflict that they assumed the pink triangle would elicit. For many, their fear of being "suspect" as gay or lesbian largely determined their reactions to others' comments:

I was horrified: because I wore this button, my teachers, friends and even strangers might assume that I am a lesbian. It hit me! I was worried. I did not want my image to be shattered because I wore the "silly pink button." I surprised myself; although I support gay and lesbian rights, the thought of being recognized as a lesbian was horrifying. I realized through this exercise that I am not willing to put my reputation and image on the line. Whereas I support the needs and rights of gays and lesbians, when it came down to it, I would not want to be thought of as one.

Some students examined their own internalization of the oppression and stigma our society visits upon homosexuals. Other students vividly discovered their own biases or intolerances and expressed their discomfort in this recognition. Many students found that their fear of others' reactions impeded their ability to address their own or others' homophobic reactions, and thus they distanced themselves from personal exploration.

One response to this confusion and fear was to make it quite clear to others that wearing the button was simply a class exercise and that they themselves certainly were not homosexual. Most students who adopted this behavior did so almost unconsciously and later regretted its political implications:

I had already decided that I would not mention that I was wearing it for a class, partly because I felt that this would give false justification to others for my wearing it, and partly because I was really wearing it because I am a supporter of gay and lesbian rights, and others should know that. My answer to my friend thus began with an explanation of the symbol's origins in the concentration camps of Hitler. I proceeded to tell him that I was wearing the pin to show my support of the gay and lesbian groups and people. Then I did something very strange and troubling. I not only over-emphasized that it was a classroom assignment, but found that I was zestfully and vehemently trying to prove that I was not homosexual or of the gay community. I told him that I was still looking for a female companion—a girlfriend if you will. I guess I did this just to confirm that he knew that I was not gay, that the pin had nothing to do about my own sexual orientation. This was childish and hypocritical, it seems, and I was ashamed of myself after I ended the short conversation.

Fear of being stigmatized pervaded many students' experiences and accounts. The tension between wanting to challenge their own and others' prejudices about homosexuality proved to be quite a powerful experience, full of troubling reactions, conflicting feelings, and new layers of meaning.

Some students addressed these conflicts by challenging (or promising to challenge) their own confusion and the negative reactions of others. Several announced a renewed commitment to apply the lessons they learned earlier in the course to some sort of social action, on at least a personal level. They expressed a desire to go beyond the particular assignment and, although the comments are not expressly political, they do reveal students' willingness to adopt a personal relationship to the issue:

I experienced a wide range of *stressful emotions*. This gave me a much better (though very simplistic) appreciation for what it must be like for gay men and lesbians who have come out. They face this kind of anxiety and trepidation every day of their lives. This exercise tested my fortitude. *I've always made a point of making sure people know that I was straight.* I'm not going to continue to play along with the system in this manner. I'm going to wear the pink triangle pin on my backpack from now on . . . if people are going to judge me and form misconceptions about me, that's their business and their problem. If they want to know my sexual orientation, they're going to have to have the courage to ask.

This student and others have begun to generalize the experience of the exercise. For them, the activity opened new layers of meaning, particularly as it is related to dominant-subordinate relations and to internalized messages about oppressed/ stigmatized groups.

DEBRIEFING AND DISCUSSION OF THE EXERCISE

In the first class session following the button-wearing activity, all students met in groups of four or five to discuss their experiences and to share the ideas they had written in their papers about the exercise. Then the entire class gathered in a circle for open discussion. It was agreed to try to report and discuss, in turn, the same themes dealt with in the individual reports—preparatory feelings, actual experiences wearing the button, intellectual and emotional reflections.

Students quite honestly shared their trepidations, fears, and anxieties, including primary concerns about "what others might think of me." The fear of being labeled and stigmatized as a sexual deviant was as prominent in this discussion as it was in students' private papers. In addition, two students publicly reported that they did not wear the button because they did not believe in the ideas and ideals of the gay liberation movement and thought that identifying with such a movement would be hypocritical for them. Another student reported that he wore the triangle on his shirt, under a sweater, effectively concealing the triangle from others; he thus was able to articulate his own feelings, although not the reactions of others. These and other reports were met with apparent acceptance by the entire group assembled.

In discussing their actual experiences wearing the pink triangle, students reported the range of incidents noted previously in their papers. Some met with no reactions at all and had to bring their identification vigorously into the open to gain a reaction. Others were asked interesting and provocative questions by their peers. Some indicated their frustration with their own response to peers, especially those who found themselves going out of their way to indicate that they themselves certainly were not gay. One young woman was embarrassed that she had "protected" herself from her friends in this way, and a young man expressed considerable frustration and irritation with himself for "betraying his initial agenda and plan." Both felt that by stating explicitly that they were not gay, they had taken themselves and their friends off the hook. They demonstrated at least to themselves how frightened they were to be thought of as gay and expressed how annoyed with themselves they were for being so frightened. Other students nodded, chuckled, and appeared to appreciate and identify with these dilemmas. It was easy, in this context, to see and discuss issues of interpersonal and intergroup conflict and the conflict-avoidance techniques most students adopted.

In open discussion, students asked each other questions and compared experiences. One young man who identified himself as not prejudiced toward gay people asked a gay man: "But why do you gay people want to identify yourselves so publicly as gay? This is a matter of private sexual preference. Why make an issue of it? Is the purpose to announce yourself so you can pick up other people?"

The gay young man responded that self-identification and collective expression of sexual orientation were a personal political act: "In doing so you overcome isolation and silence that lead to being ignored and to death." In addition, he noted, "You can set a model of openness for other gay men."

With that the discussion ended, and we thought we were finished with the exercise. The class took a break and planned to come back together in ten minutes to go on with other important work. At the conclusion of the break, three students who had been talking together indicated that they were dissatisfied with the discussion and wished to reopen it. A straight Latino male, a straight Latina female, and a gay White male noted that one of the final prebreak comments, the one suggesting that the motive for public identification might be to facilitate "picking up sexual partners," had been offensive and required discussion.

The young man who had initiated the earlier exchange indicated that he had simply asked why, reiterated his belief that he was not prejudiced against homosexuals, and stated his view that sexual behavior should be private. The gay student responded that the issues were far more complex. For instance, he said, "I could ask you why do you Jews [the first student was assumed—correctly— to be Jewish] always identify yourselves and draw attention to the Holocaust?"

"That's clearly different," the first student responded. "That was a terrible event that was not a matter of choice." At this point, an intense in-class conflict suddenly erupted: the "there and then" discussion of others' reactions to the buttons had become the "here and now" reality of our class.

The discussion quickly escalated in emotional tone and attack-defend comments. Other students jumped in. Communication skills such as reflective listening were forgotten, mutual concern vanished, and intense emotions were released. Students leaned in their seats toward the two primary "discussants," and everyone became excited and nervous; the situation appeared explosive.

At this point we instructors checked with each other to decide what to do. The discussion felt out of control, and we felt temporarily caught off balance and immobilized. We were fearful and did not want to witness further anger and explosiveness, but we did not want to cover up important issues and drive conflicts and the possibility of learning from them further underground. Some intervention was necessary.

Without having time to evaluate the instructional (or even social control) effectiveness of the idea, we intervened:

Hold it! We have here an example of a substantial conflict. Do you want to just have it at each other, to escalate the level of conflict from what now seems like a debate into a fight, or shall we try to use some of the conflict management, dialogue-creation techniques examined in this course? We could ask these two young men, if they are willing, to sit face-to-face in the center of this room and talk to and with one another about these issues. We can help them, and the rest of us, listen to and really hear one another. So now we have another challenge or choice in front of us. What do you two want to do? How do the rest of us want to be involved?

At this juncture we were not sure if it was indeed possible to (re)establish a learning opportunity in the classroom. If possible, could it be controlled? Would this fishbowl dialogue work? What was meant by *work*? What would a suitable and educational outcome look like? What was meant by *control*? This "out of control" moment provided a real test for whether the process of conflict management and dialogue we had examined in previous sessions would really "work." At any rate, it was a risk that had to be taken.

The class agreed to this process, not necessarily out of considered choice, but because everyone was somewhat frightened and some were angry. The two students also agreed, the gay male more vigorously than the straight male because he felt trashed and wished to work on the issues. The latter student did not want to risk challenge and attack and was ready to leave the scene. Our inclination was to push both young men a bit, on the assumption that they would not suffer from this activity any more than they had already suffered in the conversation and that true two-way engagement might benefit everyone.

Ground rules were established. The two students were to sit in the middle of the room, to state their positions to one another and mirror these positions, and to restate each other's position in his own words and check for accuracy. Then they could respond to each other, still mirroring. They began. One of us stood very close to each of them, occasionally placing a hand on one or the other's shoulder—both as an indication of support to them and as a measure of control of the classroom scene. We also ensured that they followed the ground rules.

In the beginning the dialogue that ensued was very fragile and difficult. Both young men remained stubborn, defensive, hurt, and occasionally angry. Slowly some of these feelings and postures melted as probing but compassionate questions were asked and answered and as they and the rest of the class were assured that these issues could be dealt with. When the discussion was opened to the rest of the class, some students used the opportunity to express support to both students. Others acknowledged sharing particular viewpoints on homosexuality and sexual oppression. Now the atmosphere became more relaxed, and comments were made that were supportive of each person's individuality, although not necessarily of their ideas.

When it seemed appropriate, we ended the discussion with the following commentary:

We have tried a new procedure to deal more openly with intense conflict, and it has permitted us to hear and appreciate each other's views more effectively. The techniques we used here today have been discussed in general earlier in the semester, and they probably have applicability to a broad range of interpersonal conflict situations. But we are not quite done. It has been easy, in the liberal environment of the class, and in this moment of crisis, to support a gay sexual orientation and to empathize with the personal hurt and challenge that have occurred. But will we still express caring and concern for him tomorrow? What about our other colleague? Knowing that he has serious personal questions about public expressions of homosexuality, that he is not an outright bigot, are we prepared to support his political viewpoint as well? Will we scapegoat him as the lone bigot among us, decide not to talk with him anymore, not care for him or deny that piece of him that is within all of us? Both men are out on a limb in this class right now and both took a risk in stating their concerns openly. We need to think about whether we have limits on the kinds of diversity we will tolerate or support.

In the ensuing weeks several class members went out of their way to express support to both young men's feelings and positions. Both young men became more open and obviously felt supported, rather than punished, for their expression of feelings and for the risk they took in the "experimental dialogue."

REFLECTIONS AND CONCLUSIONS

This particular exercise was an extraordinary learning event, which illustrated the value of the overall course design. The positive outcomes were partly the result of an open and engaging classroom environment in which students were taught the dialogic skills necessary to fulfill classroom norms of honest communication. The "spiral" effect of the exercise design, which utilized writing and personal reflection and small and large group discussions in successive stages, helped students examine and integrate their feelings about a difficult issue several times over the course of several days. Certainly the willing and even courageous participation of this particular group of students contributed to the success of the exercise. But another part was serendipitous. It was in some sense "lucky" that a "teachable moment" occurred, that the exercise and discussion created such strong feelings that a "real time" issue erupted in class, and that we came up with a meaningful way of dealing with the issue. It was fortunate that it worked out in a way that advanced understanding rather than misunderstanding, learning rather than retreat, overt discussion rather than covert snickering or back stabbing, and increased closeness and caring rather than isolation and exclusion. Why did it happen this way?

The explosion of a real time "teachable moment," the passionately expressed conflict and the ensuing involvement of the class, could not have been predicted. Many of us who work with issues of intergroup conflict hope for just such events to occur. Once it occurred, of course, we felt compelled to try to take advantage of it. Failing to do so would have constituted a failure to live up to the norms and agenda of the class; it also would have taught a negative lesson regarding honest confrontation and exploration of overt conflict. Thus, as instructors, we had to take the risk of escalating issues even further in an effort to draw maximum learning from the event (Berkeide and Segal 1985). Nevertheless, the issues were strong and scary, and the risks evident.

In reflecting about the success of this particular exercise, we have identified several factors that may have contributed to its value as a teaching tool. Some of these—the classroom atmosphere and norms, the design of the exercise, the commitment of the students, and the dynamics of the "teachable moment"—have already been discussed. In addition, the fact that the coinstructors were of different gender and ethnicity demonstrated to students that people who appear to be very different in their experiences and communication styles can communicate effectively and be supportive of each other. Our differences provided a sense of safety for us as instructors as well. When one of us was unsure about what to do, we could rely on the other to step in and move the process along (Kramer and Martin 1988). Finally, the use of conflict management and dialogue-creating processes that were already familiar to the students from prior classroom exposure contributed to their ability to trust that the conflict, though heated and at times painful, could be dealt with in appropriate ways.

Students addressed many of these contextual or procedural factors in their final evaluation papers when they assessed their personal learning experience as well as their participation in the class. Students' comments referred to the overall classroom atmosphere, the ways in which they were challenged by what seemed to be a non-traditional type of classroom, and the skills and insights learned. They also wrote of their personal growth and new social awareness about their group memberships:

I was constantly evaluating my thoughts and feelings and trying to make sense of the confusions I had never felt before. . . . At times I wanted to give up, but I persisted. The class has made me think about myself.

For one of the first times, I was in a class where I was forced to *actively* take part in the learning process.

More specifically, several students reported that norms such as active listening, respect for each other's opinions, and constructive use of conflict contributed to their learning:

I have become more willing to listen and accept others' comments before challenging them, as opposed to listening and challenging simultaneously. Lately through experience, I have noticed that through constant conscious effort, this process has become more ingrained.

I have learned to deal more directly with conflict situations, to give constructive feedback, and to not just let things happen and let them pass me by.

Some students struggled with the innovative norms that unfolded in the class and felt a bit defensive, particularly early in the semester.

I almost feel like I never reached the point where I found my niche in the class. Perhaps this is a good sign though. I never got so comfortable that I stopped really thinking.

We discussed many times that certain people seem to feel intimidated at times by the atmosphere of the class. I am glad that we discussed this issue in class because I felt less self-conscious about participating later on.

Many students stated that the course taught them new insights about self and others and new skills. The effort to examine group process even in the midst of controversial or difficult discussions contributed to this learning. Other common themes were the opportunity to look at one's behavior in groups and the struggle to participate actively without dominating discussion. Some students found particularly enlightening the efforts to look at gender, racial, and other dynamics in classroom exchanges and how these patterns might have reflected differences in power (Henley, Hamilton, and Thorne 1985; McIntosh 1989).

Some students cited content-specific learnings and related them to their lives. Others discussed specific events or feelings in class that provided insight into themselves or the nature of conflict. Others simply mentioned points or skills they carried away with them and might use in the future:

The class has allowed me the ability to improve my communication skills when dealing with conflict situations.

The techniques I learned about interpersonal confrontation were new to me and proved quite successful in confronting [an acquaintance]. This was the first time that I was able to have a "positive" confrontation with someone.

Students felt that the course stimulated growth and change inside and outside the classroom. Many students wrote about how their self-concepts changed over the semester. Specifically, some students found that the course caused them to reflect on their interpersonal styles in the classroom and their racial/ethnic and other group identities (Crumpacker and Vander Haegen 1987; Kochman 1981):

Previously, I had given very little thought to the fact that as a white male no matter what my social or political orientation is, I am part of a dominant group within society.

As an African American male who considers himself liberal minded it was somewhat difficult to find that some of my views could be more accurately categorized as oppressive to others.

It has also helped me to begin to understand the paradox of my Jewish community: we are quick to help the Jew who is in trouble, yet as a Reform Jewish movement, we have yet to respond with action to the cries of injustice emanating from the Black, gay and lesbian, and Central American communities. Why is this?

Several students commented on the value of the assignments and how they led to personal growth. In addition to commentary on the value of the pink triangle exercise discussed earlier, others wrote about the value of other assignments in helping them integrate intellectual and experiential learning:

The first paper provided a means for dealing with a conflict within a conflict. . . . I tried to write about an extremely difficult problem at a time when it was extremely difficult for me. The result was that the paper was not academically the best, but it created personal growth by enabling me to be more objective in a situation when avoidance would have been quite easy.

The mid-semester paper was perhaps my greatest challenge, for its "vagueness" baffled me and forced me to delve deep within myself and find the appropriate resources in order to complete it.

Students' and instructors' learnings from this particular exercise and from the overall classroom experience can be summarized as follows:

1. Learning about one's own often denied feelings about "difference," about the fear of being labeled and stigmatized, and about the power of peer norms and the pressure to conform.

2. Learning about the range of responses to oppression and conflict.

3. Learning that underneath our "liberal" views or unprejudiced stands on issues we may still have internalized the values of an oppressive society.

4. Learning about the necessity (and difficulty) of openly confronting one's own and others' prejudices, conflicts, and oppressive behaviors.

5. Learning new ways of fostering the ability to listen and dialogue about heated and emotionally intense conflict.

6. Learning the importance of class and instructor heterogeneity and teamwork in working on issues of intergroup and interpersonal conflicts.

7. Learning the importance of developing classroom norms and skills that can support the constructive use of conflict so that students can learn to apply these experiences and skills to the realities of a high-conflict society.

8. Learning about the complex factors required in creating just solutions to conflicts at all levels of social organization (micro-, mezzo-, and macrolevels).

9. Learning about the necessity of knowledge in the form of a theoretical base and relevant information and in the form of experience and skills to deal effectively with conflict and issues of injustice.

These learning experiences reiterate the importance of going beyond intellectual discourse in the classroom and dealing forthrightly and proactively with students' feelings. They speak to the necessity of integrating content and process in course design and of creating a classroom process (ways of dealing with interactions, communication, and authority) that reproduces some of the phenomena and principles we wish to teach about. Finally, they drew attention to the vitality of using conflict and "teachable moments" as we teach and learn about systems of oppression, conflict, and social change.

NOTE

1. Portions of these descriptions also have appeared in Chesler and Zúñiga 1991. During this same period political prisoners were required to wear red triangles, Jehovah's Witnesses lavender triangles, émigrés blue triangles, convicts green triangles, asocial prisoners black triangles, gypsies brown triangles, and Jews gold triangles. If a Jew was also a member of another category, the gold triangle was superimposed on the other symbol (Kogon 1973).

4

Latinos in the United States: A Framework for Teaching

Robert M. Ortega, Christina José, Ximena Zúñiga, and Lorraine Gutiérrez

This chapter describes an interactive approach for promoting awareness of ethnic identity and intragroup relations among Latinos in the United States. With this approach, students and facilitators interact through dialogue. For example, during the first session, the facilitators or guest speakers present a brief history of a specific Latino group. Afterward, students reflect upon this specific history and relate it to their own lives. In the discussion that follows, the differences and commonalities of their personal backgrounds surface, fostering a better understanding of diversity and identity.

Over the past two decades, the demography of Latinos living in the United States has shifted dramatically. Latinos are people of Latin American descent from Mexico, Cuba, Puerto Rico, and Central and South America. Latinos living in the United States are also very heterogeneous beyond national origin. Other factors that differentiate Latinos are recency of immigration and migration, geographic location, and citizenship status. Latinos speak English or Spanish or both, and if they identify at all in ethnic terms, their identification ranges from strong to weak. The increased visibility of Latinos in the United States requires that people in this country become more sensitive to cultural and ethnic diversity. Traditional education fails to take into account ethnic diversity; therefore, people are inadequately prepared to interact in culturally diverse contexts. Rarely are opportunities provided that foster reflective experiences about one's own culture or ethnicity. While multicultural learning is necessary in contemporary society, there are few available teaching models or pedagogical frameworks for implementing change.

To understand the experience of Latinos in the United States, we must incorporate two perspectives into this approach: biculturalism and critical consciousness. Biculturalism is fundamental to the immigrant experience because of the constant contact between dominant and subordinate cultures. Exploration of these mutual influences is necessary to come to terms with one's own identity. Critical consciousness refers to a psychological state of awareness about one's place in society and ways in which political issues penetrate individual experience. It leads to a better understanding of how relationships between social groups can be changed in the direction of greater equity (Gutiérrez 1989).

The dialogues focus on four domains of influence: sociocultural, sociostructural, interpersonal, and personal. These shape experience; therefore, they provide the framework for analysis and comprehension of both diversity and identity. Also vital to the promotion of dialogue among Latinos and between Latinos and non-Latinos are pedagogical strategies of experiential learning, such as fostering a feeling of safety to promote self-disclosure, examining personal experience, and creating a multicultural context.

The multicultural context is imperative for a thorough exploration of ethnic identity, intra-group relations, and inter-group relations. This environment allows the discovery of existing commonalities and differences between and within groups. The experience of being Chicano, Puerto Rican, Cuban, or Central or South American must be examined in relation to the Anglo majority, to other ethnic and racial groups, and to one another. Therefore, it is very important to actively recruit students from diverse backgrounds, particularly Latino students of different national origins, to provide for multicultural learning and inter-group dialogue between Latino and non-Latino students, as well as among the Latino students themselves. This classroom context not only brings many of the broader issues closer to home for students, but allows for a richer integration of personal experience and analytical material. Latino facilitators and guest speakers of diverse Latino backgrounds also enhance the multicultural context.

This course has been offered three times as a seven-week, one-credit undergraduate seminar through the Intergroup Relations and Conflict Program at the University of Michigan.[1] The class met two hours per week and was taught by instructors of different Latino descent: Mexican-American (Gutiérrez and Ortega), Mexican (José) and Chilean (Zúñiga). In one instance, the course was co-facilitated by two of us. Active student recruitment was done through word of mouth, fliers, and campuswide advertising.

CULTURE, CRITICAL CONSCIOUSNESS AND EMPOWERMENT: APPROACHES TO MULTICULTURAL TEACHING

We postulate that two distinct perspectives must be integrated for a better understanding of Latinos living in the United States. The first emphasizes the notion of biculturalism, suggesting that knowledge about one's culture and the position of one's own culture within a dominant society is important for multicultural learning. Here the emphasis is on developing an awareness of differences and similarities in cultural expression. This approach discourages the view that Latinos are an easily identifiable, monolithic group. To avoid stereotyping and oversimplification, we argue that a multicultural approach must strive to illuminate the richness in history, the cultural expressions, and the issues facing various Latino subgroups. As one of our Latino students announced to the class:

Now I know that to be Latino is not necessarily knowing how to speak Spanish. The most important factor is to feel Latino.

To feel Latino, we argue, in part requires that people are able to come to terms with their own cultural identity.

The second perspective combines critical consciousness and empowerment. It suggests that knowledge about the historical inclusion of Latinos into mainstream U.S. society, as well as current sociocultural barriers to societal participation, fosters an understanding of the ways in which minority status and powerlessness define Latinos in the United States. This has important implications for the configuration of the Latino identity and for multicultural learning. Here, the emphasis is on promoting a dialogue between and among Latinos and non-Latinos. As one student noted:

The most important lesson I learned in this class is that racism and segregation cannot be ignored. I've found from discussions with Latino students that to ignore the issues that are affecting many people who feel hurt and oppressed and discriminated against by someone else's words or actions, this is wrong! Issues should be brought out into the open and discussed and debated.

Experiences such as invisibility, acculturation, underrepresentation, isolation and marginality, oppression, and cultural resistance are often the focus of attention and examination in class discussions.

Collectively, these perspectives present the argument that a multicultural approach must portray culture and ethnicity as dynamic and ever changing, as a consequence of differences in expression and in experiences of living in a white, European-dominated society.

CONTEXTUALIZING LEARNING

Essentially, we use the bicultural and critical consciousness/empowerment perspectives to identify and explore issues of ethnic identity among Latinos, as well as among any other group participating in the class. We think it is vital to incorporate historical, structural, interpersonal, and personal factors in the design and development of a course of this nature. Our students have learned to explore these issues by utilizing a domain-specific approach as well as by reflecting upon the dialectic inherent in the "majority-minority" experience. Empowerment theory assumes that societies consist of separate groups possessing different levels of power and control over resources. The focus of empowering practice is on the experience of oppressed groups whose individual members are hampered both concretely and psychologically by their lack of access to power and resources. It is assumed that one way in which members of less-powerful groups are controlled is through ideologies that engender a state of false consciousness. This false consciousness encourages individuals to develop incorrect notions regarding the nature of the individual in society, notions that prevent them from taking action to improve their lives. The belief that a society that allows the token advancement of some Latinos improves the structure of opportunities for all Latinos is one example of false consciousness.

DOMAINS OF INFLUENCE

The Sociocultural Environment

In our discussion of Latino subgroups in the United States, we find it useful to think about the larger influences that contribute to the definition of Latinos both as individuals and as a group. For example, we indicate that an understanding of Latinos requires knowledge of cultural experiences as well as experiences of daily living. To uncover this information, we think it is useful to begin by exploring regional and historical differences. In this sense, we are interested in the social environment of Latinos, as influenced by their past and current living conditions. During the first two classroom sessions, we ask the students questions such as, "What significant historical events distinguish a particular Latino subgroup from others?" "How did these historical conditions shape the inclusion and level of participation of a particular Latino subgroup into mainstream social institutions?" "What regional differences and similarities might exist among the Latino subgroups and between Latinos and other minority groups as well as between Latinos and the white majority, in terms of cultural practices, values, and beliefs?" and "How has the general functioning of Latino subgroups been affected by their relationship with the United States?" Both the assigned readings and classroom dialogue are ways to approach an understanding of Latinos from a broad, bicultural perspective. In addition, this context allows one to examine a range of issues that have great impact on Latinos living in the United States. Questions focusing on the social conditions, high rates of mobility, socioeconomic class differences, and experiences of discrimination due to language and cultural differences help to further an understanding of Latinos. In general, this context brings attention to problems that Latinos experience as a result of not being an integral part of the community, disrupted social support networks, diminished resources, and limited access to educational and employment opportunities.

The Sociostructural Environment

Another domain for understanding Latinos in the United States focuses on structural factors encountered by those living in this country. Structural factors refer to actual accommodations as well as barriers to integration into U.S. society. For example, an early history of Latinos in the United States reflects incidents of segregation, the denial of equal access to community resources due to language barriers, and deportation in waves due to inconsistently enforced policies. It is a history of oppression that today is evidenced, structurally, in the large numbers of Latinos undereducated and uneducated, underemployed and unemployed. Within this context, then, we make the assumption that the various sociopolitical conditions under which Latinos live contain systems of explicit and implicit rules, roles, and a power structure that govern the place of Latinos in society. By understanding such arrangements, we argue that one will better understand the socialization experiences of Latinos in terms of the actual settings in which they reside. Institutional racism emerges as a relevant concept here because this context prompts questions centered around whether or not laws, rules, or norms of a given community are oppressive, depersonalizing, stereotyping, or otherwise hampering the ability of Latinos to integrate into society while preserving their ethnic identity. In general, an important emphasis is on exploring the way society is structured and how this structure fosters or impairs the growth and development of Latinos and Latino subgroups.

Interpersonal Relationships

A third domain focuses on interpersonal influences acting upon Latinos living in the United States. This refers to the influence of direct social contacts at home, work, school, church, or wherever people encounter overt or covert normative pressures. Here, one might reflect upon the content of non-Latinos' beliefs about Latino culture as determinants of the socialization experience of Latinos. In general, this context encourages an examination of conversations among non-Latinos about Latinos, among Latinos themselves, and between Latinos and non-Latinos, as a way to gain a deeper understanding of their day-to-day experiences. Questions such as "What messages (good and bad) are given that are unique to Latinos?" "What do you think are the motives behind these messages?" and "How might these messages affect Latinos?" are examples of the ways to explore and uncover interpersonal sources of influences as they relate to Latinos. As a Latino student once commented:

This kind of class should be made more available to the majority of the students at this university. So many people have stereotypes about Latinos and, with a class like this, more accurate information would be available.

Another student noted an additional observation:

It is interesting to learn more about people from different backgrounds. I learned a lot from other students. The class structure provides a positive atmosphere. Giving Latinos and non-Latinos the opportunity to learn from each other is the most positive aspect of the class.

Direct contact, then, and substantial dialogue facilitate avenues for challenging stereotypes and breaking down barriers.[2]

Personal Level (Self-Definition)

The personal level refers to the Latino experience as revealed by Latino individuals. It is a way to approach the issue of how Latinos contribute to defining themselves and their experiences of living in the United States. It is an important focus to consider since a common position is that Latinos bring problems onto themselves. We do not support this perspective. It is characteristic of victim blaming in that it blames Latinos and other minority groups for their oppression. In exploring the personal context, we direct attention to adaptive coping patterns, positive self-perceptions and attitudes, and sustaining cultural values and beliefs as important factors influencing the Latino experience.

Within this particular discussion, the extent to which external social forces act on Latinos in ways that are beyond their control must not be underestimated. Self-definition must be seen within the larger context of the social environment. Any discussion of the personal level of experience that ignores the social and political context runs the risk of blaming Latinos for their social and economic circumstances in the United States. Our position is that one must view the Latino experience as dependent upon the interaction of all of the contextual experiences that we have presented. That is, we prefer to view the Latino experience as influenced by the broad social environment, the structural conditions, interpersonal relationships, and self-definition.

Exploring these four domains in the classroom is useful in demonstrating the complexity of the Latino experience. At the very least, it suggests that in order to understand Latinos with any degree of competence, we must obtain sufficient knowledge regarding the critical components and properties related to each domain. The framework is not meant to convey one theory of the Latino experience. It is, however, intended to point out, systematically, the dynamics associated with understanding the Latino experience.

TEACHING PRINCIPLES

Four principles became central to our teaching as we tried to facilitate a process in which students could safely explore their cultural identities in a multicultural environment. These principles are critical in developing such a context, and we present them in the following discussion.

Dialogue

Minority groups have been part of what Paulo Freire (1972) calls "a culture of silence," whose perspective is never taken into account. It is therefore important to listen to minority students. As one of our students so eloquently commented:

As Latinos, we are a group of individuals whose lives have been permanently altered due to the exploitation and the cultural assassination of our people. We are a group that has been held down through individual and institutional discrimination, stereotyping, stigmatization and prejudice. We have been put in a constant cycle of oppression through mistreatment and misinformation that has led society to develop a "norm" of oppression which leads to justification of their behavior toward us. But, we are also a proud people who have overcome immense odds and opposition that will one day lead to true freedom for our people.

We believe that many Latino students have similar feelings and that they need an opportunity to express them. The presence in the classroom of Latino students of different national origin, from different regions of the United States, and of different social classes also provides the opportunity to compare and contrast experiences of assimilation and resistance to assimilation, as well as to explore commonalities and differences. However, Latino students also deal with other "cultural" identities, based on race, gender, sexual orientation, ties to "homeland," proficiency in Spanish, migration history, and other factors, and it is important for these aspects to be explored as well.

The interconnection of race, ethnicity, gender, social class, and other forms of oppression must be stressed as students explore the meaning of ethnicity among different Latino subgroups. Dialogue between Latino and non-Latino students encourages both groups to examine the diversity of experiences present in the classroom. Active participation in discussion by both men and women, Latinos and non-Latinos, immigrants and native-born Latinos is consistently encouraged. Each session starts with an opening round to encourage personal sharing and storytelling and is concluded with a review and summary of the session. The session ends after students are asked to make closing and feedback comments. In sum, the course, by design, becomes an opportunity for students to voice and reflect upon their ethnic and cultural experiences, as well as a forum for building bridges across cultural and ethnic differences.

A Safe and Supportive Learning Environment

Because we believe in listening to each other's experiences and perceptions as a "way of knowing" (Belenky 1986) and in dialogue as a way of "critically intervening in (our) realities (Freire 1981), efforts are made to create a safe and supportive environment. Students are encouraged to share stories (e.g., they are asked to talk about their name, la familia, their ancestors, something about their heritage they feel proud of); to talk about personal experiences as Latinos and minorities on campus (e.g., they are asked, "What is it like to be a Latino at Michigan compared with your hometown?" and "How do you experience prej-

udice and discrimination?)''; and to explore the impact of their Latino identity/
cultural identities in other aspects of their lives (e.g., career choices, interracial
marriages, bilingualism, political representation). The facilitators also use personal experiences and ethnographic material to support a point or to raise further
questions. They also point out commonalities and differences among and between
Latino subgroups to account for variations and differences in the Latino experience.

In addition, we have seen the course break the feelings of isolation that many
Latinos experience in college. One of our students stated:

What I did like was that people could come together and just talk. We talked about
everything. I love to talk. I feel like I can go out to UM and just be myself—a Latina.
I now realize that it doesn't matter what others think about, as long as I like who I am—
a Latina. I am even more proud of who I am.

Students typically develop long-lasting friendships and support networks as a
result of this course.

A Multicultural Context

This course has attracted both Latino and non-Latino students. The majority
of the Latino students have been of Mexican descent, although students whose
parents are originally from Central and South America, Puerto Rico, and Cuba
have also enrolled. Through campus-wide advertising this course has also attracted students of European, African, Asian, Latin American, and Native American descent.

The ethnic/racial diversity of the Latino students in our classes is quite revealing of the issues facing Latinos living in the United States. Latino students
are racially diverse, and the differences among them in skin color and physical
characteristics are strikingly evident in the classroom. Latino students also differ
in whether or not they identify as "people of color," and this raises questions
in the classroom as to what kinds of alliances ought to be built between Latino
students and other minority students.

Integration of Personal Experience with Ethnographic and
Analytical Material

Class activities and assignments are designed to help students integrate their
own experiences into the larger context of the Latino experience in the United
States. Exercises, written assignments, research topics, and readings help students establish connections between the experience of a particular Latino
subgroup and historical, structural, and psychosocial factors. They also encourage them to compare and contrast their individual biographies with those of other
Latino and non-Latino students in the class. For instance, initial class activities

have included student interviews of one another to stimulate discussion about migration patterns, national origin, ethnic heritage, demographic characteristics of family of origin, language or languages spoken at home, contact with other Latinos before coming to college, and so on. Another activity asks students to list characteristics of their own ethnic and gender groups. This activity provides an excellent forum for discussing stereotypes and exploring issues of group membership and group identity. It also helps students recognize positive and negative images they have internalized about the groups to which they belong.

Assignments have included reviewing census data for basic demographic information about Latinos in the area where students grew up or currently live. Discussions focus on observations and comparisons that students might have regarding the socioeconomic status of Latinos in that region compared with what is described in the readings. In other instances, we have asked students to reflect upon their ethnicity or engage in a values-clarification exercise that challenges students to explore salient values that guide their daily lives. The students are then asked to compare such values to traditional Latino and dominant society values as a way to evaluate their level of acculturation.

Students are also asked to write weekly journals reflecting upon the readings, classroom discussions, and events outside the classroom. Facilitators read the journals and provide feedback. Journals are also used to evaluate the content of the course in terms of what was helpful and what needs to be improved.

SUMMARY AND CONCLUSIONS

This chapter presents an approach to multicultural learning that has evolved, in part, from our teaching and student experiences. A framework for exploring issues of intra- and intergroup relations is provided, focusing on the Latino experience but applicable, with modification, to other groups. The major premise of the approach is that in a multicultural learning context, Latino students can explore their cultural identities by mutual sharing and comparing of cultural experiences. The view of a monolithic Latino community is replaced by the idea of diversity, which counteracts stereotyping and oversimplification of the Latino experience.

Historical, structural, interpersonal, and personal perspectives are identified as essential parts of a multicultural approach. We believe that elements of these domains are influential in the lives of Latinos in the United States, especially in shaping their identity. More specifically, identifying and exploring issues of ethnic identity with and among Latinos requires a conceptual framework that is capable of dynamically examining the multitude of influences acting upon cultural and ethnic experiences. By utilizing a domain-specific approach, students recognize the dialectic inherent in the interplay of these influences and the effects of this interplay on self-definition, as a member of a subgroup, and as an ethnic minority. Our impression is that such an approach better equips all students to challenge, in constructive ways, misconceptions about ethnic identity.

Beyond awareness and sensitivity to cultural differences, this chapter additionally emphasizes the need to become conscious, through open dialogue, of actual experiences of Latinos. By bringing both Latinos and non-Latinos together to talk about, share, and raise issues or problems, facilitators can create an environment of real life learning, self-examination, and, for some, an atmosphere for change. Another educational focus relates more to the disempowerment of Latinos within the dominant society. When Latinos and non-Latinos are brought into contact with each other, there is a heightened awareness of discrimination and prejudice against ethnic minorities and the consequences of such practices. The contact encouraged by interpersonal interaction becomes a mechanism for Latino students to increase their personal, interpersonal, and political power (Gutiérrez and Ortega 1991).

We emphasize four pedagogical principles to promote multicultural learning and consciousness-raising: maintaining a safe and supportive learning environment, seeking a multicultural context for learning, and blending an academic format with open dialogue in which students can learn from and challenge each other.

It is important to note that two social network outcomes emerge from teaching a course of this nature. First, students find themselves in a social environment that provides an opportunity to establish ongoing contact with other individuals who have similar interests or backgrounds. This is particularly important to those students who otherwise experience some sense of ethnic isolation. Second, students who do feel alienated from mainstream academic life are able to use the classroom setting to share their experiences and to dialogue with others. In this setting there is an opportunity for mutual support, validation, and understanding which has the potential to improve the overall academic experience of all students (Gutiérrez 1991).

NOTES

1. This mini-course is part of a larger undergraduate initiative on Intergroup Relations and Conflict at the University of Michigan, Ann Arbor. For a more detailed description of other educational components of this program refer to Chapters 1, 3, 5, and 20.

2. For broader analysis of the impact of intergroup dialogues in challenging separateness and misinformation, see Chapter 20.

5

Reflections on the Teaching of Multicultural Courses

Luis F. Sfeir-Younis

Most universities have not yet fully diversified their student populations, and the few that have made some gains in that direction are, by and large, reporting difficulties in creating a classroom environment and an institutional climate that foster the full academic and personal development of students of color, women, and other underrepresented groups. Students from such diverse populations are still the target of prejudice and discrimination and feel that their presence at the university is unwelcomed, that their class participation is discouraged, and that their personal and cultural contributions go unrecognized. A culture of dialogue that encourages and rewards students to participate in, and learn from, the cultural experiences of others has not been favored.

This chapter offers a few basic thoughts that could prove helpful to faculty interested in moving away from teaching practices that exclude and ignore diversity (monocultural teaching) and moving toward a teaching and learning mode that recognizes differences and incorporates such differences to enrich the educational climate in the classroom (multicultural teaching). These recommendations could serve as a framework or a set of principles for designing and teaching multicultural courses. These recommendations are based on my experience of several years teaching Intergroup Relations and Conflict, a course that provides students with the opportunity to develop a multicultural vision.

THE INTERGROUP RELATIONS AND CONFLICT COURSE

This course examines the nature and patterns of intergroup conflicts and promotes the development of skills to deal with conflict in cooperative, just, and peaceful ways. It includes a systematic analysis of the historical origins and the structural causes of significant and persistent conflicts among dominant and subordinate groups that are characteristic of monocultural societies. Racism, sexism, homophobia, anti-Semitism, and the like are studied within the context of such unequal power relations. Students examine the ways in which such isms act as mechanisms to oppress and exclude others, create walls to fruitful relationships among people who are different, and limit or prevent the full development of our human potential. A central course objective is for students and teachers to envision alternatives to monocultural ideologies, conceptions of reality, and behaviors and to carve out the foundations of a multicultural self and society.

The course is divided into three main parts, and each part is subdivided into sections corresponding roughly to one week. Each section contains key ideas, readings, exercises, and evaluation instruments geared to generate cognitive learning about the topics under discussion, affective skills to promote better and deeper dialogue among students and opportunities for self-examination and development. The instructors' pedagogical style, student-to-student and student-to-faculty relations, language and communication patterns, role of conflict and power, issues of trust and safety, and overall class dynamics change during the course.

The setting of this course is special: classes are taught within the living-learning environment of the residence halls.[1] Its pedagogy is participatory, interactive, and multicultural.[2] Students, about 150 undergraduates per term, are mostly first-year undergraduates, of whom 55 percent are women and about 40 percent are students of color. Two-thirds of the students live in the same residence halls where we teach the course. They are expected to attend a ninety-minute lecture and a discussion session each week and to participate in a dialogue group.[3] The course is taught with the assistance of several graduate and undergraduate students and residence hall staff who vary in involvement and experience and who come from diverse backgrounds.[4] Also, this course is purposely linked to other programs and institutions throughout the university.[5] In addition, this course is documented by a teaching and research team.[6]

MONOCULTURAL VERSUS MULTICULTURAL TEACHING

Monocultural teaching

- does not recognize diversity and differences in the classroom;
- matches course content, readings, assignments, tests and evaluations, and the language of presentation to the experiences, ways of thinking, knowledge, and learning style of the dominant population;
- excludes and ignores the contributions of women, students of color, and other subordinated groups;[7]
- tries to prevent and diffuse conflict in the classroom;
- does not recognize how instructors' social identity impacts students and the knowledge that they are imparting;

- places power and authority with the teacher, creating an unsafe and distrusting environment for women and students of color;
- blames women and students of color for possible lower performance and participation;
- sees any concessions to a diverse student population as compromising excellence.

A monocultural classroom makes for poor and conflictive faculty-student and student-student interactions and creates a climate that hurts and disempowers women and students of color and makes them the target of racism, sexism, and other forms of prejudice and discrimination. Monoculturalism unfairly singles out, excludes, ignores, or discounts students on the bases of gender, race/ethnicity, or sexual orientation.[8] It establishes one set of accepted behaviors and expects everyone else in the classroom to assimilate to it. Monoculturalism is also costly to dominant group members for it encourages ignorance, it limits the scope of their social experiences, and it promotes distorted conceptions of reality and self. In a way, monocultural teaching replicates within the classroom existing societal patterns of dominance and subordination.

Departing from monocultural teaching requires much self-examination, a redefinition of the role of the teacher, an expanded view of education, learning new teaching skills, and a re-evaluation of one's vision of a multicultural society. In addition to the faculty's level of readiness, institutional support and resources are needed.

Multicultural teaching assumes, based on experience:

1. An individual's gender, race, ethnicity, and cultural background significantly influence her or his worldview and the way he or she experiences and understands course content and classroom experiences. That is, individuals from diverse backgrounds have diverse styles of learning, communication, and conflict.

2. Power relationships in the classroom define, in large part, students' participation, sense of trust and safety, and classroom interactions. The teacher's responsibility is to create a classroom environment that fosters the full participation and development of all students. Changes in class participation and interaction require changes in power relationships.

3. A non-deficit approach to education that recognizes, validates, and incorporates the insights, perspectives, and cultural knowledge of diverse student populations benefits all students in the classroom.

A multicultural classroom is therefore one in which:

- the teacher is aware of how her or his cultural identity impacts learning and classroom dynamics;
- the content, readings, language, assignments, tests, and evaluations reflect diverse cultural styles;
- the classroom norms and ground rules are reflective of cultural diversity;

- the participation of all students is sought, and culturally diverse styles of communication and participation are recognized;

- differences are appreciated and welcomed, and ways of using differences to enrich everybody's educational experience are sought;

- power is shared among teacher and students so that everyone feels trust and safety;[9]

- conflict, both overt and covert, is used constructively to negotiate differences, establish honest dialogue, and increase learning;[10]

- classroom process and dynamics are as much a subject of study as the content and readings discussed in class, and they serve to enhance and generate new knowledge;

- excellence comes with diversity.

A multicultural classroom is participatory, fair, liberating, enriching, and humane. It represents the greatest challenge to our educational system today.

THE MULTICULTURAL VISION

The most important purpose of multicultural teaching is to help students develop a new quality of mind, a different way of conceiving reality, a higher-order thinking, a multicultural vision. Without such a vision, it is impossible for students to conceive of an alternative social and personal reality. This quality of mind is indispensable to those who wish to participate actively in the social, economic, political, and cultural life of our increasingly diversified society. It is also invaluable as a resource to contribute to the constructive resolution of many conflicts and problems that naturally emerge in a diverse classroom and social system. The multicultural vision is critical, imaginative, and intercultural.

The multicultural vision is critical in the sense that it encourages a mode of thinking that not only checks the logical consistency and the factual evidence in support of arguments but also encourages students to reevaluate their assumptions and the assumptions of the society within which those facts and arguments are generated. It exhorts students to become suspicious of power, economic interests, and the media and suggests that knowledge rooted in historically specific social realities may be social constructions designed to serve the interest of powerful groups in society. Critical thinking is a very useful tool in the first stage of a multicultural course when the most important task is to expose the history, the structure, and the ideology of a society and its institutions characterized by dominant-subordinate relations that promote prejudice and discrimination, hurting, excluding, subordinating, and ignoring diverse populations. It also makes students from dominant groups become aware of the self-inflicted injuries caused when oppressing others.

Multicultural visioning is imaginative in the sense that it allows students to understand the meaning that the larger historical and social scene has for their inner life. It reveals to students that their personal problems are often reflections of larger social issues. That is, if they were to belong to different social groups in a society and/or live at a different point in history, they might experience problems differently and have a different quality of life and a different sense of identity. It is a valuable skill to possess when the task of a multicultural class is to examine one's own values and behaviors and assess one's responsibility in reinforcing and perpetuating domination or resisting such oppression.

The multicultural vision is intercultural in that it indicates that the social world is experienced differently by various cultural groups within society. It forces students out of the straitjacket of thinking only in terms of the predominant or ethnocentric views of reality. Students also see how racism, sexism, and other isms are some of the dominant group strategies used to silence and subordinate others' cultures and individual voices. This dimension of multicultural thinking helps students recognize diversity and welcome differences. It recognizes that even though there are many commonalities among us as human beings and as citizens, as a result of historical, cultural, and social experiences, individuals from diverse cultural backgrounds possess different views of reality, modes of thinking, and styles of communication and learning. It is a valuable thinking tool when, in a multicultural classroom, students from one cultural group are invited to consider the views of others as valid as their own ways of viewing reality.

Multicultural teaching that promotes a multicultural vision is focused on dismantling the ideologically repressive apparatus of a monocultural society and helping to voice the views of the subordinated groups. Enlightening dominant-group members to the historical and ethnic particularity of their world view and deconstructing a reality based on the illusion of universality, evolution, and certainty are central to this task.

One who possesses a multicultural vision affirms the cultural roots of her or his own views and identity, retrieving what is lost or silenced in one's own cultural heritage, recognizing differences and refusing to rank others as culturally inferior or superior. This individual seeks to discover within his or her own culture what may allow for a connection, a sense of empathy, a common experience enabling one to appreciate and celebrate differences and be able to experience, even if not completely, the reality of others. It allows the person to be able to participate in somebody else's culture without invalidating one's own. Conflicts with members from other groups are seen as opportunities to participate in concerted action, to expand cultural learning, and to develop self-understanding. Finally, one possessing the multicultural vision is able to participate and negotiate an overlapping reality, a set of values, norms, and procedures (i.e., a multiculture) that allows persons of different cultures to participate in each other's culture and engage in common action. The task of creating and strengthening a multiculture represents the greatest challenge to our society today.

The multicultural vision is therefore concerned with laying the foundations for an alternative future. It is not enough to contribute to the critique of existing forms of society; one must envision options potentially open to us all. The multicultural vision allows us to do both.

Figure 1
Environment/Administration

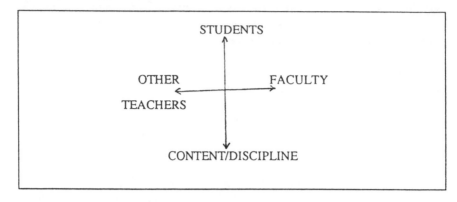

MULTICULTURAL TEACHING AS A
COLLABORATIVE PROCESS

For multicultural teaching to be effective, it must be collaborative. The idea that the teacher is the only one doing the teaching has to be abandoned in favor of the realization that many others contribute directly or indirectly to the students' learning experiences. It becomes a critical task in multicultural teaching to identify the key players in the learning process and recognize the role and the contributions of others, including those of students, to the teaching process. Others may greatly enhance teaching and provide greater resources and opportunities for a multicultural experience for all those involved. Figure 1 identifies key participants and illustrates this collaborative notion.

It is also important to realize that each participant in the teaching process has unique needs, interests, values, styles, and visions about this endeavor. One needs to validate these differing views and contributions and seek out ways of resolving each party's conflicting visions and needs in ways that enrich the course. The central idea here is that one cannot design and teach a course with a monocultural frame in mind, a frame that does not recognize and integrate the contributions of others. Thinking of all participants and figuring out ways of incorporating all the parties' perspectives make the process of designing and teaching a multicultural course collaborative and thus multicultural. In the sections below I suggest some ways to implement this model by identifying some issues that are particularly relevant to all parties involved, in particular students, teachers, and the administration.

Students

It is important, first of all, to know who your students are and where they are in terms of their values, educational career, socioeconomic status, gender, race/ethnicity, and age.[11]

Second, it is educationally sound to realize that students are usually at a stage of personal development and at a stage in their life cycle in which the issues they face, the moral dilemmas they seek to resolve, and the goals and purposes they pursue are of a different nature from those of the teacher and ought to be taken into consideration when designing and teaching the course. It is hard for students actively to listen to others, for instance, when they are at a stage in their lives when they want to be heard by others. It is difficult for students to consider the notion that their success in life depends heavily on the power of the groups to which they belong when they are at a point in their psychological development when they need to attribute their accomplishments to their skills, talents, and motivations.

Third, whether students come from diverse backgrounds or not makes a great difference in the learning process in the classroom. Students of diverse backgrounds are usually the best teachers of other students. In fact, sometimes students of color are expected to contribute so much to the education of dominant group members that they hesitate to enroll in multicultural courses. Proactive efforts at recruiting students of color should be made to enhance knowledge and multiculturalism in the classroom. Their contributions should be acknowledged and rewarded.

Finally, it is also important to realize that different groups of students experience the course differently, based on their gender, race, ethnicity, sexual orientation, and other group identities. Students from different identity groups frame the course, conceptualize ideas, respond to them, relate to discussions and class exercises, and expect different things from the course. For example, a close reading of course evaluations reveals that most students from dominant groups consider their course experience valuable if they were exposed to the culture and ideas of others whereas students from subordinated groups expect honest dialogue and concerted action to come from the course. Students also relate to the teaching staff and other students in diverse manners. I have found, for instance, that often students from dominant groups expect the teacher to be an expert whereas other students expect advocacy. Students' prior personal and cultural experiences condition their overall learning and resistance to learning. Students resist for different reasons and in different ways. For example, most of what traditional teachers consider unacceptable behavior in the classroom, like small talk, reading newspapers, sleeping, coming very late or leaving early, joking, and others, I consider indications not only of the quality of my teaching but as signals that students give to resist ideas or processes in the classroom that make them feel threatened, confused, or uncomfortable. Communication patterns and styles of conflict differ among students from different cultural groups. Without making generalizations, I have observed, for example, that male students engage in conflict as a way to develop trust, to confirm an experience, to assert themselves. Women students and students of color, on the other hand, do not engage in open conflict as an expression of trust, to affirm an experience, and to create a sense of community.[12]

Teachers must be aware of, and must learn how to validate, such different approaches and reactions to the course. The course can then be designed and carried on in ways that provide opportunities for all involved, and the educational task and objectives of the instructional staff can in some ways differ for each identity group. Therefore, a multicultural course must offer multiple ways of learning, learning goals and assignments, and forms of grading and evaluation that reflect culturally diverse learning styles. One cannot possibly teach multiculturalism in a monocultural way. Or put in another way, how far our class goes into multicultural learning depends on how multicultural the class really is.

The Teacher

Multicultural teaching begins, first, with the realization that the teacher has a major role in empowering or disempowering students in the classroom. The type of interaction that the teacher has with a student is a major determinant of the student's learning and performance in class.[13]

Second, a multicultural teacher needs to begin with an examination of his or her values, beliefs, and visions of life, including prejudices and discomforts with certain issues. Defining her or his social identity and the socialization messages that originate from the groups that have defined identity is important, for the teacher's values, beliefs, ideas, and experiences are the filters through which the course material is presented to students. There is little separation between the subject matter and the self, despite myths of neutrality and objectivity. Multicultural teaching begins not with the judgment of others but with an examination of self.

Third, it is also critical to recognize that students react differently to the revelation of the teacher's values, beliefs, or emotions about a particular issue. On many occasions, I have noticed that white male students became uneasy when my values were made explicit, for they felt that I ceased to be neutral and feared that this alleged lack of neutrality might interfere with their learning. On the other hand, women and students of color really appreciated the fact that my values were public, even when they disagreed with them. For students from dominant groups, to be neutral means (1) to be objective by separating the idea from one's values and (2) to give equal time and attention to opposing views. For example, when we talk about rape, these students would prefer that I provide equal amounts of time to the rape of women and the rape of men. On the other hand, neutrality, for students from subordinated groups, means (1) to make your personal values and assumptions explicit and (2) to provide more support to the ideas coming from members of relatively powerless groups.

Fourth, the course is experienced in significantly different ways by students depending on the instructor's identity group. The content of the course, the student-teacher interactions, class dynamics, and the overall atmosphere of the class vary based on the race, ethnicity, and gender of the instructor.[14] For

example, one end-of-term evaluation read: "You do a much better job at expressing the experiences of subordinated group members than in expressing the
points of view of dominant groups." Often students examine or even reject ideas
presented in class based not on the logic of the argument or the evidence, but
on who presents the idea.

Fifth, one's legitimacy in the classroom often depends upon one's gender or
ethnicity. I have observed that faculty of color and women have to put forth
greater effort, especially in the first weeks of classes, to create an atmosphere
of respect and to be considered as legitimate and as expert in a field as a white
male faculty member. As a faculty member of color, for example, I have discovered that I am not alone in having to give serious thought even to how to
dress for class.

Finally, what makes multicultural teaching so challenging is that the teachers,
as well as the students, and their interactions with one another may become as
much the subject of attention, evaluation, and learning as the topics themselves.
The teacher becomes part of the subject matter. "Now I understand," confessed
a colleague of mine, "why students are asking me personal questions. It has
never happened to me before."

Other Teachers

Other teachers include co-teachers, guest speakers, teaching assistants, and
students. The key idea here is to make sure that one creates a diverse teaching
team and that such a team works collaboratively. To ensure diversity in our
teaching team, I have become more proactive at announcing positions for teaching
assistants, I have to redesign the interviewing process, and I have received
permission from my department to hire graduate students from other departments
or colleges. I have also invited qualified student services staff to join our teaching
team. We also incorporate undergraduate students to facilitate dialogue groups,
guide group exercises, and assist graduate teaching assistants. It is also important
to bring in a diverse group of guest speakers and other guests.

A diverse teaching team is of great value for new ideas, experiences, and
styles of teaching to be incorporated into the course. Teachers of diverse backgrounds become important role models to students of similar backgrounds. For
example, students of color, in general, and Latino(a) students, in particular,
never fail to mention with pride that having me, a Latino, as a teacher has been
a powerful role-modeling experience. A diverse teaching team, as a team, also
serves to role-model the very multicultural behavior we are teaching to students.
It is also of great import to white students to see people of color and women in
positions of authority. It often helps to eliminate negative stereotypes of minority
groups. I find that having a diverse group of co-teachers helps complement my
teaching and compensates for my own personal and cultural limitations. A diverse
teaching team, however, requires more genuine communication, coordination,
and meetings to ensure that the diversity of the team translates into a multicultural

Figure 2
Four Possible Teaching Environments

		CONTENT	
		Mono-	Multi
PROCESS	Mono-	Purely Monocultural	Affirmative Action
	Multi-	Participatory Teaching	Genuinely Multicultural

experience that could enrich our teaching and the students' learning in the classroom.

The Content/Discipline

Multiculturalism enriches and brings about more excellence in our disciplines or fields of study. The teaching of multicultural issues requires the incorporation of a new educational paradigm, which requires a greater knowledge not only of content but also of multicultural process skills in the classroom. Not only do the theories, findings, methodology, and history of the subject matter need to be studied and analyzed, but also the manner in which the teaching is done and the relation of students and teachers toward that subject matter become as important a focus of analysis as the content itself. A focus on process may also bring about new knowledge, especially knowledge about the experiences of groups whose histories have been silenced.

Therefore a movement toward multiculturalism requires changes in content and process. Changes in the topics under study and the readings (e.g., including readings by or about people of color or women) or changes in the pedagogy (an increase in students' participation; recognition and validation of diverse ways of thinking) may increase the degree of multiculturalism of the course, but a truly multicultural course requires improvement and integration of both. Along these two dimensions, process and content, four types of teaching environments exist. This idea is illustrated in Figure 2. A purely monocultural class assumes homogeneity in its student composition (i.e., it is not diverse or does not recognize its diversity), its content is mostly Eurocentric, and its pedagogical process is hierarchical and non-participatory. In an affirmative action class the content is multicultural, but not the process. Typically, the faculty searches for readings by or about minority groups and women, but class interactions, student participation, and styles of learning, communication, and thinking are not changed.

In a participatory class the content, readings, issues discussed, and intellectual paradigm remain unchanged, but the teaching style and class interactions are more participatory, interactive, and diverse. In a genuinely multicultural class both content and process are transformed in ways that reflect the interests, behavioral styles, and learning modes of a diverse student population. In a course in which class interactions are an integral part of the subject matter, diversity is welcomed, new knowledge is generated, and new ways of conceiving reality are integrated, which may help stretch the paradigm of the discipline.

The University Environment/Administration

The community, in general, and the university administration, in particular, contribute greatly to teaching, for they consciously or unconsciously set the frame, the context, within which classroom teaching and learning take place. Much of what happens on campus, in the residence halls, and in other classes affects the way students relate to one's class. In one term, we taught our course during a period when major incidents of racism were taking place in the very residence halls in which our classrooms were located. In another term, students were protesting the administration's perceived lack of commitment to diversity. More recently, the Gulf War was the greatest concern in students' minds. I have found it very useful not to teach the class as if those events did not exist but to incorporate them into the design and teaching of the course. Readings, illustrations, guest speakers, dialogue groups among contending parties, and extended office hours to talk about the issues have all enriched the classroom experience.

The administration also contributes to the classroom climate by the degree of commitment to diversity and multiculturalism. The degree of multiculturalism of a class depends not only on the willingness of faculty (and students) but also on the degree of commitment to multiculturalism on the part of the university administration. The administration controls the resources, the incentives, and the influence to encourage or discourage discourse on these matters.

A discrepancy between the values of the teacher and the values of administration on the need for multicultural teaching may have serious implications for teaching, the students attitudes toward the class, and the faculty member's career. Four basic situations, or types of fit, that may occur between the class (or the teacher) and the institution (or the administration) are illustrated by Figure 3.

Boxes 1 and 4 represent cases of perfect fit, in which the goals of the class and the institution are in agreement. In Box 1 there is no interest on the part of the faculty or the administration to move away from monoculturalism; it is the most common situation in college classrooms today. In Box 4, talent, skills, and institutional support and resources are dedicated to the multicultural task. Monocultural teaching reinforces the prevailing division of labor and separation of goals between faculty and staff whereas multicultural teaching requires a common vision and a teaching partnership between them. Multicultural teaching invites staff to participate actively as an equal partner in the teaching endeavor.

Figure 3
Administrative Support for Classroom Multiculturalism

		CLASS	
		Mono-cultural	Multi-cultural
INSTITUTION	Mono-cultural	1	2
	Multi-cultural	3	4

Boxes 2 and 3 are of great interest, for there is a lag or a conflict between the readiness of the faculty and the support of the institution. Such lack of fit has an impact on class interactions and on faculty staff relations. When faculty have moved their courses along multicultural ways without the support of the administration, as is the case in Box 2, they run the risk of marginality, of not getting tenure, and of being accused of political correctness. In instances where the administration encourages the faculty to teach in more multicultural ways, as is the case in Box 3, faculty may resist such efforts by taking on the role of "defenders of the faith," resisting interference in the classroom, crying about the loss of autonomy, and implying that diversity is a politically expedient agenda that comes at the expense of excellence and rigor in the classroom.

A partnership between faculty and the administration needs to be sought. Multicultural programs that are genuinely supported by the administration have the greatest chances of success. Even though most diversity efforts at our universities have started from student movements, whether the president or deans of the university are seriously behind such programs is of critical importance. Such support from above adds legitimacy to multicultural courses, helps increase enrollment of dominant-group members in multicultural courses, and allows the course to be taken more seriously by both students and other colleagues.

In conclusion, the central task of multicultural teaching is to provide learning opportunities for students to develop a multicultural vision. The multicultural vision allows students to critique present social conditions, to reflect on the impact social forces have on self and others, to develop skills that incorporate and welcome diversity, and to participate in the construction of an alternative just and non-violent multicultural society. To be effective, the task of multicultural teaching has to be done in multicultural ways by recognizing, validating, and incorporating the contributions of all key participants to the teaching process: students, teachers, and the administration within the context of the university and community environment. Multicultural teaching calls for a teaching partnership, a collaborative alliance, between all parties involved.

NOTES

I wish to acknowledge the support of the Intergroup Relations and Conflict Program, the Program in Conflict Management Alternatives Center (PCMA), the Faculty Against Institutional Racism (FAIR), and the Pilot Program at the University of Michigan. I also wish to acknowledge the constructive criticisms and suggestions from the editors, Dick Meisler, Mark Chesler, Ratnesh (Biren) Nagda, and Elisa, my wife.

1. All the members of the teaching staff either live in, or have their offices in, the residence halls. The teaching assistants (TAs) perform the dual role of teachers and of resident directors or resident advisers in the same dormitories in which they teach. Several student services professionals, mostly from the Housing Division and the Office of Minority Affairs, have volunteered as TAs for this course. My office is also there. This creates a living-learning environment, a sense of community, which allows learning to spill out of the classroom into students' personal and social lives. Students also benefit from greater knowledge of, and access to, their teachers.

2. Throughout the term we use a series of large group, small group, and individual exercises, simulation games, films and videos, role playing, guest speakers, surveys and testing, and case studies designed to help students better understand the more abstract theories and concepts presented in lectures and in the readings. The exercises also help students create their own conceptions of social life and apply these ideas to their daily experience.

3. A dialogue group is the face-to-face meeting of one or more groups to explore commonalities and differences. These groups are broadly defined by race, ethnicity, religion, gender, sexual orientation, and class origins. The typical dialogue group consists of about fourteen students, seven from each group. Examples are dialogue groups between whites and people of color; blacks and Jews; men and women; white women and women of color; and gay men/lesbians/bisexuals and straights. Students meet for five sessions of two hours each, facilitated by two trained undergraduates. We believe the dialogue groups provide an opportunity for students to learn from each other, to take the material in class a step further, and to raise questions better handled in small groups. They also learn to identify and manage intergroup conflicts. Such groups have become an essential element in building a multicultural community on campus. Please refer to Chapter 20 in this book.

4. I do the lecturing, but the course has many teachers. I am supported by several teaching assistants, graduate students, and other staff from the residence halls. Moreover, we count on the assistance of over a dozen facilitators, mostly undergraduates, who facilitate dialogue groups of students who are socially different. We make every effort to ensure that our teaching staff is diverse in terms of race/ethnic, gender, and sexual orientation background.

5. We work in close cooperation with the residence hall staff to help plan activities open to everyone that are tightly linked to the content and experience of this course. For example, there is a seven-week film series associated with this course in which the films are carefully selected to match the topical sequence of the class. We also participate in activities with minority peer advisers, the Office of Academic Counseling, the Office of Minority Affairs, and the Sexual Assault Prevention and Awareness Center.

6. In the last three years, this course has been documented by a teaching and research team that helps to improve the pedagogy of the course. It also seeks to assess how students

who select Intergroup Relations differ from students who do not and to evaluate the ways in which this course impacts students' lives and learning.

7. In addition to women and students of color, the category "subordinated groups" often includes the elderly, children, students with disabilities, gay men, lesbians, bisexuals, the poor, international students, and other underrepresented groups. When in this chapter I refer to "women and students of color" I also mean to include all other students from subordinated groups.

8. See, for example, Hall and Sandler 1982, and Edna Bonacich, "Racism in the Deep Structure of U.S. Higher Education: When Affirmative Action Is Not Enough," in *International Perspectives on Education, A Research and Policy Annual*, Greenwich, CT.: vol. 1, ed. Abraham Yogev (JAI Press, 1989).

9. Teaching, in general, and multicultural teaching, in particular, are greatly enhanced if hierarchy and coercion are reduced in the classroom and students are empowered to take responsibility for their learning in a trusting, safe, and liberating environment. Students from different identity groups find a different meaning and value in power, trust, and safety. Moreover, while these aspects are strongly interrelated, in a class with a diverse group of students and teachers a change in one dimension may not necessarily lead to a corresponding change in the same direction of the other two dimensions. Finally, students from different groups have different expectations about the teacher's role in balancing out these critical dimensions.

Equalizing power between faculty and students, which is highly recommended in interactive teaching, may, in some instances, lead to the deterioration of trust and safety by a particular group of students in the classroom. This may occur because of the institutional inequality between teachers and students in general, but also because of the inequality between groups of students in the classroom. Thus, an uncritical empowerment of students in general may result in a greater empowerment of students of dominant group memberships and the loss of safety and trust on the part of students of subordinated groups. In several situations white students have felt very empowered by experiential-interactive exercises in the classroom (the empowerment of those already in power), while students of color have not. Empowering of students in a multicultural classroom takes place in relation not only to the teaching staff but also to each other, that they are empowered differentially by reducing the gap between students of dominant and subordinated groups.

10. It is not uncommon for faculty and administrators interested in the teaching of multicultural issues to be motivated by the desire to diminish or to prevent conflicts in the classroom and the university community. There is some truth, but much illusion, in this expectation. Much of the conflict that emerges in classrooms, both overt and covert, results from the monocultural way in which courses are taught and the material presented. Women and people of color and their experiences and contributions are absent or denigrated in most texts or courses in just about any subject. Exclusion, misinformation, and denial of such contributions anger, cause despair, and alienate students and thus create much conflict, especially covert conflict, which often goes unnoticed by the faculty. It is wishful thinking, however, to think that conflict will disappear the more we talk about these issues and the more multicultural the class is. In fact, one of the most important aspects of multicultural teaching is to help make covert conflicts overt so that they can be used constructively, in ways that bring about more learning, more awareness of others, and greater opportunities for unity among groups and personal development for students.

11. Every student in our class is expected to fill out a personal information form that provides us with information about student background data as well as some of his or

her values and expectations about the course. It also asks what contributions the student could make to this class.

12. Tannen 1990, offers an excellent examination of gender patterns of communication. Kochman 1981, offers a very useful comparison of black and whites styles of class participation, communication, and conflict.

13. See note 8.

14. See Chapter 17 in this book.

Part III

Courses on Racism, Sexism, and Diversity

Over the last two decades, many courses focusing on issues of racism, sexism, and heterosexism have been designed and taught on college campuses across the country. In some institutions, these courses form part of the requirements for an undergraduate or graduate degree. In others, a struggle continues among faculty about the utility of such courses in the curriculum. With or without broad institutional support, however, the courses that direct attention to the lives of those populations, which may not be considered part of the "mainstream," offer students different ways of thinking about core concepts addressed in their other courses.

The chapters included in Part Three present our authors' strategies for presenting this content in vastly different units. Aleinikoff, for example, teaches in the Law School and gives examples of the importance of helping law students reflect on their assumptions about race and racial policy in the United States. Myers's course on Lesbian Studies, in contrast, is housed in the large undergraduate college. Both authors offer insights on the presentation of course content, through assignments, lectures, and discussions, to individuals who have had limited experience in thinking about diversity.

Throughout Part Three, authors note their dilemmas with "balancing" material. For Moya-Raggio, the concern is with the balance of gender and ethnicity in her course on Latinas. In the Butter and Siefert chapter, the emphasis is on translating their goals of awareness, appreciation, and action into specific race, gender, and ethnic content in a public health course. Bryant places his emphasis on the instructor's awareness of White cultural hegemonic thought and its influence on the teaching and learning styles of students in his unit, Natural Resources, and others. Wong's chapter presents a balancing of the need to increase the awareness of students from Asian American backgrounds as well as non-Asian Americans.

The variety of approaches to present issues of diversity is apparent in these chapters. Also apparent is that the nature of the balancing act differs based on the class composition, past learning experiences of the teachers, and the institutional and societal climates. In all of the chapters, however, there is an emphasis on linking the course content to other present and future learning that class participants will engage in. Diversity, as applied in these courses, continues to signify an appreciation for difference in a larger context.

6

Anti-Racism and Multiculturalism in a Law School Class

T. Alexander Aleinikoff

Let me start with a disclaimer. Law professors, as a rule, are not trained teachers. Most law professors begin their teaching careers with a Juris Doctor degree, awarded at the end of a regular three-year law school program, and perhaps some real world lawyering experience. When I started teaching ten years ago—following a three-year stint at the Department of Justice in Washington, DC—I was given a class list and a room assignment, but no formal instruction in classroom teaching. The demands of simply keeping up with the assigned material in one's first years of teaching mean that little time can be spent on pedagogical method. Thus, most law instructors begin by adopting a teaching style they witnessed as law students. By the time we have gotten our courses under control, we have developed a teaching style—haphazard and usually unexamined—that becomes difficult to change. Nor, it should be said, do most law professors believe that change is required; after all, contracts are contracts, property law is property law. What could a "multicultural" approach add, except to clutter an already crowded curriculum with appeals to "special interest groups" that do not advance the ultimate goal of teaching students to "think like lawyers"? To the claim that traditional teaching styles and subject matters make some students uncomfortable in the classroom, the law teaching profession generally responds that a good class needs tension and discomfort in order to spark the hardheaded, clear-eyed analysis required of lawyers, and, in any event, students must learn to overcome their feelings of discomfort in order to be successful professionals.

In this chapter, I describe the goals, methods, and subject matter of a course that I have been teaching at the University of Michigan Law School for the past three years. Currently entitled Race, Racism, and American Law, the course examines aspects of the history of American race relations and racism and the

law's responses, both as a legitimating device and a force for reform and transformation.[1] Most of the content of the course deals with discrimination against
African Americans.

GOALS

Law school classes are often taught as if there were but one audience in the
classroom consisting of basically similar students interested in learning a (generally foreign) set of legal norms in order to become respectable practicing
attorneys. I now believe that this is a mistaken assumption. In each course there
are likely to be a number of audiences who respond in a variety of ways to the
subject matter under consideration and to issues of class, race, gender, and power
that implicitly or explicitly pervade legal materials (Crenshaw 1989). Whatever
the accuracy of this broader claim, it is beyond dispute that students approach
the Race, Racism class from several different (and conflicting) perspectives that
challenge a teacher's ability to construct a coherent set of pedagogical goals for
the course.

Simply stated, my primary goal—beyond teaching the relevant legal doctrine—
is to help students become more reflective about their (and their culture's) assumptions about race and race policy in the United States. I also seek to create
a (relatively) safe space where students, in an atmosphere of goodwill (if not
trust), can exchange ideas and perceptions about the nature of the color line in
U.S. society. Crucial to this goal are the recognition and valorization of experiences of students of color, who often feel silenced or alienated in the law school
environment. Finally, I hope to make my underlying themes for the course—
that racism is deeply embedded in American society and that law has been part
of the problem and can be part of the solution—persuasive to the students.

These are difficult goals to attain simultaneously. First, while class participation by students of color is crucial, it is important that they not be called on
to "testify" to the "minority perspective" on a particular issue. When white
students speak in class, others do not assume that they are presenting the "white
perspective"—or even *a* white perspective. To arrange classroom discussion so
that white students believe that a student of color who offers a viewpoint is
speaking for all students of color is to lose the particularity of that student and
to miss the rich diversity of thought within nonwhite communities. Second,
while I seek to challenge students to confront their implicit and usually unexamined assumptions about race, there is a real risk that white students will feel
that they are being condemned as bad people, as "racists." Few, if any, white
students believe themselves to be either intrinsically bad or racist, and they are
likely to become defensive rather than reflective if the problems of the world
are blamed on them. Third, the views of students of color must not be seen as
privileged or beyond debate. Such a position leads whites to keep opposing views
to themselves (thereby not subjecting them to scrutiny); and it also, I think,
sends a message to students of color that a (white) professor does not take them

seriously enough to engage them on their own terms—particularly if the professor is constantly asking white students to justify their views. Yet rejecting or challenging the views of students of color may itself be perceived, rightly or wrongly, as based on the non-minority professor's assumption that he or she knows more about racism (or whatever) than the victims of race discrimination. That is, it can be seen as an example of exactly what the course attempts to challenge: the definition of subordinated groups by dominant groups.

There are no easy answers here, and I am certain that I have not been as successful as I would like in avoiding these problems. Perhaps they simply cannot be avoided, given the charged nature of the issues and three hundred years of American racism. In the next section, I will present some illustrations of things I have done in the classroom to achieve my goals for the course.

METHODS

Because recognizing and investigating the non-majority perspectives support the goals of the course, I include a wide variety of material written by African American authors. There is no "party line" here; on the contrary, I think it important to recognize the diversity of voices within the black literary and intellectual tradition. Accordingly, the materials include selections by Martin Luther King, Jr., Malcolm X, Shelby Steele, William Julius Wilson, Booker T. Washington, Derrick Bell, and Zora Neale Hurston. Many of these materials are new to both black and white students.

I also ask the students to read a book from a list I give them of works by black authors. The selections include fiction (e.g., James Baldwin, Ralph Ellison, Zora Neale Hurston, Toni Morrison) and non-fiction (e.g., bell hooks, Martin Luther King, Jr.). It is a course requirement that they prepare a short essay on the book they have read, reflecting on some aspect of the work that ties into the themes of the course. The paper is graded pass/fail. Prior to writing the essay, they must meet for at least one discussion session with other students who have read the book. By all reports, the book-discussion-paper requirement is quite successful in sparking thought. I must concede that the assignment itself raises an interesting set of questions. Will students assume that one black author speaks for all blacks as to the nature of the "black experience"? Does such an assignment tend to deny the selected books respect by viewing them as "windows" on subordinated cultures rather than works of literature to be analyzed and appreciated as are other works in the literary canon? (One student reported to me her objection that the local bookstore placed many of the books on the list in a separate "black fiction" section, rather than "integrating" them into the general fiction section.)

To help develop a sense of trust and openness in the classroom, I have experimented with several classroom exercises that put students in small discussion groups. One year I started the class by distributing a short list of questions asking students to identify their race and how they know it, to state how significant their race is in their daily lives, and to mention one experience where race seemed particularly important. After being given time to jot down some notes, the students were divided into small groups to discuss their answers. Two students in each group were asked to take notes in order to summarize the discussion the next day in class. The exercise was quite revealing. As might be expected, students of color reported that their race tended to be of great significance on a day-to-day basis, while white students generally led their lives without thinking much about their race (unless they were in situations in which they were a distinct minority). Students were interested in their knowledge of their own race and had not thought much about how they knew "what they were." The exercise obviously produced discussion about the social construction of race and the nature of the color line in American society. Not only did it show that the course would take seriously the experiences of students of color, but it also helped white students see that they were generally unreflective about the (unrecognized) privileges accorded to whites in this society.[2]

SUBJECT MATTER AND COURSE CONTENTS

When I first offered the course, it was entitled Race and Gender Discrimination. (At that time, it had a set of materials on sex discrimination that have subsequently been dropped because of other Law School offerings dealing with those issues.[3]) While the materials deviated from traditional law school race discrimination courses (being more historical and sociological), class discussion often focused on analysis of various models of U.S. anti-discrimination law. As I taught the course, read new scholarship by minority law professors, and listened to the comments of many students of color responding to the course materials, I came to realize that the word *anti-discrimination* had an ideological content: it seemed to assume an underlying norm of color blindness, namely, that the use of racial classifications is objectionable or irrational because race is a morally irrelevant characteristic upon which to distinguish one human being from another. Under this account, "discrimination" means drawing a false and harmful distinction between persons who are intrinsically similar.

This model of race discrimination law tends toward an assimilationist goal, which is not friendly to the celebration of difference implicit in a multicultural approach. Moreover, it began to appear too "conceptual" to me; it responded to a theorist's need for tidy categories and elegantly simple rules, but it didn't seem closely enough tied to the reality of American racial domination and white supremacy. From an "anti-discrimination" approach, affirmative action becomes a problem of "reverse discrimination" (after all, if the problem is defined as the use of racial classifications, then whites should be able to state a claim for relief if they can point to a policy that harmed them solely on the basis of their race). Claims for cultural diversity, self-determination, and empowerment simply don't compute: if nothing distinguishes blacks from whites except the irrelevant fact of skin color, then talk of racial solidarity is morally objectionable or, at best, meaningless.

It has become increasingly clear to me that there are important differences between whites and blacks, based not simply on the usual statistical measures of equality (income, unemployment, life expectancy, imprisonment, child mortality, and poverty levels), but also in terms of how they understand U.S. culture and history, the Constitution, and the future of race relations. A legal approach that denies these differences seems woefully inadequate in responding to the causes and effects of great inequality or promoting respect for cultural diversity. Furthermore, rather than seeing the primary problem for race law as the use of racial classifications, I now see the primary issue as the startling strength of an ideology of white supremacy (held both consciously and unconsciously by whites). Accordingly, the course has become increasingly concerned with the history and nature of racism (the "white mind"), social policy, and cultural difference. Reflecting this shift in emphasis, it is now entitled Race, Racism, and American Law. In shifting focus from anti-discrimination to *anti-racism*, the class looks more broadly at strategies for achieving racial justice, rather than an abstract ideal of equality.

I adopt an historical organization for the course materials, beginning with slavery and the drafting of the Constitution in 1787. We then consider racism (in the North as well as South) in antebellum America, important Supreme Court rulings protecting slavery, Reconstruction and the Civil War Amendments, the era of Jim Crow, and, finally, the modern civil rights era ushered in by *Brown v. Board of Education*. I find that such an approach puts current discussions of race policy (particularly affirmative action) in a very different light and also forces students to come to grips with the central place of racial subordination and racism in American history. I further believe that the historical organization lets "the facts do the talking." Rather than hearing descriptions by an instructor about the nature of American race consciousness, students can "discover" it themselves in the historical record. To many, much of the information and analysis is new and eye-opening. The resulting "destabilization" of deeply held but unexamined assumptions about this nation's past and present is a crucial aspect of the course, and I find that the historical approach offers a less threatening (but effective) means of investigating such assumptions than does directly challenging student positions on current issues of social policy.

Finally, there is the issue of the stance of the teacher to the course material and class discussion. It should be apparent from what has already been said that I have strong views on many of the questions raised in the course. I do not bury them in class. I think it important, however, not to be seen as self-righteous or as dismissing opposing views. I therefore try (not always successfully) to offer my views as hypotheses to be analyzed and discussed. In an attempt to help make students feel more able to participate, I also readily admit my own discomfort in raising particular questions and my concern that my views may simply reflect the assumptions of the majority culture in which I grew up. These kinds of concessions are rare in a law school class, and they are difficult for me to make. At risk is the professor's very right to speak at all: his or her presumed expertise may be lost. Yet these concessions are also liberating, removing the mantle of having to "know all the answers," and undermining the hierarchical structure of classroom discussion, which often reproduces the dominant-subordinate status of the groups that the course is investigating.

PEDAGOGICAL PROBLEMS AND OPPORTUNITIES

As a number of the chapters in this book demonstrate, some of the best teaching moments are unplanned events that disclose assumptions or issues that have been present under the surface of class discussion but never openly addressed. I will briefly describe one such moment from the course.

During a discussion on current race policy, a white student concluded a comment by stating that since racial discrimination had only recently been outlawed, given time, African Americans would be able to advance much as other ethnic minorities in the United States have. From the speaker's perspective, the comment was anything but derogatory. He was asserting an equality of the talents of blacks and other groups, and he was recognizing that for most of American history, blacks had been burdened by stultifying discrimination. But the comment was heard quite differently by some students of color. One stated that she was "insulted" by the comment and that the discrimination visited upon African Americans could not be compared with that suffered by white immigrant groups. Another black student stated that he was "tired of the comparison of blacks and white ethnic groups." Underlying these students' remarks was concern about the question that whites continue to ask blacks, "My parents [or grandparents] made it in the face of discrimination—why haven't blacks?" The obvious implication of such a question is that any lack of success must be blamed on African Americans, not the system (which, according to the usual white story, rewards hard work). So the white student's equation of black and other ethnic groups was heard as another example of "blaming the victim."

The white student responded to the forceful statements of his black classmates by further defending his position, not by indicating that he had not intended to insult anyone.[4] Class time expired at this point and could not be expanded because another class was about to enter the room. As the class folded up books and notebooks, an African American student said to me, "Shame on you for letting the discussion end as it did."

I knew that the incident could not just be dropped. I think that too often faculty treat each class hour as a separate, sealed block of time and that an "unfortunate" classroom event is limited by the bell that ends the hour. To me, what had happened in class was "unfortunate" to the extent that it inflicted harm—as it clearly did, to both the white student and the black student responders (and no doubt to others who remained silent). But it was not an "unfortunate" event or topic of discussion. Clearly, nerves had been struck; an issue had surfaced that must have been present in many students' minds. The conflict raised the possibility for both analysis of the particular issue as well as a discussion of the classroom environment. In any event, I knew that the controversy had to be addressed. That kind of exchange usually has a fundamental effect on a course; it would be a different class the next day because of it.

Based on past discussions with thoughtful teachers at the university, I decided that I had to confront head-on the way we as a class were talking to each other. I thus began the next day by stating that the discussion the previous day had clearly inflicted pain. I think such an express recognition—which, I must concede, I felt awkward delivering—was necessary. Constitutional courses glibly discuss problems of race discrimination as if they existed somewhere far removed from the lives of the students. To many students, such discussions have an otherworldly character that seems bizarre and alienating. My acknowledgment of the pain that the prior discussion had caused was an attempt to say to those students that I understood that "intellectual" discussion is not always abstract and cost-free, that I recognized the risks they are taking in exposing their reactions to the class. I hoped that it also communicated my view that passion and commitment, frequently dismissed as "emotion" (read, anti-intellectualism), have a place in a law school class. This last message is hard to get across in a law school atmosphere that so values "objectivity" and "neutral principles," thus devaluing or dismissing assertions of personal views as either softheaded or self-interested.

I then addressed the difficulty of constructing a classroom environment in which people felt safe to speak their minds. I acknowledged that white students may feel hesitant in taking what is perceived as a "non-politically correct" position for fear of being labeled a racist and that students of color may also feel uneasy about revealing views that would be seen as challenging prevailing cultural norms. The most I could ask for, I said, was that students proceed upon the belief that participants in the discussion are speaking in good faith. Finally, I presented my views on the substantive issue that had sparked the controversy.

The rest of the hour was somewhat subdued, and I am quite sure that my presentation was the cause. But over the next few class hours, the class bounced back, and a number of controversial positions were put forward and debated throughout the rest of the term. I am not sure that my talk "saved the class." Nor can I be certain how the class would have gone without such an intervention. But it marked a dramatic change in my sense of responsibility for classroom environment. I think that law professors typically try to protect students (and themselves) by not addressing difficult issues on which feelings run high. Since it is obvious that these issues are present whether or not they are openly considered, it seems to me that professors must find ways to ventilate them without adversely affecting the learning experiences of members of the class.

I conclude as I began. I do not consider myself to be an expert on pedagogy. In my learning-as-I-go, I have stumbled, changed directions, sought advice, and worried. I am far from where I began, but also far from a set of definitive conclusions about teaching race-based materials. Perhaps my experience will help others interested in teaching these charged and difficult issues to realize that they need not be experts to try, although they must remain learners if they are to succeed.

NOTES

1. Creation of the course was sparked by comments by students of color about the lack of curricular offerings on civil rights law.

2. At one time, I asked students to keep a journal noting racial issues and the use of race in the news, entertainment, advertising, and daily interactions. I have since discontinued the requirement, in part because I now believe that it imposes unequal burdens and benefits. Students of color generally need no special incentive to notice the role of race in the world around them; indeed, many feel a need to insulate themselves from the microaggressions, messages, and insults they regularly experience. To ask them to keep a record of such events can be painful. The white students, I believe, most benefit from the journal requirement, which forces them to be self-conscious of the cultural messages implicit in everyday life.

3. There were, of course, costs to dropping the gender-related materials. The legal norms defining and sanctioning race and sex discrimination are not identical, and the differences are illuminating. Furthermore, discussion of gender and race allows students to see "women of color" as a distinct category of analysis.

4. Not that this response would have been adequate. All too often, white people (and particularly professors) think that lack of bad intent is an affirmative defense to speech or conduct that harms. Since bad intent is rarely present in the classroom, all manner of harms, then, need not be remedied. What needs to be explored is how professors structure courses and discussions in ways that inflict harm without being aware of it.

7

Our Lives, Our Histories

K. Scott Wong

The teaching of Asian American Studies on college campuses began only two decades ago. Its birth took place in 1968 when students on the campus of San Francisco State College organized a strike to demand courses that were more socially and culturally relevant to their lives. As part of the general shift in social attitudes of that time, this sentiment eventually spread to other campuses, and the first Asian American Studies courses were offered. In a few notable cases, academic programs and departments were established. A key foundation of Asian American Studies was its close link to the Asian American community. Many of the early activists/scholars in the field and their students were involved in local community issues and organizing for change to benefit Asian Americans. Developing at a time of increased social activism, Asian American Studies was thus infused with a commitment to the community and social justice.

My own interest in Asian American Studies is rooted in my family's origins in Philadelphia's Chinatown. Although my father's occupation took us away from Chinatown for long periods of time, we maintained close ties to the community since my grandparents and other family members continued to live there. I was raised in a very positive Chinese American environment and was always encouraged to appreciate my Chinese American heritage. My Asian American-ness, however, was not a consuming interest for me, nor was it something that I felt I needed to "get in touch with"; it was simply what I was.

During high school, however, I came to realize that there were books that dealt with the Asian American experience and people who gave the issues of Asian American ethnicity and history serious thought. My first realization of this occurred in a bookstore when I came across the paperback edition of *"Chink!" A Documentary History of Anti-Chinese Prejudice in America.*[1] The cover photograph is what initially captured my attention: a young Chinese American male with longish hair stared out at me with a cigarette hanging from his lips, and in his chopsticks was a mouse and a small snake coiled on his plate in front of him, a representation of the stereotype that Chinese ate rats and snakes. "What is this?" I wondered, puzzled, disturbed, and frankly, rather angry. I thumbed through the book and soon realized that it was a history of anti-Chinese racism in the United States. Although I had certainly encountered prejudice because of my ethnicity, I had never thought about it as being part of a historical process. Buying that book was the beginning of my search for a deeper understanding of the Chinese presence in America.

I later went on to college and majored in Asian Studies, which satisfied that part of me that felt a connection to Chinese history and culture. After college, I eventually went to graduate school at the University of Michigan, again concentrating in Asian Studies with the goal of attaining a Ph.D. in Chinese history. The discovery of two books, however, would eventually steer me into a serious pursuit of Asian American Studies. While browsing in the used book section of the campus bookstore, I came across copies of *Aiiieeeee!: An Anthology of Asian American Writers* and *Yardbird Reader 3*.[2] Again, the pictures on the cover caught my attention: young Asian American males, long hair, jeans, a hipness that was usually associated with other writers, usually African Americans or whites, especially those of the beat generation or of the sixties. It was like looking into a mirror. Never before had I seen on book covers people like myself and the other Asian Americans I knew. These images struck a chord that had never been struck by the likenesses of the Confucian sages whom I had encountered as an Asian Studies major! The literature contained in these volumes was incredible, like nothing I had ever read. It was angry and lyrical; it touched on many of the things that I had come to hold important in my life; it addressed issues of race and ethnicity, growing up Chinese/Japanese/Filipino in America; it even displayed a special fondness for Asian food and the culture that surrounds that food. It was also my first understanding of being "Asian American" instead of merely "Chinese American." There *were* common experiences that tied various Asian groups together. These stories and poems were about my family and me, about the Asians I knew, not about distant Chinese statesmen in the twelfth century. Eventually, I moved away from Chinese history to concentrate on Asian American Studies and soon developed a course that I began to teach at the University of Michigan.

When I began teaching the course, however, I was confronted with a unique case of generational and cultural discontinuity. The Asian American students in my classes did not readily identify with an Asian American community. In fact, a trip to a Chinatown would have been as new to them as it might have been for many of their white classmates. Instead of taking my course in order to claim, with pride, their identity as Asian Americans, many students came in hopes of discovering and understanding their identity as Asian Americans. Unlike the students of the sixties, they were not demanding that their courses include the study of people other than famous white males, but instead were wondering what they had in common with the Chinese railroad workers, Japanese and Filipino agricultural laborers, or Korean grocers in New York. What did the internment camps of World War II have to do with these students, who were born and raised in the affluent suburbs around Detroit? Rather than having to convince so-called majority students that the histories of Asian groups in America were worthy of scholarly inquiry or that knowledge of another segment of the American polity would be beneficial, I had to show Asian American students that their histories in this country were worth looking into, and, most important and perhaps most difficult, I had to persuade them that they were part of that history. I believed, however, that once they began to take hold of the material, to see that their lives were part of a larger, fascinating scheme of history, they would feel empowered with the knowledge that they were not alone in their experiences as Asians in America. My role, therefore, was to hold up a mirror for Asian American students to gaze into, to provide them with the means to reach an understanding of themselves and of their relationship to our society as a whole, and once the understanding had begun, to provide a vehicle for its articulation.

As noted, many of my students at the University of Michigan came from rather affluent backgrounds. Their parents were professionals, often doctors, lawyers, or engineers. They had been well brought up, were sent to private high schools, dressed impeccably, and often told me that they had never directly experienced racism. Their parents expected them to go to college, just as they expected to find high-paying jobs upon graduation. Believers in, and perfect examples of, the "model minority myth," these students were initially resistant to learning about a history that was strewn with racism and anti-Asian attitudes. Furthermore, it was a historical experience that was ongoing, a fact made painfully apparent with the murder of Vincent Chin in Detroit in 1982. A history like that was a far cry from the expensive shops of Bloomfield Hills and their parents' tennis clubs.

The problem, therefore, was finding a way to take them out of their comfortable college classroom environment and make them see other facets of the Asian American experience, to find their way around what I had discovered was, for many, uncharted territory. After a few semesters of reading mediocre research papers and book reviews, I came upon the idea of family histories. I asked students to get in touch with their parents or grandparents and start asking about their immigration experiences, their adjustment to American life, their hopes for their children, and so on. The main guideline was to keep in mind what they were learning in the course as they interviewed family members. At first, some of the students felt that this was a rather insipid assignment; they thought that they already knew what their families had undergone and accomplished. As the semester progressed, however, many of the students began to come to me with probing questions arising from their family history. Some asked me if it was possible that their fathers could have been "paper sons,"[3] if their mothers or grandmothers would have been affected by anti-miscegenation laws, or if I could help locate the internment camp in which their grandparents had lived for three years during the Second World War. Suddenly, they began to realize that they had not heard all there was to hear about the family, that they did not even know why they were in Michigan rather than in Korea or Taiwan.

Not all of the students chose to interview family members; some, instead, chose to concentrate on themselves, to write their autobiographies as Asian Americans. In these cases, results were equally revealing. Those who believed that they had never encountered racism suddenly recalled those ugly moments in their childhood when they tried to understand why they were being called "Chink" or why "gooks" were not asked to play with the other children at school. More recent experiences took on new meanings as they questioned why their dates assumed that "Oriental girls" knew how to please or why Asian males were assumed to be engineering majors without social skills.

Believing that their affluent parents had always been so, students found out that their fathers, bringing only the fifty dollars allowed by the Korean government, had come to the United States in advance of their families in order to find work, which was frequently an arduous process. Despite a medical degree from a prestigious Korean university, one father could not practice medicine in the United States without recertification, which meant five years of studying English while he swept the floor in a grocery store to pay his rent. One student discovered that her grandparents, with children in tow, fled the war in China by crossing the border into Burma. There the family stayed for a number of years, saving money to make the journey to a safe haven in America, but never amassing enough to bring the grandparents, who later died in Burma.

As their own stories became clearer to them, some students began to tell me how much they appreciated this assignment, that it had been the most meaningful paper they had ever written. For many, it was the first time that they had really spoken to their parents about their lives. Long-held assumptions were proven true or false, as students came to understand themselves and their families in new ways. When they looked at the lives that they had researched, the lives of the immigrants in their assigned readings became more accessible to them. Their grandparents, parents, and they themselves were these immigrants. The lives of the struggling immigrants or the faces behind the barbed wire of the internment camps were theirs or their families'. Others wrote about their realization that they were very much part of American society; born and raised in America, they were as American as anyone else, regardless of ethnicity. In most cases, the students began to have a sense of historical connection with other Asian Americans because they had come to see the very real similarities in their lives and the lives of others.

When I came to the University of California, Santa Barbara, as a Dissertation Fellow in the Asian American Studies Program, we gave a similar assignment to students in the survey class on Asian American history.[4] The differences in Asian American demographics on the West Coast as compared with the Midwest, however, allowed for marked differences in the nature of the family histories and autobiographies and demanded certain changes in the manner of teaching as well. It is essential to understand that the term *Asian American* is a fairly new term, coined in the 1960s in relation to the civil rights movement and rising ethnic awareness. However, the term *Asian American* encompasses a large variety of people. In terms of national origins, it includes Asians living in America whose ancestry is traced to China, Japan, Korea, the Philippines, India, the various nations of South and Southeast Asia, and the Pacific Islands. In most respects, skin color is the main feature that these people share in common. The histories and cultures of these nations are very different and unique, and these differences must always be acknowledged. Aside from the inherent differences due to national origins, the amount of time a family has spent in the United States will certainly have an effect on the identity of a particular Asian American. A fourth-generation Chinese American will very likely view his life in America differently than does a recently arrived immigrant from China, not to mention a new immigrant from Vietnam. Therefore, the historical and generational similarities and differences among the Asian American groups will affect how they relate to each other and to the larger American population. Because the Asian American population in California is much larger and more diverse than in other parts of the country, courses on the Asian American experience taught there must especially attempt an all-encompassing approach to the teaching of the Asian presence in America.

The nature of this larger and more diverse Asian American population in California could be seen in the family histories and autobiographies. There were still stories of the children of immigrants who had passed through Angel Island or who had spent years in the internment camps or had relatives who once picked asparagus with the other Filipino farm workers, but I also read many more stories by students who had left Vietnam in 1977 in overcrowded and leaky boats, spending three years in refugee camps in Thailand or Malaysia before finding sponsors in the United States. I am still struck by a young Hmong, who, prior to his arrival in the United States, had no conception of reading and writing since his was a preliterate society and who was now writing about his flight to America on a personal computer!

The assignment in California was also handled in a different manner for non-Asian students. At Michigan, I allowed the non-Asian students to do their own family histories or autobiographies since I believed their stories to be worth researching as well. It was decided in Santa Barbara, however, that since the course was about Asian Americans and because it fulfilled an ethnic studies requirement, non-Asian students were to interview Asian Americans in order to come to some understanding of what it is like to be an Asian in America. There is, perhaps, no better way to arrive at some level of multicultural understanding than to talk seriously with someone of another cultural or ethnic background. This approach turned out to be quite successful as some non-Asian students admitted this was the first time they had interacted with an Asian American other than in passing. Even if this assignment represents the most time that a non-

Asian ever spends with an Asian American, it is hoped that a new level of awareness and appreciation will have been gained. As racial and ethnic tensions increase in this country, on college campuses and elsewhere, it is essential that students talk to each other with the intent of understanding each other. Therefore, students who took both quarters of the survey class (pre- and post–1965 Asian American history) had to interview someone of a different racial background each quarter. This was mandated in order to increase the range of their multi-cultural contact.

A major issue that often arises in courses that focus on the history of people of color in the United States is the reaction of Euro-Americans to the materials presented in lectures, films, and the readings. The term *whites* is often seen as hostile and value-laden, and *Caucasian* as too clinical. Some of us have begun using the term *Euro-American* to denote those Americans of European origin. This is also a way to stress that the term *American* is not bound to color; in other words, Asian Americans are just as "American" as those Americans of African, Latin, or European descent. More important than the terms used, how-ever, is the content of the material presented in the course. Asian American history is not a pleasant history. It is a history filled with violence and injustice, often at the hands of Euro-Americans. It is essential, however, to create an atmosphere in which Euro-American students can deal with the material without feeling threatened or "blamed." At the same time, they should also be en-couraged to acknowledge and come to grips with the history of white racism in America. These are not issues that can be softened or ignored in order to maintain a "comfortable" classroom. There may be a few students who will feel that the course is being presented from a point of view that maintains "these are the evils that whites have done to Asians." This, of course, is not the purpose of Asian American Studies, yet the historical process must be laid bare in order for students to come to new realizations about the history of their country and want to make it a more just place in which to live. But it must be done without creating an atmosphere of "we" versus "you."

Strong negative reactions on the part of Euro-American students to the course content can create a tension in the classroom that can be very intimidating to Asian American students and hinder the learning process, especially in cases where Euro-Americans outnumber Asian American students. It has been my experience that Euro-American males may seek to dominate or direct class discussions, often to the detriment of Asian American students, especially Asian American women. In these cases, one may have to deflect some of the aggression of the more assertive students and draw the less assertive students into the discussion. If need be, the instructor may have to meet with the various "fac-tions" (should the situation reach that extreme) separately in order to establish a degree of equilibrium in the classroom. In other words, the aggressive students may need to be asked to back off a bit and the less assertive students encouraged to speak their minds. If one purpose of the course is to help Asian American students empower themselves through the knowledge of their history in America, then the most logical place in which to first exercise that newfound empowerment is the classroom.

I have come to believe strongly in the efficacy of these assignments. They open up students to new insights about themselves, their families, their friends, and their society and give them a sense of historical connection to their own ethnic group and to the lives of those around them. As America becomes more ethnically diverse, it is essential that our students appreciate and understand what kinds of lives their fellow Americans have experienced. Their research shows them how stereotypes serve only to reduce, falsify, and invalidate real human lives. We owe our students this much.

As scholars and educators, we spend so much time with texts and ideas, creating paradigms and looking for meaning, that we often assume that our students live in the same intellectual environment that we do. More often, they do not. This course has been as rewarding for me as it has been for many of my students. Through their experiences of self-discovery, I learn not only about the specifics of their lives, but I get a glimpse of Asian American history in the making. Their stories are what the texts of a few years hence will focus on. By seeing what experiences these students have endured and what concerns them now, I have found specific parallels and contrasts in the earlier history of Asians in America. When shown this, the students are more apt to appreciate the lives of those long gone because they have come to understand their own lives as history. I, too, have come to a better understanding of the patterns of Asian American history by placing my own life in relation to theirs. So long as we acknowledge the value of our students' lives, I believe we can be honest historians in the classroom.

NOTES

1. Cheng-Tsu Wu, ed. *"Chink!"*: *A Documentary History of Anti-Chinese Prejudice in America* (New York: World Publishing, 1972).

2. Frank Chin, et al. eds., *Aiiieeeee! An Anthology of Asian American Writers* (Washington, D.C.: Howard University Press, 1974); Shawn Wong and Frank Chin, eds., *Yardbird Reader, Vol. 3*. Berkeley: Yardbird Publishing Inc, 1974.

3. In 1882, the first of a series of Chinese exclusion acts was passed by Congress prohibiting the immigration of the Chinese working class. The 1906 San Francisco earthquake, however, destroyed most of the city's birth records. Many Chinese in the United States took advantage of this and claimed to have been born in America, thus gaining American citizenship. This status would then allow them to bring family members over from China irrespective of class. The term "paper sons" refers to Chinese men who purchased papers (i.e., birth certificates) linking them to Chinese American fathers, thus facilitating their immigration. The exclusion of Chinese laborers continued until 1943.

4. I went to the University of California, Santa Barbara, in the fall of 1989 as a Dissertation Fellow in the Asian American Studies Program under the directorship of Professor Sucheng Chan. Aside from writing my dissertation, I co-taught survey courses on Asian American history with Professor Chan and taught a course on the history of

the Chinese in America. Professor Chan had been assigning family histories to her students for a number of years. In fact, the Asian American Studies Program at UC-Santa Barbara is currently in the process of publishing a series of collections of these student papers. Since coming to Williams College, where I teach courses on Asian American history, comparative American immigration history, and the history of race and ethnicity in America, I have also assigned personal or family histories with equal success. Here, my students have taken this opportunity to produce not only written family histories but have produced videos, photo essays, and illustrated texts as well. A brief set of guidelines for the writing of family histories or autobiographies can be found in Part Eight.

8

"A Circle of Learners": Teaching About Gender, Race, and Class

Linda Frankel

In my teaching I continually struggle with the question, How can I create a "circle of learners"[1] (Horton 1991: 150) that accommodates the different needs and experiences of the participants yet encourages all to approach the materials with a broader, multicultural vision? My goal as an educator is to guide a diverse group of individuals through a process of active and shared learning to a deeper understanding of the gender, race, and class dynamics that undergird our social worlds. This requires carving out a space in the classroom that encourages students to test out new ways of thinking and new behaviors.

For both the students and me, taking risks with new material and different classroom experiences has proven challenging, frustrating, exciting, and enlightening. The continuing odyssey toward increasing diversity and inclusiveness has challenged me as a teacher and scholar in several ways: to incorporate more inclusive materials and theoretical approaches in course content; to acknowledge and respond to the impact of differing mixes of students on the learning process; and to try out new teaching techniques that support active learning, integrate critical and emotional understanding, and allow for constructive outcomes of conflict. For the students the challenges have been to confront ideas and realities that undermine comfortable, accustomed ways of thinking; to become aware of the impact of the interpersonal dynamics of social differentiation on classroom behavior and the learning environment; and to become active learners who can call on intellectual and emotional skills to guide them through confusion and conflict.

In this chapter I highlight some of the risks and rewards encountered on the pathways toward inclusiveness and multicultural learning that my students and I have explored. If we can take these risks in the relatively protective environment of the university classroom, perhaps we can begin to work out better ways to understand our differences and our conflicts in society. If we can do this in a context that addresses both the emotional and intellectual components of our understanding of diversity, then the outcome, I believe, can be a potent force for change.

For three years I taught an evolving Women's Studies course on Gender and Society: Sex, Race, and Class. The fourth version, taught in the Residential College, explored gender, race, and class in the U.S. South.[2] With each successive experience teaching this material I became more aware of the classroom undercurrents and dynamics that accompanied the students' wrestling with these ideas and issues. Many factors, including students' expectations, class size and composition, the gender and style of the instructor, and the difficulty (abstract/ concrete dimensions) of the material played a role in determining to what extent the learning outcomes reflected multicultural qualities. I discovered that managing a multicultural course requires not only shaping the content and responding to variations in class composition that influence the learning process, but also creating a supportive context and concrete strategies that enable students to acknowledge and grow with conflict.

CONTENT

I focused my Women's Studies courses on the structural features and cultural patterns that support gender, race, and class-based inequities in our society. My goal was to look at the linkages and overlaps, as well as the differences among these three arenas of social hierarchy. I also highlighted the forms of individual and collective action that characterize women's attempts to survive, struggle with, resist, and change oppressive conditions in their lives. I chose reading material that illuminated the contrasting or shared experiences of women of different racial-ethnic groups and classes across a range of topics, including women's paid and unpaid labor (employment, community work, and domestic labor); poverty (class and race issues, including a critical look at the conceptualization of the feminization of poverty); race, sexuality, and violence (forms of racial and sexual control such as lynching and rape); movements of struggle and resistance (gender and race relations in national, community, and workplace organizing); and feminist theories and strategies relating to diversity.

Each time I taught these courses, I modified the syllabus in response to my previous classroom experiences and my growing awareness of the significance of race in defining women's experiences. Instead of simply comparing the experience of black and white women in each area I increasingly moved to choose material that illuminated the direct and indirect relationships between differentially situated women. For example, I used selections from *Like One of the Family* (Childress 1986) and *Between Women* (Rollins 1985) to examine the relationships between black domestic workers and their white female employers. I wanted students to understand that it is not only black women whose lives are affected by the social construction of race. I also used films and outside speakers to give students more visceral exposure to multicultural issues and diverse perspectives. The film *Metropolitan Avenue*, for example, takes us into lives of neighborhood women fighting to preserve city services by forming alliances in their multiracial, multiethnic urban community.

Another change occurred in the way I sequenced the material. Instead of beginning with highly theoretical pieces on racism and feminism, I entered into the content through more experientially based writing on the nature of racism (Gwaltney 1981; Anzaldúa and Moraga 1983; Moody 1968) and through readings that addressed the need to confront racism, sexism, and classism in the classroom and the university (Bunch 1987; Andersen 1988a; Rich 1979a). I felt that this would be more accessible to predominantly white groups of students and give them more substance with which to evaluate theoretical claims. Also, I tried to move dialectically between content that emphasized the negative aspects of domination, exclusion, discrimination, and hierarchy and a more positive focus on marginalized groups as active agents of protest or culture. Students found it depressing when the readings moved from racism to poverty to violence against women to occupational discrimination to sexual harassment. Therefore, I integrated material on work and family strategies, activism, and comparative policies into reading and discussion throughout the semester to create a better balance. I tried to avoid leaving discussions of resistance and social change to the end of the term when students are often immersed in group projects or other assignments and are less energized to engage in these discussions.

ASSIGNMENTS: JOURNALS, ORAL HISTORIES/ AUTOBIOGRAPHIES, PROJECTS

In addition to classroom activities, the written work I assigned was geared toward the dual goals of helping students to process multicultural content and giving them an opportunity to engage in a collective work process. Because each group of students manifested different learning styles and agendas, I found that different assignments took on more significance or value as part of the total learning experience.

Each semester I tried to provide a mix of individual and collective writing and projects. As I have incorporated more multicultural materials and methods (and as class size permits), I have used journal writing as a forum for students to think through the ideas and feelings that arise. Keeping a weekly journal gives students a space in which to address themes from the readings, to connect these ideas with their own experiences, values, and assumptions, and to reflect on, and process, the content and group dynamics they take away from class sessions. Students who are reticent about speaking in class particularly benefit from this assignment. This format presents a safer way to engage the material and can sometimes serve as a foundation for making one's concerns and ideas more public as the semester progresses.

Another type of assignment I have used allows students to apply some of the core concepts identified in class and readings to a more accessible piece of writing such as a novel or autobiography about a group other than one's own (e.g., Angelou 1970; Kingston 1976; Yezierska 1925; Campbell 1990; Marshall 1981; Walker 1982; Arnow 1954). For example, I have asked students to compare the experiences and perspectives of a black woman growing up in the rural South (Moody's *Coming of Age in Mississippi* 1968) with those of an upper-class, white, southern woman (Durr's autobiography, *Outside the Magic Circle* 1985). Both women played active roles in the civil rights movement, but their positions and life experiences were very different. This contrast illuminates the complex interweave of gender, race, and class relations.

A variation of this assignment, which elicits more creativity and active engagement on the part of students, calls for students to conduct a life history interview with someone who is different from themselves along any of a number of dimensions: race, religion, ethnicity, generation, class, gender, sexual identification, and so on. I ask students to walk a tightrope between how the informant frames his or her own life experiences and how the material that emerges fits or alters the analyses we have been discussing in class.

Finally, I asked students to work together in small groups to research and organize a presentation on a chosen topic for the class. Students coalesced into small groups around broad topics that interested them, such as violence, education, families/parenting, and health. Within these broad areas they selected a particular focus for their individual research, which was submitted as a final paper. At the same time they coordinated their efforts with fellow group members to create a unified class presentation that related their topic to the gender, race, and class themes covered during the semester. This arrangement gave individual students a chance to bring their particular expertise to bear in the small group as well as to have the experience of working with their peers to produce a coherent presentation that covered the multiple dimensions and perspectives of their group's theme. I felt that students would be relieved of some of the anxiety of depending on the performance of others by the fact that their final paper could reflect their own individual work.

We used some class time for small group work, but most of the preparation took place outside class. Students turned in planning sheets describing what they wanted to do and how they were accomplishing their goals. They also turned in periodic evaluations concerning group process issues—participation, attendance, task orientation, and so on. I met with each group as requested to give guidance, but I left the main responsibility for coordination and monitoring progress to the students. I have used this approach several times. At times it worked spectacularly well: the students came up with a product that conveyed true collaborative effort, communicated information and analysis that reflected a multicultural approach to their topic, and presented the material in a creative format. For example, one semester a small group performed a very powerful, collectively written prose poem exploring the cross-cultural dimensions of women's experiences. The presentation concluded with a class ritual in which a light was passed around the circle as each class member expressed her or his vision of a more peaceful, multicultural future. The fusion of intellectual insight and emotional connection achieved in this presentation provided one of the most inspiring classroom moments I have experienced.

At other times group efforts have produced less satisfying results; students simply divided up the topic into three separate subtopics and didn't do much to provide linkages or creative insights. The degree to which individual students were able to engage in true collaboration varied. This assignment also involved some costs to the amount of material and energy that were devoted to the readings and time we spent together as a whole class.

Even when the results were less than inspiring, though, students reported that they valued the opportunity to work more closely with others. Many of their most important learning experiences took place in this context, where they had more autonomy and could potentially confront and work through personal and intellectual differences. Yet, as I will illustrate, this assignment also provoked an incident of classroom conflict. I found that students generally needed more preparation, tools, and opportunities to practice cooperative work during the course of the semester, as well as more guidance on how to structure their presentations.

TEACHING MODE AND LEARNING EXPECTATIONS

Although I spend a lot of time seeking new materials and making adjustments in course content and assignments, this doesn't tell the whole story of my odyssey toward a more multicultural classroom experience. The more experience I have gained in using these materials, the more cognizant I have become of the role that my personal teaching style and students' learning expectations and preferences, as mediated by relations of gender and power, play in shaping the educational outcomes.

Hierarchy versus Cooperation

In the classroom I utilize a great deal of discussion guided by directive comments, questions, or intervention when students have wandered too far afield. The mode of classroom dialogue I favor is better described as a conversation than as a debate (Shapiro 1991). I try to facilitate an atmosphere of shared participation and collective responsibility for exploring the ideas triggered by reading, films, observation, and experience. My style, though seemingly loose and flexible, is undergirded by a guiding dynamic that seeks to empower students to see the multilayered, complex interactions of social realities. I present myself not as someone who offers authoritative answers but rather as someone who has spent a lot of time thinking about issues and can thus offer guidance to those who are forging their own explorations.

Survival in the academic culture has required that I develop the ability to engage in the pervasive argumentative, assertive style of debate. As a teacher I try to encourage dialogue that is nuanced, contextual, and shaped by the shared goal of greater comprehension, as opposed to one built on defending stark assertions in a conflict-driven process. Yet I find that when students (generally male) challenge my legitimacy by criticizing my style, it is difficult not to revert to the "display" mode to reestablish my authority (Tannen 1991; Maher 1984).

My attempts purposely to downplay my authority in order to leave space for students to take greater charge of the learning process sometimes leave gaps when students are unprepared to do so. For example, I have required that pairs of students facilitate a class discussion by preparing some questions and monitoring the discussion. This has proven difficult for many students who are unaccustomed to taking this role. It requires a great deal of restraint and patience not to revert to old patterns.

Students' comments on end-of-term evaluations have reflected ambivalence about the issue of control. Some students have asked that I be more assertive or directive while at the same time acknowledging that they have learned new skills:

Linda has distinct teaching methods which have both positive and negative aspects. She delegates power evenly between herself and the class members. This is good because we should have a strong role in what happens. . . . She also exposes us to new ways of examining info or situations and new ways of working with classmates. . . . The bad side of this is that she sometimes lacks control of the class . . . class members need an instructor to take control.

Even though, to a large extent, students self-selected into my courses on the basis of interest in the content and some positive sense of the proposed teaching method, they were sometimes not fully prepared for the parallels between the nature of the inquiry and classroom dynamics. That is, even students who expected to take a more active role in the learning process found it difficult to deal with the often-challenging emotional content of a course that is infused with multicultural concerns.

Gender in the Classroom

This problem was further compounded by gender relations in the classroom. As the literature on female managers makes clear, women in positions of authority call forth confused and ambivalent reactions (Kanter 1977). In order to make sense of the anomaly of a woman with public power, those with whom they interact attempt to cast them into more familiar roles, for example, "mother" or "battle-ax" (what Kanter calls the "iron maiden," 1977: 236). Therefore, the ability both to nurture students and to model respect for engaging in challenging intellectual work without being forced into a confining role is a constant struggle (Schuster and Van Dyne 1985: 165–71).[3]

No doubt my particular response to the gender (female), class (upper middle), and ethnic (Jewish) components of my own experience has played a role in shaping the interactional modes that I find comfortable. I experienced these gendered power dynamics as a female student and scholar striving to find my own voice in a male-dominated academic culture. My personal struggles to move beyond them, shaped by feminist theory and practices, sensitized me to the need for a process of empowerment for individuals and groups that experience marginality.

Impact of Diversity

Translating this awareness into my classroom teaching has made me conscious of classroom dynamics both between myself and the students and also among diverse students. Differences in class composition in these courses presented different opportunities and challenges. For example, when four black women took one of my small Women's Studies classes, several good discussions resulted. These students were able effectively, but without hostility, to challenge the white students to rethink some of their perceptions about race and push them to reflect critically on the quality of their interactions with blacks in the class. In another class, in which almost half of the white students were male and one class member was a black female, both the racial and gender dynamics were more troubling. In a racially homogeneous class of white students the challenge was both to make them aware that they have a racial identity and to explore some of the other kinds of diversity below the apparent homogeneity: gender, ethnicity, sexual preference, age. Returning women students in three of my Women's Studies provided another dimension of diverse life experience that added greatly to discussions.

In order to address these differences and to work through some of the discomfort, I have tried to incorporate more evaluative and process-oriented classroom activities into my teaching. I devote more class time to process issues, and I have also followed the example of some of my colleagues, who use small and large group tasks and cooperative and experiential exercises to supplement class discussion.

Students with more traditional expectations as well as those seeking alternatives have much to gain from a classroom climate that is built on trust and power sharing, and that aims to integrate intellectual and interpersonal growth. But I have found that I cannot assume that these gains will come automatically or without struggle, as demonstrated by two classroom conflicts—one centered on gender and the other around race—that highlighted the most recent version of this series of courses.

GENDER, RACE, AND CLASS IN THE U.S. SOUTH

Far beyond my other classroom experiences, this course reflected many of the tensions and promises of multicultural teaching. In a very dramatic fashion, classroom dynamics during the term mirrored the often painful and difficult issues about which we were reading.

I did not particularly anticipate overt conflict. In fact, my generally conciliatory style accommodates differences while sometimes prematurely dampening emergent conflicts. Yet I knew that the materials we were going to deal with were not easy or familiar for most students. Therefore, as I did in my other courses, I handed out and discussed a modified version of Lynn Weber Cannon's (1990) "Ground Rules For a Course on Minorities," a useful tool that I learned about during a curriculum integration workshop at the Center for Research on Women at Memphis State.

We began the first component of the course by asking, "Who Speaks For the South?" (Painter 1984). Our discussion centered around what it means to reconstitute the writing of southern history by moving the experiences of women and blacks to the center from the margins of the story. Next we moved on to an examination of myths and stereotypes, how they emerge and are perpetuated, what functions they serve, what material conditions support them. I find the film *Ethnic Notions* to be a very powerful, but sometimes overwhelming, complement to readings about racial and sexual stereotypes. Our next several sessions were devoted to recent scholarship on slavery, centering on the experiences of female slaves and white mistresses. The topics that followed included race and gender in the Reconstruction period; race, sexuality, and violence (with a showing of *The Klan: Legacy of Hate*, which covers its history and contemporary reemergence); poor whites; textile industrialization and labor strife; class and power in Appalachia; and race and gender in the civil rights movement. None of this material was easy, and most of it was new to students.

Conflict in the Classroom: Gender

During the first week, a female student wrote in her journal:

I hope this class becomes more emotional. It is important to study something from an academic viewpoint, but it is much more meaningful when the class is emotionally involved. That is, getting angry at the information, having academic debates and having strong feelings about the issues. A class like this could accomplish a lot more than an intellectual study of a region. It could also do a lot of consciousness raising and stereotype challenging. And on this campus, in this country at this time, those are vital things to have happen. Remaining removed and intellectual about a topic is an easy way not to be affected by it. In a class like this, that shouldn't happen.

Her words proved prophetic as she played a role in moving the class toward confronting the parallels between what we were reading and how we were interacting in the classroom.

In the beginning of the semester several of the six male students in a class of fifteen challenged texts and challenged my authority, even though I de-emphasized this aspect of my role. Although not all the men were vocal, there were several who were particularly assertive and sometimes domineering. Their styles tended to be in the debate mode. While their input was intellectually stimulating, the effect of their self-presentation and manipulation of the discussion sometimes disrupted true dialogue and prevented wider participation. I found that much of the discussion became an interchange between particular individuals and me or a debate between two students. I found myself torn between valuing some of their insights and spending my energy controlling their strong influence on the discussion by trying to draw out quieter students who I knew from journal entries had important insights to share.

I tried many different techniques to equalize the participation and shift the conversation in a more productive, group-oriented direction. I spent one entire class session and additional time throughout the semester on group process, exploring various dimensions of group dynamics—participation, feelings, power, tasks, norms, and decision-making strategies. One technique we used was the fishbowl exercise. This allows half the class to observe from an outside circle while the other half discusses in the center; then the two groups switch places. It gives everyone an opportunity to analyze patterns of interaction as well as to receive feedback about his or her own behavior from peers. The fishbowl provoked the following observation by the woman student cited above:

There were some disturbing dynamics going on. I noticed that the first group to gather in the center was a 5:2 female to male ratio. Yet, the two males still managed to dominate the discussion despite the fact that the facilitator was a woman and that facilitators usually talk more than others. . . . Both men frequently interrupted the women speaking, and one would often paraphrase what the women were saying and then present it as a point for all. Generally, the same happened when I was in the center. . . . These dynamics are typical of most other classrooms, and it makes me think that it wasn't just chance.

Following this exercise, a small group of women students, including the one quoted above, approached me in my office about this problem. I suggested that we make this a focus of discussion for the entire class. At the next class meeting, I introduced the issue of gender imbalance in the classroom and suggested that we might spend some time examining this issue together. After my brief introduction, the concerned women presented their thoughts and asked if others shared their views. There was a very mixed response. Some students interpreted the problem as a ''personality issue,'' some of the male students became defensive, some of the other female students did not feel they had been silenced but were willing to accept that other women felt that way. One student described the session in her journal in this way:

The discussion turned to an emotional brainstorming session that included everything from the levels of authority shown to a male versus a female professor, to the different degrees of respect and receptivity shown to both male and female members of the class. Examples of bantering across the room, different patterns of discussion facilitation,

communal and individual resources and general group disrespect were all mentioned. . . .
We concluded that the awareness of these types of dynamics were crucial to their improvement. Linda's final quote about "learning to learn" struck me as quite significant,
and it is something that I have subsequently pondered in all of my classes since then.

There was no unanimity about the source of these difficulties, yet there seemed
to be agreement that the problem was worth monitoring and that we would try
various strategies to ensure that everyone felt comfortable participating in the
discussions.

While our group discussion about gender did sensitize the group to issues of
inclusion and the etiquette of participation, it did not signal the end of the gender
issue. A few sessions later, during the section of the course that focused on
Appalachia, we viewed the film, *Coal Mining Women*. In the discussion that
followed I posed a leading question about the difficulties these women had in
being accepted by men in an occupation that depended heavily on male bonding.
One of the male students in the class took this as an indictment of the behavior
of all males. He launched into an angry speech about the feminist orientation
of the course and his feeling of being held personally responsible for all sexism
simply because of his gender. His outburst surprised and shocked many of the
other students, including some of the other men. I was surprised, too, but I
knew from reading this student's journal entries and from his previous class
participation that he was seriously trying to grapple with the material. I decided
it was important in my response to legitimate his expression of his feelings but
also to remind the group that our ground rules for the course did not support
blaming individuals for participating in discrimination simply because they were
members of majority groups. I emphasized that our approach should be to understand the particular circumstances and structural arrangements that have perpetuated different forms of inequality and to examine the often-conflicting
perspectives of those representing advantaged or disadvantaged groups. While
it might be appropriate to discuss how this knowledge affects our own perceptions
and behavior, I concluded, it certainly would not be appropriate to make judgments about individuals on the basis of an ascribed characteristic such as gender
or race.

This issue of "feminist bias" had been brewing throughout the semester.
Earlier in the term a male student wrote in his journal:

The most irritating thing about the course is that the gender issue is only being discussed
from one point of view. It seems that the female role is the only one discussed. . . . It
seems that in their effort to revise white, male dominated history, female historians are
quite reactionary and give unfair bias to the female perspective. Someone must do it
objectively!

Yet this same student wrote in his end-of-term evaluation:

I have never had the opportunity to discuss problems within a group before and am happy that I have had the opportunity now. . . . I did not agree with all the points made by some of the women in the class when they pointed out that the discussion seemed to be dominated by men. However, I understood their points and would not have considered them had we not discussed the problem.

Although this conflict was not easy to experience, it nevertheless did cause all of the students, male and female, to reconsider in a deeper way the issues raised in the course content. The conflict sharpened awareness of the parallels between reading about the discourse on gender differentiation and hierarchy captured in the readings and experiencing it interpersonally in the classroom setting.

Conflict in the Classroom: Race

The second overt conflict in the semester occurred around the usage of a racial epithet by a white student as part of an experiential exercise designed for a small group presentation. For me, this conflict raised important questions about when and how to intervene when students' actions can have damaging effects, however unintended.

Prior to the presentation in which this occurred, a small group of three white students came to my office to explain how their group project was taking shape. The female member of the group explained briefly that she had made up an experiential game to illustrate how black sharecroppers were disadvantaged in their transactions with white landowners by poor education and illiteracy following emancipation. She proposed to divide the class into two groups—black farmers and white landowners—each with its own private language that the other could not understand. For these languages she had made up words for ''money,'' ''seeds,'' ''black person,'' and ''white person.'' The word for black person in the white language was *niger* (not spelled the same as *nigger*, but the pronunciation was left ambiguous), while the word for white person in the black language was *honky*. When I questioned the use of these words, particularly *niger*, she argued that this reflected the conditions blacks faced at the time. She felt sure that no one would misunderstand the purpose of choosing this word or object to the way it was used. We discussed the provocative and offensive nature of this word, and I suggested that the group needed to do more thinking about the advisability of using it in class. When the students left, it remained unclear what they intended to do about my suggestions.

At the following class session this group of students began their presentation with the game. The class was divided into two groups, and sheets with the instructions and code words, tokens for money, and bags of ''seeds'' (beans) were distributed. The students began trying to sell their produce, using only the few words they were allowed. During this chaotic process when students were running around, shouting out strange words, and trying to make the best deals they could, the only black student arrived late to class from her job. She was handed an instruction sheet and sat on the sidelines observing. When the game had gone on for a while, the student presenter reconvened the group and tried to frame the game in the context of the disadvantages black farmers in the post-emancipation period faced due to illiteracy and lack of educational opportunities.

The black student challenged her use of the word *niger* and strongly expressed her feelings about the insensitivity of using this word, especially without asking her ahead of time. The white student was dismayed and countered that she had not intended any hurt but had used the word solely to illustrate the oppressive conditions that prevailed at that time.

During this discussion I did not say much, but it was clear that many unresolved feelings had surfaced. At this point, however, I decided that the other two students should continue with their portions of the presentation so that this group's project could be completed without interruption. Also, I thought that everyone, including myself, needed some time to process the events. The other two students gave very standard "lectures" about their topics, and the whole group seemed distracted and bored. After class, the two women talked again, but each seemed to be reiterating her own position without much clarity.

Over the next few days until the following class session I spent several hours on the telephone talking with the two students and consulting colleagues. One colleague, a black man with training in intergroup relations, agreed to mediate a group discussion if the black student and I felt that would be useful. However, I sensed that the black student didn't feel that this was necessary but rather wanted me to take some responsibility for dealing with the issue in front of the class. She was very disappointed that I had not intervened forcefully in class or prevented this from happening. I realized that although there could be differing viewpoints about the way the word *niger* was used in this particular instance, the fact remained that there was only one black person in the class and therefore the impact on her was the only real issue. As she argued quite adamantly, "Why didn't the students consult me?"

Part of the reason she was not consulted lay in her somewhat marginal position in the class, not entirely attributable to (although compounded by) her status as the sole black member. Her employment caused her consistently to arrive late to class and to be absent more frequently than is desirable in a discussion-oriented class. Despite her outspokenness and valuable participation when she was present, this circumstance kept her from developing into a fully contributing member of the class. It also affected her participation in her own small group project. This was a structural problem that probably should have been acknowledged and dealt with early in the course.

At this point I had to focus on her legitimate feelings to help us all understand what had happened. Although I worried about how to frame the discussion, I knew we had to devote the next class session to processing this conflict. A black female colleague suggested I use Audre Lorde's piece on "The Uses of Anger" to validate the black student's feelings. I began the next class with a short statement to set the tone for discussion. First, I took responsibility for my actions.

I said that it was the responsibility of the teacher to set limits and that refusing to do so gave tacit approval to the outcome. Further, I said that an overzealous desire to empower students was not as urgent a priority as making sure that this doesn't happen at another student's expense. I suggested that it was naive, insensitive, and perhaps arrogant to presume to know someone else's feelings. Such presumption could break the trust the group had developed and disrupt the learning environment. I pointed out that the classroom does not exist in a vacuum and that it is wrong to assume that classroom activities will not reverberate differently for students with different experiences in the world. I reminded the class of the video we had seen at the beginning of the semester, *Ethnic Notions*, which gives an intense picture of the long-standing toxicity, hurtfulness, and demeaning intentions of racial epithets. Finally, I talked about choosing to see conflict as negative or productive. Drawing on Lorde's brilliant piece, I suggested that we try to grow through this experience. As Lorde (1987: 7) says, "Guilt and defensiveness are bricks in a wall against which we all flounder; they serve none of our futures."

A very open discussion followed about what happened. Rather than restricting the focus to the two women at the center of the problem, we started at one end of the circle and went around until everyone had a chance to contribute his or her reflections. The black student did not need to be "protected"—she was very articulate and honest in expressing her views—but, rather, she needed to be validated in a setting where the issue was taken seriously by the group as whole but, perhaps more importantly, by the instructor.

This incident raises legitimate and interesting questions about when it is useful or appropriate to use derogatory language in an educational context. From the point of view of the white student the purpose here was clearly not to inflame but rather to illustrate the negative consequences of racial discrimination. Yet someone was hurt. We must work hard to ensure that learning about difficult issues does not unwittingly inflict greater pain.

Since this happened near the end of the semester when students were busy working on their projects, this episode did not appear in the journals. In their evaluations of this group's project, however, the white students did not mention this incident but did write about how interesting and enlightening they had found the game. The black student wrote the following in her evaluation of the course:

The students were given too much responsibility . . . for some decision-making. Students used taboo words in the class while the teacher sat and did not respond. . . . There needs to be more control from the authority figure. Being able to respond to different projects and presentations enlightened me about how much still needs to be done as far as race relations between blacks and whites are concerned. However, the class did allow adequate room for thinking without the pressure of censorship and not saying the right thing.

This event reinforced the critical importance of the process of learning and the need continually to reestablish trust through communication. It also helped me to clarify my own role as both a facilitator and role model in the classroom. In their model for "connected teaching" M. F. Belenky et al. (1986: 227) point out: "A connected teacher is not just another student; the role carries special responsibilities. It does not entail power over the students; however, it does carry authority, an authority based not on subordination but on cooperation."

For some of the students and for me, this experience also reinforced awareness that the classroom is not isolated from the larger university context and from the larger social world as experienced by these students. Although the goal of creating a circle of active learners is a good one, it can also have exclusionary effects if the larger realities are ignored. For example, how is the circle affected if a student who is a single parent is forced to miss many classes because her child is ill? What is the impact on a small group project if the job of one of the students prevents her from meeting with other students outside class time? How does the routine late arrival of a working student to class influence the group dynamics? When the students in these examples are black, as they were in these cases, the goal of making the classroom more inclusive is elusive. These difficulties reflect socioeconomic class as much as race, but given the smaller number of black students, the impact on classroom heterogeneity is more devastating.

Clearly, for students to be able to participate equally in the circle of learners, they must receive adequate support. Otherwise the university will remain an elitist conclave open only to those whose family and financial circumstances permit participation. That, of course, is a broad institutional concern. But what responsibility do the professor and the fellow learners bear to a particular student? Ignoring the problem sets up a dynamic that stigmatizes and penalizes the student whose circumstances are different, while allowing for different levels of participation may cause resentment.

In a traditional classroom where students are required only to listen to lectures, do the required reading, and submit exams or papers, these problems do not present much of a dilemma. The student can work out an individual arrangement with the professor or take an incomplete without affecting the other students or the structure of the classroom. In a classroom built on cooperative learning and discussion or experientially based pedagogy, the integrity of the group and the learning experience of all the students are affected by the contribution of each. I don't have a solution to offer at the level of the specific case except to stress the need for greater sensitivity to these dynamics between the in-class and out-of-class realms.

EVALUATION

Too often we—students and faculty alike—measure the success of a course by the immediate outcomes and nuggets of knowledge we carry away. Faculty in particular may be dissuaded from experimenting with new forms of classroom organization when conflict arises. Even though teaching is devalued in large research universities, student evaluations of faculty performance are factored into decisions that affect one's career. Without support it may appear dangerous for both instructors and students to take risks. Nevertheless I have found that while students sometimes resent the amount of time spent on process issues, they generally conclude the semester with an appreciation of the benefits derived from these efforts, particularly as new insights emerge from working through conflicts. If we cast our teaching aspirations in a wider net, we may find that the impact of these alternative teaching goals may reach beyond the immediate experience of the class. This may be true both in terms of providing students with some life tools for working cooperatively in groups and understanding conflict, but also in the sense that students will have a more personal investment in, or relationship to, the critical ideas/content of the course. Not infrequently, I think, students have a delayed reaction to course material based on their own developing experience as workers, citizens, community participants, and family members. We need to understand this rather than focus too narrowly on initial resistance or evaluations that don't capture all the important dimensions of the learning process. Instead, I would argue, we need to support one another over "the long haul" (Horton 1991) to continue to create more inclusive and democratic circles of learners who can bring these skills and values into their lives and communities.

NOTES

1. Myles Horton (1991: 150) uses this term in his autobiography to describe the educational approach put into practice at Highlander Center, a training ground for community activists in labor, civil rights, and environmental movements during the past sixty years.

2. Units such as the Residential College, a small liberal arts college within the University of Michigan, and Women's Studies that systematically build these learning skills into their curriculum from introductory courses on up create an important supportive base for successful multicultural teaching. Yet both are also beleaguered units within the wider university context—underfunded, undersupported, and constantly required to explain and justify their methods and rationale. These conditions create difficulties for the faculty, who are often stretched to their limits by multiple, sometimes competing, demands. They must meet the needs of the students while compensating for institutional inadequacies and maintaining their own research productivity in a climate that rewards scholarship rather than teaching.

3. More recent feminist writing has attempted to deconstruct mothering and to revalue female values and activities. An example is the notion of the "teacher-midwife" who engages in "connected teaching" (Belenky et al. 1986).

9

Multicultural Teaching in Public Health: A Course on Gender, Race, Ethnicity, and Health

Irene Butter and Kristine Siefert

Addressing multiculturalism as it relates to public health poses a number of complex dilemmas. The concepts of race, ethnicity, and gender, intrinsically controversial themselves, are sources of additional controversy in health-related research; debates over interracial and gender differences in mortality and morbidity abound in areas as diverse as infant mortality and cardiovascular disease. Moreover, epidemiologic models of health and disease assume complex and interactive relationships among disease-producing agents, host vulnerability, and the environment. For many health problems, research findings are inconclusive or contradictory; causal pathways and the relative importance of various risk factors remain to be determined. However, an emphasis on one causal factor over another in theories of etiology—genetic endowment versus environment as the critical factor in neonatal mortality, for example—can have profound implications for policies and programs. If racial differences in infant mortality are seen as genetic in origin, less emphasis may be placed on reducing environmental risks to pregnancy outcome through improved prenatal care and other health and social services. Similarly, if estrogen is thought to confer protection against coronary artery disease—a long-accepted theory that is currently being challenged—women may not be considered at risk for cardiovascular disease or even included in relevant research (Collins and David 1990; Yankauer 1990; Kirchstein 1991).

In addition, risk factors such as social class or poverty, well known to be strongly associated with health status and disease outcomes, are difficult to measure. Given current methodological limitations, there is no way, for example, to calculate a poverty-specific infant mortality rate. Nevertheless, the factors associated with infant mortality all have the common denominator of poverty, and this association has been well documented for at least seventy years (Kotch 1986; Lathrop 1919).

BACKGROUND OF THE COURSE

Despite the importance of the debates surrounding race, ethnicity, gender, and class in public health, the significance of these variables has not been systematically addressed by curricula preparing students for professional public health practice. Accreditation standards for schools of public health contain no mention of the need for specific content addressing race, gender, or class (Council on Education for Public Health 1986); and an informal survey of schools of public health undertaken by the authors found few courses focusing specifically on any of these variables. At the University of Michigan, Gender, Race, Ethnicity, and Health is a course developed by the authors to meet the need and student-generated demand for such content in the public health curriculum.

The course evolved from an earlier course, Sex and Gender in Health, which arose as a result of student and faculty interest in the late 1970s. Faculty research interests, student demand, and the development of a dual master of public health-master of social work degree program with a concentration on child and family health led to the development of the present course, which was first offered in 1988. The need for such a course was further reinforced by the findings of a schoolwide Task Force on Race and Racism (Task Force on Racial and Cultural Concerns 1990). The report summarized a survey sponsored by the task force that found students lamenting the lack of course content addressing race and racism in public health courses and the cursory reporting of health-related data, classified by race, without discussion of causes and consequences of racial disparities. These findings underscored that our course should address interests and needs articulated by students.

Gender, Race, Ethnicity, and Health is a three-credit, full semester course offered jointly by the School of Public Health and the School of Social Work. The course examines the influence of gender, race, and ethnicity on health status, health behavior, and health care delivery; it emphasizes critical appraisal of existing research, identification of gaps in current knowledge, and practical application of theoretical and empirical observations to promote the health of underserved populations. Course objectives include using a multidisciplinary framework to familiarize students with a distinguishable body of knowledge on gender, race, and ethnicity in health; engaging students in the analysis and evaluation of relevant research; and promoting the use of laws, policies, and other action strategies at multiple levels to promote social change and social justice. The course format is a combination of lectures, discussion, and small group exercises; course requirements, described in detail below, include participation in an integrating session for one of three course modules, writing analytic papers, and keeping individual process journals, which are submitted periodically throughout the term.

TEACHING GOALS

Three major teaching goals guide Gender, Race, Ethnicity, and Health: awareness, appreciation, and action. The first teaching goal is to increase students' awareness of the influence of race, ethnicity, gender, and class on health and health care through the acquisition of relevant knowledge. This is done by explicitly focusing the content of the course on non-dominant groups, rather than by comparing and contrasting such groups with the dominant majority. Thus, course readings and lectures center on the health status and health care experiences of women and people of color, rather than on the overall distribution and determinants of health status and access to health care resources in the general population.

The second teaching goal is to promote increased appreciation of diversity as it relates to health and health care through heightened awareness of one's own and others' attitudes, values, and beliefs. Key concepts such as race and ethnicity are not defined at the outset of the course; it is assumed that the concepts are value-laden and that there are no uniform definitions. Instead, students are encouraged to examine their own definitions of these concepts as they evolve and change throughout the course; to explore such issues as the origin of their own and others' beliefs and biases and the differences between visible and hidden diversity; and to consider how each of us is oppressed in some way and how we in turn consciously or unwittingly oppress others. Accomplishing this goal demands the full and open participation of a diverse group of students.

The third teaching goal is to promote social change and social justice through the undertaking of specific actions at the individual, group, organizational, community, and societal levels. Students are asked to consider, propose, and attempt to apply strategies for change at all of these levels by examining examples of effective and ineffective efforts in order to identify those elements that determine success or failure. Students analyze their own experiences, case studies and examples from the literature, and the experiences of the instructors and guest presenters. Other strategies that are used to accomplish these three teaching goals are described below.

PEDAGOGY

Three dimensions of multicultural teaching are of importance from the very start: (1) the identity (gender, race, class) of the teachers; (2) the identity (gender, race, class) of the students enrolled, and (3) the style and content of the teaching. While these three dimensions are interrelated, congruence is not always present. Students generally outnumber the teachers in a given course, and therefore there is more potential for diversity among the former than the latter. The mix of students in a class with a multicultural focus and the proportions in which students are distributed by sex, race, and class are also crucial. Course content is likely to be a product of teachers' backgrounds and student mix.

We are two white females offering a multicultural course on Gender, Race, Ethnicity, and Health. We have searched and continue to search for new conceptual frameworks and literature exploring the linkage among gender, race, ethnicity, and health. As organizing frameworks for exploring this relationship, we focus on asymmetry, hierarchy, and structures that reflect domination/subordination, privilege/exploitation. Models for restructuring the course toward these themes have been derived from the literature on curriculum transformation (Andersen 1987; Cannon 1990b; Collins 1989; Dill and Zinn 1990; Higginbotham 1988). We also continue to question the literature concerned with the relationships between gender, race, ethnicity, and health and the emphasis placed in this literature on biogenetic versus sociocultural/environmental factors, and/or their interrelationships.

Since we first offered the course, we have continually broadened the scope of diversity through literature, films, and experiential material. Each year we involve our students in further diversification of the course content. Our students have contributed health-related articles, case studies, and suggestions of films specific to their backgrounds, for example, health practices of Latino populations, experiences of males in female-dominated occupations, access barriers to health care for African Americans, and offensive treatment given to individuals of different sexual orientation. Men continue to be a minority of the students enrolled in our course. Their presence has always been of fundamental importance in our teaching goals, and their small number presents a challenge to class dynamics. Women students need to express themselves freely about the effects of male domination and paternalism on women's health. Male students are expected not only to listen and try to understand but also to respond to women's perspectives and to discuss health issues from their own perspective. We strongly believe that increased awareness and better understanding of health problems (and how they are influenced by gender, race, ethnicity, and class) will come about only when all voices participate in an exchange of viewpoints and experiences and all shades of perspectives are incorporated in the dialogue. Our goal of all-inclusive participation and sharing prompts us to keep searching for new and more effective teaching strategies.

OUR ROLE IN THE CLASSROOM

Our primary purpose in teaching this course is to facilitate change through learning from and about each other and about ourselves. The learning process draws on substantive health content derived from literature, films, and experiential material. Emphasis is placed on identifying, questioning, analyzing, and possibly changing the attitudes and values implicit in the materials we discuss and in our responses to the materials. Classroom strategies are oriented toward mutuality and helping each other examine and understand our differences, as well as community, for example, aiming to respect and transcend our differences so that we can build the kinds of coalitions needed for social justice and social change. We like to think that the course can stimulate the beginnings of change on two levels: working toward change of the structures inimical to individual and societal health and changing ourselves and our relationships with others.

A principal task for us is to create a class environment characterized by safety and trust and to facilitate strategies of sharing and communication. We start out with modeling self-disclosure by sharing very intimate and private aspects of our background, orientation, and experience. We encourage intimate sharing by all class members and stimulate participation by talking with the class as a whole, small groups and individuals, both the silent ones as well as those tending to monopolize class discussions. Students are encouraged to describe incidents or forms of oppression, discrimination, or exploitation they have experienced and also to identify their own roles as oppressors. Discussions are oriented to ways of coping with the former and methods of extinguishing the latter.

To help accomplish the purpose of learning and change, we rely on three main devices. These are requirements of students in the form of short, analytic papers, integrating sessions, and process journals. An example of an analytic paper would be an analysis of a personal experience in a health-related job setting, with respect to interracial, gender, and/or class relationships. Integrating sessions are classes where students are completely in charge of synthesizing aspects of course materials or developing a new interpretation of a particular conflict, bias, inequity, or discriminatory action in greater depth. The process journals are tools that help students to clarify attitudes and values about gender, race, ethnicity, and health and also to record changes in attitudes and values as these occur throughout the course. Each assignment stipulates that students address racial, gender, and ethnic differences and analyze the structures and individual behaviors that allow these differences in health to be maintained.

HOW COURSE CONTENT IS AFFECTED
BY CLASS COMPOSITION

The starting point of our multicultural teaching endeavor was to develop course content organized around diversity and health. The courses we had taught previously were typically focused on mainstream literature, centered around public health in general, norms, and the concept of "generic person" or "generic populations." As noted above, the goals of the new course are to promote awareness and appreciation of diversity, not just by adding content material on non-dominant groups as illustrations of deviations from norms, but by dismissing norms as meaningful concepts and by placing non-dominant groups at the core of the course. For example, in our study of AIDS, we focus explicitly on the experiences of women, people of color, and different ethnic groups with the disease, before examining the more general characteristics of AIDS in our society. While we have started the process of revising course content toward greater diversity, much remains to be done in adding ethnically more inclusive material and in integrating conceptual frameworks with social work and public health practice.

We attempt to attract a group of students representing diverse gender, racial, ethnic, and sexual orientation groups. The more multicultural the participation in this course, the greater the chance of promoting appreciation of diversity. At first we engaged in a broadly based advertising campaign, by posting fliers describing our course all over campus so that students of varying backgrounds could learn about it. Because of the dearth of multi-ethnic courses offered on this campus, it did not take long for the number of students interested in taking the course to exceed ideal class size. Typically, class composition is heterogeneous and includes African Americans, Latinos, Asian students, an occasional Native American student, and students with different ethnic backgrounds, religions, and sexual orientations. In our experience, course content preceded and helped determine the class composition. Inasmuch as we solicit multi-ethnic course material from our students each year, class composition is more likely to influence course content of the following year.

We are attempting to develop a unified approach in presenting the material to different groups in our class. For example, our unit on genocide compares and contrasts the Tuskegee studies in which African American males were deprived of treatment for syphilis to Nazi experiments in concentration camps. By proceeding in this way, we hope to enhance awareness and understanding of the parallels of different forms of oppression and the common elements required for prevention and resistance. Implications of these two forms of genocide are explored from the perspectives of health professions and through role playing and focused group discussions; students are guided to formulate positions, to analyze structures, and to compose action strategies that would guard against repetition of such destructive occurrences.

In this course, classroom dynamics differ considerably from those of other courses. A relatively small portion of class time is devoted to formal lectures, and these go beyond, rather than cover, the readings. The literature that students are expected to read serves as background for class sessions, which are used primarily for sharing insights and experiences in small group discussions and with the entire class. There is opportunity for critical feedback, which strengthens efforts toward coping, changing, and renewal. Emphasis on communicating and sharing our differences lends itself to a mutual opening up to the foreign, unfamiliar, and unknown and to a better appreciation of our own oppression relative to that of others. We stress the point that rivalry among oppressions and the ranking thereof according to magnitude or greatest cruelty are counterproductive and ultimately devoid of meaning.

RATIONALE BEHIND ORGANIZATION

Our course is organized around three modules. The first module addresses gender, race, and ethnicity as predisposing variables of health status, health behavior, and attitudes toward health. The second module looks at gender, race, and ethnicity as predisposing variables of the providers of care and of health care delivery. The focus of the third module is on social change as we address strategies for the individual, institutional/communal, and national level of change. Students are challenged to think creatively about options for strategies for change at all these levels.

Each module ends with a class organized by a group of students who collaborate in integrating the material covered in the particular module. The idea is for students to analyze the key issues in greater depth, to expose controversy and contradictions, and to involve all members of the class in further deliberations. The integrating sessions have taken the form of debates, dialogues, role playing, attempted conflict resolution, and so on. This exercise forces students to analyze and synthesize and to become actively involved with the material. We use the integrating sessions as a device to empower students inasmuch as they take complete responsibility for planning, organizing, and conducting these classes. Many students report that integrating sessions provide the richest learning experiences of the course.

Two short analytic papers are required, on assigned topics, derived from modules 1 and 2. In one of these exercises students are given a series of advertisements from newspapers with health-related content and are asked to analyze the overt and covert meanings of these ads as well as the accuracy of the information presented and methods used to influence, appropriately or inappropriately, the behavioral responses of the target audience. Underlying assumptions or biases and repercussions of the sales techniques used, in the context of gender, race, and ethnicity, are also addressed in the exercise.

A third assignment is based on attitudes, values, and experiences as stated in the process journals at the beginning and end of the semester and is intended to trace attitudinal changes related to the course. Students are asked to discuss attitudes, values, and experiences related to sexism, racism, ethnic pride, affirmative action, gay rights, and so on, and to analyze the impact the course had on changing or reinforcing their perspectives. The teaching goal is that with the use of journals, students would be encouraged to sort out their own values, and in the process more awareness would be developed, which in turn would generate higher-quality communication and more sharing as well. The journals turned out to be provocative tools for learning, soul-searching, and heightened levels of awareness.

In each of these assignments we look for evidence of learning, creative thinking, and novel ideas regarding differences, conflicts, and possible reconciliations.

ASSESSMENT AND EVALUATION

We consider it important to incorporate a multicultural perspective in our teaching as part of our personal and professional efforts to contribute toward social change. We view our teaching as a means of empowering ourselves and others and as a way of collaborating with our students to overcome oppression and to promote social justice. Faculty colleagues in the School of Social Work, which co-sponsors the course, have been quite supportive of our efforts, but the reaction of our colleagues in the School of Public Health has presented a dilemma. Although a few individuals have been supportive, the majority have not. Sadly, we have had some faculty members actually question the validity of race, ethnicity, and gender as variables; other colleagues have made it clear that they consider the material we cover to be of dubious value. A few have made outright racist, sexist, or homophobic remarks. Few advisers in the School of Public Health have directed their students to the class; some have actually discouraged their students from taking it.

It is likely that the difference in colleagues' reactions in the two schools is the result of structural factors; the School of Social Work's accreditation standards require content on women and on ethnic minorities of color in the curriculum (Council on Social Work Education 1979). In addition, the formal course evaluations used by the School of Social Work include questions about inclusion of content on race and gender and on the instructor's sensitivity in conveying such content. Nevertheless, the result of this active and passive devaluation has been isolation, marginality, self-doubt, and anger. The content of the course itself and the feelings that such sensitive material engenders are also stressful, and at times we have questioned whether we want to continue teaching the course.

The intrinsically sensitive nature of multicultural teaching combined with a non-supportive environment creates fertile ground for frustration and conflict. We have learned to expect occasional student outbursts because a certain form of oppression was in their opinion overemphasized or because feminism was considered to be a movement that causes alienation from men or because a film shown in class was partly sexist or classist or contained homophobic elements. Over time we have learned to anticipate such occurrences and have become better prepared to handle these situations.

It is encouraging, however, that the School of Public Health has formed a schoolwide Task Force on Racial and Cultural Concerns and that a workshop recently held in the school on adding racial content to public health courses drew a large number of interested faculty participants. Continued efforts along these lines should improve colleagues' receptivity to the course.

Student response has been a major source of support and encouragement. Formal student evaluations have been consistently and uniformly positive; in fact, the course is among the most highly rated in the school. Since the course is sponsored by both the School of Public Health and the School of Social Work, each school's standard evaluation questionnaire is administered. These questionnaires consist of a series of statements about the course and its instruction; students are asked to indicate the extent to which they agree or disagree with each statement on a five-point scale, with 1 indicating strong disagreement and 5 indicating strong agreement with the item. On the item "Overall, this is an excellent course," the median response was 4.86. On the items "The instructor is sensitive in handling minority issues and content" and "The instructor is sensitive in handling gender issues and content," the median responses were 5.0 and 4.98, respectively.

In addition, we have had the pleasure of observing our students actually undertake actions based on what they have learned in class, ranging from attempts to eliminate prejudice and bias in certain individuals to forming coalitions to combat racism and sexism. One student outlined an article for a nursing journal on the ethical implications of Nazi medical experimentation. Another student systematically introduced the topics of racism, sexism, and homophobia into conversations with other students in her department lounge in an effort to sensitize students she overheard making prejudiced statements about women, people of color, and lesbian women or gay men. Another student actually filed a discrimination complaint with the university's Affirmative Action Office. Reviewing the students' process journals at the end of the term and learning about the impact of the course on students' attitudes and values have been a source of encouragement. Many students admitted a willingness to reevaluate attitudes and values; felt more comfortable with talking and asking questions about gender, race, and ethnicity of those from different cultural backgrounds; and adopted new ways of thinking about sexism, racism, and other issues by shifting from individual to institutional forces.

Despite the lack of support by public health faculty, class size has grown from twenty-five to over forty students, forcing us to place a limit on enrollment. Student comments on evaluations have included the recommendation that the course be required for all students in the School of Public Health, and an increasing number of students from nursing and other units of the university have enrolled on the basis of our student recommendations. The enthusiasm and appreciation of our students have been a major source of inspiration and have strengthened our resolve and commitment to offer the course.

Teaching about race and gender in public health has affected our perceptions of ourselves, our role in the university, and our research. We have become more aware of our own biases and shortcomings, and we make more conscious and active efforts to overcome them. We have taken a more active role in the university's efforts to combat racism and sexism by participating in various organized activities and by advocating for individual students who have experienced racial or gender-related discrimination. Our research has been influenced by our involvement and has moved from including gender and race as variables to focusing on the impact of racism and sexism in our areas of investigation. Although the professional rewards for this type of work are not always commensurate with the required effort, the personal rewards have been substantial.

10

The Latina: A Teaching Experience

Eliana Moya-Raggio

> The dominant white culture is killing us slowly with its ignorance.
>
> Ignorance splits people, creates prejudices. A misinformed people is a subjugated people.
>
> Gloria Anzaldúa 1987: 86

The Latina, offered for the first time during the winter term of 1986, began almost as an experiment, to explore with students their notions about women within the Latino group as well as to expand and clarify previous knowledge or to remedy the lack of it.

FOCUS AND OBJECTIVES

The focus of the class was to be on ethnicity and gender. I wanted students to enhance their comprehension of the historical experiences of the major groups of Latinas in the United States: Chicanas, Mexican Americans, Mexican immigrants, Puerto Ricans, Cubans, Colombians, and groups from Central America, as well as the Dominican Republic. I was especially concerned with the issue of identity, preservation of culture versus assimilation, and the role women played in that process. To a large extent, women from these groups are caught in a permanent confrontation between their identities as Latinas and their identities as women; they struggle to preserve a voice and an identity within a powerful dominant culture. Aware of the complexity behind the presence of these varied groups of people in the United States, I hoped to work with students to enhance their knowledge of the historical, economic, social, and political issues that had contributed to this complexity in the United States.

On the issue of gender, I was especially interested in exploring notions of universal womanhood and sisterhood and submitting them to close scrutiny from the perspectives of class and race or ethnicity. It was important, I thought, to remedy the failure to explore these connections that I had already observed and encountered in Women's Studies Programs in general. I considered that the diversity of women's experiences within a given societal organization was essential to comprehend the complexity of systems of subjugation.

Even more, I was interested in bringing Latinas and their history and culture in the United States to the surface, to unearth a history largely forgotten or ignored—a history of labor struggle, of social participation, and of concern for women's issues. I thought that the names of Emma Tenayuca, Lucy Gonzáles de Parsons, Jovita Idar, Luisa Moreno, and Dolores Huerta needed to be placed properly within Chicano culture and history, in the same way that Lolita Lebrón, Josefina Villafañe, Julia de Burgos, and Luisa Capetillo, together with hundreds of Puerto Rican women, needed the recognition they deserved.[1] My intention was for students to understand that although women's liberation in the United States has had an impact on the Latino population, each group of Latinas is the inheritor of an important tradition of women's struggle for justice and dignity, as women and as workers; also I considered it essential to challenge the notion of passivity so commonly ascribed to Latinas as well as to recognize the strength to survive and resist that they exhibit when confronted with a powerful dominant culture.

The fact that the so-called Hispanic population shares a mestizo culture, where Native American, African, Spanish, and other European origins collapse to form an ethnic and cultural component of vast proportions, makes it difficult to present the material exclusively from the perspective of race. Ethnicity, even though not homogeneous, seemed an appropriate approach for the ample diversity we encounter within Latinos in the United States; it was important to do justice to the cultural, linguistic, and human plurality represented by a Quiché woman of Guatemala, a Mexican of Aztec descent, an Argentinian of Jewish or Italian heritage, a Colombian of Spanish origin, or a Puerto Rican of African roots.[2]

The recognition of such a variety of female voices constitutes an essential component of the course. I thought about the course in terms of a truly humanist experience, which would make every effort to unveil reality and destroy myths. I believe that a truly well-educated or enlightened individual is tolerant of differences, whether they are encountered in his or her own society or between societies. Ethnically diverse points of view help to eliminate the shallow monocultural perspectives that so limit students' education. My own experience in teaching Spanish and Latin American culture and literature had given me personal insights into teaching about other cultures and into the complexity of introducing undergraduates to other ways of thinking about the world.

Latinos or Hispanics, to use the official label given by the U.S. government, constitute the second largest minority in this country and share a common culture. They are, nevertheless, not a homogeneous group of people, easily identifiable by the color of their skin, but rather a heterogeneous group, with vastly different backgrounds and experiences. This sometimes acts as an impediment to achieving a united voice within the United States. Although the history of their presence in the United States differs for each group, they respond, in general, to one given political and economic structure that has affected them all, a worldwide economic system of periphery and center. Countries and people are structurally positioned according to this organization. Historically the Hispanic people of the Southwest have known the consequences of territorial expansion over the land that was "lost" for them, a loss that marked the beginning of a process of deterritorialization. The metaphor of the lost land has been creatively expressed in the struggle over a language and an identity. Later on, motivated by a series of economic and social factors, Mexicans crossed the border between Mexico and the United States—sometimes as a desired labor force and sometimes as an unwelcomed one. While Puerto Ricans during this century have experienced a constant movement of people between the island and the continent, groups such as Cubans and Central Americans owe their presence in the United States to dramatic political upheavals in their countries—movements and changes that need to be considered within the broader perspective of the role played by the United States vis-à-vis the individual countries or regions from which Latinos have arrived.

These facts contribute to the different self-perceptions of these groups and in some cases to the distances among them. Few issues bring them together; for example, few attempts on campuses around the country are successful in uniting all Hispanic students when the need arises. Fair-skinned and blue-eyed and speaking fluent English without the trace of an accent or dark-skinned with dark eyes and speaking a halting English or none at all, well off or poor, professionals or laborers, Latinos do not always constitute an easily recognizable group. Although the loss of an accent may constitute a tremendous achievement for some, for others it represents the loss of the only tangible, permanent experience of an ethnic/cultural identity. Regardless of their appearance and the language they speak, they are a fragmented people, usually caught between the mirage of total assimilation and a romantic holding on to an idealized past. The true challenge remains preserving an identity while achieving full participation and a fair place in Anglo society.

CLASS COMPOSITION

The composition of the class has been an important factor. The number of Latino students has increased consistently during the four-year period the course has been offered; in fact, Latinos constituted half of the total number of students the last time the course was taught. Of this group, usually one or two were males while the remaining were Latinas of Mexican, Puerto Rican, Colombian, Guatemalan, or Peruvian national origin. These students were an excellent source of fresh, new perspectives. Their presence, even when it was small, produced conflictive feelings in Anglo students, which were seldom discussed openly in class, but often expressed in the journals. These conflictive feelings ranged from apprehension to surprise, from curiosity to frustration. Will the instructor be partial to Latino students, since she is a Latina? Are they going to dominate the class? Are their experiences of any value to me? These were only a few of the questions that ran as a subtext in the first journal entries.

The gender composition of the class is another important aspect. The majority of students have been females, and males have been present in very small numbers, four being the most registered for the course in a semester. Of the four, two were Anglos, and two were Latinos. This presence has been an added source of information for the group in the case of the Latino male students and sometimes a source of conflict in the case of the Anglo male students.

Readings: Different Texts

I wanted the class to be as participative as possible, so that students could talk to each other as well as talk to me about their findings, their readings, their thoughts and ideas. Keeping that in mind, reading assignments were distributed to groups of three students each week; those students were responsible for presenting to the class the major ideas of the material read; also all students read the material so they could engage in a fruitful exchange with the presenters. The three students were responsible for initiating class interaction by presenting to the class their own understanding and opinions of the assigned readings. My role then was facilitator; I provided information when and if it was needed, and I usually took notes on the most salient points that students raised in their interaction with one another. Usually those points were further clarified, discussed, and expanded with added informational material during the class. The class met for one and half hours, twice a week, which helped to give enough time for students and for me to complete points of discussion.

Aware of the fact that the course would introduce students to vastly different areas of knowledge, aware that it would require of them careful, critical thinking and that it would challenge previously held ideas about Latino groups, I wanted the format to be different, more open than the traditional classroom so that it would enable students to reflect upon their own experiences (or lack of experiences) with Latinos, whether in their school years, their college days, or in their life in general, in their hometown, city, or area. I wanted them to think about their learning of American history and how the history of the Southwest, Puerto Rico, and so on has been presented. So, whenever possible, I would pose questions to the class in relation to their educational or life experience. Expecting students to develop awareness of the old and new presence of Latinas in this country, I tried to make them think about Latinas they might have encountered: a classmate in high school, a person at their place of employment, a roommate, a student in one of their classes, a friend of their parents. I discovered quickly that very few, if any, among the Anglo students had come in contact with Latinos, except for those who mentioned the cleaning woman from Guatemala at their parents' home or the men who washed dishes at the local restaurant where they had worked.

Paulo Freire (1985: 3–4), the Brazilian educator, says that the act of studying is an attitude toward the world . . . "it cannot be reduced to the relationship of reader to book or reader to text. . . . Studying is, above all, thinking about experience, and thinking about experience is the best way to think accurately."

He adds that to study requires a sense of modesty as well and, perhaps most important, he believes that "the act of studying assumes a dialectical relationship between reader and author . . . [which] involves the author's historical-sociological and ideological conditioning, which is usually not the same as that of the reader."

Precisely this issue became a crucial point in the class—the invitation to study in the Freirian sense, to read from the perspectives of Latinas and Latinos, "to leave home" to abandon the familiar, truly to approach the experiences of people who, although in the students' midst, remain largely ignored in their history, their language, their struggle, their will to survive. I encouraged students to consider that, to a large extent, this lack of knowledge of Latinas reduces them to invisibility.

The course showed three films to students. *La Operación*, a film about the issue of involuntary sterilization of women in Puerto Rico, is placed within larger economic and social context. Usually I invite a graduate student from the School of Public Health's program on population to introduce the film and to guide the class in the discussion of the issue presented. This has proven to be an excellent contribution to the class. Another film is *El Norte*, which conveys with clarity the many problems Central Americans face when immigrating illegally into the United States. A third is *Salt of the Earth*, a classic film about Chicanas' participation in a miners' strike in New Mexico. I have also shown *Double Day*, a 1975 project of the first International Conference on Women in Mexico City, which presents the problem of double daywork for women in Latin America (in other words, how women add to their jobs outside the home the full responsibility for domestic work and maintenance within their own home). The value of that film resides in its ability to show the many social levels and ethnic groups of Latin America.

Films have proven to be an excellent tool for this class. Students were asked to take notes on what they saw to connect the images with the material read in class and to express themselves in terms of the issues presented and the relevant features of the film.

I thought of the class as essentially an interdisciplinary course. The reading material reflects a variety of perspectives on the same issue: Latinas. Several poems and Sandra Cisneros's *House on Mango Street* (1991) provide a literary perspective with the extraordinary story of Esperanza's childhood, taking readers into a succession of vignettes that depict the experience of growing up as a Latina. Equally important is the story of a Guatemalan Quiché woman as told by herself in *I, Rigoberta Menchú* (1984). This story has motivated many students to develop further their interest in this subject as well as to value a new form of literature that combines immediacy and authenticity with the power of a narrative and leaves lasting memories in the reader. Students also read several poetic texts by Bernice Zamora, Lorna Dee Cervantes, Julia de Burgos, Julia Alvárez, Sandra Estévez, and others.

It has proven difficult for students to read the historical background material written by Chicanos or Puerto Ricans because the authors' perspective diverges and departs so profoundly from the one students have been given, because they never before took a close look into the process of territorial expansion, or because they had never considered the other side of that process—the feelings of people newly incorporated into a vastly different system of cultural institutions. Many of them for the first time confront a different writing of history.

Writings such as Rodolfo Acuña's *Occupied America* (1972) or John Chávez's *The Lost Land* (1984) are the work of people fully identified with the position of Chicanos as a people with their own history, and they challenge students to abandon the comfort of one-dimensional, stereotypical perspectives. These are works in which the vision given implies a looking from the outside in and from the inside out. The same is true, sometimes, with the writings of Gloria Anzaldúa and Cherríe Moraga, both Chicana feminists and lesbians, or Iris Morales's testimonial piece on being the daughter of Puerto Rican parents who did not speak English (Morales 1974). All these authors—men and women—write through what has been called by Chela Sandoval (Anzaldúa 1990: 51–75) "oppositional consciousness," that is, the place from which peripheral, oppressed people describe, explain, and try to make sense of their own experience.

Reading these materials, students tend to engage in a process—somehow productive and challenging for class discussions—of resisting or denying the reading material. This reaction is not limited to the historical background material, but extends to several assigned articles by Latino scholars. The first and most common disclaimer has to do with "lack of objectivity," the assumption, of course, being that a Latino researcher cannot be objective since he or she is analyzing problems too close to his or her experience; the other tendency is to devalue an article through different strategies: it is limited in scope, unsatisfactory in the sample, has a weak conclusion, and so on. Usually the most devalued articles are those that confront students with the destruction of pervasive biases or stereotyping in regard to both ethnicity and gender, such as characteristics of Latino families, sterilization of Latinas in California or of Puerto Ricans in the island, and discriminating labor laws.

Considering all these issues, I believe that the way I assigned the readings by groups, inviting students to express their reactions openly, helps everyone in the group. The Latinas in the class usually legitimate the material with their own knowledge and feel a sense of pride in being in a class where their perspective is presented; the Anglo students process their discomfort and gradually learn to appreciate the right of others to their own perspectives. Nevertheless, in many instances the discomfort is kept inside and expressed only within the journals.

This, in turn, presents me with the problem of being the only reader of that expressed discomfort and forces me to decide how or if I should bring it into open class discussion.

Guest speakers have been equally important for the class. Selected from within the academic community and also from the community at large, they have provided extraordinary examples of conflicts, challenges, and different forms of discrimination experienced personally or by their families. They have included community professionals, faculty members, women of Central America in sanctuary with several church organizations, and, in some instances, campus visitors like Moraga.

ASSIGNMENTS

A journal seemed an ideal form of exercise to facilitate the process of critical thinking, to help students work out their thoughts, ideas, prejudices, and biases. The journal (minimum eight pages, biweekly) was to be an instrument of self-reflection, of critical thinking about assigned readings and class discussions, and also of awareness, so that conversations with relatives or friends, reading of newspapers and magazine articles, TV programs, and so on could find a place in their process of thinking and rethinking, of discovery and learning. The journal has been a confidential document between students and instructor, in order to encourage honest and free expression of ideas and feelings. I have always returned it as quickly as possible, with abundant comments and questions; students continue to develop their ideas from one entry to the next, and they answer the questions I pose or bring up new ones themselves. In many cases, the journals have provided me with essential material for class discussions. The journal has given me a guideline of the direction in which students are progressing. It has pleased me that over the term, the journal offers an opportunity for a continuous dialogue with students, a dialogue that may be extremely satisfactory or extremely frustrating. Although not everyone writes at the same level of involvement or critical reflection, it is, overall, an excellent tool when used well.

Students' initial reactions to this assignment have been mixed. Some seem to have a relative familiarity with the format of the assignment because they have written journals for other classes, although with slightly different characteristics. For others, it has been a bit of a struggle and takes time to develop the ability to think globally, to establish connections, to integrate their readings with the world around them. The syllabus provides students with clear instructions about what is expected from their journal; they need to have a clear understanding that it is not a reading log or an outlet to vent their frustrations and anger.

In spite of any initial difficulties, the journal becomes an excellent instrument of careful reflection, of critical apprehension of knowledge, and of the ability of students to begin to establish connections between an academic text and their own experience. Here is what some say about the journals:

I liked the journals, they helped me comprehend ideas and get a chance to express myself.

I have learned a great deal. Of particular value is the journal we turn in every two weeks. In the journal I struggle with ideas.

Another assignment of the class was an interview with a Latina. This became the favorite assignment for many students. Latino students often wanted to validate the experience of a woman whom they had known—someone important in their lives such as their own mother or grandmother. Anglo students often saw it as an opportunity to approach a human being with experiences vastly different from theirs. One term, a group in the class, with the help of a student from the School of Social Work, interviewed members of Latin Americans for Social and Economic Development (LASED), a Latino organization from Detroit, with extraordinary success. Each student, or group of students working together, conducted an interview with the subject on an issue of interest and presented it in class. Some students were especially interested in the educational experience of Latino women or issues related to their incorporation into the labor force or their views on family and child-rearing and migration.

The process of the interview was broadly discussed in class. Students were to select their subject, but first to explain clearly the reasons for the interview, the nature of the class, and why the woman's contribution would be important. Students were to reassure the woman that her name would never be mentioned (each student selected a fictitious name for the person) and also to explain to her that a second conversation might be necessary for clarification of points. Students were told to be considerate of the needs of the interviewee; if she did not want a tape recorder used, the student should respect that. Students were also encouraged to seek their subjects from a large pool of women in the area and to look for age, educational, social, and economic differences.

Students collected the informational data from their subject and wrote a paper in which the material of the interview and a portrait of the person interviewed were incorporated. I asked them to reflect upon their feelings of ease or unease while conducting the conversation and to include a paragraph on those reflections in their paper. Time was set aside in the class for students to talk about their experience in interviewing the Latina and their feelings as outsiders or as members of the same ethnic group. Each student selected a person in the class with whom to share the transcript and the paper, so when the student presented an interview to the class, class members could contribute further observations. Many of these interviews and papers have been kept at the Women's Studies Program library and the American Culture Program library. The most exciting result of this exercise was that it provided students with the possibility of confronting in practice what they had been reading in theory during the class.

Students were pleasantly surprised to see that most women were very willing to talk about their experiences and that they felt empowered by this validation of their lives. The women who reacted with the most interest in sharing parts of their life experience seemed to be those who had had fewer opportunities to express themselves, those who had been, for too long, silenced by internal and external constraints and whose voices, actions, and struggles had remained obscured by forces from within their own culture or by forces from the outside dominant culture.

Here are student comments on this assignment:

I think what I learned the most from this interview and the many processes around it is how much more I need to learn, despite how much I have learned already. The first lesson I learned in this process was how few Latinos I knew in general, and even fewer Latinas. This made me begin to question why this was so, and I realized the extent to which my upbringing and the institutions I live and work in—especially the University of Michigan—have prevented my contact as a white woman with other women of other ethnic backgrounds.

The experience of doing the interview was a good one for me, at an intellectual as well as emotional level. I hope it was a good experience for M. too. I felt torn between feeling a separation from her because I had my tape recorder and "background reading material," as if I were a scientist, while at the same time feeling the warmth of just chatting with an acquaintance. In spite of the uncomfortability of feeling like you are putting someone on the spot, doing it is a great experience. Not only does it give you a lot to think about with regards to class material, but for me, interviewing M. especially, because she is an older woman, has given me a new perspective on myself and my life.

Finally, students wrote a research paper; many times the interview and the journal contributed to their developing an interest in a given area, which was further researched in their final paper. Many students became interested in pursuing the problem of education for Latinas, considering the forces within their culture that raise obstacles as well as the obstacles found within the educational system; others have written excellent papers on the place of women within the world of the migrant agricultural workers; some have written papers on the issue of language and the "English as official language" movement and its effects on women; still others have written papers on women's testimonial literature or on the literature written by Latinas.

My intention is that all assignments of the class relate to, and complement, each other, enabling students to develop a well-founded and organic perspective on the issues presented. Their own readings and critical reflection, their participation in class discussion, their getting to know a Latina and having the opportunity to talk extensively with her—all these experiences enhance the view that gender is a category of analysis that needs to be considered along with class, race, ethnicity, nationality, sexual preference, and religious identification.

GENERAL AND PERSONAL REFLECTION

The course exists within difficult boundaries, and the difficulties of teaching it are related not only to the general position of a minority program such as

Latino Studies within the larger context of departmental and program offerings but also to the position of the persons who usually teach such a course.[3] Many are women, and almost all are themselves members of a minority or disadvantaged ethnic or racial group. In my own case, the diversity I bring to any class I teach has nothing to do with the color of my skin, but rather with my origin. I am a Latin American in close touch with my roots; my origin also has to do with my life experience as a university-educated woman of the middle class, who, at a personal as well as a professional level, has had to struggle to survive in a vastly different culture; it has to do with my education in Chile, which, in turn, contributed richly to shaping my vision of the world, although I have seen that education subtly devalued many times. In some cases, this devaluation is based on ignorance and deep-seated prejudice about certain areas of the world.

There is no doubt that my Chilean education is the rigorous basis upon which I have continued to expand my knowledge. But nobody sees this because the only degree with prestige seems to be the one granted by a U.S. institution. This, in turn, poses the added problem of whose knowledge is transmitted and how distant, insignificant, and poorly known is the cultural production of people who inhabit the vastly different world of Latin America.

Will multicultural teaching contribute to diminishing this distance, or will multicultural teaching involve exclusively some curriculum changes (e.g., inclusion of one book) without ever forcing us to question the very foundation of the hierarchical system in which we teach?

After long years of experience teaching in the United States, I know now that it is not easy to be the one (sometimes it feels as if I am the only one) to introduce students to culturally or ethnically diverse points of view. Interestingly, I have done this by teaching Spanish from a cultural perspective closely tied to its status as a Third World language. In conveying the diverse and multiple issues embedded in the language of Latin American literature, history, and culture, one runs serious risks of being misinterpreted, but that is the price to be paid within an educational system that has for too long kept a monocular perspective and where examples of a shallow education, devoid of any critical perspective, are often encountered.

The act of study demands a sense of modesty, says Freire (1985: 4), and for students the dilemma presents itself in being modest and reading, for the first time in most cases, new, critical perspectives on a history they thought they knew, and in approaching, with equal modesty, the specific situation of working-class women of color and recognizing and respecting their struggle against forced sterilization, poor working conditions, nonexistent child care facilities, and so on. Students need to discover how to learn about what they have been made to fear, ignore, or simply avoid; they need to learn to validate the efforts of people who want to provide their own perspectives or their own culture. This proves to be a difficult task for many of them.

A lack of ethnically and culturally diverse points of view makes for an uneasy encounter with difference and diversity at many levels, from discomfort with the simple presence of Latinos in the classroom to difficulty accepting Latinos' interpretations and perspectives.[4] There is a degree of political confrontation with what has been previously learned or not learned, with the considerable gaps in students' historical knowledge, and with the culture of silence, which results from unequal structural relations. A class such as this, which focuses on the experience of people who have been displaced or marginalized, who have been subjected to external and internal colonialism, lays bare the lack of experience students have in critical thinking about these issues and in approaching a variety of perspectives with open minds.

To read Chicano history written by Chicanos is to read about dispossession and a territorial expansion with all the characteristics of internal colonial domination. This comes as a surprise to many students, and some of them have great conflict accepting that position. The same happens with the history of Puerto Rico and its colonial status. The lack of experience in looking critically at some essential historical facts within the history of their own country makes for an uneasy beginning for some. Precisely from the very beginning of the class, therefore, I invite them to leave behind the familiar and to begin to enter into another territory, an ethnic group.

When the person teaching such a class is herself a Latin American, like myself, or a Latina, she becomes an observer and participant in the process of learning through a profound identification with the subject matter. There is no doubt that being a Latin American in the United States is an experience different from that of being a Latina, and this difference includes place of birth, the experiences of formative years, education, and in many instances, social and economic factors; nevertheless, there is a point of encounter for both—a higher degree of comprehension of the experiences of the Latina when both the Latina and the Latin American are able to find the common threads that run through their ethnic identities and are forged in contact with the dominant culture.

The experience, nevertheless, of my own exile or displacement differs dramatically from the internal exile of Chicanas or Puerto Rican women or other Latinas. In some cases this displacement has been imposed on them, with a consequent loss of language, culture, and ethnic identity. I, instead, moved with my identity intact, closely tied to my native language, which I have preserved in speaking to my son and daughters, in which I teach most of the time, and in which I write. I have never experienced the type of linguistic repression Anzaldúa (1987: 53) describes when she writes, "I remember being caught speaking Spanish at recess—that was good for three licks on the knuckles with a sharp ruler" and when she recalls her mother saying, "I want you to speak English," fearful that the preservation of Spanish would diminish her daughter's opportunities in Anglo society. But I have experienced the limitations imposed by the use of a language different from my own. Teaching this course has made me acutely aware of the necessity to use that borrowed language, English, to convey the experience of women with whom I have a very special connection; therefore, I have wondered and continue to wonder if, with that borrowed language, I can do justice to the wealth of experiences, triumphs, and defeats of each and every Latina in this country.

The class has contributed to broadening and enriching my own Latin American identity, from the narrow margins of simply being a Chilean. My life in the United States and my teaching in this country had already expanded my perception of being a Latin American, giving it a continental dimension that is not so well defined when one lives in her country of origin, but that is enhanced by exile. In this country I have had to respond, from a broader perspective, to a consistently limited view about the part of the world I come from. In turn, to teach The Latina has profoundly altered my own vision. I am aware of the artificial separation and distinction that so many wedge as barrier between the Latina in the United States and women from South or Central America. Although I remain scrupulously aware of the different contexts that shape these women's struggles, experiences, and visions, I am interested in examining the common historical, cultural, political, and creative threads that unite us. I am interested in discovering the new language of women who struggle to preserve a voice so often threatened by economic systems, by the terror of military regimes, by rigid patriarchal structures, by racial, ethnic, or linguistic discrimination.

Finally, I must address some of the reasons this class focuses on women. Most students are, to a greater or lesser degree, familiar with women's issues within their own society and culture. The tendency is to believe that all women have the same experiences and face the same problems. Although true to a certain extent, such a way of thinking does not account for social, economic, and racial differences.

The process by which the particular history of Latinas is reconstructed for the course makes up the major core of the material. In other words, it is important for Latino students (as well as for Anglo students) to know that women within that ethnic/cultural group have had strong participation in the shaping of their own history. This is a process of empowerment for many of the students in the class, especially for female students who are able, for the first time, to feel a connection with other women of their own group; it is also a point of departure for analyzing and better understanding the present and reinforcing the notion that, as Latinas, they do have an important contribution to offer to Women's Studies programs and to women's organizations and movements. This awareness of their own cultural heritage encourages many students to affirm and/or to confront the traditions inherited from their female predecessors.

Latinas, to a large extent, find themselves occupying a subordinate status within the dominant United States culture and within their own culture. As women they may share with Anglo females the need to define their position in a society shaped by male values, and they may share in the feminist perspective's analysis of questions of gender and sexuality, but there are important differences vis-à-vis the mainstream feminist perspective on issues of race, culture, and class. To complicate matters further, Latinas feel torn between the support they give their male counterparts in their common struggle for racial and social justice and their oppression as women within their own cultural group.

> The culture expects women to show greater acceptance of, and commitment to, the value system than men. The culture and the Church insist that women are subservient to males. If a woman rebels she is a *mujer mala*. If a woman doesn't renounce herself in favor of the male, she is selfish. If a woman remains a *virgen* until she marries, she is a good woman. For a woman of my culture there used to be only three directions she could turn: to the Church as a nun, to the streets as a prostitute, or to the home as a mother. Today some of us have a fourth choice: entering the world by way of education and career and becoming self-autonomous persons. *A very few of us.* As a working class people our chief activity is to put food in our mouths, a roof over our heads and clothes on our backs (Anzaldúa 1987: 17, emphasis added).

To convey to students this double struggle that takes place both inside and outside a cultural realm is of utmost importance and is plagued with difficulties. It is a comforting thought, for many, to relegate women's oppression to the realms of another cultural/ethnic group, to think of machismo as a typical characteristic of Latino culture, the major culprit in the subjugation of women. Without denying its existence, I invite students to read some of the literature published by Latinas in this regard, to familiarize themselves with machismo as a stereotype and with machismo as a masculine role shaped by the position of a group within a given structure. It becomes important for students to understand that it is not an absolute or inherent category since the expression of it varies broadly from group to group, according to economic/social position, and is affected by such factors as whether or not a wife is employed outside the home. Machismo is ultimately an expression of the power relations between racial minorities and the dominant society.

The knowledge that most students have of women's issues seldom includes the experiences of poor women who belong to an ethnic/racial group and who experience a different set of problems inherent to their gender, ethnicity/race, and class. At this point, when the commonality of gender does not suffice to explain differences, the course looks closely into the issue of marginalized cultures and an incipient critique of the traditional forms of knowledge.

Students have approached this course, for the most part, with enormous desire to learn, and some of them have answered as follows in their course evaluation when asked if they would recommend the class to others:

> Yes, it is not simply a course about Latinas but, indirectly, about all aspects of our world. This course breaks stereotypes, furthers reflection and allows for some gaining of truth.

> Yes, it is an unusual, thought-provoking class. Its content and structure are refreshingly different.

> Yes, this course had an impact on me which I will carry with me from now on—this is not often true of college courses.

I would strongly recommend it because you learn so much; it is a very enlightening course. Every American should go through this.

Teaching this class has been both a rewarding experience and a frustrating one at times, but always a challenge. I have approached it with a sense of enormous responsibility to do justice to women who have, for generations, struggled to survive—with their families or by themselves—women who defy with their lives the image of passivity and submission so easily encountered in relation to them.

NOTES

1. Emma Tenayuca and Lucy González de Parson, Chicana labor leaders; Jovita Idar, feminist educator and journalist from Texas; Dolores Huerta, from California, vice president of the United Farm Workers of America; Luisa Moreno, a Central American, who joined the Chicanas in their struggle for better working conditions; Julia de Burgos, a feminist writer from Puerto Rico, published in the journal, *Revista de Artes y Letras*, published monthly in New York; Luisa Capetillo, author of several books on women's issues, an important voice in the history of feminism in Puerto Rico; Josefina Villafañe, medical doctor and suffragist of Puerto Rico; Lolita Lebrón, an activist in the movement for the independence of Puerto Rico.

2. To expand on this issue see Flores and Yudice 1990.

3. For an expanded view on the issue of course and curriculum, see Carby 1989.

4. *Diversity*, like several other words used in the context of race and ethnicity, is not accurate. I agree completely with Guillermo Gómez-Peña on the need to find a new terminology; he adds that the language of cultural institutions and funding agencies is ethnocentric and insufficient. See Gómez-Peña 1989.

11

Lesbian Studies and Multicultural Teaching: A Challenge in Diversity

Patricia Myers

This chapter explores the interconnections among race, gender, and sexuality within the context of a Lesbian Studies course taught in the Women's Studies Program at the University of Michigan during the winter and fall semesters of 1989. It was a unique course at the University of Michigan because of the teaching method, the students drawn to the course, and its lesbian content.[1] Practical Feminism: Lesbian Studies was an undergraduate seminar course on lesbian lives and culture attended by a mixture of gay and straight students, taught by a white, lesbian-feminist graduate student.[2]

Emotions about teaching a Lesbian Studies course in a homophobic cultural context ran from fear to terror. Imagine preparing to teach a course about lesbians at a large midwestern university, an environment where "Kill fags," "Homosexuality is a sin," and "Lesbians hate men" are oft-heard phrases in and out of the classroom; where plexiglass display cases of a gay student organization are routinely vandalized; where advertisements for gay social or political events are regularly defaced or destroyed; where the university office charged with meeting the needs of lesbians and gay men is publicly challenged by conservative students and university administrators; and, most recently, where hateful comments are written on five consecutive blackboards in one of the university's most heavily populated classroom buildings.[3] As a publicly visible lesbian on the Ann Arbor campus, I had already been exposed to homophobia and threats of violence against lesbians and had certainly had my share of nightmares: bricks through my window, assault while leaving a demonstration or classroom, job loss, and castigation for my "bias" by university officials. Now I had been hired to teach an introductory course on lesbians to undergraduates, a first at the University of Michigan. Certainly, I feared, I would be debated, tested, and dismissed or, worse, harassed (Goleman 1990; Herek 1989; James Kim 1988; Miessner 1989;

Secor 1990). Fortunately, my fears were not realized, and the course was a success.

FEMINIST PEDAGOGY

Make sure to keep atmosphere open to differences.

I really appreciate the interpersonal/experiential focus of the class.

I thought the best class discussions were when we were learning from each other.

There were times when discussion got tense and unpleasant, but it seems like more intervention on your part would not have been a good idea.

I would have liked for you to step in, and clarify things, and mediate more between points of view.[4]

Feminist and experiential teaching goals and strategies can be incorporated into many classroom settings and seemed the most useful framework for exploring lesbian issues within an academic context. My background in teaching both experiential and lecture-based courses and in small group facilitation demonstrated the importance of the practice of teaching.[5] Lecture courses can be an effective way of conveying a concise body of knowledge to a large number of students. For many courses, however, particularly those addressing minority cultural history, small group discussions may be a more effective method of processing information. Allowances for differences in class composition and life experiences of students should be addressed in the course planning and implementation. An instructor cannot plan an effective course with the assumption that all of her or his students share a common history. These kinds of assumptions perpetuate the myth that all students are white, heterosexual, middle-class or upper-class men, a myth that further stigmatizes any deviation from this norm.

Educational theorists suggest that feminist teaching—and other radical pedagogies—should involve "both the cognitive and affective areas of human learning" (Schneidewind 1990: 269; Lowney 1989). Critical analysis and synthesis are important tasks for many university courses. But how does an instructor encourage and reward the integration of practice and theory, the synthesis of the personal and the political? How might a course expose students to differing experiences of oppression and identity formation in a way that can be linked to their own histories? These questions frame much of my teaching at the University of Michigan, but were particularly important in my design and teaching of the Lesbian Studies course.

Feminist pedagogy goes a step beyond radical pedagogy in that gender is a fundamental category of analysis. It engages students in an educational process that is respectful of differences, particularly gender-based differences. Feminist teaching is an inherently political process that emerged from human rights activism of the late 1960s and 1970s and remains connected to grass-roots political activism. It seeks to ''admit and utilize the variances in students' contexts as well as to undermine the traditional concept of education as the collected wisdom of the past, which is by definition patriarchal and therefore ignores the experiences of women and other oppressed groups'' (Ryan 1989: 40). The voices of lesbians and women of color are often silenced or invalidated, and even descriptions of feminist educational theories and practices often lack an explicitly anti-racist and anti-heterosexist stance (Aptheker 1981; Bacca Zinn et al. 1990; Bulkin 1980; Klepfisz 1982; Smith 1982). Feminist pedagogy challenges the traditional academic biases that have relegated women's experiences to the intellectual margins. Thus, descriptions of multicultural teaching techniques, including information on the integration of sexual orientation into the curriculum, serve a critical need.

Many resources were utilized in the design and teaching of the Lesbian Studies course. These resources included materials from Women's Studies Programs at the University of Michigan and elsewhere (Albrecht and Brewer 1990; Bunch and Pollack 1983; Culley and Portuges 1985; Fischer 1981; Jenkins 1990; Krupnick 1990; Weiler 1988; Women's Issues Commission 1991); anthologies of essays on African American Women's Studies (Anzaldúa 1990; Moraga and Anzaldúa 1983; Hull, Scott, and Smith 1982; Ransby 1990; Smith 1983; Spelman 1982); published and unpublished syllabi from Lesbian Studies courses (Crumpacker and Vander Haegen 1987; Cruikshank 1982: 3–21; Escoffier 1990; Parmeter and Reti 1988); and analytical or autobiographical materials written by lesbians and women of color (Clarke 1983; Chapman 1987; Pence 1982; Stein 1989; Woo 1983; Lorde 1984).[6] These resources allowed me to frame the overall course and the specific components of it so that students and I could undertake a more complex and realistic examination of the intersections of race, gender, and lesbianism.

STUDENT ENROLLMENT

My own reasons for taking the class were because I knew so little about lesbians and their movement, and I was interested in women's issues in general. No big deal, right? HA! When I happened to mention the class to anyone, the typical response was a widening of the eyes and the question, ''*Why* are you in *that* class?'' I realized that every time I told someone new, my sexuality was on the line. When whoever I told had made doubly, triply sure that I wasn't myself a lesbian, they would tell me (in a whispered voice) of someone they suspected of being a lesbian. The next popular question I got was, ''How can you *stand* to sit in that class knowing that all of those lesbians are there?''

Taking the class for credit yet I feel I'll learn a lot being so unfamiliar with the topic.

I want to learn about lesbian life and culture because I have a sister who is a lesbian.

I can contribute, it appears, a unique perspective as (once again!) the sole woman of color who is also questioning her sexuality.

Don't know if there's much I can contribute except a good example of a willing-to-learn, dumb college student trying to be as open-minded as possible in today's society.

Table 1
Students Participating in the Lesbian Studies Course

	Lesbian Women	Gay Men	Bisexual Women	Bisexual Men	Heterosexual Women	Heterosexual Men	TOTAL
African American	2	1	1		1		5
Asian American	2	2				1	5
Latina/ Latino	2				1		3
Native American					2		2
Jewish	5	1	5		11	2	24
Caucasian	17	4	14	1	25	7	68
TOTAL	28	8	20	1	40	10	107

My main goal for this class is to learn more about lesbians and lesbian communities. I've never studied this (my) culture before and I would just like to know more!

The Lesbian Studies course met two hours weekly for seven weeks to discuss course materials and participate in experiential activities. One section of the course was offered in the winter of 1989 and two sections were offered in the fall of 1989. For the purposes of this chapter, the course will be considered as a single entity.[7] The Lesbian Studies course, like other courses that explore minority experiences, drew in a range of people.[8] The ages of the participants ranged from sixteen to fifty-eight. Differences in previous exposure to lesbian issues and expectations and reasons for taking the course varied as well.

Lesbians and gay men registered for the course to learn more about their cultural, social, and political history and to discuss the issues openly. Some of the women, self-identified feminists, registered for the course to increase their awareness of lesbianism, particularly as it related to gender issues. Some of the students had a gay sibling or parent and were interested in furthering their understanding of homophobia and the obstacles that often face lesbians, gay men, and bisexual people. Some of the students, primarily those who were themselves gay or who had a gay relative, had a high interest level and knowledge base. Some students had never been exposed to these issues, but were taking the course simply because they needed the credit and the course fitted into their schedule. Thus, I could not assume that all students shared an equivalent understanding of homophobia or homosexuality, nor could I presume that all were equally committed to exploring this contemporary social phenomenon in a unique, supportive environment.[9]

OVERVIEW OF THE LESBIAN STUDIES COURSE

This is probably the most ignorant thing I'll ever admit to, but the first time I really thought anything about the existence of lesbians was in this class.

Be a little more understanding towards the heterosexuals in the class.

I liked all the exercises. I'll remember much more from this class than others.

The course began with a historical overview of lesbianism in the United States, emphasizing the importance of considering lesbians in all areas of human interaction, including academic and political arenas. Gender, race, ethnicity, and religion were discussed in the third and fourth weeks of the course as fundamental characteristics in the development of identity and community.[10] This framework encouraged students to understand more fully the complexity of the interrelationships among sexuality, gender, and race.

An exploration of the intersections and divisions of oppression reveals similarities and differences in experience. Because many lesbians, gay men, and bisexual people must integrate their newly identified homosexuality into an identity that is already molded by gender, race, and class, it is impossible simply to discuss homosexuality without connecting it to other forms of oppression. This challenges the prevailing notion of a hierarchy of oppressions, which often rates race, sex, or sexuality as being more or less important, significant, or fundamental. Cherríe Moraga (1983: 52) writes: "The danger lies in ranking the oppressions. *The danger lies in failing to acknowledge the specificity of oppression.* The danger lies in attempting to deal with oppression purely from a theoretical base." Overt and covert discrimination against people of color, women, and lesbians exists in some shared areas: economics, education, politics, employment, social interactions, and medicine. However, the specifics of treatment, expectations, experience, and outcome vary with the situation. For example, high-quality health care may mean choosing between bankruptcy or a lack of the necessary treatment for a poor Latina lesbian, but may simply mean a shift in spending habits for a wealthy, white gay man. Their experiences may become more nearly parallel, however, if the gay man were diagnosed HIV-positive and lost his job, insurance, and housing. Ideally, students incorporate new information about the impact of racism and sexism on lesbian lives into an understanding of sexual development and the implications of "coming out" as a lesbian.[11] Many lesbians must consciously address and discard the antihomosexual teachings of family, community, and culture to embrace their stigmatized identity, and this was the focus of the last weeks of the course.

Positive images of and for lesbians must be created and distributed at the same time that negative information is reacted to and rejected. This was, in part, the agenda of the Lesbian Studies class and was explored in the final weeks of the course when discussing intracommunity issues of sexuality and future visions. In fact, the final activity for the course was a small group brainstorming of what the world might be like if it were free from the various forms of oppression. This gave the students a final opportunity to associate what they had learned in the course with their personal opinions and beliefs. The importance of linking academic information to students' experiences influenced my choice of reading materials, assignments, and classroom activities.

COURSE READINGS

I read the whole coursepack in the first week! It's great to have an anthology which covers *so* many perspectives.

I enjoyed the poetry, the cartoons, the literary writings—the more scholarly articles were good/helpful too, but not as much fun (which shouldn't be a surprise).

Too much reading to expect for each class.

Each section of the course, through readings and discussion, raised the critical terms and issues in the field of Lesbian Studies.[12] Readings consisted of an introductory text on homophobia and a coursepack of photocopied articles (Pharr 1988). Since no interdisciplinary Lesbian Studies textbook exists, I developed a collection of essays that drew materials from a wide range of disciplines and sources. Drawing materials from a range of perspectives and disciplines presented its own difficulties. How could I competently teach issues raised from viewpoints and experiences I did not share? Writings exploring the experiences of lesbians of color were critical to the visions and goals of the course. The integration of materials written by women of color, as opposed to appropriation or assimilation, is a constant tension in feminist education and theory, and a balance was sought in the Lesbian Studies course. By speaking to particular issues instead of from the positions articulated in these readings, I attempted to engage students in a discussion of oppression based on color and culture without assuming the "expert" position.

Students were asked to complete approximately thirty pages of reading before each weekly discussion. These readings consisted of theoretical materials in addition to an occasional literary or artistic piece. In an effort to break the silence regarding the life experiences of lesbians, particularly lesbians of color, autobiographical narratives were an integral component of the coursepack. Whenever possible, essays that articulated personal experiences within a social context were highlighted. Students were encouraged to apply theoretical concepts to these accounts of individual women's lives, with a particular focus on the impact of gender and race on lesbians' experiences.

Students were asked to evaluate the readings, assignments, and exercises at the close of each term. I utilized a university-wide evaluation service that analyzes and compares evaluations for approximately three thousand University of Michigan courses and developed a four-page, detailed evaluation form. Students seemed especially moved by the more personal readings and less interested in the longer, more theoretical pieces. A number of students were concerned about the large amount of reading required for each class meeting, but discussed plans to continue reading the collection after the course had ended. Overall, students indicated that they found the articles challenging, educational, and engaging.

COURSE ASSIGNMENTS

The autobiographical essay was a great assignment! It really helped me to articulate my experience, and see the connection between myself and others.

This took a lot out of me (I did the pink triangle.) Was refreshed. Learned intensely.

The bibliography made me see that lesbians in society today are doing what everyone else is doing. They are living like normal people.

The most valuable aspect of the bibliography was learning that there is stuff out there on lesbians.

The bibliography was good—it wasn't too much work for a 1 credit course but gave me a chance to see how much information was out there.

The bibliography was a vital part of creating more visibility for Lesbian, Gay, and Bisexuality issues.

Students were asked to complete two written assignments. These requirements also attempted to integrate individual experience with theoretical materials. Students were asked to write an autobiographical essay as the first assignment. A primary goal of the autobiographical narrative was to give the student a chance to engage the materials in the course, in addition to initiating a student-instructor dialogue. Students had three options for this assignment: write their own "coming out" story; write about their growing awareness of homophobia; or wear a Pink Triangle for a day, signifying their support of lesbians' and gay men's rights, and write about their experiences.[13] Students submitted poetry, fictional letters to family members, descriptions of the struggle to accept their own homosexuality, stories of reactions to friends who are gay, and descriptions of their experiences wearing the Pink Triangle. This assignment encouraged students to examine and articulate thoughts and feelings in an informal atmosphere. These writings are extremely valuable and can be incorporated into many classroom activities and discussions.

The second assignment was to complete a short bibliography on any topic related to lesbianism. The research required was minimal, but gave students an indication of the abundance or lack of available materials. Students generated approximately one hundred bibliographies, which included such topics as lesbians in the arts, gay themes in adolescent novels, lesbian erotica, workplace discrimination, lesbians in sports, and lesbian mothers. The bibliographies were combined into a resource manual, which has been distributed to a number of students, staff, and faculty at the University of Michigan. Feedback indicates that this has been an invaluable resource in designing and implementing courses and trainings on lesbian issues, encouraging lesbians to share their experiences in academia as lesbians, and making the course itself an agent for social justice.

EXPERIENTIAL EXERCISES

The Multiple Choice Exercise got people in the class talking to one another right away. The first class focused on us talking to each other directly rather than through you.

Hard to choose just one answer but helped me to really think about my feelings on certain topics.

Multiple Choice was the best exercise—we realized how different the categories or labels or definitions are—but also that we can still agree on some things.

A set of exercises exploring multicultural issues formed the core of the classroom activities. Informal discussions, debates, small group discussions, and structured exercises were all utilized to examine stereotypes, misconceptions, and experiences with regard to the various course topics. Consistent with the structure of the course discussed above, I developed or adapted exercises to address the needs of this particular group of students. Structured exercises, with clearly articulated rationales and expectations, helped students synthesize course materials and challenge stereotypic beliefs. The Multiple Choice Exercise, conducted the first day of class, focused on defining the categories of "lesbian" and "feminist," among other things.[14] This was an effective tool in explicitly identifying student assumptions and expectations of the course. Students were asked to congregate under an "answer" that best fit their response to a trigger statement. For example, 43 percent of the students defined a lesbian as a woman who "loved" other women, 30 percent understood lesbianism as political "identification" with other women, while 8 percent thought lesbianism was primarily a sexual choice. The rest agreed with none of the above. Differences in understanding of the category of lesbian significantly impacted experience and interpretations of exercises, discussions, and readings. Likewise, feminism had various meanings: 42 percent of the students felt the liberation of both women's and men's lives was the focus of feminism; 30 percent believed feminism addressed the needs of women as an oppressed class; and 21 percent thought feminism was too narrow to address issues of race, class, age, and sexual orientation. The remaining students chose no answer. The exercise also asked students questions about group roles, expectations of the course, other students, the instructor, and anticipated levels of participation. This gave the students a chance to introduce themselves briefly to one another and to discuss topics of interest.

The Line Exercise was intense and scary, it was eye-opening and perhaps served to bond the class together in our differences/struggles—we all have *some*.

It was embarrassing for participants.

Good for opening up the class for risk-taking.

Good icebreaker. Challenging, though.

Students were also asked, on the first day of class, to participate in an exercise that used an imaginary line to demarcate different social/political categories. This exercise introduced students to some of the course themes and to each other.[15] As students crossed the line, differences in socioeconomic status, age, race, language, disability status, and sexuality were revealed to class members.[16] Questions of identification, that is, what a lesbian is or who a lesbian is, have often been an initial step in non-academic and scholarly writing or talking about lesbians (Crumpacker and Vander Haegen 1987: 66–67; Diffloth 1987; Richards 1990; Cook 1979). Being identified as a lesbian or a gay man raises issues of privacy, choice, political expediency, safety, and accountability for homophobic behavior. Within the Lesbian Studies course, however, the negative consequences for being "deviant" shifted onto the heterosexually identified students, and some expressed concerns about being misunderstood, stereotyped, held responsible for the behavior of all heterosexual people, or dismissed as irrelevant. Some of the heterosexual students continued to struggle with this "minority" status within the Lesbian Studies course through defensiveness in discussions, frustration and anger at the gay students, or a newfound empathic understanding of "how homosexuals must feel in the rest of the world." The implications of disclosing one's lesbianism or being otherwise identified as gay are not limited to the college campus, however. The political significance of identifying historical or public figures as gay has been debated recently in the popular media as "outing" (Bronski 1990).[17] Classroom concerns, though less dramatic, have similar implications. In the end, however, students found taking risks in this initial class meeting useful. The information shared in both exercises laid critical groundwork, because many students had no previous experience in a Women's Studies course, and none of the students had taken a Lesbian or Gay Men's Studies course. These exercises are useful introductions for the students and a way of collecting information to assist the instructor in future planning.

During the week of exploring sexism and its impact on lesbian identity development, students were asked to participate in a "guided fantasy" that explored traditional gender socialization by asking students to imagine a world in which gender roles were reversed (Wells 1976). This generated a discussion of the specific ways sex-role socialization and enforcement can impact women as a group and lesbians in particular. It also reinforced an awareness and understanding of "compulsory heterosexuality," an important concept of the course (Rich 1980). In her essay, Adrienne Rich carefully documents and analyzes the ways in which heterosexuality is systematically encouraged, reinforced, and rewarded throughout an individual's life, including such vehicles as children's books, toys, and games, television programs, greeting cards, advertising images, parental expectations regarding marriage and reproduction, and social institutions including religion, law, education, medicine, and the military. The readings, discussions, and exercises emphasized the social construction of the "natural," a revelation necessary in a course that seeks to enlighten and change society.

Brainstorming was effective in making us stop and realize the many guises of oppression and mapping out the distinctions in society.

Privileges aren't necessarily enjoyed by *all* members of a particular group.

I felt uncomfortable.

This was extremely helpful in tying different issues together—I have already referred back to our list and am sure I will do so in the future.

This had the potential to be the most informative and interesting, but it didn't work for me.

Social mechanisms that uphold the oppression of different minority groups were discussed following brainstorming of some common privileges associated with race, sex, and sexual orientation (McIntosh 1988). Students were encouraged to generate lists of specific and general mechanisms that maintain power differentials, in addition to listing and discussing the specific privileges attached to being white, male, heterosexual, Christian, and able-bodied. Discussions following brainstorming of privileges have been particularly spirited, as students negotiate ascribed privileges and personal responsibility. These discussions of the fundamental impact that the social environment has on an individual's opportunities, choices, and aspirations encouraged students in the Lesbian Studies class to examine more thoroughly the need for, and the difficulty in creating, coalitions among minority groups.

The Concentric Circles Exercise was interesting, but a bit intimidating.

Great! There was a lot of room for differences in experience. Honest and accepting atmosphere.

Good, but not enough time to fully respond to the questions.

Students' early learnings about gender, race, and sexual orientation were examined in an exercise entitled Concentric Circles, named for its discussion format.[18] Students were placed in two circles: the inside circle faced the outside circle, and each student had a partner in the opposite circle. Five groups of comparable questions were read, asking students to share with their partner the early messages they received from influential adults about racial groups, gender roles, sexuality, situations in which they have been perceived as prejudiced, and strategies for social change. Each person had three minutes to respond to the questions asked, then that student's partner had the same amount of time to discuss her or his experiences. This exercise attempts to illustrate some of the interconnections of oppression, particularly in the messages we received as children and young adults, in addition to outlining the differential impacts of race, ethnicity, gender, class, and sexual orientation. Students found this to be an eye-opening, challenging activity.

The fishbowl format for small group discussions was the most helpful because it gave space to talk about things in a safer small group, yet the whole class could hear.

It generated the most new and interesting discussion.

It was a great chance to ask all those burning questions.

This was my favorite exercise.

One of the most helpful formats for small group discussion puts a small group of students (six to eight) in a circle inside a larger group of students (the rest of the class). In order to participate actively in the discussion, students must move to the inner circle and leave it when finished. The discussion is carried out among the smaller group of students, simulating a more intimate setting, but all have the opportunity to listen. Students seemed appreciative of opportunities to hear stories from their peers and to share their own. Students, anonymously, wrote questions on index cards, which were then posted on newsprint as potential discussion topics. Some students were particularly interested in questions of lesbian parenting, sexuality, politics, coming-out stories, and tensions that might exist in interactions between lesbians and their parents, colleagues, and friends.

CONCLUSION

The course helped me to fine tune my awareness of the interconnections. I'm more aware of how homophobia and sexism are related.

All these isms are too over-rated and talked about too much.

I'm less homophobic.

I did not recognize heterosexism as such a great problem as I do now.

Can people be forced to confront their own racism?

This chapter concentrates on the teaching method, practice, and content of a Lesbian Studies course at the University of Michigan, but many of the components of the course can be, and have been, effectively integrated into other courses that explore discrimination or oppression. The exercises described here are useful in initiating discussions of sexual orientation, among other topics, particularly in introductory courses in African American Studies, American Culture, English, political science, psychology, sociology, and Women's Studies.

Students in the Lesbian Studies class expressed both frustration and delight with the course content and method. For some, it was the "best course I have taken at this university." Others found the combination of unfamiliar content and experiential method overwhelming. Personal exploration of attitudes about lesbianism and homophobia was difficult in a predominantly formal, academic setting. Some students might have been better served by the Lesbian Studies course had they been exposed, through informal discussion groups and individual reading, to some of the issues before registering for the class. However, other students, particularly the lesbians, had read much of the material and discussed many of the topics, albeit not in an academic setting. A richer understanding of diversity necessitates conflict, mistakes, and patience with the educational process. The experiential teaching methods used in the Lesbian Studies course effectively engaged students from a wide variety of backgrounds and expectations in a learning process that all found valuable.

The challenge to reconsider strong beliefs about gender, race, and sexuality is a primary task of many courses addressing multicultural issues. All components of the course attempted to synthesize information about lesbians into an existing framework that often, in other settings, minimizes or dismisses the particular contributions of people from different minority groups. The voices of lesbians of color, in particular, were emphasized in the readings, discussions, and exercises of the Lesbian Studies course. Developing and teaching courses with a multicultural focus at the university level are critical efforts toward social change. These courses can help to disrupt our own oppressive attitudes and those of our students and the institutions in which we work.

NOTES

1. The Women's Studies Program at the University of Michigan had an approved, generic course entitled Practical Feminism. The Women's Studies Advisory Committee, the governing board of the program, offered the Lesbian Studies mini-course under this title in order to avoid conflict with the regents of the University of Michigan. Leaving the main course title Practical Feminism protected those students who were concerned about the appearance of the word *lesbian* on their official transcript. It is ironic, given the title of the course, that an early women's liberation slogan was "Feminism is the theory, lesbianism is the practice." Since 1989 a 300-level, full-term Lesbian Studies course has been approved by the University of Michigan's Curriculum Committee based, in part, on the "highly rated" and "well-enrolled" Lesbian Studies mini-courses.

2. My preferred phrase for talking about gay people as a group is "lesbians, gay men, and bisexual people." I believe that the increasingly popular phrase "lesbians and gays" reinforces lesbian invisibility in a sexist context by equating "gays" with men. I use the term *gay* inclusively to describe both lesbian women and gay men. Similarly, *homosexual*, while overly clinical, is used to describe both women and men.

3. *The Michigan Review*, a conservative University of Michigan student newspaper, has written a number of stories that criticize gay activists and the Lesbian-Gay Men's Program office. The blackboards were unofficially reported as containing the following "messages": "Help rid our world of disgusting filth such as gay's [*sic*]," "Homosexuals are not people but abominations," "Tired of gut-wrenching faggots," "Decent people must ban [*sic*] together to stop the homosexual movement," and "Do you want a healthy environment to raise your children in? Then join the fight against homosexuality." A similar flier was discovered on one of the campus bulletin boards: "Rape all Dykes. Straight White men are #1!"

4. Unless otherwise noted, these comments are quotes from student assignments, evaluations, or feedback.

5. I have taught several introductory courses in the Women's Studies and American Culture Programs at the University of Michigan in addition to two upper-level experiential courses in the Women's Studies Program. I have also served as a "diversity" consultant to college-wide teacher training programs. I have been an educator on homosexuality and homophobia on college campuses in Michigan for the last twelve years and have facilitated a number of small discussion groups on these issues.

6. A subcommittee of the Women's Studies Program surveyed academic institutions comparable to the University of Michigan to determine the number and kinds of courses offered exploring lesbian issues. We found that 64 percent of the surveyed institutions had offered a Lesbian Studies course, 45 percent on a regular basis. Eighty-six percent of the courses offered were humanities courses, with literary courses comprising over half of the offerings.

7. The Lesbian Studies course was taught during two successive terms to three sections of students. Modifications in the readings and classroom activities were made between the terms and according to the numbers and interests of the students in each section.

During the winter term, I established small discussion groups for the participants to facilitate more intimate exchanges since this was a fairly large group. I dropped these small discussion groups during the next term—primarily because the course was smaller, but also because the groups were difficult to coordinate, facilitate, and manage.

8. Demographic and background information on student participants was collected anonymously on index cards on the first day of class. Students were asked to indicate, among other things, their sexual orientation, age, racial and ethnic background, and previous exposure to lesbian issues. There were 107 participants in the three sections of the course: sixty-two during the winter term, twenty-six and fifteen in the fall term sections. An additional twenty-five people attended the class more than twice during the term.

9. The focus on lesbian issues was unique. The Women's Initiative Group at the University of Michigan (WING) collected information about course content on race, gender, ethnicity, and sexual orientation in eighteen introductory fall 1989 courses, primarily in the social sciences. Issues of sexual orientation, according to 51 percent of the 846 students surveyed, were never mentioned. When mentioned at all, these issues were mentioned positively only a quarter of the time. Individual lesbians and gay men were not mentioned 67 percent of the time (Vandewater and Stewart 1991).

10. The Lesbian Studies class focused on lesbians, and not gay men or bisexual people, for two reasons. The Women's Studies Program tends, at this point in its history, to focus on women to promote visibility and parity. This course was able to explore both the specific impact of sexism on lesbians and the obstacles that lesbians and gay men share. Second, other courses offered at the university have been more focused on the experiences of gay men.

11. "Coming out" is short for "coming out of the closet," a phrase describing the lifelong process of identifying, accepting, and disclosing one's homosexuality in a homophobic culture. Lesbians have collected and documented our "coming-out" stories in a number of books and articles. For examples, see Baetz 1988; Beck 1982; Hall 1989a; Holmes 1988; Ramos 1987; Stanley and Wolfe 1989.

12. The field of Lesbian Studies includes works across a range of disciplines. For examples in the history of sexuality, see Braverman 1990; D'Emilio and Freedman 1988; Duberman, Vicinus, and Chauncey 1989; Faderman 1981; Kehoe 1986. Literary and

critical works on lesbians include Foster 1975; Freedman et al. 1985; Jay and Glasgow 1990; Zimmerman 1985. Social science scholarship on lesbians includes Darty and Potter 1984; DeCecco 1985; Krieger 1983; Phelan 1989; Wolf 1979.

13. This exercise is described in detail in Chapter 3 in this volume. Pink Triangle buttons are widely available as a symbol of lesbian and gay men's liberation.

14. This exercise was adapted from an exercise introduced to the author by Dr. Beth Reed, professor at the University of Michigan School of Social Work.

15. See Chapter 21 in this volume for descriptions of The Line exercise. This exercise was first introduced to the author at an "Unlearning Racism Workshop," facilitated by Ricky Sherover-Marcuse, Ph.D., at the University of Michigan, 1987.

16. For discussions of the possible implications and considerations in self-disclosure, see the following: Barale 1989; Beck 1981; Cruikshank 1982: 3–21; D'Emilio 1987; Newton 1987.

17. A discussion of the personal, political, and legal implications was also a highlighted segment on the January 28, 1991, "L.A. Law" television program.

18. The Concentric Circles exercise was adapted from an exercise distributed through the University of Michigan's Office of Minority Affairs.

12

The 1988 Presidential Campaign and Multicultural Education

Bunyan Bryant

Multicultural education may be viewed as a critique of white cultural hegemony. Multicultural education not only is a critique that helps both whites and people of color understand and appreciate the richness of diversity of cultures and their contributions, but also is a direct challenge to white cultural hegemony; it attempts to lessen the impact of white cultural hegemony on people of color; it attempts to affirm the existence of people of color by making them aware of the importance of their own culture. Through multicultural education, new and more powerful cultural paradigms can emerge within a curriculum that is respectful of both Western and non-Western cultures. Yet this will not be easy; conservatives will resist such efforts by stating that the already overcrowded curriculum does not lend itself to other cultural perspectives. It is clear that this struggle over the curriculum will continue to take place and has to be won; it is fundamental to the success of multicultural education.

Our brightest youngsters at our most prestigious and predominantly white universities are often exposed to multiple forms of white cultural hegemony in both subtle and not so subtle ways. For black students to learn about western literature, science, and the arts presupposes that the only meaningful knowledge is that of Western authority; the conspicuous absence of intellectual contributions by blacks is a denial of black metaphysical being. Although in studying Western civilization, black students are exposed to the Aryan model, which presupposes that Greek civilization evolved from nowhere to make significant contributions to the world, evidence suggests that Egyptians, Semites, Phoenicians, and others either had colonialized or had influenced Greek civilization. Thus, much of Greek civilization was built upon previous cultures (Bernal 1987). Thus, education based on white cultural hegemony is a form of global plagiarism. Because black students are seldom exposed to roles that former slaves played in the Civil War, they are unaware that this war could not have been won by the North without the help of black soldiers (Du Bois 1972). Black students are forced to adapt to Western cultural arrogance that attempts to shape their world view as being less than equal to that of their white counterparts. It is not that Westerns have failed to contribute significantly to civilization, but taking credit for the lion's share of the world's cultural contributions, without recognizing the contributions of others, is the height of white cultural arrogance.

White cultural hegemony steeped in Western civilization provides the conceptual basis for whites to think they are the sole contributors of worthwhile knowledge and thus brighter and more creative than their black counterparts. White cultural hegemony assumes not only that blacks are inferior, but that their cultures are as well. To threaten white hegemony may unleash the most vile forms of racism, such as jokes, discrimination, physical intimidation, and violence. If multicultural education empowers people to seek self-expression through traditional institutions, we can expect manifold resistances from whites to protect their dominant world view. Yet it is important that multiculturalism help whites to modify their world view to take its proper place in history. Multicultural education should not only be a critique of Western culture, but celebrate the positive aspects of various cultures and their unique contributions. In teaching multiculturally, one should be aware of the adaptive (White 1949) and problem-solving (Orozco 1983) contributions of multiple cultures. Adopting the best of each culture can improve and enrich the lives of all of us. If multiculturalism fails to challenge white cultural hegemony, then we can expect to find little resistance from whites, and at best it will be tolerated with little or no significant impact.

The more subtle forms of white hegemony keep blacks from being recognized by faculty or heard in classroom discourse. Minority students are often alienated when their contributions to discourse are taken less seriously, or their ideas are seldom legitimated in discourse until their white counterparts repeat them as their own. Under such conditions black students often retreat to a silence, leaving their white counterparts with the impression that they agree with their logic (Delpit 1988). Black faculty whose ideas are not taken as seriously as those of their white colleagues or whose ideas may be legitimated only by their white colleagues (or white students) in team-taught courses often become both frustrated and demoralized. Once in a while a white student asks rhetorical questions or pretends to be confused or challenges me not because the student wants to know, but because the student wants to play a game of one-upmanship; this can be frustrating. At times students fail to do their best work or to take the course seriously, yet they expect to get an A. In these instances, students attempt to take advantage of the course and of me for their own selfish ends. To have students take my courses less seriously than others and to have them attempt to take advantage of me and the course often has made me angry and defensive when dealing with them. I do have to be conscious of my feelings.

While power corrupts, so does powerlessness (May 1972)—with both blacks and whites finding themselves intricately involved on the twin horns of this dilemma. Because of the assumptions that whites make about people of color, which form the conceptual basis for racially corrupt behavior, whites operate under false premises, which lead them to believe they are more civilized and thus superior. Yet blacks who feel powerless may also experience corruption in that visible manifestations of their powerlessness take on the form of alienation, anger, and oftentimes despair. Racial protest in and outside the classroom is an educational curriculum of consciousness to empower students to challenge and curtail white cultural hegemony. Such challenges are normal for oppressed people in their quest for justice.

My struggles as a teacher have centered around letting go of a considerable amount of my personal power in the classroom by having students engage in a number of simultaneous small group discussions while I move from one small group to another, playing the role of participant-observer. Using small group discussions as an alternative to lectures as much as possible and encouraging students to create their own learning both have been empowering to students. The question becomes, How do I deal with my own corruptness resulting from my own loss of power? Placing more emphasis upon small group discussion runs against the authority-dependent relations between faculty and student. The struggle is, How do I maintain respect from students expecting authority-dependent relations in the classroom? How do I maintain respect from my colleagues who view well-organized, fifty-minute lectures as the only avenue to academic rigor? As a teacher, how do I deal with white cultural hegemony in the classroom? How do I deal with a racist student in class with little support from other students? How do I try to protect him or her from being scapegoated? How do I make an intervention and simultaneously respect the student as a human being, even though the student's beliefs are radically different from my own? How do I support a black student who is emotionally toned (expecting some support from me) without giving the impression that the black student and I are at odds with the rest of the class? How do I deal with the issues of helping students develop social change skills, when they may in fact use these skills later on to help frustrate or thwart civil rights efforts?

While none of these questions is easy to answer, one answer to the last question is structural in character: the university has to increase its enrollment of minority students for equal access to information to defend against those who would want to hinder or thwart social justice. While the more visible forms of white hegemony seldom appear in class, subtle forms are often in evidence. My course, Presidential Campaigns, does not pretend to be a model or panacea for other courses. There were shortcomings, to be sure, as we engaged each other in discourse. Through dialogue, some students may have become more conservative or more liberal or remained where they were. Presidential Campaigns is a course that I have taught twice, and hopefully one can glean important insights from my experience to be helpful in teaching students from diverse backgrounds.

COURSE DESIGN AND DESCRIPTION

Because there has never been a recent presidential candidate like Jesse Jackson, who has deeply stirred the emotions of black America, I felt that 1984 and 1988 were ideal times to teach a course on presidential campaigns and multiculturalism. Why was it difficult for white Americans to support Jackson, even though he spoke to white, middle- and working-class issues more than other candidates did? This difficulty did not become clear until I attended a presidential debate in Des Moines in 1987. As a member of the board of directors of Prairiefire, located in Des Moines, we cosponsored a presidential debate along with several other organizations. Prairiefire is a nonprofit organization, dedicated to resisting farm foreclosures. During this presidential debate among Democratic contenders, white farmers (99 percent of the audience was white) gave Jackson a standing ovation and yelled, "Tell it like it is, Jesse." They whistled for him. Yet I noticed that some farmers were wearing Dukakis hats and some were wearing political symbols of other candidates. I heard one farmer tell another one, "I would vote for Jesse, if I thought he could win." What a contradiction, I said to myself as I felt my anger rise. These farmers, however, were not unique; thousands of whites across the country fell victim to the self-fulfilling prophecy of "I would vote for Jesse if he could win." This issue was raised and discussed a number of times in the course—that is, why could not whites vote for a black when blacks usually voted for whites?

Even though Jesse Jackson had a better environmental platform than his Democratic and Republican rivals in both 1984 and 1988, I felt that there would be too much resistance to teach such a course in the School of Natural Resources. Therefore, I tried the path of least resistance by getting permission to teach Presidential Campaigns under the auspices of the Center for Afro-American and African Studies (CAAS). In addition, minority students were not identified with Natural Resources; many were identified with the CAAS. Therefore, it would be easier to recruit them if the course was taught in the CAAS. Although attempts were made to recruit other minorities, they were less than successful.

The first time this course was taught was in the winter term of 1984 during the Democratic presidential campaigns when a number of Democratic contenders, including Jesse Jackson, competed for the party's nomination. Although most people failed to recognize or understand Jackson's appeal, it was rooted in the civil rights movement and liberation theology. Combining civil rights organizing strategies with religious symbols, he was able to forge a coalition between progressive white groups and the black religious and nonreligious sectors. Jackson's campaign provided opportunities for black students in particular both to understand and to use the political process to bring to center stage critical discourse regarding the plight of black America. The second time the course was taught, blacks, Jews, gentiles (as in the first course), and one Asian were able to engage in substantive, though tense, discourse. Each time the course was taught, students were asked to adhere to two ground rules: (1) respect for one another and (2) a commitment to work through a conflict until each side understood the other's perspective. It was all right to disagree as long as they understood why they were disagreeing. These two basic ground rules were referred to several times throughout the courses; they served as reference points for students to take stock of their behavior and how their behavior was affecting those around them. It was easy to refer to ground rules when students became emotionally toned, and thus it became easier to handle conflict. Additionally, this pedagogy was an attempt not only to provide students with a different educational experience, but to encourage them to take charge of their learning and to challenge more traditional pedagogies that fostered authority-dependent relations. A typical class is as follows:[1]

10 min. Miscellaneous announcements and information related to course logistics.

20 min. Excitement sharing: students reported to the whole class new learnings or insights regarding their respective campaigns or candidates. Also, students reported on their trips to Iowa and Illinois during this time.

35 min. Hypothesis testing: hypotheses were stated by the instructor to stimulate large group discussion or some of this time was used for short lectures. (Some days were devoted to lectures, some of which were given by outside experts.)[2]

10 min. Break.

35 min. Small group discussion: students selfselected into various campaigns to plan a panel presentation based upon their candidate's platform. Each campaign group had to research and obtain a thorough understanding of a variety of complex issues that made up the various platforms and be able to defend them. Two sessions around midsemester were devoted to panel presentations.

10 min. Evaluation: in the whole group, students evaluated the class in terms of strengths and weaknesses. Students talked about their learnings and excitement as well as things they were less excited about.

PEDAGOGICAL TECHNIQUES

Class Composition

A special attempt was made to get a large number of black students in class. Posters were placed in the Center for Afro-American and African Studies and around campus; fliers were sent to colleagues to inform black students who might be interested in the course. Fliers were given to students; they were encouraged to pass on the information to others by word of mouth. As one-third of the forty students in class were black, it was an unique experience for both blacks and whites; neither black nor white students nor the Asian had ever been in class with large numbers of blacks since being at Michigan. As was expected, black students, along with a couple of whites and the Asian, supported Jesse Jackson's campaign. What was unique about this experience was not that there were significantly more black students in class than in most other university classes, but that white hegemony was indirectly questioned, using presidential campaigns as the vehicle. Not only did the existence of a critical mass of black students empower them to be heard in discourse, rather than relegated to political impotence, but it changed the normal pattern of discourse between black and white students and made it more symmetrical, rather than asymmetrical. Because black and white students had to deal with each other on more equal terms, ideas surfaced by black students could not be easily dismissed or trivialized. Blacks, Jews, gentiles, and Asian had to deal with issues of racism raised within the various campaigns and news media; they had to deal with each other and why they supported their respective candidates.

Experiential Learning

This course was unique in that it was experiential and used a variety of pedagogical techniques, including computer conferencing to empower students in the learning process. Although students were required to attend class once a week for two hours, they had to assign themselves to a presidential campaign. This self-selection took place after representatives from various campaigns were invited to class to give a ten-minute presentation about their candidate. While some students participated in activities such as fund raising, voter identification, voter registration, phone calls to get out the vote, writing press releases, organizing for their candidates to visit Ann Arbor, and coordinating media campaigns, others took on major roles in various campaigns such as managers at both the local and state levels. This hands-on experiential approach to learning made up a significant portion of the course, allowing students, who would otherwise never have dared to become involved, an opportunity to be a part of a political campaign. In addition to working in various campaigns, students were required to learn about their respective candidate's platform (as well as other substantive information pertaining to electoral politics) and be able to debate its merits both in the classroom and on the computer conference.

Excitement Sharing

At the beginning of each class, students were asked to share information about their candidates that they had recently read in newspapers, magazines, or journals or that they had discussed with friends. This technique was a quick way of bringing each other up to date with respect to a variety of issues raised by candidates. We usually spent anywhere from ten to twenty minutes on this process. Students reported not only information about their candidate, but exciting events they experienced in their local campaigns and trips to Iowa and Illinois. Students, mostly of Greck ancestry, who supported Dukakis and supporters of Simon went to Iowa for a couple of weekends to work in their respective campaigns. The Simon supporters also traveled to Illinois to help rejuvenate his campaign. Although students supporting the Jackson campaign planned to go to

Iowa, this trip never materialized. Traveling across country to work in various campaigns was not a requirement of the course; this was something students felt they needed to do. While black students and a few white ones did not travel across country, they worked hard in the local Jackson campaign. They were ecstatic when Jackson won not only Ann Arbor but the state of Michigan. Although Jackson had won a number of primaries in the South, this was the first time he had won a major northern industrial state. The students felt they were making a part of history.

Computer Conferencing

Computer conferences allowed students to connect with one another wherever they were, allowing them to interact outside time and space limitations of the classroom. Students at home (if they had a computer and modem), on campus at one of the public computer stations, or at their campaign headquarters readily conference with one another. Computer conferencing allowed students to make contributions at their convenience without waiting for other speakers to finish, and they could work at their own pace (Turoff 1975). Computer conferencing allowed students to talk and listen at the same time; students entered information about their campaigns or issues of importance without feeling that their communication stream would be interrupted. Not only did the conference allow for self-activated communication, but a student who was asked a question did not feel pressured to respond immediately as in face-to-face discussions (Vallee et al. 1975). Because students were reading different materials, they were empowered to make significant and unique contributions to the conference; the structure of the reading assignments supported maximal participation and symmetrical relations among students and between students and faculty.

Computer conferencing allowed students to integrate knowledge with feelings. Too often, the educational process de-emphasizes feelings and detaches us from them as if we cannot learn from them. Below is an example of how student feelings were expressed through conferencing. The candidates were about to enter Super Tuesday's primaries and caucus, involving approximately twenty states—most of them southern. While the southern strategy was to use this day to thrust a southern candidate into the limelight to offset the influence of the Iowa caucus and the New Hampshire primary, it was about to backfire. When it looked as though Jackson would do extremely well on Super Tuesday, because of the large number of potential black voters in the South, white students wanted Jackson to consider the vice presidential candidacy position:

Jesse Jackson can be the V.P. nominee if he can demonstrate that he can help to elect a Democratic ticket. If a ticket with J. J. is electable and he does want to be the V.P., then there is no reason why he wouldn't be the V.P. or the presidential nominee; he must broaden his base among white voters. Even if he is unable to do that, the amount of support J. J. has gotten should ensure him of an influential role in the next Democratic administration.

I think that J. J. has just as many delegates, votes and as much viability as anyone to be the V.P. candidate. I don't think that the Republican old boys will give it to him though because they will do anything to keep the Democrats out of office. I wish this weren't the case, but unfortunately that's what I believe. This however, is NOT, NOT, NOT a reason not to work for and support J. J. He is a serious candidate for all types of people and helping J. J. will help all of us.

Let's quit playing games. Jackson is too close in the delegate count to be asking what Jesse wants. HE WANTS TO BE PRESIDENT. He leads in the popular vote. HE WANTS TO BE PRESIDENT. If this were any other candidate there would be different ways people would be projecting how this candidate would or could get the nomination. Since this would be the case, and since J. J. has so much support behind him, at this time he and we should be thinking of only the latter possibilities. Forget the party bosses! Let them come to him in June or July or whenever the darn convention is. The only thing that he said he wants is that HE WANTS TO BE PRESIDENT. Support that!

Computer conferencing allowed students to integrate their thoughts and feelings, and the faculty felt that it improved the quality of in-class discussions. Classroom discourse indicated that students had done considerable thinking and reflecting about various campaign issues. Yet most white students felt that Jackson couldn't win because he was black. Jewish students felt that Jackson was anti-Semitic; they couldn't understand why blacks would support a person who was racist. Even though many of the white students believed what Jackson had to say and even though many of them turned out to hear Jackson on his visits to Ann Arbor, they still clung tenaciously to their own candidates because they supported the prevailing societal view that ''Jackson can't win because he is black.'' Considerable debate took place on whether people should vote for Jackson because they believed in what he said or vote for the person who could win. The latter opinion won out.

Discourse in Small Groups

Small group discourse was used extensively throughout the course as a way of maximizing group participation. Authority-dependent relations were discouraged, enhancing independence of thought, personal autonomy, critical thinking, and quality interaction with peers (Abercrombie 1970) and faculty. Because the classroom was student-centered, emphasizing student participation and symmetrical relations among students and between students and faculty—thus fostering self-affirmation and empowerment—an atmosphere was created for students to take charge of their own learning. Through this process, they liberated themselves from the shackles of authority-dependent relations by becoming actors, not spectators, and by coming together in human solidarity, creating a belief that they could make a difference by participating in their respective presidential campaigns. Active participation in learning required students to make perceptual shifts from being the object of knowledge to being the source of knowledge, from being authority-dependent to being self-empowered, and from being passive participants to being active learners and teachers (Abercrombie 1970). This approach was not always easy.

Discourse in Large Groups

Although lectures were given on occasion, the basic role of the teacher was facilitator—encouraging dialogue among students from various campaigns.[3] Too often, faculty view students as having little meaningful information to contribute. The lecture thus renders students passive; the lecturer turns the classroom into a spectator sport (Palmer 1983), placing the lecturer at center stage. Because lecturers reinforce asymmetrical relations between themselves and students, the educational process is not liberation, but control. Therefore, many of the large group discourses were based upon hypotheses generated by me. These hypotheses, based upon current campaign events, were used to structure the discourse. For example, I would state: "My hypothesis is that the black voters of Illinois will vote against Paul Simon when he runs for Senate again because he did not drop out of the Illinois primary, thus spoiling it for Jackson" or "My Hypothesis is that Ed Koch will be defeated in the next mayoral election because of his attack on Jackson" or "My hypothesis is that Jackson will win Super Tuesday because of the black southern vote" or "My hypothesis is that Dukakis will be defeated in the general election because he is running away from the liberal ideology." Hypotheses like these triggered intense discourse. On the last day of class, however, the discourse heated up—not in the computer conference, but in the classroom.

Black students stated that the media were racist; Jackson's resounding defeat in New York, spearheaded by Ed Koch, angered them. While blacks pointed out the racist attacks of Mayor Koch, Jews in the class were quick to criticize Jackson's Operation Push, his relationships with international Arab groups, his anti-Semitic statements made in the 1984 presidential campaign, and his association with Arafat. Black students, on the other hand, felt that Jackson had apologized more than once for the anti-Semitic statements, there was little else that he could do, and these statements happened during the 1984 campaign. Blacks felt that at the heart of the matter was Jackson's policy on the Middle East; especially Jackson's support of a Palestinian state, something the Jews could not forgive. Although none of the black or Jewish students changed their minds regarding Jackson, they were able to engage in discourse, although intense.

The Structure of Course Content

Empowerment means that students not only take the initiative for their own learning, but become excited about learning. They are more spontaneous in their interactions within and across racial lines and with faculty; they are more motivated to go beyond academic requirements of the course; grades become secondary; students, regardless of racial identity, feel they can make a difference in the world in which they live. All of this is reflected in discourse. Because students read different articles, their chances of making unique contributions within and across campaigns were increased. Because they read different materials, the discourse among students was more symmetrical in character within and across racial lines; all became experts on sections of their candidate's platform. By reading different articles, students increased their chances of empowerment within small group discourse, and increased their chances for collective empowerment as they reported and debated their candidates' platforms with the whole class at mid-semester. For black students, Jesse Jackson was a symbol of empowerment, and his campaign provided an easy vehicle for them to raise issues of the history of oppression and racial injustice in the university and larger society. Jesse Jackson became the living textbook for black students, who interpreted his meaning and mission in class.

Course Evaluations

While structured readings were important, so was the building of small group affinity to enhance both learning and empowerment. Evaluations were important because cerebral activities were de-emphasized, providing rare opportunities for students to express their feelings regarding the seminar. Because evaluations were critical to the learning process and empowerment, a onetime evaluation at the end of the semester, although important, would have come too late for any meaningful changes to take place. A onetime evaluation would not have allowed students to exercise their power over the pedagogical process if it was failing to meet their needs. Ten-minute evaluations at the end of each session were solicited to generate data to improve the seminar. Evaluations were usually very positive, and suggested changes were minor.

Grading

In addition to opportunities to evaluate the course on an ongoing basis, students were given opportunities to evaluate their own and each other's performances in their respective campaigns. First, in preparation for the last class, students were given three evaluation forms of approximately four pages each. Students, where possible, self-selected themselves into trios within their campaign group. One form was used for self-evaluation, and the other two for peer evaluation. Once the forms were completed, they were used as a basis for evaluative discussion. Therefore, each person in the trio engaged in self-evaluation and peer evaluation. Completed evaluation forms were handed in and used in the grading. Second, mid-semester grades were based upon students' platform presentations of their respective candidates. Students worked in small groups during classroom time to prepare panel presentations. Third, each student analyzed a presidential primary or caucus based upon readings, class lectures, and discourse. Some decided to analyze more than one primary or caucus. In fact, most of the Jackson supporters analyzed Super Tuesday, and one student obtained permission to hand in her paper late because she was interested in the outcome of the New York primary. Students were asked to focus on why their candidate did so well or so poorly and what events changed people's minds to vote or caused them to withdraw their support from their candidates. What mistakes did candidates make? How did the media treat their candidate? Fourth, because the computer conference served as an electronic log, students were graded on the number of times they participated in the conference and their knowledge and analysis of campaign issues. Many of the entries into the conference were thoughtful; they showed that students had spent considerable time thinking about these issues. Last, students were graded on classroom participation. They were required to come to class, except in those cases where students decided to stay in Iowa or Illinois for an extra day to do campaign work.

SUMMARY

Although the pedagogical emphasis in this course was upon discourse, there were several short lectures to disseminate information. The overall critical variable was empowerment. By focusing on different material, students were able to make the perceptual shift from being the object of knowledge to being the source of knowledge, shifting the locus of control from the teacher to students. Through debate, white cultural hegemony was questioned, and white students were forced to deal with black students on more symmetrical terms. Debate forced white students to pay attention to the devastating impact of white cultural hegemony as reflected in many of the issues the Jackson campaign addressed. Therefore, teachers of students from diverse cultural and ethnic backgrounds should not only divide materials to be read among students, but provide articles and books written by black, Hispanic, Asian, and Native American scholars to help empower minority and majority students. The above pedagogical techniques are particularly important to use when students of color are small in number.

The class was structured to maximize student participation and empowerment as reflected in both large and small group discussion and the computer conference. Discussion gave students time to use each other as resources. It gave them a chance to engage each other in meaningful discourse, both in the classroom and on the computer conference. The class did question the assumption of white cultural hegemony. On the last day of class, four Jewish students—all male—came to me and told me (a black faculty member) how they appreciated the class. One remarked that he had "never experienced intelligent black people before" and that the only blacks he had been exposed to were in a lower-class neighborhood in Boston where his father worked as a dentist. This student now had a new image of black Americans.

NOTES

1. A Computer Conference on Presidential Campaigns was taking place during the course. Each student in the class was responsible for logging on once a week to engage

in substantive discourse. Students would generate new ideas resulting from their experiences or from what they had read, or they would in some cases continue the discussion that had been started in class. The computer conference helped students organize their thoughts about issues, and its content was used for grading students.

2. Lectures, some of them given by outsiders, were followed by discussion. A few days students did not meet in small groups. Before midsemester the campaign was the basis of much of the small group discussion. Following midsemester, however, small groups were sometimes mixed: representatives from each campaign formed the makeup of groups to enhance political discourse.

3. Lectures were given on such topics as the U.S. farm crisis; differences between caucuses and primaries, their strength and weaknesses; black voting patterns since 1960 and political office gains; the delegate selection process; superdelegates and their rationale; role of the media in presidential campaigns; rationale for Super Tuesday. Most of the lectures were short. Emphasis was placed upon discussion.

Part IV

General Courses Giving Attention to Diversity

It is not uncommon to overhear contemporary college and university instructors comment on their concern that they have not been adequately prepared to incorporate issues of race, gender, sexual orientation, ethnicity, and class into their courses. Most of us were trained during a time when courses contained standard content, and one merely had to choose from among the list of acceptable resources to design a course. As the "experts," our knowledge of the essential resources was rarely questioned. The incorporation of multicultural elements in a core curriculum was, simply, not a concern.

The very concept of the core curriculum is now under fire across the country, and faculty are increasingly called upon to include more content on ethnicity, sexual orientation, gender, and race into core courses throughout institutions of higher education. The authors in Part Four present their thinking on how this has best been accomplished in their courses. They represent departments of English, sociology, mathematics, architecture, women's studies, biology, and social psychology.

Sutton's chapter focuses on teaching students to think in new and creative ways about their interactions with their projects and the individuals who will eventually use the fruits of their labor. Aliaga identifies fifteen principles leading to the effective teaching of mathematics. Kleinsmith's acknowledgment of racial bias in science education, along with his involvement in his daughter's education, has led to the development of an interactive program to teach biology. This program and its impact on the test scores of African American and Latino students are reported in his chapter. Story demonstrates how an introductory composition course—required of virtually all first-year undergraduate students in U.S. colleges and universities—can be broadened to include the works of major authors of color. In the Gerschick chapter, a dialogue between the author and class participants sets the stage for reflections on the question of how faculty from European American backgrounds can best address multicultural process and content. Larimore echoes some of Gerschick's reflections in her analysis of a course on Third World women, with an emphasis on allowing participants to learn from a variety of sources. Finally, Douvan and Veroff share the insights gleaned from teaching a course in social psychology and illustrate the differences that can occur with the same course content when the class composition changes.

Each of these chapters provides teachers with valuable tools for thinking about the incorporation of multicultural content and process issues in general courses in higher education. The authors honestly discuss concrete innovations as well as successes and failures in their ongoing work in this area.

13

Seeing the Whole of the Moon

Sharon E. Sutton

Design studio—the centerpiece of architectural education—is a workroom where students spend ceaseless hours crocheting incongruous facts into highly personal visions; an inner sanctum where devotees invent dreams to solve the problems of humankind; a Brigadoon where they draw, build models, ride skateboards, prepare late night meals, sleep, discuss projects, work one-on-one with student and faculty mentors, and boast of all-night marathons. Quite unlike other learning environments, this is assuredly a space where a student's social imagination could be expanded to perceive the interdependence of all people, places, and events—a place where a student's internal landscape could be filled to embrace the wholeness of human existence. Unfortunately, this rarely happens.

While blessed with potential, architectural education is, as well, cursed with the reality of training future technicians to build a physical infrastructure for the status quo. Circumscribed by nationally established performance criteria, its curriculum equips graduates to reconstruct an essentially unjust world where professionals achieve stature, but others—too many of whom are ethnic minorities—subsist without housing, jobs, education, personal safety, or even hope. A library filled with glossy images of grandeur, a teaching methodology driven by the comparative virtuosity of individuals, a coveted connection to the world of art unconstrained in its search for beauty—all this encourages aspiring architects to see not the whole of the moon, but rather a waning crescent, where only the privileged can access their services.

WHEN AND WHERE I ENTER

My fascination with the paradox of architectural education began in the fall of 1968, when I was one of twenty-six African American students admitted to

Columbia University's School of Architecture. Our enrollment was a result of a bloody occupation of administrative offices staged earlier that year by student activists to dramatize racist policies at the university. As the halls of ivy curtsied to the demands of social justice, the architecture school—not surprisingly a major player in the occupation—lurched forward into new experiments. Banished was the traditional curriculum in which students imagined all clients to be like themselves—white, male, and middle class. Not only were there these twenty-six, mostly working-class African American students (the enrollment of women was still minuscule), but many assignments focused on real clients, particularly disadvantaged folk left unserved by professionals.

During that time, a major concern in schools as well as in the profession was how to create housing for all U.S. citizens, and this concern was buoyed up by a never-fulfilled promise of massive federal funding. Not only at Columbia but all around the country, schools of architecture hired social scientists who pioneered courses to help students understand the relationship between culture, environment, and the capacity for developing as productive members of society. Most architectural students of that era balked at being pigeonholed into the role of technocrat, insisting that the simultaneous participation in political and economic issues is an essential precursor to good design. They balked at the image of a lone virtuoso artist, insisting that sensitive, holistic design solutions require teams of people, including the client. They balked at the idea of neutrality and objectivity, insisting that all actions reflect cultural values.

But alas! The Vietnam War and an oil embargo subverted the quest for social justice. During the seventies, the country lurched from one economic crisis to the next—crises that had an especially severe impact on architects. Housing subsidies vanished, construction costs skyrocketed, many offices closed, untenured social science faculty were let go. The architectural profession mirrored the mood of a country in which more than a few people blamed the poor, rather than international events, for soaking up resources (Harrington 1984: 31–38). Conservatism took hold, and a newly enthroned crew of technocratic experts erased the expansive vision of architect as social planner. Proclaiming that architectural education could not be wasted on social work, they reerected distinct boundaries around the formal (physical) aspects of building. Whether it be learning to watercolor a building perspective, to make leakproof roofs, or to use history or philosophy to generate physical form, the architect's domain, they asserted, was in the craft of construction. The "why" or "for whom" of building was another problem altogether.

But, I wondered, how will narrowly trained technicians learn to take responsibility for their actions, especially when they are called on to assist in parceling out limited resources to competing interests in a multicultural society? Will they, for example, help one client to amass large quantities of income-producing property, even though that action may leave others without decent, affordable housing? Will they participate in designing massive security systems to protect some while others are left unprotected from those who have resorted to criminal behavior? Will they offer their services to a few to indulge in energy-consuming life-styles while others risk their lives defending the sources of energy?

How will narrowly trained technicians respond to these dilemmas? Will they see that their actions as individual professionals ultimately affect the common good? Will they help to set a moral context for using the environment? Will they accept responsibility to serve the whole of society where justice and injustice are often divided according to race or gender?

I agree with Henry Giroux who, in reflecting on Paulo Freire's philosophy, says that education is part of a larger ethical, social, and cultural enterprise in which teachers are morally responsible to help students engage in a struggle for a more humane world (Giroux 1985: xiii-xviii). In my view, a multicultural democracy is inconceivable unless all citizens—regardless of race, gender, or class—have basic human rights. Yet if "children [are] born into neighborhoods where inadequate medical care leaves babies dying at double the national average, where public schools spend only a fourth for each student of what is spent in richer districts, where even substandard housing is out of reach for many fully employed families, where drugpushing and violence rule the streets, you can be sure that citizens' rights have been violated from birth" (Lappé 1989: 46). Multicultural education makes students aware of this violation and seeks to engage them in a struggle to correct it.

The design studio experiences that I have initiated in the University of Michigan's Architecture Program invite students to participate actively in a moral debate regarding the equitable distribution of environmental resources. The experience that I describe here was offered during the winter term of 1990 to students in the fifth and sixth years of a six-year professional program in architecture. Their assignment, which extended a project begun in my class a year earlier, was to develop prototypes for housing and the use of open space in an impoverished, crime-ridden neighborhood in Detroit. A church-based development corporation was the client for their services. Students would take a broad look at the social, economic, and physical conditions of a twelve-block area. They would make recommendations for redeveloping the community without gentrifying and, therefore, displacing existing residents—an enormous task to accomplish in a fifteen-week period, especially since real people intended to use our recommendations.

In this chapter, I juxtapose an overview of my teaching philosophy and the performance parameters of the particular environment in which I teach in order to reveal how I (and my students) risked failure by pursuing this type of assignment. I describe the teaching method that I used, one student's project, the outcome for the client, and, finally, a student's evaluation. Although design is a unique form of inquiry, I believe that the educational approach that I describe can be applied in varied academic settings.

THE MISSION I BRING

Nourishing the Moral Imagination of Students

"Sometimes people like Abraham Lincoln, Malcolm X, and Martin Luther King are assassinated for insisting that we reexamine our way of being. . . . Serious education . . . has a way of forcing continual confrontation with our basic moral commitments and, more unnerving, with our failures to meet those commitments" (Purpel 1989: 8). To bring such a confrontation into the design studio, I use as my blueprint the liberation of creativity. All creative people reexamine and restructure existing images and ideas because of a persisting dissatisfaction with the way things are. Artists question accepted systems of order, consider the unrealistic, search for an escape from the predictable.

Yet, as geographer Yi-Fu Tuan (1989) points out, creativity or imaginativeness and morality are uneasy bedfellows. Creativity suggests "a tendency to indulge in fantasy and be irresponsible" (Tuan 1989: 3). In the last decade, the view of imaginativeness held in architectural schools and professional publications has often been flamboyant self-indulgence. However, our work as architects has a moral impact on society. "Anyone who looks at the earth can see that it has been differentially altered—in some places carelessly, in other places with imagination, and in still other places with an excess of imagination; that is, in irresponsible fantasy. Already I have used words that imply moral judgment. As we study the human use of the earth, moral issues emerge at every point if only because, to make any change at all, force must be used and the use of force raises questions of right and wrong, good and bad" (Tuan 1989: vii). My goal is to help students realize that their creative work has a moral impact on society, that, in accepting responsibility for the effect of their decisions, they are enriching their aesthetic imagination with the moral perspective that is needed to achieve academe's fundamental mission of justice and truth.

Understanding Your Connectedness to Others

"There is seldom, if ever, a school or university that sets as one of its prime, continuous, and long-range goals the cultivation of human caring and concern. The tragedy of this policy is to truncate the human spirit, especially that part which yearns for connection and involvement" (Purpel 1989: 41). The class that I am describing was dedicated to cultivating human caring and concern, to expanding the human spirit, to creating a sense of connection and involvement among people whose differences of race and class often block a sense of relatedness. If we were to accomplish these goals, my students needed to understand the difference between being sentimental and being compassionate.

"According to Purpel," I explained, "sentimentalism is . . . an inward, almost nostalgic, feeling that leaves the external context of the problem unchallenged— and weighing heavily on the shoulders of individuals (Purpel 1989: 43). It's saying, 'What a shame these poor people don't have good housing.' Sentimentalism causes guilt, powerlessness, a sense of personal inadequacy. It creates an asymmetrical relationship between you (the savior) and your client (the victim). You separate yourself from the problem. You think of what you are giving but not what you are getting. Your solutions may address the immediate problem of shelter or open space, but they will not bare the structural weaknesses that have caused the extreme deterioration of this neighborhood.''

"Compassion," I continued, "reaches outside the self to articulate the social, political, and economic context of a problem. Compassion is informed and morally responsible (Purpel 1989: 42). It is like saying, 'As long as housing is a commodity that feeds the interests of a wealthy few, then many less powerful people will surely be without it.' In looking for solutions, create a 'we' that includes your clients; make sure that they define their own solution; understand how they are helping you; acknowledge the privilege and responsibility of your advantaged position; develop a generosity of spirit that limits your need for a bigger share of the pie. To quote Bellah et al. (1985: 194), 'Generosity of spirit is . . . the ability to acknowledge an interconnectedness—one's debts to society— that binds one to others whether one wants to accept it or not. It is also the ability to engage in the caring which nurtures that interconnectedness.' ''

Creating an Empowered Community of Action

If ours was to be an effective community—able to learn, grow, and take action—then each person on the designer/client team must feel an inner sense of power to bring about change within the context of the group. This feeling is not something someone bestows upon you. It—being empowered—is something you have to have the courage to reach inside for. When I first made the decision to work with students on behalf of disadvantaged people, I presumed that high-achieving students in a first-rate university would claim, as their birthright, an incorrigible capacity for being subjects rather than objects of change. After all, they would soon graduate to leadership positions. It was the disadvantaged folk who would experience a sense of powerlessness.

This presumption proved far from true. In fact, the survivors of a competitive, individualistic educational system have so focused on pleasing the teacher that most have forgotten how to take control. Some may even be annoyed at being asked to participate in determining the direction of the class because it slows up the fast pace of finishing first. Besides, how can students collaborate with peers who have been viewed for so long as "the competition"?

In the pedagogical approach that I take, students are asked not simply to resolve an assigned problem, but to decide what is the problem. Stepping back and waiting for students to define the problem that needs to be studied are the most difficult challenges that I face. Myles Horton once advised me: "If you want to succeed immediately, start doing things for people so they'll see a result. If you want to succeed in the long run, let people do for themselves."[1] But this is hard advice to follow. Within the fifteen-week semester is there time for students to reverse their habit of following rather than leading, to exercise their right to make mistakes without fear of failure, to recapture their own power and begin to use it? It seemed quite impossible, but if we were to share a concept of empowerment with our clients—the people who were really without power— the students would first have to experience it themselves.

A CONTEXT THAT MAGNIFIED THE RISK TO MY STUDENTS AND ME

In the fall of 1989 students in the University of Michigan Architecture Program were 68 percent males, 78 percent United States–born whites, 9 percent United States–born ethnic minorities, and 13 percent foreign-born. Sixty-seven percent were in-state residents, probably from suburban areas or small towns; virtually all were full-time students in their early twenties.[2] In short, the student body was mostly white and mostly male, with little exposure to other ethnic groups or to urban life.

All students earning a master's degree from the Architecture Program are required to take a six-credit–hour design studio that meets twelve hours per week for each of eight semesters. While beginning studios introduce a broad range of concerns encountered in the general practice of architecture, advanced studios focus on specialized problem areas and reflect the expertise of the faculty at any given time. In recent years, assignments have emphasized either sociocultural, technical, aesthetic, or general design issues. Previously there had been a fairly even distribution among the types of assignments with less emphasis on socio- cultural issues and more on technical ones. By the time I offered this course, however, there had been a radical shift in emphasis for several reasons, including a redirection of new leadership and faculty retirements. During this semester most studios focused on aesthetic issues with less emphasis on technical ones; mine was the only studio offering that had a sociocultural focus.

Although assignments may involve an actual site in the local area that students can visit, most do not involve an actual client who can be interviewed about a specific set of needs. Rather, the professor creates a theoretical circumstance or program to involve students in exploring a given dimension of architectural design. Students become clients for one another as they critique each other's projects so their own values become the baseline for designing. Recently the use of theoretical sites and programs has increased at my school not only because the less experienced faculty who are replacing tenured, practicing architects lack access to real situations, but also because of a prevailing belief that reality limits creativity. When assigned a theoretical problem, students can be unconstrained in shaping their response.

Students select upper-level studios via a lottery system that is a litmus test for the faculty's personality and specialty area since the ratio of faculty to students is quite generous. No more than sixteen people are admitted to any studio.

However, if there are several very popular offerings, some faculty members may attract only a few students or suffer the embarrassment of a canceled section.

Throughout my teaching career in four different schools I was assigned, without exception, to entry-level design studios—an assignment given to most of the few women who teach in the nation's ninety-nine accredited architectural schools. (According to the Association of Collegiate Schools of Architecture Task Force on the Status of Women in Architecture Schools [1990:1], women represent 15.7 percent of the nation's architecture faculty, and only 2.8 percent of these women are tenured.) However, in the second semester of my thirteenth year I finally earned the honor of teaching an advanced studio. Given the reality of being in a hard-to-get position, given the lottery system, given the prevailing lack of involvement with real clients or sociocultural issues, given the reality of being a black female professor in a white male profession and school, you can well imagine my trepidation in deciding to offer an applied assignment involving housing and neighborhood design in an inner-city area.

My fears were well grounded. After I announced the studio, I heard late-night comments by students about the fatal flaws of the proposed course: too practical, too many calculations to figure out cost, too much teamwork. Most outstanding was an objection I had not anticipated: an aversion to developing a prototype. Architecture, according to my informants, must be unique, never prototypic. I circulated a flier to respond to these comments (see Myths & Facts in the Appendix to this chapter); however, by the first day of class only one architecture and one urban planning student had signed up.

Fortunately, the enthusiastic commitment of these two students was worth its weight in gold. They proposed to spend the week finding a contingent of students, and soon enrollment increased to six—three architects, two urban planners, and one landscape architect. However, there were drawbacks. As you might imagine, these were not six folks who needed to be "converted" to social concerns; they were already equipped with social vision. Then, although six were enough to run the studio, my department considers only the number of architecture students served. Consequently my activities record for the semester clocked in a large deficit. Finally, I was concerned about developing a competent, holistic solution with so few students. On the other hand, the class began with a smidgen of that hard-to-achieve inner sense of power, probably because of the student-led effort to create the class.

A SYLLABUS WRITTEN THROUGH CONSENSUS

I began the class by distributing a handout that contained a list of activities for students to complete in order to become familiar with the neighborhood, the services requested by the development corporation, and my sociopolitical perspective on housing and neighborhood development. Over a two-week period students used this background information to define their personal goals and develop a plan of action.

During this period we toured the neighborhood, talked to the executive director of the development corporation, and attended a church service to meet the people in the congregation who had taken a leadership role in the corporation's earlier development activities. However, most of our class time was spent in intense debate. A major sticking point was what services to provide. A "request for services" from the development corporation asked for a house prototype and a design for open space, but the context in which these elements would be built was critical. Unfortunately, no overall plan or preliminary studies existed.[3] How would six students be able to conduct the studies, develop a plan, then complete designs?

We put up a long length of brown wrapping paper on the wall and began adding ideas written on yellow paste-ons. Long after the other studios had dismissed, our debates bubbled on. Over the two-week period, the paste-ons were rewritten and reorganized until finally an ingenious plan took shape. The studies that we needed would not be completed in the studio. Instead we would decide what information was required, then parcel out tasks to students in other classes (e.g., a political science student completed a survey of housing needs in the neighborhood to fulfill his requirements in a survey research course). This additional help would combine with volunteers in the community to yield a significant group of researchers, leaving class members free to concentrate on planning and design. Based on personal goals and the "problem" as we had defined it, three class members chose to develop a neighborhood plan, two chose a housing prototype, and the other chose open space design—a plan of action that was heartily approved by our client.

After consensus was reached on what was to be done and by whom, I wrote an official syllabus and a flier to be used to secure additional student help. Armed with these tools, we carried out a process that included extensive site visits and discussions with neighborhood residents as well as three formal presentations to the church-based community development corporation. The outcome of the class was a set of sixteen drawings that were donated to the development corporation. The information contained in these drawings served to shortcut the work for an architect who was hired later on, enabling him to provide more extensive professional services for the monies that were available.

DEBUNKING THE MYTH OF THE LONE
VIRTUOSO ARTIST

The work that resulted from this class was generally of very high quality—an assessment confirmed by the guest architects who attended and critiqued presentations at the end of the semester. However, one project stands out because it defied the elitist conception of a lone virtuoso artist that is currently so prevalent in the architectural profession. Completed by a Third World woman who took the issue of cost control with extraordinary seriousness, the design proposed prefabricated housing modules, which she felt would yield the greatest economy.

During an initial presentation, this idea provoked a great deal of snickering because the audience (other students, faculty, and representatives of the development corporation) imagined a stereotypic trailer park. There were also more serious questions about how the unit could get trucked into a city and whether they would comply with local ordinances. In the following weeks, the student persisted in investigating her idea—collecting detailed information from several manufacturers, visiting and photographing installations, making exquisite sketches of the existing houses in the neighborhood in order to understand their visual composition. By the second presentation, the preconceptions began to lift as it became clear that prefabricated modules could be combined in a pleasing, multistoried fashion and that the quality of their interior construction actually surpassed typical low-cost housing. For her final presentation, this student produced a well-conceived plan showing the entire process of delivery and installation, ways that the client could combine one module with other modules to create several different complexes, and elements that could be added by residents, as well as her sketches to show the match with existing buildings.

In addition to being excellent by architectural design standards, this solution reached my highest sociopolitical goals for multicultural education. Merging aesthetics with a moral commitment to keep cost at a minimum, this student created a scheme in which she graciously shared with the client her power as designer to produce housing that accommodates individual preferences. In addition, her cultural perspective as a witness to poverty allowed her to take a fresh look at something considered unacceptable and, in so doing, helped all the other students to question their role as the gatekeepers of good (but expensive) taste.

ACHIEVING DIGNITY FOR THE WHOLE

In this chapter I have described a sequence of events in the field of architecture that led to my particular view of multicultural education as an admittedly subjective effort to engage students in the struggle for human dignity. To participate in such a struggle, students' social imagination must be enriched with moral vision, with an understanding of the wholeness of human relationships, and most of all, with an inner sense of power to bring about social change. Within the context of architectural design, multicultural education involves students in seeking a more equitable distribution of environmental resources, and housing is an essential resource for human survival.

The course that I described involved students in an applied housing and neighborhood design project in an inner-city community—a risky assignment in a school where the dominant focus was theoretical and aesthetic. Although finding students to participate posed an enormous challenge, eventually a small group of highly committed students used their creativity to parlay input from a much larger group. The best lesson came not from me, but from a student who resisted teasing to unmask the myth that a good architect works as a lone virtuoso artist.

Architectural design has unique features—its intuitive and visual approach, its small one-on-one classes, its concreteness. However, the approach that I have outlined can be applied to other subject areas. One principle inherent in the approach is not to teach students about cultural differences, but to involve them in a relationship with people who are different from themselves. Another principle is not to present students with a syllabus or finite set of teaching materials, but to engage them in formulating their own goals and action plan within a given moral framework. Both of these principles erase the traditions of teacher as "the one who knows" and learner as "the one who does not." In my view, a more equitable internal structure in any class is a first and fundamental step toward achieving dignity for all the peoples of humanity, which is surely the ultimate goal of multicultural education.

One student sums up the experience of seeking her "whole of the moon" this way:

The strengths of this course are that it gave me an opportunity to develop personal interests, to take leadership, to be experimental, to learn without being told what to think or believe, to learn about that part of myself which guides and influences design decisions. It also gave me an opportunity to learn self-evaluation and personal goal-setting . . . but, to be honest, I have been trained to be dependent on letter grades. . . . There were times when I wondered how I was doing—feeling uncertain of my progress . . . but when the confusion was over, something had grown and changed a little.

I was very excited about taking this course, and I was not disappointed. I feel like I really learned some things that are important to the development of a designer-planner and a person—a better Whole.

APPENDIX

Myths & Facts

Housing and Neighborhood Design in Detroit

Myth 1: There is no creative work in this studio!

Myth   All the creative decisions for the *Housing and Neighborhood Design* project were made by last year's class. The only work that remains is "grunt" work.

Fact   This project is in a conceptual stage. In fact, neither plans nor preliminary studies have been done. An architectural firm will eventually develop the technical details of the project, but student assistance is needed to explore ideas with the client and to "stir up the pot" for what *could* be in this neighborhood.

Myth 2: A prototypic building is *never* architecture!

Myth   This studio requires a prototypic house design which cannot be considered "architecture" because each site and client require a unique solution.

Fact   It is true that a prototype is required for the *Housing and Neighborhood Design* project, and it is also true that many prototypes lack design quality. However, there is nothing inherently bad about a prototype—it's the designer, not the tool, who determines quality. An imaginative designer might conceive of a house as a "kit of parts" to be variously assembled for different sites and clients.

Myth 3: This is a number-crunching studio!

Myth   The *Housing and Neighborhood Design* project will require tedious cost estimating because a low-cost solution is required.

Fact   It is true that design solutions in this studio must be cost-effective. However, we will approach this task in the broadest way, looking at economies of social relationships as well as economies of building. A consultant will be on hand to provide students with "rule of thumb" methods of determining the latter.

Myth 4: This studio requires teamwork which will stifle creativity!

Myth   Since there is only one large project for the entire semester, everyone will be forced to work on a team which makes creativity impossible.

Fact   Studio requirements will be determined by students. If students agree to work individually, then the class will be organized in that manner. If students agree that teamwork is best, the instructor will make every effort to assign tasks that enhance the individual skills and creativity of each person.

Why not join up?

You can make a difference and still be creative

NOTES

1. Quote is from my conversation with Myles Horton at Highlander Research and Education Center, New Market, Tennessee. November 4, 1989.

2. I obtained enrollment data in a telephone conversation with the University of Michigan Registrar's Office during the summer of 1990.

3. Interestingly enough, a confidential plan for the area was made public by the press just after the class ended. Although this plan, which includes a golf course, lakes, and parks, has "some housing for people with low incomes, there might not be enough for all those who currently live there. They would have to be relocated to homes elsewhere in Detroit." Needless to say, the church-based development corporation was not consulted by those who created the plan.

14

How I Teach Mathematics to Minorities

Martha Aliaga

Most African Americans avoid science and mathematics courses early in life, in part because most go to large urban schools where they receive poor education (Task Force on Women, Minorities, and the Handicapped in Science and Technology 1989). Research indicates that the development of potential scientists and engineers begins very early. The great majority of students who pursue an undergraduate degree in a scientific or math-related field have already made that decision by grade twelve. In college, migration is almost entirely out of, not into, the science/math education pipeline.

New conceptions of science and mathematics education involve teaching that is highly interactive, engaging students actively in making sense of ideas and applying what they learn to solve personally and socially relevant problems. Learning is a dynamic process in which meaning is developed by searching for relationships. Knowledge must be conceptual and interconnected. Students attain more "meaningful learning" when teachers employ a variety of integrated pedagogical techniques. The key to meaningful learning is to tie new information to other things students are learning or to the concerns of their personal lives.

The National Research Council's Mathematical Sciences Education Board (MSEB) has made a directed effort to eliminate underachievement and underrepresentation of minorities in mathematics through its national project, "Making Mathematics Work for Minorities." As part of the program, six strategy workshops were conducted in different regions of the country. A few of the recommendations made at these workshops address issues of teacher performance:

- We will encourage teachers to become sensitive to their own behavior in the classroom and to realize that their behavior has an impact on the performance of students, especially minority students in mathematics. In-service training and summer programs will be developed to help teachers develop strategies to teach minority students, understanding that no minority group is monolithic.

• Teachers will be encouraged to appreciate the importance of their own knowledge, attitudes, and teaching skills in order to develop competent students with positive attitudes toward mathematics.

Asa G. Hilliard III (1990), of Georgia State University, one of the speakers at a regional meeting of "Making Mathematics Work for Minorities," analyzed six successful mathematics programs and identified the principles and characteristics common to them all: questioning is the focus of the pedagogy, not lecturing; student-based knowledge is the basis for lesson construction; students experience a feeling of competence; teachers teach students the meaning of what they do. Hilliard also suggested "remedies" for unsuccessful teachers:

1. Increase the mathematics knowledge of mathematics teachers.
2. Teachers must have successful pedagogy. Master teachers must provide teacher training.
3. Teachers must have access to quality training sites and have access to teaching demonstrations in different settings with different teachers. Videotapes were suggested as a medium for capturing these demonstrations.

THE BRIDGE PROGRAM

As a native of Argentina, I am myself a minority in the United States. I have taught mathematics and statistics at all levels (kindergarten through the doctoral level) in four different countries for twenty-five years. This discussion will focus on my experiences in one undergraduate program at the University of Michigan, the Bridge Program.

The Bridge Program was established in 1975 to prepare incoming students academically for the fall term. The program lasts seven weeks during summer session and is offered by the Comprehensive Studies Program (CSP). CSP, which is part of the College of Literature, Science and the Arts, provides special support services that meet the needs of minority students in all undergraduate colleges at the university. Founded in 1983, its principal aim is to assist student achievement through a variety of intensive programs focused on instruction, counseling, and mentoring.

Although the Bridge Program is open to all students, the ones who participate are usually minority students with Scholastic Aptitude Test (SAT) composite scores of less than 950. Most of these students come from a small number of schools in Detroit, although some are from other cities within and outside Michigan. In my classes, approximately 85 percent of the students are African Americans, and approximately 15 percent are Latinos. Students enrolled in the Bridge Program are only conditionally accepted for fall enrollment, pending successful completion of the program.

I have been involved with the Bridge Program for nine years at the University of Michigan. Of the sixty or so students admitted to the program annually, twenty are placed in my algebra and trigonometry class (Math 109). Although most of the students have taken pre-calculus or calculus in high school, their math is weak, and, with few exceptions, they lack the necessary preparation to cope with the stressful life at the university. Students' careers beyond the Bridge classroom have been tracked since 1986. In the past five years, three former Bridge students have graduated in mathematics education.

MATHEMATICS TEACHING STRATEGIES

The following strategies proved successful with my Bridge students. I believe they are appropriate for all mathematics learners:

Development of Internal Perceptions, Attitudes, and Expectations of Students

Believe that each student can achieve. I tell students that I believe in them from day one. I reinforce it continuously when they achieve, either with words or by writing notes on their papers when I correct them. This theme is central to the success of the Bridge course and is reinforced throughout the literature (Carl 1989; McBay 1990; Anderson 1990). The principles embodied in the self-fulfilling prophecy are essential to this entire initiative.

Response Interval

The most effective time for learning, retention, and ability to utilize material at a later time is the developmental "moment of readiness." Therefore, that is the time when I respond to questions, solve problems, and straighten out mistakes in learning. This is consistent with the "cognitively guided instruction" (CGI) approach that Hilliard (1990) listed.

Availability of Instructor

It is necessary for students to believe and experience that I am truly available to help, clarify, or redirect at any time. This pattern will avoid several situations that detract from learning: students' feeling that they are interrupting, annoying their teacher, or taking up too much time, and students' getting an answer later, when it doesn't matter anymore. This also encourages questioning and the necessary thinking and debating to get to the right answer.

In-Class Response to Questions

I feel it is important to make sure that no questions are unresolved at the end of any class. If possible, all problems must be settled and issues clarified while they are important. Of course, sometimes the problems need research or more contemplation, and, in those cases, the discussion is continued in future classes.

Use of Testing Mechanisms for Continuous Feedback

Students must be tested on material while still at the beginning of the learning process so that problems can be corrected before they become an erroneous part of mathematical thinking and understanding. I return tests immediately and then discuss them before the material becomes overlaid with the next levels of learning. I distribute solutions to daily quizzes when students hand in the quiz.

Use of Paced Segments of Information Designed to Conform to Student Learning Patterns

I disseminate all information about mathematics in sequences and sizes that mirror students' learning ability. As their incremental knowledge increases, I can move faster and in larger conceptual blocks. I check to see that each student understands. If some students don't understand a concept, I explain it in a different way and give another problem to that student individually. I continue until I am sure that everyone understands. I often have a few students put the same problem on the board to explain how they got their answer. Once I know that the basic concept is clear, I move more quickly through the unit of study. Again, this is consistent with CGI.

Relevance of Material to Real Life and Students' Futures

There is usually an explanation of the pertinence of material to students' own lives now and in the future. I emphasize visualization of mathematical concepts to bring them down to daily life and to make mathematics exciting and meaningful.

Outlining the Necessary Requirements for Success to Increase Confidence and Motivation and Communicating a Positive Future

It is essential to create and maintain an idea of a future in which further successes are assumed. The motivation and optimism of students rise when the future and their chances for success in it are communicated in specific, sequenced examples that are grounded in real experience. I describe how they will succeed in the future by specifics, rather than by sweeping statements such as, "You will need four more years to graduate." For instance, I ask them individually what their career goals are; then, we examine the steps needed to achieve this goal. We make realistic predictions of the content and difficulty of future courses and relate them to the experience of the current course. In this way, looking at things selectively and specifically, we discuss how to succeed in the field of interest. Studies indicate that people are more apt to experience optimism and eagerness to act when they can imagine themselves succeeding. General supportive statements do not produce the same long-lasting visualization of future success and students' ability to get there. The most effective method to produce that state is to enable students to envision a very specific, sensory-grounded future.

Incremental Learning

I am very careful to "build from the ground up," never going to the next floor before there is a good foundation below. My quizzes test all previous material, with emphasis on the most current. This approach counters the idea that all previous assumptions about mathematics are unimportant or that class "starts over" with a new instructor.

Grading

Grading is not important to me, although it is to the students. (The joy of learning is what counts in mathematics!) When correcting tests, no partial credit is given. An average grade could be attained if the students get partial credit for their assignments and tests. My students are required to finish all problems on all assignments and tests. This training is reflected well in their final and midterm exam grades; the performance of my students generally surpasses that of other students in the course.

Real life recognizes only the correct answer to a problem, and experience supports the use of mathematics in the real world. The experience of attempting fully to solve a problem taps capabilities not otherwise used in developing and using cognitive and problem-solving skills and increasing the habit of persistence. If the students knew they could just give up when the going becomes difficult, they would not have the same opportunity to increase important abilities.

Group Problem Solving

Most students in the Bridge Program have gained admission to the University through individual effort; they are used to studying alone. However, these independent study habits are a disadvantage in the competitive academic atmosphere at the university. The advantages of study groups include built-in peer support and the practice of speaking aloud the language of mathematics.

Students work in groups of four at round tables. They debate with, and question, each other to arrive at correct solutions. The group must share, discuss, and agree on a shared answer; then, it is presented as the group's proposed solution to the problem. This means that the group must review the mathematical principles involved over and over and that students learn them more fully as they try to convince the other group members about their own suggested answers. The group gets a communal grade. The groups are self-selected; this results in groups composed of students who are acquainted with each other and are of varied academic abilities.

Use of the Course as a Resource

If questions come up, I redirect the questions back to the asker or to the rest of the class. There needs to be a variety of methods to enable students to depend on their own understandings and abilities to move all the way to a solution. Also, it is worth using the class to expand the student awareness of resources other than the teacher. Should no one have the answer, I provide it or provide a source to find it.

Changing the Classroom Atmosphere

The atmosphere to be encouraged is the antithesis of the traditional classroom. In order to increase learning and confidence, students are encouraged to participate, talk, debate, disagree, and argue. This is not an environment in which everyone waits politely for me to reveal the answer or only one person talks at a time after raising a hand and waiting to be called on. People must work for their opinion to be heard, for their right answer to be acknowledged. It is not chaotic, but it is full of energy, outspokenness, and people daring to extend themselves and take risks.

Another departure from the traditional setting is that students are encouraged to take risks and make mistakes, to ask questions and show their ignorance. We are looking for mistakes! is a theme that prevails. Students are not encouraged, explicitly or implicitly, to be cautious so as to hide their lack of knowledge. Quite the opposite: make mistakes! To that end, I make it clear all semester, particularly at the beginning, that mistakes are not a reflection of who the students are, what they can or cannot do, or how intelligent they are. It is only a measure of what must be learned to fix the mistake and increase the understanding. I say at the beginning: "I do not yet know your names, and, for right now, it is not important that I do. I do want to get to know each of you personally outside this learning environment, but, in here, your questions and your learning are the most important thing to me and for you. If you think that I am pointing you out personally when you ask a question, then you will not learn. I will not remember who asked or who made a mistake, so you can feel free to make mistakes. That is the way you learn." Also, I emphasize the principle that it is all right to show lack of understanding because the rest of the class will also learn from it.

Review Sessions

During my twelve years of teaching in the Comprehensive Study Program, my students reached marks near the top and, on several occasions, in the top of the class. (In winter 1991 one of my female students received the highest score in Calculus 116.) Consistently in the students' evaluations I read the same thing, that the review sessions helped them to learn the material. The review sessions became mandatory for the first time in 1991. This decision was based on my observations that students need to get a feel for how much time is necessary to devote to their course work in order to learn it thoroughly.

I provide a place called Math Land where students can meet regularly with me to complete routine study activities and where I present a more challenging set of problems than those presented in class. I usually do not answer questions but guide the group to find them. Students come in, sit down, and start working on their problems. When a student finishes the first problem, she or he raises a hand and I bring that student together with another student who has also finished the problem. The two students then compare their answers and work together to come up with a common solution to the problem. Once they agree, they raise their hands, and I check their work; I may ask a few questions to make sure they understand their work. Then, if the solution is acceptable, the two students go on to the next problem. If the solution is not acceptable, I say, "Not Yet!" and the students go back to the drawing board. This method gets students actively thinking and talking about the material. This cooperative learning not only encourages elaboration, a key to long-term memory, but has positive motivational effects as well. Students prefer this manner of group selection (as opposed to self-selecting with friends) because they find themselves in groups with peers who are close to their own abilities; these peers often become their friends.

Graphics

Research shows that once students visualize a problem with a graph, the problem is easier to solve (Beckman 1989; Goldenberg 1988; Leinhardt et al. 1990). I teach students how to understand graphs without laboriously plotting points. Using the properties of the functions, they calculate limits, derivatives, and estimated areas. Students learn how to "see" the graph just by looking at the formulas, graphs of polynomials, rational functions, absolute values, logarithms, and trigonometry functions.

I move slowly through the early stages of explaining a concept, developing the concept step-by-step and working through a problem on the board. I even use my body as a teaching tool. For example, I try to help them get beyond simple rote application of an algorithm to a deeper understanding. Using body language, I describe the effect:

What is the difference between the graphs of: y = /x/, y = 3/x/, and y = ½/x/? If y = /x/:

If y = 3/x/ then, for the same /x/ value, the y value is three times larger so:

If y = ½/x/ then the y value is ½ for the same /x/ value:

YES TO MATHEMATICS!

I am aware that students who come to the University of Michigan seeking a career in mathematics do not often start in the Bridge Program with Math 105 (pre-calculus). To open the door to mathematics for Bridge students takes a lot of effort and time. We need to support these students who are both in a foreign atmosphere (a college campus) as well as on new academic ground (more advanced mathematics).

My belief is that no student should leave the university without some exposure to mathematics. Everyone can do mathematics! It just has to be taught in a way that builds a student's confidence in his or her mathematical abilities. Mathematics education offers unlimited access to careers in a technologically powerful society. Self-expectations and personal achievement in mathematics cause students to view themselves positively as learners. We have to treat them with dignity and respect. Overall, we have to care.

Each day in my teaching I incorporate tips about how to succeed on campus (e.g., where to find computers on campus, where to find the best ice cream, how to select classes and teachers based on schedules and location, how to succeed without cheating). Students have the opportunity to share phone numbers if they like. We take time out to talk about study responsibilities (e.g., where to study, how to study, when to study, how much studying is expected per lecture hour). In addition to giving them survival techniques (which will benefit their performance in my class and their other classes), I am showing them that I care about them as individuals.

The summer Bridge classes are my most enjoyable, as they are free of the hectic social atmosphere of the fall. I have time to inform, to empower, and to inspire. The reward for me is always the same: the students say, "Bridge was a great experience and a fundamental step in staying at the U of M." In fact, 70 percent of Bridge students eventually graduate.

15

Racial Bias in Science Education

Lewis J. Kleinsmith

What is the most dramatic change that has occurred in the typical introductory college science classroom over the past twenty years? Faced with such a question, the average person might think about the numerous scientific discoveries that have occurred during this period and would therefore conclude that the answer must involve major differences in the material taught today versus what was taught twenty years ago. Given the constant barrage of newspaper, magazine, and television reports about the latest scientific breakthroughs, such a belief is not surprising. It is, nonetheless, inaccurate. If one were to examine twenty-year-old introductory college textbooks in most of the natural sciences (e.g., biology, chemistry, or physics), the typical non-scientist might be surprised to see the extent to which the major principles of twenty years ago are still the major principles of today. Of course, our understanding of many details will have improved, a few older concepts will have been discredited, and a few important new concepts will have emerged. Yet the continuity and consistency of the major scientific concepts over the past several decades are striking; these concepts are built upon hundreds of years of observation and experimentation, and, in fact, the resulting edifice of scientific knowledge changes relatively slowly and systematically.

If the content of our introductory science classes has not shifted dramatically over the past twenty years, then what dramatic change, if any, has occurred in the typical college science classroom? The answer is related not to what we teach, but rather to whom we are teaching it. As an undergraduate pre-medical student in the early 1960s, I couldn't help but notice that my fellow science majors tended to share two things in common with me: they were white, and they were male. When I went to medical school in 1962, I counted a total of 202 white males in a class of 208. Today, of course, it is hard to believe that such a gross disparity ever existed. Thanks to the civil rights and feminist movements, society's view of who may aspire to the scientific and medical professions is no longer as constrained as it once was, and our population of college science students therefore exhibits a much healthier ethnic, racial, and gender diversity than it did in the not-so-distant past when I was a college student.

What impact, if any, has this increasing diversity had on the science classroom? In other areas of the curriculum, where subjective values play a prominent role, the increasing ethnic, racial, and gender diversity of our student clientele has inevitably led to controversies about the subject matter of the curriculum itself. If, for example, a course in great books focuses predominantly on authors who happen to be white males (just like the makeup of my medical class), does this judgment concerning the nature of "great" literature reflect some objectively verifiable truth, or might it simply represent the ethnocentric opinions of a faculty that consists largely of white males? As a biologist writing about the science curriculum, I cannot resolve such complex issues; I offer this example only to illustrate a unique difference between the natural sciences and other areas of the curriculum. By definition, scientific "truths" are to be ascertained by independently verifiable experimentation. If, for example, students do not believe Isaac Newton's equations describing the rate at which an apple falls from a tree under the influence of gravity, they can perform the experiment themselves and confirm (or refute) his calculations. A hundred people dropping apples from trees will all obtain the same basic results, regardless of their race, color, or gender, but they certainly won't agree on which books are the greatest books ever written!

Because of the central role played by objective criteria and independent verification in the natural sciences, it is a common belief among science educators that their disciplines are race- and gender-neutral. My purpose in this chapter is to challenge such a belief. Although I discuss only one way in which the natural sciences fail to live up to the claim of race and gender neutrality, it is a failure that, if allowed to remain uncorrected, will have dire consequences for the future health and survival of our country.

THE PROBLEM: UNDERREPRESENTED RACIAL GROUPS IN THE SCIENCES

The problem I wish to address can be stated quite simply: if the natural sciences are race- and gender-neutral, how can we explain the historic underrepresentation of people of color and females in technical and scientific professions (Malcolm 1981; Dix 1987)? In spite of various affirmative action efforts, the crisis in the production of scientifically skilled blacks and Latinos is especially severe and shows little sign of improving. In fact, the percentage of black graduate students steadily declined from the mid-1970s into the early 1980s; in 1982, blacks earned only 3.6 percent of the nation's doctoral degrees while comprising more than 15 percent of the overall population (Pruitt 1984; Staples 1984). In 1982 Latino enrollments joined black enrollments in the decline (Pruitt and Isaac 1985). Since current demographic projections indicate that blacks and Latinos will constitute close to half the population of the United States by the year 2000 and a majority of the work force by the year 2020, the continued failure to utilize this enormous reservoir of human talent in the scientific and technical professions would have disastrous implications for the economic health and competitiveness of this country in the twenty-first century.

For this reason, it is of vital importance to address the question of why blacks and Latinos are so severely underrepresented in the scientific professions. Although multiple factors may be involved, such disparities certainly raise the question of whether or not science education itself is racially neutral. My own experiences in grappling with this problem over the past ten years have led me to the reluctant conclusion that science education tends to illustrate a pernicious form of institutional racism referred to as indirect institutionalized discrimination (Feagin and Feagin 1986; Chesler and Crowfoot 1990). This brand of institutional racism refers not to conscious, deliberate attempts by individuals to discriminate based on race, but rather to organizational practices that have a negative impact on racial minorities even though the community norms underlying these practices are, on their face and in their intent, fair and racially neutral. Hence it is not discriminatory intent, but rather a discriminatory outcome, that defines this kind of institutional racism. The danger inherent in this particular brand of racism is that the individuals involved in carrying out such organizational practices may be fair-minded in their personal beliefs and hence unaware of the discriminatory impact of their actions.

Because natural scientists pride themselves on their objectivity and fair-mindedness, the suggestion that they are involved in any type of racial discrimination is bound to be controversial and to elicit cries of protest. It is therefore crucial to analyze the data and experiences that have led to such a conclusion. To begin with, the fact that academic achievement in the sciences is relatively poor for blacks and Latinos is well documented. Recent data collected by the National Assessment of Educational Progress (NAEP) reveal that the disparities in science achievement for blacks and Latinos can be traced to the secondary and elementary school level; assessments carried out in 1986 revealed that the average science proficiency of black and Latino students is at least four years behind that of their white peers and that by age seventeen, only 15 percent of the black and Latino students demonstrate the ability to analyze scientific procedures and data compared with nearly one-half of the white student population (National Assessment of Educational Progress 1988).

Given this background, it is perhaps not surprising that black and Latino students interested in the sciences encounter difficulties at the college level. At the University of Michigan, where an intense effort has been made during the past two decades to increase the enrollment of underrepresented minorities, considerable data have been collected concerning this issue. Analysis of retention rates and academic performance for this group of students has revealed some disturbing signs. One especially distressing finding that emerged shortly after black and Latino students began to appear in increasing numbers on campus in the early 1970s was their below-average representation and academic performance in the sciences. In my own discipline, for example, it was discovered that the average grade for black and Latino students in our introductory biology course was almost two full grades below the overall class average. Since this introductory biology course is a prerequisite for all students interested in pursuing careers in the health sciences, opportunities in some of society's most prestigious and lucrative professions were effectively being closed off for this population of students at the very beginning of their college education.

Was this racial discrepancy in academic performance a manifestation of indirect institutionalized discrimination? It is certainly easy to deny this possibility by arguing that outside factors (e.g., inadequate preparation by the public schools, lack of student interest and motivation, and so on), rather than the educational policies and practices of the university itself, were responsible for the observed racial gap in performance. While it is certainly true that the performance gap might not exist if students of all races came to college equally well prepared and interested in the sciences, this argument does not let educators off the hook. The more relevant issue is whether or not the educational practices of the university itself contribute to the discriminatory outcome. To answer such a question, we simply need to ask whether or not changes can be made in the way we teach that would eliminate the discrepancies in performance observed among different racial groups without altering the scientific content of our courses, without lowering the academic standards employed to assess performance, and (ideally) without singling out any group of students for special treatment. If changing the way we teach can accomplish these objectives, then by definition the racial gap in performance observed before such changes were implemented must have been the result of our educational practices. In other words, we would be forced to conclude that by definition, the initial gap in performance was a manifestation of institutional racism.

THE INTRODUCTORY BIOLOGY EXPERIENCE AT THE UNIVERSITY OF MICHIGAN

When I first became aware in 1982 of the gap in performance between black and Latino students and the rest of the class, it occurred to me that the basic problem we were encountering is not specific to introductory biology; it is encountered in most large introductory lecture courses in which faculty must lecture to audiences of several hundred students of widely differing background, ability, and interests. I know that when I design my lecture material to challenge the best-prepared students in the class, the more poorly prepared students quickly get lost; on the other hand, if my lectures are instead focused on the needs of the students having the greatest difficulties in the class, the slower pace makes it difficult to cover all the necessary material, and the better-prepared students soon become bored. Faculty who teach such large introductory courses quickly experience the frustration of trying to walk this tightrope between the needs of various student constituencies.

The underlying problem, of course, is that we are simply expecting too much from the lecture format. Lectures are an important tool for providing an overview of the subject matter, but they cannot ensure that all students will come away with an equivalent level of knowledge. If the goal of an introductory course is to provide all students with a roughly equivalent understanding of basic principles, then the great variability in student understanding that is virtually unavoidable following a lecture to several hundred individuals must somehow be made up outside class. This is especially important in introductory courses, since the concepts involved provide the foundation of the following courses in the discipline.

But what can be done outside class to help all students achieve a roughly equivalent understanding of basic concepts? Over the years, we have experimented with several approaches. The most obvious, recommending that students study the appropriate sections of the textbook, suffers from two serious limitations. First, reading is a largely passive experience deficient in both feedback and interaction; this deficiency is largely insurmountable because a book has no way of knowing whether the student understands what he or she is reading. The second limitation is that printed words and diagrams are static, while biological principles tend to involve dynamic interactions occurring in time and space. Many important biological principles are therefore difficult to convey in textbooks.

In addition to textbook assignments, we have also experimented with two other approaches for helping students outside class. One involves weekly open-ended review sessions in which I respond to students' questions and difficulties by elaborating upon the concepts that are confusing them. The second approach I have tried is passing out old exams so that students can practice applying the principles I have been teaching to the kinds of problems they are expected to understand. To my surprise, neither of the preceding approaches has led to a detectable improvement in overall class performance on exams. The lack of improvement in student performance after being given access to old exams has been especially surprising, since the types of problems used on exams are quite similar from year to year. In talking with students about how they go about studying from old exams, it has become apparent that they spend more time memorizing the old answers than trying to figure out the reasoning that allows one to discriminate between correct and incorrect responses. Hence they are unable to generalize what they have learned and apply it to new situations.

This is where the problem stood in the summer of 1982, when serendipity suddenly provided me with a novel insight. My twelve-year-old daughter, who had just taken a two-week course in computer programming, developed a simple riddle program in which the computer asked a series of questions and provided funny replies in response to answers chosen by the user. It suddenly became apparent that this simple kind of interaction could form the basis of an educational program in which the computer's responses were designed to educate, rather than amuse, the user. If the program were well designed, it might in fact mimic the kind of Socratic feedback that I would provide to individual students sitting in my office as I was trying to help them understand a basic concept.

Armed with this idea, I solicited and soon obtained university funding for an experiment to see if microcomputer software could be developed to help students having difficulty in introductory biology. After examining the types of software that were commercially available at the time, it quickly became apparent that existing materials did not meet our requirements and that we would therefore need to develop our own programs. During the next year I began to learn about computer programming, first from my daughter and later from two computer-literate students who happened to be working in my laboratory on other projects. As I developed some rudimentary programming skills and began to think in detail about the educational objectives of the project, I saw that two distinct types of software were required.

The first category of software to be developed consisted of programs designed to provide students with experience in applying the concepts and principles developed in lecture, exactly as they are required to do on our examinations. Although the large size of the class dictates the need for multiple-choice tests, the questions we use tend not to be of the rote memorization type that students typically encounter in high school. Instead, our questions generally require students to analyze, synthesize, and/or extrapolate from the information provided in order to draw the appropriate conclusions. It is difficult to acquire such skills by simply going to a lecture or reading a textbook. I therefore decided to create a series of interactive "problem-set" programs in which students are presented with a broad spectrum of multiple-choice questions typical of those found on our exams (in fact, most of them were taken from old tests). Moreover, the sequence of questions and the order of the multiple-choice answers are randomized; hence students cannot simply memorize patterns like "The answer to question number nine is choice A," as they often do when studying from old exams. In this way, a virtually endless array of problem-solving exercises can be made available. The most important difference between these programs and simply looking at old exams, however, is that when students choose an incorrect answer, they are provided with feedback specifically designed to point out the error in their reasoning and/or to provide clues to the appropriate approach.

In the original version of the problem-set software, students were automatically advanced to the next question after they had picked the correct answer (although they were first given an explanation of why the answer was correct in case they had chosen it for the wrong reason). Students quickly complained that they wanted to be able to return to the question again, even though they had chosen the correct answer, to find out exactly why other responses were incorrect. Now that our problem-set software functions in this way, I have repeatedly heard from students that they learn more from choosing wrong answers than they do from the correct ones. This unexpected insight into how students learn suggests that the use of our software develops critical thinking and reasoning skills in a way that cannot be done by simply looking at old exams and seeing what the correct answers are.

The problem-solving programs, which represent the first category of software we developed, were designed to give students experience in applying principles and concepts with which they already had a basic familiarity. The second type of software we have produced is targeted at a slightly different problem: teaching complicated concepts involving dynamic interactions of various biological components in time and space. At best, textbook diagrams can illustrate a few static pictures of such processes, and lecture presentations using a blackboard or overhead projector tend to be even more cumbersome. Although good film loops can overcome this problem and illustrate dynamic concepts and interactions quite well, films are noninteractive presentations over which students have little control. We have therefore begun to develop a series of "animated tutorials" that utilize the animated graphic and interactive capabilities of the microcomputer to create programs in which students not only can watch dynamic, computer-generated animations of complex biological processes, but can stop and start the action at any point, jump forward or backward, adjust the speed, observe the animations with or without explanations, and finally test their understanding of the processes involved by instructing the programs to ask them questions along the way.

Although preliminary versions of our programs were tested on a limited number of students as development proceeded, it took almost two years before a sufficient number of "problem sets" and "animated tutorials" were refined to a degree that justified testing them on all five hundred students in the class. In order to facilitate student use of the software, a special room designated the Biology Study Center was outfitted with fifteen microcomputer workstations, and the software was made available through a user-friendly network that requires absolutely no prior knowledge of computers. When a student sits down at a computer, he or she is simply confronted with the message, "Press any key," and from there on everything is explained and run automatically from a series of menus. Although a graduate student teaching assistant is always present to answer questions, student queries almost always concern the biological subject matter rather than how to run the computers or programs. Use of the Biology Study Center software is not required of students, nor is their attendance monitored in any way. Students are simply told that this study facility is a resource available for them to use outside class as they desire, just as one might go to a library to study.

Shortly after the Biology Study Center opened in the fall of 1984, beneficial effects began to become apparent (Kleinsmith 1987; Johnston and Kleinsmith 1987). One particularly interesting item concerns minority student attitudes toward the use of computers. When the biology software project was first proposed several years ago as a possible approach to dealing with the problems of minority students in introductory biology, the question was raised as to whether minority

Table 1
Student estimates of the amount of time spent using the Biology Study Center
software prior to the first exam in 1986 (data obtained from an anonymous
questionnaire).

	Percent Responses	
Amount of Time Spent Using Software	Black and Latino Students (N = 14)	Other Students (N =455)
none	0%	3%
under 3 hours	0	8
3 to 10 hours	21	44
10 to 20 hours	64	39
over 20 hours	14	7

students would feel comfortable going to computers for help. Some of our colleagues suggested that computers are impersonal and dehumanizing and that a lack of prior experience with computers might cause minority students to shy away from trying to use them. The data that we have now collected, however, indicate that such fears were unwarranted. When asked on our anonymous questionnaire how many hours they had spent using the Biology Study Center software, black and Latino students, in fact, reported a greater use than the class as a whole (Table 1). When asked how valuable they found the software in helping them study, these students again gave extremely positive responses (Table 2). The written comments of minority students about their experience with the software were equally striking. One such student wrote that the programs "were very helpful and . . . fun to do. They also helped me to study for things I wouldn't have normally studied for. Thanks for the computers, hope my exam shows how much they helped." In a similar vein, another student went on to say, "It's the best way to study for the course and provides very thorough understanding of the material." Such comments and the associated questionnaire data clearly revealed the absence of any significant barrier to the use of computer software among black and Latino students.

The most exciting finding to have emerged regarding the behavior of black and Latino students, however, is a dramatic improvement in exam performance. Table 3 summarizes the mean score on the first examination in introductory biology before and after the initial version of this software was introduced in 1984. Note that the mean for the class as a whole improved about 10 percent during the first two years of software use (1984–1985) and improved even further

Table 2
Student estimates of the value of the Biology Study Center software in helping them to prepare for the first exam (data obtained from an anonymous questionnaire administered after the first exam in 1986).*

	Percent Responses	
Estimate of the Value of the Software	Black and Latino Students (N = 14)	Other Students (N =442)
very valuable	100%	86%
valuable	0	13
somewhat valuable	0	2
not at all valuable	0	0

*Students not using the software are excluded.

Table 3
Class performance on the first examination in introductory biology before and after introduction of the Biology Study Center software in 1984.*

	Mean Exam Score	
Time Period	Black and Latino Students	Total Class
1979-1983	48.0 (3.7)	65.6 (3.4)
1984-1985	65.5 (0.7)	75.0 (0.7)
1986-1988	80.1 (1.2)	82.3 (1.5)

*Cell entries are averages of the annual mean exam scores for each time period (the numbers in parentheses are standard deviations showing the variability in class means for each period).

after 1986, when the software was made more widely available by placing it at various public workstations around campus in addition to the Biology Study Center. But what is even more striking about these data is the improvement for black and Latino students. Note that prior to the introduction of this software in

1984, their performance was almost 20 percent below the class mean (roughly two full grades). By 1988, after students had been strongly encouraged to use the software, this difference had virtually disappeared. Although it might be argued that the academic qualifications of our incoming minority student population are simply improving, the average incoming grades and SAT scores of the black and Latino student population in our biology course have not, in fact, changed significantly.

It should be emphasized that the improvement in exam performance observed during the past three years cannot be explained by any obvious change in the difficulty of the exam or in the effectiveness of the lecture presentations. Since the exams consist largely of problems designed to test the ability of students to apply the basic concepts and principles discussed in lecture, the kinds of questions used on the exam can be made quite similar from year to year (just as the kinds of problems used on a math test can be similar from year to year). Moreover, the number of questions and their distribution over the various subject areas stay basically the same. In terms of the effectiveness of the lecture presentation, I have been teaching the introductory biology course for twenty years, and after experimenting with content and style during the first ten years, the subject matter and my lecture notes have remained basically the same during the past ten years. In addition, the standardized student evaluation forms administered every year have revealed no significant change in the perceived effectiveness of my lectures during the past three years. It therefore seems reasonable to conclude that the dramatic improvement in minority student performance observed in the past few years is related largely to the effectiveness of the tutorial activities in the Biology Study Center.

One of the most appealing features of the experiment described in this chapter has been that the Study Center is not a remedial facility or an activity designed only for minority students; it is a facility utilized by the vast majority of the class as a learning resource center. Hence minority students are not subjected to the indignity of being sent to a special facility for remedial help. They are simply taking advantage of a general service designed to provide all students, regardless of differences in background and experience, with the opportunity for achieving a roughly equivalent understanding of the basic principles of introductory biology.

EPILOGUE

The most striking conclusion to emerge from my experiences has been that the racially biased outcomes previously observed in introductory biology could be eliminated by educational changes directed at improving the academic performance of the class as a whole, not just minority students. This discovery is of crucial importance for science educators because many of our introductory science classes have long had the reputation for being, and even prided themselves on being, "weed-out" courses that eliminate large numbers of students from pursuing careers in the sciences. Although weeding out students who currently don't perform well in introductory science classes may be the easiest thing for faculty members to do, such practices are socially irresponsible in an era in which our country no longer produces enough scientists and engineers to meet its future needs, and, as we now see, such behavior perpetuates an insidious form of institutional racism as well. To keep the horticultural metaphor intact, our universities and science faculties need to spend less time weeding out students and more time cultivating them.

NOTE

Funding for the Biology Study Center project was provided by the following administrative units of the University of Michigan: (1) the Office of the Vice President for Academic Affairs, (2) the College of Literature, Science, and the Arts, (3) the Department of Biology, (4) the Center for Research on Learning and Teaching, and (5) the Office of the Vice Provost for Information Technology.

16

Waking Up to the World: A Multicultural Approach to Writing

Ralph D. Story

Multicultural teaching in the university represents a very noble yet practical way of preparing the people in our institutions of higher education for achieving their mission in the twenty-first century. This is especially true in the United States, which has a genuinely heterogeneous population that is becoming ever more ethnically and racially diverse and culturally challenging. Those of us who embrace the idea of multicultural education are really trying to make the concept of a university more closely convey this definition in the contemporary world and better illustrate the "whole" that a university is supposed to represent. We are, inside and outside, more than one culture; we have been and will be, culturally speaking, more than the sum of our parts. It is only natural, then, that our educational praxes mirror this reality.

When I think of multicultural teaching, I think of the great, insightful, and learned teachers I had light years ago who enthusiastically introduced me to the concept of multicultural teaching before the term was ever fashionable. As an undergraduate I had the opportunity to read Gabriel García Marquez, the great Colombian writer, many years before he achieved world acclaim; I was also able to make numerous literary explorations of the works of Leopold Senghor (Senegalese), Octavio Paz (Mexican), Ezekiel Mphalale (black South African), García Lorca (Spanish), Isaac Singer (Jewish), Nicolas Guillén (Cuban), Vine Deloria (Native American), Alurista (Latino American), Aime Cesaire (Marti-niquian), Amiri Baraka (African American), and countless other writers. This experience made me view my education as one of the best I could have received anywhere in the world. Sadly, however—especially for those students who really didn't know of the existence of the aforementioned writers—those in the academy who could have institutionalized the idea of multicultural teaching some twenty years ago strongly resisted expanding the curricula to include artists who did not hail from Europe and particularly England. There were a few courses provided for students like me who were genuinely interested in pursuing this course of study. Nevertheless, there was also swirling within the academic milieu an undercurrent of dissonant opinion that attitudinally said these writers did not deserve being included in the proverbial canon.

My mentor, hero, and friend, the writer in residence at Ohio University from 1968 to 1972, Quincy Troupe, was my inspiration.[1] He had enough vision to see the future and try to prepare me for it by introducing me to some of the greatest writers in the world. There was also a very practical and worldly dimension to his courses; he understood long ago, as many others have now come to understand, that it is absolutely essential that the youth of the Third World (which, by the way, includes African Americans) be exposed to writers who hail from the same culture and share the same or similar experiences as they do.

We appreciate Shakespeare and Melville; minority youth who want to be writers, though, are inspired and motivated to create by playwrights like Luis Valdéz (*Zoot Suit*) and novelists like Toni Morrison (*Beloved* and *Song of Solomon*).[2] This is what multicultural teaching entails. It is inclusive and not exclusive; it is comprehensive and not limited; it is more and not less; it is enriching, motivating, inspiring, and energizing because it is, to use the words of Don L. Lee (Haki Madhubuti), "the way of the new world."[3] In very pragmatic terms, however, my approach to multicultural teaching has evolved and, in the process, has become a personal and public discovery, a signpost of intellectual growth. Here I discuss my ideas regarding multicultural teaching in the university and how, as someone who has been teaching for more than twenty years, I have embraced the idea of multicultural teaching while simultaneously achieving the more traditional and anticipated pedagogical goals of Introductory Composition.

Introductory Composition has probably existed since colleges and universities first came into being. Since it stresses writing and reading, essential tools for students in their attempt to cultivate intellectual habits, it is relatively easy— especially since today's composition textbooks, such as *The Writer's Craft,* now include writers from a variety of backgrounds and cultures—to make sure that all kinds of writers are represented in course materials. Moreover, in practical terms, it is easier to get students to submit better than average essays, which are more than just competent, if they are genuinely motivated, inspired, and provoked. The works of multicultural writers seem automatically to spark charged discussions and serve as catalysts for writing that transcends "an assignment." Inevitably, the reason these writers are more provocative than others is the fact that they are discussing issues (e.g., race, racism, ethnocentrism, bigotry) that most contemporary writers purposely avoid. These issues, however, are extremely sensitive for most eighteen-year-olds, and, as a result, an instructor consciously has to make an effort to create a relaxed and healthy classroom atmosphere for discussions. There are some very practical and behavioral practices that should be tried at the very beginning of the semester to foster such an open atmosphere; they are techniques successful teachers have used to promote group camaraderie, stressing the idea of cross-cultural similarities to a greater degree than multiracial or cultural differences. One should consider the usage of small peer groups, oral presentations, and group projects to enhance classroom discussions. I start each semester with a group project.

One of the most popular group projects I've used, an assignment that has always been enjoyable for students, involves creating a thirty- or sixty-second commercial. Almost all of us at one time or another have thought we could create a convincing or entertaining ad for a product. Students generally find this assignment enjoyable because it allows them to meet in small groups and develop a cohesiveness and camaraderie that last for the entire semester. They are required to produce as a group an ad that has a recognizable claim and appeal; they are given exactly two weeks to prepare the commercial. I've discovered that once students are placed in a group, they are forced to embrace the idea of a collective mission as well as a collective evaluation. It makes them subordinate their individual egos, work toward a common goal, and produce a finished product that inevitably turns out to be quite good. The entire class gets an opportunity to evaluate and rate the other students' commercials. This is a relatively good way of letting students understand how qualitative judgments can be converted into quantitative ones.

In 1978, I started creating groups randomly based on classroom seating patterns; this proved to be a rather weak way of creating groups. After the random selection process proved to be ineffective, I started grouping students according to writing ability by screening their diagnostic essays; a very good writer, a good writer, an average writer, and a weak writer would comprise a group. This strategy worked even better when I purposely grouped students living in the same residence hall. I found that when groups had an appropriate mixture of talents and abilities and were forced to work outside class without being able to use logistical difficulties as a reason for their lack of productivity, the group strategy worked extremely well. The assignment is also an entertaining one since, when the commercials are completed, the entire class evaluates each commercial, translating subjective, open-ended observations into numerical ratings. The end result is always pleasing because students come to understand how their assessments are just as critical as an instructor's. This is merely one example of an assignment I've used for years that promotes group harmony and teamwork.

It also is essential that young African American, Latino, and Native American students be exposed to writers who come from the same culture as they do, maybe even "look like them," so they can discover that one doesn't have to be a Caucasian to be a writer. Introductory Composition has taken on the additional responsibility—more than other courses, it would seem—of introducing students to the university as one of the first steps a student will take along the road to a liberal arts education.

If one is trying to inculcate the idea of "depth and breadth of knowledge" and of being "well read," the reading regimen should include, especially in this day and age, the work of writers from all over the world and not just the West.

There are few writers as talented as Gabriel García Marquez (*One Hundred Years of Solitude*, 1970) writing in any language, at any time, or in any place. The same could, and should, be said about Toni Morrison (*The Bluest Eye*, 1972), Chinua Achebe (*Things Fall Apart*, 1959), Vine Deloria (*We Talk, You Listen*, 1970), and many others. Traditionally, none of these authors would be included in a literature or writing course because, until the postwar era, literature basically meant English literature and very little else. In sum, all students should be exposed to the very best written material in the world in order for them to be truly educated. Correspondingly, if we want to say we are educating "some of the best students in the world," we must consider what it is to be a learned person. Since ancient times, a learned person has been one who is knowledgeable of other cultures and capable of interacting cross-culturally with all those with whom she or he would come into contact. It should be clear that the educated person of the twenty-first century will have to possess the same attributes: a worldly background and an attitude that allows for the appreciation of, and respect for, more than one culture. This is as close to the ideals of a "university" as we can come; we just need to practice what we preach!

My primary purpose in Introductory Composition is to teach students how to write with a sufficient amount of technique and a variety of inventive approaches to perform better than average on any kind of writing assignment they encounter during their first two years in the university. I have only a number of weeks to accomplish this task so whatever students read is, ultimately, not as important as the written material they generate about what they read or discuss. I would also hope that I'm teaching students how to think critically and how to embrace more than one point of view. Using the works of a variety of writers from a variety of cultures and places is one way of accomplishing these goals.

There are other issues, though, like race and gender, explored in many of the readings for my course, that should be addressed. The racial and ethnic composition of the class has little, if anything, to do with this pedagogical aim except to make sure there is a wide sample of all kinds of writers and writing from many cultures. The only necessary characteristics or attributes for a professor are (1) to know the material comprehensively and (2) to be prepared for any and all sorts of questions regarding the material and the writers. There is, of course, a tremendous amount of background reading that has to be done in order to be truly prepared; nevertheless, if an educator is open-minded, is interested in her or his students' mastering the material, and has a grasp of cross-cultural norms, folkways, and so on, she or he can teach a course dealing with any issue.

Race is a concept I deal with candidly and without any hesitation. African Americans have had to feel relatively uncomfortable, whether they wanted to or not, discussing this ideological concept because the subject always seems to emerge in predominantly white educational settings. My approach to any subject matter is typically grounded in history, so one of the very first items I expose my class to is history written by African American scholars from an African American point of view. There is an excellent quote by John Henrik Clark in his essay titled "The Meaning of Black History" that places the idea and ideology of "race" within a specific time frame:

Nature created no races. Nature created people and people did not refer to themselves as belonging to a race until the rise of the colonial system and of the slave trade concurrent with that system. People belonged to groups and religions, they belonged to clans, they belonged to regional groupings, they belonged to blacksmiths' guilds and carvers' guilds, but they did not belong to a race in the general sense that we are now talking about. This concept was created to justify European colonialism. I am not saying that prejudice is a European invention but I am saying the Europeans began prejudice based solely on color of the skin. The European could not acknowledge the role that the African played in the making of the "New World."[4]

For many freshpersons, however, these ideas, for example, African American scholars and the historical antecedents of race, are very new and very provocative. Definition essays (e.g., Define the concept of race, define the concept of class, define class stratification) and argumentative essays (e.g., Which is the best predictor for the life chances of African Americans: class or race?) that require comparative analyses of different views and research are excellent writing assignments for the discussion of these ideas. To be sure, for those who are interested in becoming multicultural educators at the university level, a far-ranging and diverse reading background in African American, Native American, Latino, and world history is absolutely essential. Freshpersons and sophomores, in particular, will have numerous questions regarding the origination of ideas from scholars they have never heard of who express opinions and discuss facts to which they have not been exposed; the only way to be adequately prepared from a classroom standpoint is to be extremely well read. It is not an impossible task, however, since so many of the historical works that one needs for this preparation are in print and readily available.

I also approach gender historically, with a tendency to use more social science writings than works of literature. Ashley Montagu's *The Natural Superiority of Women* (1968) is always an excellent starting point for discussions regarding this issue. His work discusses nomadic cultures and how sexism has evolved all over the world since ancient times as a result of man's superstitions and fears. Students are astonished that they truly know so little about the evolution of ideas and that role differentiation wasn't always etched in granite. Typically, we begin by talking about hunting-gathering societies and the creation of mythologies— primarily by men—to explain the unique capacity of women to "create humans." The discussions eventually get to the images of women created by men and how various attitudes and values about both sexes have been part and parcel of our individual and collective socialization. The work of Margaret Mead, and more recently Michel Foucault, are also great sources for provoking discussions and generating very original student essays. There are other pieces that work very well: "Sexism in English," by Alleen Pace Nilsen; psychologist Karen Horney's "Conflict Between the Sexes" (1987); free-lance journalist Dorothy Sayer's

"Are Women Human? (1986);" "Dating" by Susan Allen Toth (1986); and the remarkably precise work of Angela Davis, *Women, Race and Class* (1981).

As a specialist in African American literature, I discovered early that there were more than a few genuinely gifted, yet overlooked, contemporary African American writers. Ismael Reed is a case in point. Yet, it is not his hilariously inventive fiction—for example, *Freelance Pallbearers* (1967) and *Mumbo Jumbo* (1972)—that I consulted for his views on multicultural education. He discussed his ideas on this subject, quite candidly, years ago in a collection of essays titled *Shrovetide in Old New Orleans* (1978). Reed's commentary on this issue is particularly useful because, in most instances, one understands the idea of a multicultural universe only when it is clear, institutionally speaking, that others have somehow not recognized its existence:

> If any English Department in the United States or any liberal arts department is so devoted to the experience of people, like Anglo-Saxon enthusiasm, it should be in the ethnic studies department where all the other super-race programs go on. . . . *This is not Europe and it is not Africa. It is a new civilization.* . . . This happens when a monocultural attitude approaches a multicultural attitude. Most of the Americans I talk to are influenced by variety (Reed 1978: 252, emphasis added).

Reed found out, as many African American scholars and other creative intellectuals have throughout their careers, that to champion the artistic endeavors of writers outside the mainstream almost always puts one in a confrontational and/or adversarial relationship with those in academe, especially those within it who feel themselves officially anointed or appointed as "custodians of culture." The American people, however, are a great deal more open-minded and interested in any artistic work that possesses quality and embraces the human condition in unique and original ways.

The most recent and refreshing popular culture development connected to the idea of a multicultural universe, however, is that perhaps for the very first time in American cultural history, the American people have decided that they will make their own decisions regarding what they deem to be appropriate or interesting artistic expressions. Some rather telling examples of an enlightened American citizenry, as it relates to art by Third World artists, are the commercial and critical acceptance of Spike Lee's film *Do The Right Thing* and the phenomenal— some would say, startling—crossover success of African American rap music. The subject matter of Lee's film and the thematic and rhetorical content of rap (also known as "hiphop") music would have typically provoked critics (particularly those creative intellectuals "certified" as the American intellectual elite) to dismiss both creative endeavors as much too strident, passé, or polemical to gain the attention and positive reception of the American people.[5] Fortunately for Lee and groups like BDP and Public Enemy, the American people do not share the opinions of the critics.[6] Yet those of us in academe who believe in, and work hard to institutionalize, multicultural education have had consistently to demonstrate to our colleagues that pedagogical goals, the traditional ones, can still be achieved when including the work of writers who are viewed as "nontraditional."

In terms of course design and content, if one wants really to delve into these issues in more than a cursory fashion, choosing the right text (as well as supplemental materials) is absolutely essential. One needs a text that is multicultural in terms of its inclusion of various authors, yet still addresses the course's praxis. In addition to students' generating a great deal of writing, I introduce them to the topics of black stereotypes (e.g., in eighteenth-century American literature, in early and contemporary American film and TV) and gender. I've learned from experience that a textbook, no matter how wonderful its construction or how many different writers and writings it includes, never seems to keep students' attention sufficiently for an entire semester; I've always supplemented a textbook with a coursepack, selecting articles that I enjoyed reading and thought were well written.

Introductory Composition courses at the University of Michigan are evaluated each semester, using computer-scanned evaluations prepared by the Department of English Language and Literature and the Center for Research on Learning and Teaching. They are used by the instructor and his or her mentor (most Introductory Composition sections here are taught by graduate student teaching assistants) to improve the course and the instructor's performance in the course. I've been very fortunate in this regard because I've always had the kind of rapport with my students that would allow for genuine communication and actual learning from them about my successes and failures as a teacher. I've always tried to eliminate the distance between "the podium and the chairs." I think I've been quite successful because the topics I've chosen for students to write about and discuss are inherently interesting. Moreover, I treat students as young adults, not as children, and consider each and every point they make (for the most part) as a valid, legitimate contention. I don't condescend, ridicule, or chastise students in front of their peers.

I believe that educators, in general, and writing instructors, in particular, should set very high performance expectations and, without pressure or intimidation, get students to produce a great deal more written work than they think would be possible in a semester's time. At the very beginning of the semester, when the syllabus is discussed, the instructor has to make it clear that within fourteen weeks it is reasonable to assume that a student can produce six to nine typed essays and that the instructor has confidence that this will be accomplished. I also tell students that each and every class I've taught previously has written this much in a semester's time so they will, likewise, produce that much. Students are, therefore, gratified by the end of the semester because they've had the beneficial experience of electing an interesting class and they have achieved the practical goal of generating quite a bit of writing. If anything is certain about writing, the only way for students to improve is to write and write. They write essays; they are encouraged to keep journals, which are submitted periodically during the course of the semester; they write responses and critiques of their peers' work; and they are told from the very first day they're enrolled in my course (with the aid of Maxine Hairston's "Habits of Writers" from *A Contemporary Rhetoric*) that to be a good writer will take the same amount of time and energy it takes to be a good swimmer, a good free-throw shooter, or a good musician.

The twenty-first century will be technologically and visually beyond the scope of our collective imagination. We can only make sure we are ready for the future by preparing for it; we should use the technology we have at our disposal. I've found students to be enthusiastic and energetic when they've had the opportunity to see and hear something other than a lecture. One relatively standard feature of my sections of Introductory Composition is the use of visual stimuli (videotapes and, to a lesser degree, films) for classroom discussions and additional writing assignments. Since the mid–1980s, I've continuously looked for short educational segments that can supplement and/or enhance a particular piece of writing. One of the more effective visual shorts I've used is a segment from the Cable News Network program, "This Week in Japan." This thirty-minute segment is linked to an article by Herman Arthur titled "The Japan Gap" (1983), which discusses the phenomenal success of the Japanese in the post–World War II era, making specific comments about how their success is linked to their culture, values, and educational system. Students have been demonstrably excited to discuss both and have learned a great deal, more than they would from the article alone, from the cross-cultural discourse. Since both works eventually must be addressed in a midterm question, it is clear that the two goals—to make the classroom a useful multicultural experience and to be certain students are learning by measuring their performance—are achieved.

NOTES

1. Quincy Troupe's most recent work is *The Miles Davis Autobiography* (New York: Simon & Schuster, 1989). He is the author of other works, as well, but the most relevant one for this particular discussion would be his work as the editor (with Ranier Schulte) of *Giant Talk: An Anthology of Third World Literature* (New York: Random House, 1975).

2. Luis Valdéz's play *Zoot Suit* (which starred Edward James Olmos of "Miami Vice" fame in the lead role) received critical acclaim and won him a Tony Award. Toni Morrison, whose work *Beloved* (1987) won her the Pulitzer Prize for fiction is also the author of *Song of Solomon* (1978), *The Bluest Eye* (1972), *Sula* (1974), and *Tar Baby* (1981).

3. Don L. Lee (Haki Madhubuti), *We Walk the Way of the New World* (Detroit: Broadside Press, 1970). Also see *From Plan to Planet, Don't Cry Scream,* and *Dynamite Voices: New Black Poets of the 1960's* (Detroit: Broadside Press, 1973, 1969, 1971).

4. John Henrik Clark, "The Meaning of Black History," in *Blacks in White America Before 1865,* ed. Robert V. Haynes (New York: David McKay, 1972), 23.

5. Spike Lee's film *Do the Right Thing* received very favorable reviews from who are considered to be "mainstream" American film critics, most notably Gene Siskel and

Roger Ebert, the syndicated TV film reviewers. Lee's film also made money at the box office. Some time ago the sociologist Charles Kadushin, in a rather trailblazing piece of scholarship, identified what he (and others) considered to be *The American Intellectual Elite* (Boston: Little, Brown, 1974).

6. BDP (Boogie Down Productions) and Public Enemy are African American rap groups noted for their politically conscious lyrics.

17

Should and Can a White, Heterosexual, Middle-Class Man Teach Students About Social Inequality and Oppression? One Person's Experience and Reflections

Thomas J. Gerschick

> Tom felt completely comfortable lecturing on the women's movement and on the issues of rape and rape culture which some would consider as intrinsically outside of a man's ability to truly understand. Even beyond this, is the incongruity of a straight man lecturing on radical lesbian politics with the incredible assumption of authority. . . . Is it only me, or is something really strange, not to say really sexist, about this situation?[1]

As the above quote indicates, some of my students have had strong feelings about whether a white, heterosexual, middle-class man could and should teach others about oppression. This chapter describes my experiences teaching an Introductory Sociology course focusing on social inequality; I taught this course at the University of Michigan over the past three academic semesters.[2] The class consistently drew 125 students, approximately 35 percent of whom were students of color. The class tended to be evenly distributed between men and women. We addressed the issues of racism, sexism, ableism, homophobia/heterosexism, and classism. The format of the course was two fifty-minute lectures a week in addition to a two-hour small group discussion session. In this chapter I focus on the issues that concerned students raised about me personally and the larger issues that arose as a result of our dialogue.

There is a small, but growing, body of literature that addresses the question of who is appropriate to teach whom or who is appropriate to teach what at the university level (Short 1988; Beauchamp and Wheeler 1988). The National Association of Scholars (1988) argues that entertaining the question of who can teach whom unnecessarily politicizes the academy. It argues that "academic freedom is based on disciplinary competence and entails a responsibility to exclude extraneous political matters from the classroom'' (Short 1988: 7). Thus, according to the association, one's gender, class, sexual orientation, and race do not have an effect on an instructor's ability to teach; only one's competency matters.

However, studies have shown that in addition to competence and enthusiasm, an instructor's personal characteristics do have an effect on the teaching process *for some* students (see Dukes and Victoria 1989: 448–50 for a review of this research). Most often, these are the same students who tend to be marginalized by the educational system.

Today's students increasingly come from diverse backgrounds, with different needs, expectations, identities, and beliefs. As instructors, we must pay attention to these differences and seek to understand the experiences of diverse groups if we are going to be able to build truly multicultural universities in the future. Attention to these dynamics allows for the development of rapport, which is a necessity for effective teaching (Dukes and Victoria 1989). "If we cannot communicate, we cannot teach or learn. If students' and instructors' worlds are galaxies apart, prospects are poor for effective instruction" (Goldsmid and Wilson 1980: 55). Lack of identification with instructors by students of color, by lesbian, bisexual, and gay students, and by women students often leads them to feel underappreciated, discouraged, disenfranchised, and alienated. Following W. I. Thomas's (1931: 189) prescription that "if human beings define situations as real, they are real in their consequences," I maintain that an instructor's gender, class, sexual orientation, and race do matter. Yet, students' perceptions, needs, and concerns involving these issues are rarely taken into account when instructors plan their courses and develop their teaching styles (Chasteen 1987).

In order to determine the effect of my personal characteristics on my ability to reach students, each term I asked them about this issue directly. Not surprisingly, the responses varied considerably. Many of the students felt that if I were committed to the issues, enthusiastic, and knowledgeable about the subject matter, they would have no problem learning with me. However, every term there was a significant minority of concerned students for whom my personal characteristics had an effect on their ability to identify and learn with me. Their concerns raise important questions about my ability, and the ability of instructors like me, to teach courses on inequality and oppression.

CONFLICT OVER MY PERSONAL CHARACTERISTICS

Tom, as a white, straight (tell me if I'm making an assumption there) male, only needs to think about the issue of racism, heterosexism, sexism, etc. only three-four hours a week while a lesbian teaching about lesbian issues is thinking about and living heterosexism. A person of color needs to deal with this racist society every day. I guess I am not sure how a white male can relate to the oppression of others.

To me, this quote captures the lack of trust and the doubts about legitimacy I have often experienced as a white male teaching about inequality and oppression. These are two central dynamics of this issue that I confronted when teaching the course.

Trust

As a heterosexual, white, middle-class man, I am a representative of a social structure that oppresses other groups of people. Hence, from some students' perspectives, I have no business teaching others about being oppressed. Simply put, because I benefit from the current status quo, I am not to be trusted. It was difficult for me to hear such statements from students without feeling attacked and defensive. Yet, the questions and challenges regarding my personal characteristics are important because education relies, in large part, on trust. Trust cannot be expected, given the long history of relations between oppressed people and white academe. Trust must be earned, and there are particular practices that, if used, can help establish it. The following are some of the things that I used in the course to create or build upon incipient trust.

First, my willingness to discuss my characteristics helped to create a classroom environment where students were not afraid to challenge the instructor. To me, this indicated a nascent sense of trust, which allowed us to continue to explore these questions and issues throughout the term. It also indicated that students were thinking critically, which was one of the expressed goals of the course. For me not to entertain these questions would have had long-term ramifications for openness and trust. Through my willingness to discuss these issues, students' concerns were validated.

By taking students' challenges and concerns to heart and by making it one of the expressed goals of the course openly to discuss these issues, I encouraged students to challenge me, each other, and themselves. Although this seemed to be outside the realm of experience for many students, over time I found that they grew more comfortable with the practice and learned that they could trust me and the other students not to get defensive or become punitive. In doing so, my commitment to their concerns became more apparent and the bases for trust were furthered.

Implicit in our ongoing dialogue was the question of whether I could transcend the interests of my own group to understand and empathetically identify with the experiences of other people. The students also questioned whether I was willing to confront my own privilege and power as both a white male and a professor. These are important questions to ask. I think the answers provide insight into determining whether white men are appropriate for teaching such courses. In class, I stressed that although white males of this generation may not have created the oppressive social system, we benefit from it and, as a result, must be held accountable and responsible to help bring about change. To me, the process of confronting this requires critical reflection on the ways in which

I benefit from the current social structure. It also requires becoming conscious of the oppressive roles I have taken on and actively resisting the differential power and rewards that accompany such roles (Pease 1990). Confronting other men, especially white men, because I am a white man, also becomes essential to this process and provides others with an excellent indication of where one's commitment lies.

However, I also realized that my words were not enough to satisfy some students. They wanted further proof to demonstrate my commitment. Similar to what Bob Pease (1990) experienced, my anti-oppression activities on campus indicated to students over time that I was not as suspect as they thought. However, that is not to say that all students came to trust me or were convinced by the end of the course of my convictions and abilities to teach the course.

Credibility or Legitimacy

The second major issue that I faced in teaching the course was credibility or legitimacy. The way in which concerned students in the course understood legitimacy meant that if one had experienced and, as a result, understood oppression such as sexism, only then was one capable of understanding other forms of oppression such as racism. As the following quotes indicate, some students felt that I was not appropriate to teach a course on oppression because, as a white, heterosexual, middle-class man, I have not experienced any of these forms of oppression.

In my opinion, Tom, you can teach the course from a technical standpoint but you cannot relate to the situations or understand exactly how the oppressed and discriminated against feel.

I feel that you can be empathic, but you can never fully understand or relate to the oppressed, let alone sufficiently explain feelings, frustrations, and variety of other emotions. Anyone can be technical but only the oppressed group can better explain their standpoint for they are the ones who are being oppressed.

The issue of credibility and legitimacy presents a more difficult problem than the lack of trust. It is impossible for me to experience systematic oppression. Hence, there was no way for me to become legitimate in some students' eyes. Knowing that I could not change this situation, I was challenged to try to mitigate the lack of credibility. I chose to start by being honest about my life experiences, especially the privileges I have encountered. This acknowledgment contributed to building trust within the classroom. I also stressed my belief that different people have different experiences and as a result have different perspectives. These different perspectives reflect our different realities. Hence, I noted that in order for us to learn from one another, all perspectives must be acknowledged and understood. This made room for a white male perspective and became a norm in the course for all students.

Second, I tried not to play the role of "expert"; rather, I continually stressed that we all had something to learn from each other. This action resulted in reducing the hierarchy of the classroom. It also alleviated any responsibility students might have thought that I had to convey everything about the different forms of oppression. Moreover, it meant that they had the responsibility to contribute what they knew about the subject matter. Three other related strategies were guest speakers, films, and literature. Through the use of "other voices," my legitimacy became a less significant issue.

Additionally, we changed the organization of the course over the three semesters to incorporate a diverse teaching team so that we differed by race, class, sexual orientation, and gender. This allowed students to identify with different members of the teaching team, thus alleviating some of the credibility issues.

Thus, people with characteristics such as mine face two (and from some perspectives, intractable) issues when teaching courses of this nature. The issue of trust seems to be a more easily overcome problem than the issue of legitimacy. Hence, different strategies need to be used to mitigate the latter's deleterious effects.

LARGER ISSUES

There are larger considerations apart from the personal concerns of students. As part of the ongoing dialogue with the class, I challenged students to think in other ways about the questions they raised. This reinforced the practice of critical thinking and the belief that there are multiple perspectives on every issue. Given the concerned students' reasons that white males should not teach these types of courses, the following is my list of reasons why they should.

To begin by placing this in context, I firmly believe that more faculty representing oppressed groups are needed in academe. The situation presented by the course is clearly exacerbated by the limited number of such people teaching at universities. Having been traditionally marginalized by the academic profession, oppressed people have pursued other fields. For instance, according to a recent National Research Council report, the number of African Americans earning Ph.D.'s dropped 23 percent between 1979 and 1989 (Thurgood and Weinman, 1990). Our department reflects this trend in the limited number of faculty of color whom we have. Despite our attempts, we have had a difficult time hiring faculty who represent oppressed groups. Recent labor market trends have placed such faculty in high demand. Consequently, it is also difficult to retain them once they are hired.

In addition, we need to confront the expectation that traditionally oppressed people should teach classes about inequality and oppression. This expectation places an undue burden on these instructors for several reasons. First, although it is often true, we should not assume that faculty representing oppressed groups strongly identify with their group. Second, why should these faculty be pressured to teach courses of this kind at the expense of their other teaching agendas? As a white instructor, I do not face the same expectations or burdens. I have always been allowed to teach in the areas in which I am interested, rather than ones determined by the color of my skin, my sex and gender, my sexual orientation, or my social class. Third, because of their small numbers on college campuses, these individuals tend to be in high demand as role models, advisers, guest speakers, members of committees, and so on. These are extremely time-consuming obligations. Adding preconceived teaching expectations only exacerbates this problem. Fourth, to have only such faculty teach these classes lets white faculty, especially white male faculty, off the hook. It sends a message that oppression is not a white problem and that white men do not have to confront the issues and problems raised in this chapter. However, oppression is not solely the problem of oppressed people; it is a white problem, too (Katz 1988; Chesler and Crowfoot 1990; McDavid 1988). White instructors, especially white male instructors, need to show more initiative in this area to reinforce the idea that oppression is everyone's problem and that we are all responsible for eradicating it. We thus have an opportunity to become role models for other white students and instructors who are trying to understand, take responsibility, and challenge their privileged positions (Beauchamp and Wheeler 1988; Pease 1990; Chesler and Crowfoot 1990; Folsom 1983; McDavid 1988).

My experience has been that another reason for white males to teach such courses is that my personal characteristics tended to lessen some white students' resistance to discussing these issues. In this regard, my viewpoint was seen as less threatening and was less easily dismissed by them. As Audre Lorde (1981) has noted, white people challenging other white people evokes much less guilt and defensiveness on the part of whites, and as a result they get a better hearing. This dynamic is evidenced by the following two quotes from students:

Another thing I liked that other people complained about was having a white male professor and T.A. [teaching assistant]. It made me feel like the opinions were not biased. I think I would have had the attitude that, of course, you are going to say what you are saying. Since you are black, a woman, a homosexual or whatever, you would tell me you are oppressed since you would have something to gain by making myself and others believe that. Which, when I look at it is probably a racist, sexist and homophobic thing to say, but that is how my thinking was when the class started.

Although he is a white, young, upper-class, heterosexual man, I believe that fact may actually serve to somewhat validate his claims to some students, who are used to learning and accepting what comes from people with those same characteristics.

The above quotes suggest that white students may have difficulty relating to faculty who are different from themselves. While I am glad that I was able to reach these students, I am also troubled by the fact that my co-teachers may have been seen as biased. As Peggy McIntosh (1988) and Jack Folsom (1983) have reported, I did not totally succeed in creating an environment where persons of color, women, lesbians, bisexuals, and gay men could speak with as much credibility as a white male. I will continue to struggle with this, knowing that it is a reflection of a larger societal dynamic, but an important one to continue to challenge.

Finally, teaching a course on oppression provides white faculty, especially white men, an opportunity to grow as instructors and as people. As Louis Kampf and Dick Ohmann (1983) report, participation in teaching about oppression can be a process of self-education and consciousness-raising. Richard Bach once said, "You teach best what you need most to learn" (Bach 1977: 48), and this course will continue to provide me with an excellent opportunity to challenge myself and the values and beliefs that I have internalized. In addition, it will provide me with the stimulation and the environment necessary to question and challenge the privilege and power that accrue to me solely on the basis of my personal characteristics.

SUMMARY

These are some of the salient issues surrounding instructor orientation, the learning process, and courses on social inequality and oppression. The issues I raise were raised in the course as we struggled with the question of who should teach whom about what. Some, but not all, of the concerned students agreed with me at the end of the course that white men could and should teach such courses. Despite the lack of consensus, we were much more informed about the different perspectives that exist on this issue, and much learning occurred. To me, this has remained an important outcome of the course.

To return to the first question in the title of this chapter, namely, whether white, heterosexual, middle-class men should teach about social inequality and oppression, I argue strongly yes. In doing so, white men indicate that oppression is also a white male problem, they become role models for other white faculty and students, they challenge the belief that only oppressed people should teach about oppression, and they are provided with an ongoing opportunity to explore and confront the privilege that accrues to them on the basis of their sex, sexual orientation, skin color, and class. As to whether white, heterosexual, middle-class men can teach students about oppression, I give a more qualified yes. If a white man is willing to confront his status and privilege and to continue to challenge himself as well as the class, then he is in a position to teach such a course. This entails the use of numerous strategies aimed at creating trust and mitigating the lack of legitimacy that white males tend to encounter based on their lack of experience of oppression.

NOTES

I am indebted to Tracy Ore, Mark Freyberg, and Kim Simmons for the many insights that came out of our conversations as we struggled with how best to teach this course.

Additionally, I am indebted to Lynda Duke, Mark Chesler, and David Schoem, who reviewed earlier drafts of this chapter and helped shape its ideas.

1. All quotes come from course critiques or from the course computer conference.

2. I did not teach this course alone. I taught with two other persons, who were responsible for the small group meetings. Because my responsibilities included the large lecture section, I was identified by the students as the primary instructor.

18

On Engaging Students in a Multicultural Course on a Global Scale: Risks, Costs, and Rewards

Ann E. Larimore

Most students left the classroom as our discussion of two United Nations films on Namibia ended, but not five angry women students. They confronted Ximena Zúñiga, my co-instructor, and me. One was crying hard; the others all talked at once, loudly. Then it was fall term 1988; now, in the summer of 1990, I cannot recall their passionate words, but I still feel my startled and anxious reaction. It was only the fifth class meeting of the term. During the next forty-five minutes or so, Ximena and I listened to their sense of shock at the films' revelation of self-justified white South African/German exploitation of the local Ovambo peoples. These films made clear that by political control of both the natural resources and the Black Africans who were living in miserable poverty and political limbo, the White settler population had become wealthy.

Yes, we said, these United Nations films are authentic. We are not exaggerating when we explain that the current, extremely stratified form of the world economic system generates this kind of human oppression and discrimination. Yes, no matter where their class, race, ethnic group, and local community place them in the global hierarchy, women as the marginalized gender—with few exceptions—have it worse than men.

Mostly we listened while they vented their feelings of revulsion and disbelieving shock. The intensity of their feelings spent, they began to talk more quietly. We asked them to be patient and to approach the course with open minds so they could learn what issues Third World women themselves raised to challenge such situations. Finally, the discipline of our individual tight schedules reasserted itself, as we left the classroom, each on her own path.

I had not expected this particular form of response that day, but I knew from teaching Third World Women: Women in Development before that my approach asked students to engage the subject matter on a visceral level. I had to be ready for unexpected and intense reactions. I also had to be willing to deal with my own emotional reactions to their feelings.

I know the costs: additional time and both mental and emotional energy, which cannot be budgeted beforehand except by framing a professional schedule with some slack time built in. That means taking time and energy away from scholarly research work. That means recognizing that these tasks of working through my own emotional reactions and of planning strategies to bring these kinds of encounter to a positive outcome distract my attention and divert my effort away from work that is more highly rewarded by the university and academe.

The added uncertainty of whether, with this or that particular mix of students, I can bring off this kind of course successfully can lead to crippling anxiety. Here, to restore my calmness and self-confidence through reflection and consultation, team teaching with an experienced and familiar colleague is invaluable. Being able to talk through the situation together when a crisis occurs and together design a response lessens anxiety and the risk of compounding the difficulty while also increasing the likelihood of an effective response.

I have found that the senior instructor can consult productively only if he or she genuinely seeks collaboration rather than asking for a critique (mostly positive) of her or his own design. In such situations, bigger reputation, higher rank, older age, and more experience do not always indicate more inventive ingenuity or more sensitivity to the situation's nuances.

Ximena is a Latina, originally from Chile. She is finishing a doctoral dissertation about action research and social change. I am an older white American woman, a cultural geographer, who spent much of fifteen years (during the 1950s and the 1960s) doing geographical field research in East African and Middle Eastern rural areas. Since 1981, I have concentrated my scholarly work on understanding the intricate farming systems operated by village women together with men, systems that have been nearly wrecked by modernization.

I have taught an undergraduate course on Third World Women for the University of Michigan Women's Studies Program several times, offering the course every other year. Though from the United States, I ventured to do this because of my particular scholarly field experiences and because no Third World woman faculty person was available on campus to teach undergraduates about the plight of Third World women from a systematic perspective. In a previous version of this course, Ximena taught about Latin American women; in the fall of 1988 we were co-designing and co-teaching the course for the first time.

FRAMING CONCEPTS OF THE COURSE

In an open letter handed out when the course began, we told the students of our premise:

We are all connected in specific and identifiable ways to the whole world of women. Our ethnocentrism and ignorance not only divide women from women, men from women, but also Third World people living in the First and Second Worlds from those in the Third. To transcend these divisions by acquiring some familiarity with women's global situation will aid you in assessing your own situation in the U.S. at the end of the 20th century.

Our central pedagogical stance to implement these goals was that Third World women themselves know their status, situations, and conditions better than any external scholars, journalists, or politicians and better than men and male experts in their own cultures. We argued that *multicultural* must mean cultures differentiated by genders as well as by classes, ethnicities, and nationalities. That is, within any class, ethnic group, or nationality, we claimed that men and women belong to different cultural communities.

In our open letter, we said:

Government policies in every country directly shape women's lives. So we will be considering various dimensions of the structured relations between women's personal spheres and the public arenas dominated by men. THE PERSONAL IS POLITICAL AT EVERY SCALE OF GOVERNMENT.

In taking this stance as instructors, we clearly rejected and disassociated ourselves from the conventional, public U.S. stance of cultural superiority, as fashioned and reiterated by the white male elite of owners, executives, and professionals who dominate public discourse. By claiming such a stance, this white male elite justifies managing the development of the multicultural world, whether on a global, international, national, regional, or community scale. Our alternative stance rejects the reigning orthodoxy of public policy and confronts students with the question, If I adopt this stance, do I risk being judged not a "patriotic American" by those who forget that the core of U.S. patriotism is the act of loyal and informed dissent?

COURSE DESIGN

This overarching pedagogical stance to multicultural teaching gives the people being studied in the course as much authority as the instructors. As a consequence, we implemented a number of design decisions that raised our costs in time, effort, creative thought, and complicated arrangements:

1. We set the pedagogical goal of the course as learning to ask informed questions. In our open letter we said:

Genuine controversy permeates the subjects we will study, issues that we will raise; therefore we will not arrive at answers very often. We do not see ourselves as instructors to be in the business of giving answers, rather we are informed guides to lead you in sustained inquiry. . . . Our goal is to create an environment which supports questioning of self, reflection, and critical examination of our often all-encompassing misperceptions, biases, ethnocentrism, and oversimplification. We aim for an openness to all questions respectfully asked.

2. As a text we used Joni Seager and Ann Olson's 1986 *Women in the World: An International Atlas*. Its forty, copiously documented, statistical world maps show the disadvantaged status of women resulting from "development" (not the lack of it), regardless of country. These effects are expressed in various configurations that, in this course, we examined for four large regions: Latin America, Africa south of the Sahara, the Middle East, and South Asia.

3. We used documentary films made by Third World women or by filmmakers who allowed them to speak extensively.

4. We featured at least one Third World woman speaker from each region we included in the syllabus.

5. We required students to go to another university's international conference on Third World Women and Health Issues, which brought numerous scholars from the Third World.

6. We announced Third World women speakers, Third World films, and Third World events happening on campus.

7. We used a coursepack of readings selected from books and journal articles and political reporting. Third World women, scholars, activists, and journalists wrote all the articles, with some carefully explained exceptions. This principle of selection ensured that those issues that women of particular Third World regions thought crucial were emphasized. Using an anthology of readings that we organized, rather than a textbook, cost us substantial additional preparation time and effort before the course began.

8. We asked students to keep journals in which they explored their feelings and reflected on the readings. From these journals, they were required to hand in five typed pages of excerpts three times during the course. Responding to journals on both a cognitive and affective dimension requires investing substantial time and both intellectual and emotional energy. It also requires carefully maintaining an open, honest, and caring stance while framing replies to the students' writing.

9. We required students to form research groups of five to six students each. These groups wrote and presented joint research reports identifying the women's issues particular to various regions of the Third World. They did independent research in the library, assembled interdisciplinary bibliographies, and read widely.

EXPERIENCES

In the class of thirty women and three men, the students were mostly middle- and upper middle-class white Americans of various ethnic backgrounds, and one was an African American woman. One student, however, was an Arab American woman; one was an Asian Indian American woman; one was a Philippine American woman. We, as instructors, did not invoke their Third World backgrounds because we were sensitive to the exploitive implications of asking students, ethnic isolates within a class, to speak for their own ethnic communities. Moreover, we found that such students, while often informed about the status and situation of their ethnic communities in the United States, are usually uninformed about women's situations in their parents' region of origin. One reason they are taking the class is to learn about them.

We devoted a number of class meetings to discussing readings assigned for that day in two medium-sized groups (ten to fifteen people). Each of us facilitated a group. We decided not to preface discussion with an orientation to the readings to be discussed, avoiding introductory remarks so that our opinions would not unwittingly act to filter Third World women's positions. We believed that our own views would become clear during the flow of the discussion.

I now believe this strategy was flawed. Not providing a brief introduction to the discussion meant that we asked students to reveal their opinions and interpretations of the readings without assurance that we would reveal our own. Thus we were asking them to take risks that we weren't taking. This sent a message about power dynamics between instructors and students different from other messages we were sending. (In a parallel instance of unconsciously instructed, unequal power dynamics, one student commented that we should have shared more of our personal experiences since we expected them to be personal in their journals.)

We also deprived students of our interpretations of the readings to stimulate their thinking. Some, in consequence, seemed not confident enough of their own analytical and interpretive abilities to venture their views of the readings in a public forum without the instructor's in some way indicating her own thinking. Many students are accustomed to adapting their comments to fit within a "proper" framework as indicated, often subtly, by the instructor.

This pedagogical stance, I now think, resulted in discussions that were often unsatisfying and uncomfortable. Additionally, some students did not do the readings assigned, and many indicated that they thought the readings were too long. Teaching the course another time, I would provide much more structured directions for the process of reading the material and preparing it for discussion. I would also indicate my own views and welcome challenges.

Even now, I find it difficult to unravel reactions to the subject matter itself and reactions to our chosen pedagogical stance and strategies. A course dealing honestly with the current impoverishment and oppression of women in all parts of the Third World, a disturbing perspective and one at variance with the mainstream view that "development is the answer," makes difficult emotional demands on students. When the course design also asks students to rely on their abilities to make sense of the material on their own, to take the initiative for their own learning, and to manage large amounts of often confusing and contradictory source materials representing Third World women's many voices, students may well feel that the course demands too much of them.

The five angry students described at the beginning of this article stayed with the course. In fact, one of them, in her final journal, wrote:

I came into this course set to change the horrible plight of all Third World women. Even while I frowned at the multinationals for their attitudes and admonished the Peace Corps for their politically based aid it has only been recently that I have begun to examine my own ethnocentric biases. I've realized that as much as I would like to deny it, I carry fragmented stereotypes of Western superiority with me. I hate to admit that: it's embarrassing to see something like that in me when I recognize how dangerous such attitudes can be. But I suppose it is more important to recognize it now and continue to struggle against it than to deny it altogether.

The five students' outburst was the most spontaneous and violent protest that we encountered. Far more difficult to engage productively were other repeated behaviors that I interpret as veiled protest actions. These protests took the form of chronic lateness to class, more than occasional absences, complaints, refusals to do assigned work, and after-the-fact criticisms in evaluations.

For students, no matter what their stances, the course may have had emotional low points of despair at the current global scale of abuse of women. A student commented on one of the few readings by a non–Third World woman:

This article is full of hope, something I thought we rarely saw in the rest of the many readings, and which I lost several times in the past few months.

Reading of women abused, discriminated against, and marginalized in different cultural communities may have brought disturbing insights into female students' own ambiguous position in a large, elite state university that prepares students for professional careers dominated by elite white men.

I have concluded that Ximena and I, enthusiastic about past positive experiences with strategies for student participation in the classroom, expected these students to adapt simultaneously to too many novel pedagogical requirements little used in most undergraduate courses. For some this was challenging in a positive way. For others it was threatening. To ask students to move out of their sure confidence as bearers of contemporary, "mainstream" American culture to the rest of the world and consider with respect and sympathy the plight of women (and indirectly men) in very different cultures, while at the same time requiring them to behave in several unfamiliar risk-taking ways in order to earn a grade, is asking them to risk too much at once.

COURSE EVALUATIONS BY STUDENTS

We did not recognize the accumulation of risk for the students when we designed the course. The cost to us, as I see it, was receiving final course evaluations from scathing ones to accolades, with many students' articulating their complex reactions in mixed evaluations. Such evaluations do not easily inform an outside evaluator's understanding of the quality of the teaching. (I am based in a unit where teaching evaluations count heavily in awarding annual merit increases.)

At the negative extreme, one student wrote:

This is what I feel I learned from this class:

Was such a blanket condemnation balanced by the reward of two other students' evaluations? They wrote:

Ann and Ximena know exactly how to format and present this course. How else can I say it—Everyone on campus should take this course. I never took a class like this before and I can't make it clear enough—the info I learned here is invaluable. *Good Job—Don't change a thing!*

The course was an important one—everyone should take it—it really teaches us how to question the status quo.

Letting Third World women speak for themselves, rather than fitting their analysis neatly into Western frames of reference, left some students feeling that some of the material was repetitive and "too much." Of particular salience for multicultural teaching was a thread of criticism that we placed too much emphasis on commonalities and generalizations without enough attention to differences. Indeed, at the global scale, development efforts exhibit much uniformity as the extension of trading networks commercializes both small-scale industry and agriculture. Women, however, have responded to their impoverishment and marginalization by amazing and diverse feats of creative productivity in local communities and even at the regional scale.

Including more of these positive stories of women's accomplishments not only in readings but in classroom presentation would underscore the different kinds of initiatives women have taken. This might help to lighten the tone of the course because students, like many other Americans, have great sympathy for the disadvantaged but are eager to learn quickly of positive outcomes. Doing this would take a careful framing explanation; otherwise, I believe, it would risk obscuring the fact that these initiatives are, at the present time, coping strategies, rather than emerging movements that will change the political economic hierarchy constructed by modernization and development.

ATTITUDES UNDERLYING STUDENT RESPONSES

I think students respond quite differently to this kind of course content, experiencing it according to their own, often unconsciously held, general stances toward other cultures. From what undergraduates have told me and written for me during the years I have been requiring them to write journals about their study of Third World women, I find that most undergraduate college students' attitudes reflect their family's, peers', or community's general positions. Three general stances seem to stand out.

First is a stance of being sure as an American of issues and strategies for development, already knowing what development means and wanting more knowledge in order to become more professionally prepared. Moving away from this position, which I might term an "America—the Global Leader" worldview, comes very hard for most students. It means letting go of an often unconscious, absolutist view based on nationalist and imperialist ideology to begin to construct for oneself a view based on a balanced and questioning appraisal of information.

We know that learning about other cultures' behavior gives us perspective on our own: this is a hoary justification for foreign language study and travel abroad. When, during a course, a student begins to become conscious of a more accurate world perspective based on compelling amounts of systematic data, personal testimony, and reasoned argument, a dynamic process of intellectual and emotional change begins to operate. Integral to the intellectual struggle sparked by this cognitive dissonance is emotional turmoil.

Because Ximena and I were teaching about worldviews—the ultimate framing systems of linked concepts we each use to position ourselves in the complex, seemingly chaotic world around us—we were challenging attitudes at a most fundamental level. Some students, I think, will retain their original stance when challenged because they sense that changing it is too high a risk in their personal and familial context. I speculate that such denial may produce evaluations such as the extremely negative one cited above.

Not all students showed the change that this student reported in her final journal:

One theme that I briefly touched on in my first journal assignment was that of development. I mentioned that I was of the opinion, common to many Western people, that development was good for everyone no matter what. I think that the reality which we have been discovering this term negating this myth is one of the most important things I have learned. I will no longer take for granted that what the United States or the World Bank terms as a development project is necessarily a good thing for all involved.

. . . One thing I have learned is that it is not up to us to decide what is best for anyone. The only way we can really help is to listen to what the people in the situation feel is best for themselves and attempt to make their voices heard. Judgment based upon our ideals, culture, and experience will do little, if any, good, and in most cases much harm.

A second stance is being open to information and learning because of not being knowledgeable, not being engaged with public affairs. Where can these students come from except from families, schools, and communities where attention is simply not paid to the world's issues and problems or where young women, in particular, are not rewarded for paying such attention? In a course like Third World Women, such students may rapidly abandon the comfort of their ignorance. One such student wrote:

What was particularly great about the class was the encouragement to become more aware of the issues—even here on our campus. This does sound terrible (and it is rather embarrassing now), but I come from a very conservative upper-class background and problems of the "poor" never really crossed my mind. And as far as political issues and current events, I have been oblivious. Only on rare occasions had I ever read a newspaper or turned on "World News Tonight." I came to U of M not knowing what Apartheid was! Someone did explain what the shanties on the diag [wooden shacks representing

South African black poverty built by students on the University of Michigan Library's paved forecourt, the campus's central place] symbolized, but my response was one of indifference.

Believe it or not, but quite a radical change in my attitudes occurred this semester because of this course. I have taken an active interest in international political affairs now—active in the sense that I am trying to educate myself. I have gone to several of the films and guest lecturers that were recommended in the class. I even signed up to take Mazrui's World Politics class next semester! Through this class, I realized how ignorant I was and how important it is to be aware of issues around the world, especially women's issues.

Third is a stance of being aware of the world's cultural diversity, of being uncomfortable with the categorically superior position of "America—the Global Leader," of wanting more knowledge and understanding in order to help. Students wrote:

I used to think that a responsible form of development could be achieved if only developers (whoever or whatever they may be) would take time to acquire an understanding of culture and the environment. I am concentrating in anthropology and have taken some classes in the School of Natural Resources so that I may become a culturally and environmentally aware person. My goal was to eventually take my knowledge and use anthropological methods to determine and recommend culturally and ecologically sound development programs. I thought anthropologists could save the world by becoming cultural liaisons between the First and Third worlds. After taking this course, however, I no longer think this is the appropriate approach.

I wish we had talked about the incredible sacrifices being made and the tremendous love being shared unconditionally between these women [in South Africa and Latin America] and their children. It would have helped us to step out of our always too big American boots and realize that we should be learning something *from* them, not always *of* them. One similarity that most of the women we have studied have is the desire to give their children a much better life to live. Sometimes I think Americans forget this, or it just doesn't fit into their agenda. We think as if we really have nothing to improve on, but we have a lot of lessons to learn and I think that by looking at the Third World, we should see a lot more of what it is our country lacks by being the first world [emphasis added].

Teaching students with these three stances operating in one class produces continuing tension, particularly when students are asked to interact with one another. In the future, I expect to have students examine their attitudes in an interactive way so we can identify and discuss their salient features in relation to each other.

POSITIVE OUTCOMES

Despite their often negative feelings, many students progressed through the course to positive outcomes. Two themes repeated in many final journal entries—

wanting to learn and wanting to help—spoke to new sensitivities in students' perceptions of their place in the present heavily stratified, culturally diverse world. We asked students in their final journals to write the questions that they would take away from the course.

Students reported increased respect for the complexity of cultural diversity:

Third World women are not all alike. They are different in a multitude of ways. It is so important to see each situation as having its own causes and effects. What is good for women in one country, or one village, or even one neighborhood may not be beneficial for another no matter what her proximity or apparent similarity. This raises another important issue which is the Western bias with which so many people look at the Third World. So many tend to clump countries and regions together and judge what is best for them.

I have learned that the process of social change is just that, a process, which moves at a slow pace but consumes a high rate of energy and compassion. By looking at the conditions and situations of different women, all over the world, I have gained a new perspective, a more worldly perspective. Now, I can never just look at the women's movement, or feminism, as an isolated movement with one set of rules. Instead, I see it as a worldwide movement that is interconnected, open to communication, and that must celebrate differences.

Who am I? and What is my part? What part do I play in the world? What can I do, as a white, middle-class woman to improve the lives of women (and also myself) all over the world, including the United States? I also continue to question what baggage I carry and what I need to get rid of.

FINAL REFLECTIONS

As a cultural geographer trained in the 1950s, I have taught various "multicultural" courses for decades. From 1965 to 1969 for the Association of American Geographers, I developed a model world regional geography course whose purpose was to demonstrate the orderly pattern underlying the world distribution of cultural regions overlaid by the global network of independent states. I have found it to be a much more intellectually difficult and emotionally taxing project to develop and teach multicultural courses that posit cultural communities to be separated by racial, ethnic, class, and gender distinctions in a hierarchical arrangement created and maintained by White male elites and their allies.

When teaching such a course, instructors must necessarily insist that the students grapple with the falseness of the Western claim of modern White male superiority and with accepting, internalizing, and expressing authentic respect for other cultures. Students also must be asked to recognize the particular configurations of their own male-designed culture and its claims to superiority and to begin to reject those claims—an act prerequisite to behaving toward other cultures with respect.

To succeed in these multiple dimensions means engaging the students' emotions with the risk that in the academic term's fifteen weeks, only one or two will fully understand the content while others in the class will become angered and alienated. The reward for success lies in reinforcing students' attitudes of cultural respect for women whose lives are much different from their own while at the same time showing them opportunities as women to learn and help.

This, I believe, happens most successfully when students gradually learn from a variety of evidence, rather than when the instructor forces or demands, however subtly, certain views. Judiciously selected readings and testimonies by Third World women and films that accurately and sympathetically reveal these women's lives provide material that students can reflect upon for themselves. Assigning students to do research projects in which they select sources from the library provides a way for students to consult material with contrasting views. Using a variety of source materials instead of a textbook, students have a better chance of drawing widely informed conclusions about their relationship as modern Americans to women in the Third World.

Are the costs of time invested and intellectual and emotional energy spent— for both students and teachers—rewarded? Personally, I am gratified with the growth in compassionate understanding based on increased knowledge that a number of students displayed. I also take pride in expanding students' horizons so that they discover whole new realms of learning and inquiry. But, institutionally, at the moment, instructors' investments are not recognized in conventional academic terms. It is very difficult to sustain this kind of risk-fraught teaching without institutional attention and compensation. How should such efforts be rewarded? If this chapter helps to bring that question to prominence in academic discourse so that some positive institutional changes in costs, risks, and especially recognition are made, I will consider myself well rewarded.

NOTE

I'd like to acknowledge with grateful thanks the helpful comments of Diana Campbell, Max Heirich, Christine Kolars, Ximena Zúñiga, and the anonymous reviewers.

19

Social Psychology

Elizabeth Douvan and Joseph Veroff

In the wake of racist incidents on our campus and protests by African American students who pointed to the institutional racism pervasive in American higher education that permits and covertly legitimates such incidents, a significant number of faculty in the social sciences and humanities began to rethink their courses with an eye to increasing attention to the experience and reality of minority cultures. Just as some of us had tried to expand our use of readings in feminist scholarship a few years ago, we now reassessed our course reading lists and lecture notes to create or enlarge opportunities for class discussion of the plural reality and intergroup relations that comprise American society in the last decade of the twentieth century.

BACKGROUND: THE SETTING

We have co-taught a course titled Personal Organization and Social Organization for a number of years. This is a second-level social psychology course that attracts large enrollments, primarily upper-division students. We hold lectures in common, alternating turns so that neither of us lectures every week. Each of us has our own section of thirty students that meets once a week for two additional hours.

The course content, falling within the domain of social psychology, takes as its central question, What are the ways in which the social environment influences the development and adaptation of the individual? It takes a greater interest in social structure than does a great deal of current work in social psychology, and it includes analysis of both cultural and interpersonal forces. We are not uninterested in the effect of the individual on the social environment, but we take the position that the influence process in the other direction is far and away more powerful. We look for isomorphism and analogues between the personal and the social.

REINFORCING READINGS

Course requirements include two activities that are not standard in undergraduate courses: (1) designing an empirical study and collecting some data designed to test the study's hypothesis and (2) leading at least one class discussion, sharing the role with one or two other students and the instructor. Both requirements press students to collaborate. In the case of facilitating class discussion, students have to collaborate since there are only some fourteen discussion sessions and thirty students in the class. For the research projects, they are urged to work together so that they can do more significant data collection.

This is the setting in which we introduced a significant proportion of readings that dealt with the multiple realities of American life. We were impressed with the research literature that had accumulated on minority cultures since the early seventies. Although some scholars have noted the dampening effect on research on the Black family that was brought about by the Moynihan report and its critical reception, in fact scholars in the field continued to study the Black family and its socialization patterns, the development of children from minority backgrounds, the effects of discrimination and racism on the economic well-being of minority families and particularly on the self-concept and security of young Black males, the effects of racism on the sense of personal efficacy, and the implications for minority political participation. We had riches to draw on; the problem was choosing from such abundance.

This abundance led us to ask ourselves why we had used so little of this literature in the course previously. The findings were apposite for so much of what we deal with in the course, for example, the findings having to do with the twin lessons that children in the Black community must learn in order to maintain a robust self-esteem (as so many do): that Black people are the victims of systematic discrimination and have relatively little power to affect aspects of their fate in a racist society; but that within the child's life and personal quest, he or she is encouraged and helped toward the recognition and development of personal powers and reinforced and applauded for self-determination and self-assertion (Jackson, McCullough, and Gurin 1988). These findings deal with complex issues of socialization and raise highly sophisticated questions that can lead to important extensions of theory. How could it happen that so much of our teaching and so much work in our fields (social, personality, developmental psychology) have ignored this body of literature? How did the standard texts in psychology get drained of so much co-culture material that would require us to condition and contextualize our theories? Surely it is not only that psychology continues to be beguiled by a view of itself in the model of the ''hard'' sciences whose laws are stated as holding ''in a vacuum,'' that is, laws that transcend context.

We think that it is also probably partly the result of the isolation of Black studies or Latino studies. And then there is institutional racism, from which none of us is exempt. How many of us keep up with the literature not just in our own disciplinary journals but in, say, the *Journal of Black Education* or the *Black Scholar*? How many of us read a new book on the Latino middle-class family or the Asian immigrant family in preparing to teach our course on the family? It takes political pressure from students to remind us that there is a world beyond our standard academic sources that we might want to include in courses. Up until quite recently there were so few minority students in places like the University of Michigan that a teacher might go for most of an academic career without ever having more than one or two minority students in any class.

The Jackson et al. reading was used in the introductory section of our syllabus, in which we establish the theme of the social nature of personality. We propose that personality is a derivative of previous socialization and current expectations of groups in which we are or have been embedded. This particular reading underscores the differential identity influences that Black Americans experience from their families, their neighborhoods, and the society at large. It argues cogently and with empirical evidence that Black families often instill a self-concept and self-esteem in children that are robust enough to allow them to withstand the negative messages they may receive later from the larger culture and that at adolescence these youngsters reveal a complex, differentiated view of the self that reflects these various inputs.

Other readings we introduced at various points in the course to illustrate particular theoretical issues ranged from an analysis of white privilege (McIntosh 1989) to ethnography (Stack 1974) and quantitative empirical studies (Wilson 1987).

The readings we selected were only a few of many available. So we had plenty of useful, powerful readings to add to the course (though we will see later that this did not always guarantee successful discussion). We planned lectures to include reference to these readings and to others that we had not asked students to read but that were also focused on minority cultures. We knew that discussions would include some comparable issues since one of the functions of the discussions was to explore assigned readings and the concepts and conclusions they presented.

CREATING AN ATMOSPHERE FOR OPEN, INFORMED DISCUSSIONS

How discussions would go raised a number of questions. We couldn't hope that a third or half of the class would be minority members. Michigan doesn't have that many minority students. While courses like social psychology probably draw a larger proportion of minority and women students than some other courses, we knew, nonetheless, that Black, Latino/a, Native American, and Asian students would be in the very small minority in our course and that it could be hard for minority students—in their token positions—to speak up. White students from the dominant culture would probably also be somewhat inhibited, under the general rules of politeness in our culture that hold that speaking of difference is somehow rude and embarrassing. Since the dominant racist ideology frames all difference as representing a deficit in the group other than dominant Anglo culture, it inhibits any discussion of difference. Educated minority members as well as their liberal White peers also fear that any discussion of difference can be misused by racists to support their assumptions that minority cultures are inferior.

Avoiding discussion of differences doesn't eliminate them and is in itself a reflection of the belief that what is different from dominant culture is less valuable. How, then, would we both stimulate the discussion of difference and racism and at the same time ensure that minority students were not put on the spot or dehumanized? We didn't have any pat solutions going into the course, but our experience offered us a number of insights that we will keep in mind as we design future courses and/or that we will use as the base for political judgment and actions in the university community.

INSIGHTS GAINED OR REINFORCED

The first insight—one that we didn't really need to gain from this experience— was that discussing and teaching about diversity and pluralism make more sense and are more natural in a group that is itself diverse. This touches again on the theme of tokenism and its vicissitudes. By chance, one of our two sections was significantly more heterogeneous than the other. While one section had only a single minority student, the other section was somewhat richer in diversity, with three African Americans, two Asian students (one of whom was Asian American), and several Jewish students, who were aware of their minority status in a midwestern university and spoke about various aspects of their situation. This group had a definite gender imbalance (three males and twenty-two females), and this added to the diversity of the group in the sense that it provided the men in the class an unusual experience of being in a minority. For the two American males (both white, both members of fraternities) it was probably quite a new experience. Having so few men in the group was also a warrant against the common occurrence of men's dominating discussion in coed classes.

Perhaps a fifth of the group were sorority or fraternity members, and the group had both in-state and out-of-state students from urban, suburban, and rural backgrounds.

An additional vivid presence in the group was a returning student, a thirty-five-year-old woman from a working-class background who had given up a relatively high-paying job in retail sales and was mortgaging her future to get an education. She had run into all of the bureaucratic obstacles put in the way of nontraditional students (i.e., other than the eighteen-year-old, full-time residential student whose parents pay the bills) in a "major research university."

She was vocal about her grievances against the university and about her awareness of being "deviant" in a sea of eighteen to twenty-two year olds. She was also politically quite aware and sophisticated.

One other student should be mentioned in this roster of diversity in the section. (For simplicity, the more diverse section will be designated Section B.) She was a student from the Business School, a senior, who can only be described as a booster for free enterprise and the value of competition as the preferred mode for all human activity. She fervently held that individual effort is the most powerful force determining success and social status and assumed that the playing field is level. Except for her good humor, she might have been on the editorial board of the *Michigan Review*.[1] She was open and assertive about her conservative views, and it became clear early in the term that hers was a widely divergent worldview in this group. Yet no one attacked her, put her down, or ignored her. People argued with her, but they granted her a humane, respectful hearing before answering her. A number of students behaved as models of civil, respectful behavior in these exchanges. She argued and presented her case with good humor and an absence of rancor.

The other section of the course (Section A) was considerably more homogeneous. As we have indicated, the group included only one minority group member. The sex ratio was less extreme in this section, with around a quarter of the class male. Rural-urban status did come to the fore in this section but was not of great moment to many members of the group.

Minority students in the more diverse section (Section B) knew that they were not alone—that each of them had potential backing and support from the other minority students—and at the same time, they had clear individual views and experiences that would prevent their always having to feel that they spoke "for the Black community." Always to be treated and reacted to this way—as a member of a class rather than as an individual—denies one's individuality and humanity. It is as though the only thing that people see about you or react to is your skin color or ethnicity. Being one of three unique individuals who also happen to share an important group membership requires others to respond both to your individuality and your common feature.

Having a viable co-culture in the class was most clearly liberating for one of the minority students. At the beginning of the term this young woman —let's call her Martha—was very shy, very quiet, even wary. She clearly gave the interaction keen attention, but her stance and her silence signaled caution.

Within weeks Martha had heard numerous discussions touching on race, discrimination, and intergroup relations. She had heard the other two African American women (both much more assertive than Martha) speak of their experiences on and off campus. On one or two occasions she was specifically asked by one of the other women to validate a judgment or experience. By the end of six weeks, she was entering discussion in a much more initiating and self-contained way. Her shyness had dissipated noticeably. She volunteered to work with a group that was developing a research project. She has maintained a relationship with one of us, her instructor, by stopping at the office now and then to discuss things that are going on in her courses. She seems to have gained self-confidence that serves her well in dealing with the world beyond our class.

So our first important insight—not really originated in this class but forcefully represented in it—is that the setting for discussion of diversity and pluralism should itself be diverse. A corollary is that underrepresented groups should be represented by more than a token individual. The sine qua non of open discussion is a certain level of trust in one's safety in the group, and it is not possible for most people to feel safe if they are alone in representing a group or a position.

This was powerfully demonstrated for us in the contrasting ways in which discussion of the readings on racism went in the two sections. In the group with only one minority student, leading discussion was sometimes highly problematic. Individual students would assert strongly that they were attuned to difference and that racism existed in other people, that racist attitudes existed "out there." It was difficult for the instructor (with his position of authority) to confront such statements without seeming to pummel students for holding "wrong" attitudes. It was impossible for the single black student in the class to speak up at this juncture.

Once when the single Black student was absent from the class, the discussion turned to students' concern about Black prejudice in the dormitories, and what followed can only be described as an outpouring of anxiety and indignation. Students complained that Blacks had their own lounge and activities, which excluded White students. One young woman asserted that university and housing officials extended special privileges to African American students in what she described as reverse discrimination. The tone of the discussion contrasted sharply with those that had taken place in the group when the Black student was present.

This discussion also contrasted sharply with a very similar discussion in Section B, the more diverse group. In this case, the issue of Black racism arose in a different (even surprising) context. A White student said that she was afraid to talk about racism for fear that she would be accused of being a racist (meaning, we think, that she does not think of herself as racist but that her perhaps conservative, individualistic ideology would be interpreted as racist). At this point one of the Black women—a quiet-spoken but very clear and quietly assertive young person—spoke up and asked, "Now, how many of you think that there is also racism in the Black community?" She then went on to describe what had been the reaction of friends in her Detroit neighborhood when she announced that she was going to enter this university. "They told me that the university is a racist school, that I wouldn't be welcome, that it was just for Whites and why would I want to go to a place like that? So, you see, I know that there is racism among Blacks." This extraordinary, open, rueful disclosure provided an opening for several students and the instructor to point to the structural difference of racism between powerful and powerless classes. Expressing regret about racism wherever it occurs, these speakers nonetheless wanted to underline the critical difference contributed by power: holding stereotyped and racist attitudes makes more difference when the person holding them is in a position to deny opportunity to members of the group they target to oppress.

This led quite naturally into a discussion of the article by Peggy McIntosh entitled "White Privilege: Unpacking the Invisible Knapsack" (1989), in which she describes the many ways in which her position as a member of the dominant White culture exempts her from the apprehensions and alienation to which Blacks are subjected daily in our racist culture. This reading is especially apposite for helping White students understand why Blacks might be wary in settings where their sense of themselves and their culture is not automatically considered in the texture of everyday life and why being alien in a dormitory where the reference audience is always White might make Blacks sensitive to unintended slights.

A second insight from the class had to do with the relative ease of discussing various forms of prejudice and discrimination. For these bright young students at this moment in American history, it seems much easier to be open in discussions of sexism than in discourse about racism. This could be an effective point of departure for discussion of differences between forms and bases of discrimination, but we did not always feel either prepared or skillful enough to do this very effectively.

The most vivid use of readings involved the structural features of groups: being a minority or majority in a group and the effects that has on attitudes and group behavior. Class members designed exercises to involve students in these processes. Again it was easier for them to use gender than race as the differentiating characteristic, but the generalization to racial composition in groups was often possible.

INVOLVING STUDENTS

A third principle—again, one that we had credited before this experience but were more strongly impressed with after—is the necessity of providing opportunities for active learning, rather than relying on traditional lecture methods in teaching. Clearly the design of the course reveals that we are committed to the exercise method, the participatory form of classroom learning. We ask students to design and carry out a research project, and we actively involve each student in the design and conduct of at least one or two discussion sessions. These modes of learning offer students a chance to get to know each other better through collaborative work. Sometimes strong friendships develop around the discovery of common intellectual and value positions. Allowing students—perhaps, especially, students from different ethnic backgrounds—to interact in more than a single setting increases the possibility that they will make such discoveries, get to know each other as whole persons rather than only as co-students.

We are also coming to feel, after some forty years of teaching college students, that the effects of television are by no means restricted to early socialization. Contemporary college undergraduates, sitting in a large audience, listening to a presentation by someone behind a lectern, are likely, we think, to lapse into a

TV mode. They have watched and listened to thousands of hours of television presentations by the time they enter college, and their ready response to a lecturer is to relax and be entertained. They expect a polished performance from a professional performer. They expect, as one student put it, that the film (or lecture or panel discussion) will be "well edited." This places an extraordinary and recently added demand on the "performer." Active, project-based involvement in course materials seems a more compelling and effective way to make intellectual connections with contemporary students. Perhaps it always was, but the fact is that in the past we weren't challenged as much to provide imaginative alternative approaches to learning as we are currently.

In addition we are convinced that teaching students how to work in collaboration—that is, how to amalgamate two or more views and constructions of the world into a meaningful and coherent intellectual product—is an important and significant gift we can offer them. As the occupational world becomes more competitive and individualistic, it also becomes less satisfying and meaningful to workers. Our research on changes over time in the way that American adults experience their work and family roles has made clear this relationship between individualistic competitiveness and disaffection with work (Veroff, Douvan, and Kulka 1981).

It also seems to us that in many cases the individualistic construction of work is a delusion and that continuing to teach our students as though their future work will be done in splendid isolation and in competition with everyone else is to encourage distorted and inaccurate expectations. Most work is collaborative. Furthermore, social interaction with colleagues and peers is the source of a great deal of creativity and stimulation. We want to teach our students in a way that allows them to experience satisfying and creative collaborations. We think that the active involvement that projects and exercises elicit is an effective way to ensure that students learn.

Exercises designed by students themselves (albeit in consultation with an instructor) are most effective. Students identify with their peers who are trying to stage an exercise. We sometimes suggested that the students "pretest" exercises on friends to anticipate and modify procedural problems.

Some examples of exercises that effectively promoted discussion of diversity issues are:

1. The effect of minority group membership on behavior and feelings. In the class with a larger minority of males, the leaders created four groups, two in which a woman was the token and two in which a male was the token. The groups were told to imagine they were a work team facing a problem (provided in a written scenario). They were to discuss the problem and decide on a course of action. The class was asked to observe each group discussion in turn. The participants in the teams were asked to describe their thoughts and feelings after the exercise was finished.

2. The importance of religious group membership in identity. The discussion leaders asked a group of volunteers how religious affiliation affected their thoughts about

themselves and others. Would they marry a person of a different faith? Why? Why not? Raise their children in their own faith? and so on.

3. Treatment of service workers. Students were asked to role-play ordering in a restaurant. Unbeknownst to the diners, the waitperson had been asked to be either very acquiescent and attentive or assertive. Differences in the diners' responses to these styles were discussed, particularly the meaning of "knowing one's place."

The student research projects also often took diversity issues as a focus. We encouraged this focus wherever possible. Some examples of topics that opened issues of diversity were the effect of moving from a small town to a larger city (high school seniors in a rural community were interviewed about their post–high school plans); the effects of fraternity/sorority membership on behavior and self-definition; the effect of being from mixed racial parentage.

Results of the studies were not usually clear-cut, but the act of stating hypotheses, figuring out how to measure relevant variables, and thinking about what the results might mean—and doing all this in a collaborative team—was a powerful experience that often stimulated students to think about issues of diversity in new and vivid ways.

To engage students in exercises and discussions of complex issues of race and difference—discussions that may be hard for young people particularly because our culture in general would rather avoid such issues and deny difference and conflict (as though they were not somehow fit topics for civil exchange) and expect them to put their honest reflections on the table and take part in an open and honest exchange—one must clearly first establish a sense of trust, an understanding that students are not going to be punished or hurt for their views or values. They are not going to be asked to give up their identity or to change toward some common view or attitude. An open and authentic encounter with difference needs to be presented as a complex and difficult human enterprise that no known culture has ever managed very well. No human group has achieved an ideal accommodation to difference, a perfectly humane response to "the other." Therefore, this group, this class of learners, is entering a human quest as explorers, venturing into largely uncharted waters, and students' willingness to do so must be hailed as an act of courage and humanity. The situation should be made as safe as possible. It will take time together to build trust and faith in each other before they will be able to risk expressing their own views and observations.

PROVIDING A MODEL

How can one encourage the development of trust and create a safe atmosphere for students? While our experience in this particular realm of concern—trust and openness in discussion of race, racism, and discrimination—is limited, we have years of teaching experience that provide us a few principles important in creating trust in a classroom. These refer to the role of the teacher. The college teacher leading discussion must act as a model and exemplar of respectful, non-punitive, civil advocacy. When a student expresses a view with which the professor disagrees, even finds appalling, the teacher must, of course, respond with intellectual, logical, evidential argument against that view. But she or he must do so in the context of respect for the person of the student presenting the views. In this the professor is following the principle of the Quakers, who "recognize God in every person." No matter how foolish, wrong, naive, or offensive the views a person states, one must credit the person's humanity in order to make any contact or have any meaningful discourse.

This will be more or less easy for individual teachers to do and more or less difficult for any of us depending on the particular offending statement the student makes. But it is clearly true that if we wish to reach a student and potentially have an influence on the student's thinking (the purpose, we assume, of any teacher in liberal education), we can only hope to do so only by first allowing the student his or her personhood and respecting her or his integrity. In following this principle, the teacher reassures the student whose views have offended that the teacher will not use either authority or unfair tactics to put the student down, defeat him or her, or damage her or his *amour propre* in front of the class. The other students in the class learn the same things and experience a model of the kind of argumentation that the teacher hopes to encourage in discussion.

Suppose a male student makes a blatantly sexist remark or refers to a gay male with a pejorative term; the teacher cannot let the remark stand, yet does not want to attack the male student. A reasoned response says to the student, "Let me tell you why that remark is unfair and offends others and me." The situation is delicate because as teachers we have powers that can seriously affect students. A White male teacher, in particular, may find his position in such a discussion peculiar. The authors have both had the experience of searching for the *mot juste* when a woman student intervened to object to the offending statement and offer an explanation. We think that this is the ideal resolution since we are convinced that peers are often more likely to be heard and credited.

Occasionally a teacher has an opportunity to mediate a conflict between two students and model respectful and civil behavior in the role of moderator, neither rejecting nor harming either of the disputants but raising to conscious attention the kind of behavior that is expected and encouraged in educated, liberal discourse. We have each had this opportunity on occasion, an opportunity to intervene when a long-standing and rancorous difference between two students expresses itself in an argument that becomes so heated that the two interrupt each other, overshout each other, and generally do not allow or hear the arguments of the other. Here, by stepping in and holding the disputants to rules of discourse that allow each side a hearing, the teacher can again model acceptable patterns and permit the disputants to experience the difference between unproductive, disrespectful discourse and exchange that is respectful and potentially productive of genuine understanding, clarification, and growth.[2]

ENCOURAGING TRUST

Aside from the suggestion that the teacher model acceptable forms of discussion under pressure (which also requires that the teacher be up-front about her or his own attitudes and deeply held values), we have few specific suggestions for how to create a safe and trustworthy classroom atmosphere—at least few suggestions for things that the teacher can do consciously. The rest of the insights we can offer come from things that the students themselves did—more or less consciously—to create trust.

The first thing that occurred, in one of the earliest class discussions, was an exercise that dealt with trust and that required and reinforced risk taking and demonstrated that the classmates who asked a student to risk were, in fact, trustworthy. The exercise was never phrased in these terms. Consciously it was designed by the student discussion leaders to demonstrate the effect of gender on the willingness to risk. We were at an early point in the course syllabus dealing with the influence of social factors on individual behavior.

The two student discussion leaders had recruited two others to help with the exercise. The four then asked for volunteers to participate in an exercise. They chose a male and a female to participate and proceeded with what is a model exercise in trust. They blindfolded each of the volunteers in turn and had one of the leaders lead the blindfolded person on a silent journey in and out of the classroom, going up and down stairs, and so on.

The gender difference the leaders expected did not appear, but what did appear in palpable form was the trustworthiness of the leaders, their care and sensitivity in leading the blindfolded class member, and the volunteers' willingness to trust and growing relaxation and trust as the short trip progressed. It was a salutary experience for a classroom group about to engage in discussions for which trust would be a critical underpinning condition.

Our Business School woman began to establish her special role in the group early, indicating that she did not think that social structure influenced individual behavior and that it was perfectly within the individual's power to influence social structure. She illustrated with her own case: she had grown up in a working-class family (not, in fact, quite true) and was planning to become a member of the upper class by becoming an executive in American industry. Her willingness to challenge the basic assumptions of the course early on and the serious, respectful response of the instructor and her classmates again exemplified the safety of the class environment and reinforced a sense of trust.

Therefore, by the time the young women confessed that she was afraid to talk about race on campus because she was afraid she would be accused of being racist, there was a base of trust in the group that allowed her at least to bring up the topic. There was openness enough to allow one of the Black women to respond with empathy and to disclose a painful experience she had had within the Black community.

Throughout the semester, discussions in Section B were open, non-defensive, and illuminating. At the end of the course, many of the students—minority students and majority members, sorority and fraternity members, social science majors and students from other fields who had had only one or two previous social science courses—said that the course had been the best they had ever had at the university. Of course, many of the students had never had classes as small as this one, but we understood this also to reflect students' relief to discuss critical issues they had encountered in their own experience (issues that are often denied or ignored) and to be able to engage in such discussion openly in a trustworthy setting.

The students in this class were special in many ways. One young White woman whose dress, speech, and general demeanor clearly reflected her upper middle-class background, spoke of her thrill at discovering, when she first came to the university, its "terrific" (and, to her, terrifically interesting) diversity.[3] She said:

You know, in my town you knew only people who were just like you. They looked like you, talked like you, thought like you. I could tell you exactly what any person in my school thought about just about anything. If I had gone to college in the East, I would have been with the same kind of people again. But when I came out here, my first roommate was from Kansas City. Talk about different! She talked different, and she thought about different things. She is great. We're best friends, and I never would have known a person like that if I hadn't gotten out of my own little cocoon.

As we say, they were special. But probably not all that much more special than any class of Michigan students would be if you saw them in a setting that drew out their most interesting, thoughtful, responsive qualities. It was, we are convinced, the level of trust that developed in this group that allowed students to disclose attitudes and experiences and to listen to each other with genuine interest and understanding.

NOTES

1. The *Michigan Review* is a paper published by conservative students. It is comparable to the notorious *Dartmouth Review*, which has been the center of controversy on the Dartmouth campus; however, the Michigan version has never attracted the same level of attention or conflict.

2. We do not mean that passion is unacceptable in classroom discourse. We are highly skeptical of the idea of debate—that is, that a person should be able to argue any position, even one he or she does not believe. But we are teachers, and we therefore believe that civil discourse can affect people whereas refusing to hear someone will never allow us to influence that person. It should be stated clearly that this is an ideal to which we do not always adhere.

3. We are reminded that judgments are relative and are constrained by perspective and experience. Although we consider the university population very homogeneous compared with our aspirations for it, the upper middle-class, eastern suburban community that this young woman came from makes the university seem very heterogeneous in comparison.

Part V

Teacher Training and Nonformal Education

Working with teachers and professional staff who also often teach requires the development of innovative strategies on the part of facilitators. The chapters in this part embrace a variety of innovations that have been used successfully. We believe, in addition, that these have utility when adapted for populations in other educational institutions and organizations. The Zúñiga and Nagda chapter offers insights into a strategy gaining increasing use, the dialogue group. Dialogue groups have begun springing up across campus and provide students, faculty, and staff with opportunities to "face off" with dissimilar groups to discuss important aspects of their interaction. A successful experiment in teacher training, FAIRteach, is described in the Frankel chapter. This innovation provides a necessary vehicle for teachers who are attempting to incorporate a multicultural perspective into their courses, as it focuses on pedagogical as well as content, issues. The Edwards, Myers, and Toy chapter focuses on the provision of accurate information on the lives of gays and lesbians to students and staff across the campus and wider community, through the Lesbian and Gay Male Programs Office. Finally, the Schoem chapter focuses on training teaching assistants so that they, in turn, can work effectively with undergraduate student populations.

20

Dialogue Groups: An Innovative Approach to Multicultural Learning

Ximena Zúñiga and Biren A. Nagda

College students today are becoming participants, knowingly or unknowingly, in the cultural and social metamorphoses accompanying the changing demographics on campus and nationwide. As students come into contact and begin to interact with members of different social groups, the scope of their personal and social inquiry increases. Questions such as, Who am I? With whom do I want to identify? What groups do I belong to? expand to a curiosity about others: Who are they? What groups do they identify with? What do they believe in? Why are they behaving that way? As students are challenged to interact further with, and learn about, each other, questions about their interrelationship may arise: Why are my views being challenged? Why is she or he so different from me? Why are they treating me that way? How am I treating them? What impact are they having on me, and me on them?

These questions are among the many that are being confronted in a new form of student discussion—dialogue groups. A dialogue group is a face-to-face meeting between members of two groups that have a history of conflict or potential conflict. The students' seemingly personal and internal deliberations are brought out in the open to encourage joint ''thinking aloud'' with the hope of linking their personal psychological world to larger sociological processes and structures. Dialogue groups were developed as an initiative to educate undergraduates about various forms of conflict among social groups and to explore alternative ways of conflict resolution to promote understanding and positive intergroup relations.[1] This curriculum effort links academic learning and course work to the living and social experiences of students outside the classroom. The effort is guided by the philosophy of systematic instruction, substantial interaction, and meaningful dialogue among the various groups to build truly multicultural communities.

In this chapter we first look at the institutional climate surrounding the dialogue groups. Next, we provide some examples of dialogue groups and consider student experiences of the dialogues. We then discuss the ways in which these dialogue groups are organized and facilitated. Finally, we focus on the critical challenges and dilemmas in developing and implementing a pedagogy of dialogue.

THE INSTITUTIONAL CLIMATE

Dialogue groups have emerged as an effective means of challenging the prevailing institutional climate on college campuses, a climate that poses serious limitations for positive intergroup interactions among students of different social and cultural backgrounds. Although interrelated and mutually reinforcing, these limitations can be found in three general areas—institutional structure, content, and process.

Institutional forces perpetuate the lack of positive interactions among the different groups that make up the campus social mosaic. As institutions of higher education increase the representation of students and faculty of color, the possibility of building multicultural communities is not, as many students hoped during their high school campus visits, immediately and readily available. The current emphasis on augmenting minority representation, in numbers alone, is not sufficient to change the existing structures of power, authority, and opportunity in the institution.

The content of the academic curriculum is usually characterized by the dominant group's interpretation of the issues and of history; a particular view of the world is emphasized. As Anglo-European institutions of higher education are challenged to change and build diverse and inclusive communities, ignorance and misinformation about other world views, especially those of subordinated groups, needs to be creatively confronted both inside and outside the classroom.

The process aspect of the limitations refers to the actual interactions that occur between and among the various participants in the campus community. One core component of the process is the teacher-student relationship in the classroom. The classroom climate emphasizes a "banking" pedagogy, a didactic method of knowledge accumulation based on the idea that the student is an empty vessel to be filled by the expert-teacher (Freire 1972). This social arrangement not only reinforces the hierarchical relationship between the teacher and the students but contributes to accentuate the separation among students. In the classroom they are encouraged to relate to or through the instructor, rather than with each other. Moreover, a distinction is made between the intellectual and the experiential; the former is construed as belonging in the classroom while the personal remains outside.

In their out-of-class lives, students are heavily involved in interactions with other students. Separation among individuals from different social and cultural groups is the norm in these interactional processes. Recent developments at universities, such as Berkeley, serve to highlight the separateness that occurs on campuses that are rapidly becoming racially and ethnically diverse; small racial/

ethnic "quarters" are cropping up that mirror larger segregation patterns—
Harlem, Chinatown, and so on.[2] Despite the diversity in numbers, there remains
a homogeneity in the students' social networks: "It is like a college mixer where
no one mixes."[3]

These aspects of the institutional climate, separately and together, hinder
instructive and constructive intergroup relations among college students. Dialogue groups, therefore, have emerged as one possible intervention for addressing
and challenging the dire drought in positive intergroup interactions that prevails
on college campuses.

THE DIALOGUE GROUP LEARNING PROCESS: EXPERIENCES OF STUDENTS

The dialogues are a discussion format that usually occurs between members
of two self-identified social groups.[4] The most common focus of intergroup
dialogues is interracial/interethnic. Examples include Blacks and Whites, Whites
and People of Color, Blacks and Jews, Blacks and Latinos, Chicanos(as) and
Puertorriqueños(as), and Blacks and Asian Americans. The next set of dialogues
is structured around gender, such as men and women, Black men and Black
women, Asian American men and Asian American women, and gay men and
Lesbians. Dialogues involving gay men, lesbians, bisexuals, and heterosexuals
and involving lesbians, bisexuals, and heterosexual women are grouped around
sexual orientation. Last, religion is the primary focus of the Christians and Jews
group.

Students enter the dialogue group process with varying expectations, influenced by their knowledge and misconceptions about members of the other group,
their ability to confront conflict, and their relative positions in the varying dominant-subordinate power relationships. For some students, the expectation is
clearly to educate others:

As a Black woman I want to tell people my story; I want to educate people on my story.
The dialogues allow that process to occur, and it is very empowering for participants.
. . . It is great to know that someone is really listening to me (student, Blacks and Whites
dialogue).

For others, the desire to participate is colored by a deep-seated hostility toward
"the other" and a strong desire to fight for their points of view:

I entered the dialogue with a "shark" mentality. I was determined to get across my
views, and I was adamant in making my opinions be the focal point of the discussions.
There was so much hostility built up within me against the African American community.
I was under the uninformed impression that all African Americans were anti-Semitic
(student, Blacks and Jews dialogue).

For still others, the expectation is to get to know people they otherwise wouldn't talk to, much less discuss "issues" with, be it in the residence hall or in the classroom.

Students' evaluations indicate that the dialogue groups provide an excellent opportunity for individual and intergroup learning. The experiences reported by facilitators and student participants range from simply getting an idea of group differences and learning about "the other group" to questioning and challenging societal processes and structures that perpetuate the schism between the groups to developing a sense of relational identity and alliance with the other group. Some intergroup dialogues—Whites and Blacks, Blacks and Jews, gays/lesbians/bisexuals and heterosexuals, Christians and Jews, Whites and people of color—have allowed students openly to discuss stereotypes and prejudices, recognize commonalities and differences, and break some barriers in the estranged relationship. Other dialogues—Latinos and Blacks, Chicanos(as) and Puertorriqueños(as), Blacks and Asians—have allowed students not only to explore stereotypes and prejudices, but also to appreciate the diversity of experiences among "minority" groups and collectively discuss issues they face at the university. The different lessons reported by the students are discussed below.

Opportunity to Break Down Barriers

Students find that the dialogue groups offer a unique space for them to talk about issues with people they rarely interact with:

We are getting people who don't normally talk to each other or communicate with each other. I think a lot of times you have people who are talking to each other but they are not listening. As the weeks go by you can see them kind of go, "I never thought of it like that" (cofacilitator, Blacks and Whites dialogue).

As a White man do I want to talk to a Black person about racism? It can be really scary. I feel like a dialogue group is really a safe place for people to talk about difficult issues. We can sit down and can talk about these issues and learn. In our group, people were afraid at the beginning. . . . Do we want to discuss homophobia with homosexuals? It can be intimidating. But we got over the fear and we got talking (student, gays and straights dialogue).

As students become more comfortable, they are able "to ask questions they had never asked before."[5] They are thus able to get to know each other and tear down pieces of the psychological wall that separates their lives:

Our meetings served as a forum where questions could be asked of us, no matter how ignorant or insensitive they might have been, and be answered honestly. It was so strange to be able to ask those questions that were bottled up inside of you forever and not be afraid of what kind of reaction they might receive (student, Blacks and Whites dialogue).

The opportunity to talk and explore difficult topics allows students to get closer to students with whom they would not otherwise associate. In many instances, the momentum stirred up by the dialogue is such that students "would just hang around" after the session was over.[6] In some instances, the dialogue spills over into the students' living quarters.

After group that day, one of the African American students and I went up to my room to further discuss things. While we spoke that evening, he explained to me why he didn't consider America his home. This conversation may have been the single greatest learning experience I have had at this campus. It enabled me, for a moment, to step into the shoes of an African American and see the world through his eyes. I wouldn't trade that experience for anything (student, Blacks and Jews dialogue).

Opportunity to Challenge the Ignorance Inside and Outside Oneself

Students also value the peer education opportunities of the dialogue group. First, students have the opportunity to challenge the misconceptions perpetuated by segregation and prejudice. For instance, a student of color reports that the dialogue allowed him to confront some of the misconceptions White students have about minority students' college life:

I never had such a deep discussion with people of the opposite race before. I never actually realized how many misconceptions people of the White race have about minority races. For example, some of the White students thought that minority lounges were places where we sat around talking about White students or blamed them for the oppression of our race. I just assumed everyone knew that minority lounges were there to reinforce our knowledge about our culture. Some White students thought that minority organizations were groups "out to get White people." The people of color told the White students that minority organizations provide them with information about their culture they could not learn in the classrooms (student, Whites and People of Color dialogue).

The dialogues also enable students to challenge the education they have received since elementary school about their own group and other groups. As a student said, "The education we have received is so bizarre that we had to re-learn things not only about the other group but about ourselves too."[7] In this dialogue between students of different minority groups, the re-learning process included inviting speakers, reading articles, and watching videos to access information they had not received in the classroom.

Second, students are able to discover that their preconceptions about members of the other group are often ill-founded. This process can take time; yet in some instances just feeling listened to is sufficient to start challenging some of the misconceptions:

I previously thought that Christian people were completely uninterested in the Jewish faith. I saw us, Jews, always learning about their religion while they were prejudicially judging us without knowing anything about Judaism. I was pleasantly surprised to witness the Christians' curiosity and desire to better understand our religion (student, Christians and Jews dialogue).

In other instances, discovering the heterogeneity within the other group can serve as a catalyst for reframing the ways members of each group perceive the other:

I discovered that not all White students resent minorities being on campus. I thought that every White student saw me as a statistic or filling a quota. But when I asked the White students how they felt about minorities on campus, they said that they resented some of the affirmative action laws that worked against them but they did not resent minorities. One person said that diversity brings a multicultural atmosphere which will help everyone be able to relate to all types of people in society (student, Whites and People of Color dialogue).

However, a crucial step in the process of understanding the intergroup relationship is for students to critically examine their own prejudices and establish connections that allow them to refute the misconceptions:

I had always assumed that African American students had no desire to mix with students of other ethnic groups, but I soon found out that they did not try to segregate themselves at all. They just spent time with each other in order to unite. It is interesting that although many Whites do not mix with members of other racial groups, they are never accused of segregating themselves (student, Blacks and Whites dialogue).

New Insights, New Connections, New Identities

As students reflect on their own and others' experiences and the impact of group identity upon their lives, new insights and connections are made possible. In some instances, the need to vent, though at times painful, gives participants the opportunity to feel the impact of oppression in their lives in unexpected ways:

Each side began something which I later learned was called "ranking oppression." Members of each side kept citing specific examples where they felt that they were treated poorly. Each side had so much hostility, not necessarily about each other, but just in general. It was very ugly and it hurt a lot to watch this transpire. However, this spontaneous release showed me just how much we all carried different feelings of oppression (student, Blacks and Jews dialogue).

As the sharing continues and students challenge each other, they discover some consequences of discrimination and monoculturalism and ways in which these are institutionalized:

It was interesting to realize that although both groups—heterosexuals and homosexuals exist within the same American culture, we really belong to two very different cultures. The reason this is not very apparent is that homosexuals are forced to hide behind the "straight" image because society tells them they are unacceptable and denies their existence (student, gays/lesbians/bisexuals and straights dialogue).

Students also come to grips with their privileged status. White students realize the impact of race and the ways in which being a Caucasian is an advantage:

I realized that I was privileged. I don't have to endure the same daily rigors that a Black student does. Being a member of the "White group" is like having a magic key that opens most doors, whereas Blacks must use two or three keys to open the same door (student, Blacks and Whites dialogue).

In other instances, students recognize the difficulty in accepting positions of privilege. As the following comment suggests, this can be particularly so for someone who usually experiences the world as a minority despite having the privileges of being a man:

I noticed when we had the discussion on sexism that my role changed. I quieted down. I didn't say anything. I just kind of sat there. I didn't know what to say. I really wasn't used to being in that kind of position. But I think it gave a different perspective that I know what it is like to be on the other side. I think that was very good, very helpful (student, Blacks and Jews dialogue).

In yet other instances, students discover the ways in which discrimination renders some groups invisible and powerless. As a student put it, "Homophobia pushes a group of people out of sight and causes them to be forgotten or not treated with the proper respect."[8]

New Questions

As students talk to each other, share experiences, ask questions, and challenge misconceptions they have learned, they become aware of the ways in which their views have been molded by social institutions. Thus, they are challenged to step beyond their prescribed reality to allow for more openness and newer understandings of self and group identity:

After learning so many ideas and approaches to understanding God, I found myself questioning my own religion. When the Jewish students in the group asked me about what it meant to be a Christian, I sometimes found myself articulating opinions and ideas for the first time. I began to ask myself about my own beliefs even as I defended them. This experience has helped me to be more open, not only to Judaism, but to all religions different from my own (student, Christians and Jews dialogue).

This process of redefinition can be painful and difficult to confront. For some, it involves dealing with internalized hatred and shame. It requires trust in the dialogue process:

Coming to a dialogue like this, I realized that I would have to face certain stereotypes that I had. For me, these stereotypes pertained to my own group (gay/lesbian) and not to the other. I was raised heterosexually. I grew up with the same ideas and misconceptions everybody did. I was enculturated by the same society that enculturated the heterosexual members of my dialogue group. Although I am a member of the gay community and have had considerable exposure to it, I still hold some of the stereotypes about it. I was afraid that the other gay members would be too militant . . . that they would feel that their role was to educate or change the heterosexual members of the dialogue group. I found that this was not the case. Members of both groups engaged in dialogue, and members of both groups changed (student, gays/lesbians/bisexuals and straights dialogue).

Building Coalitions—Possibilities and Limitations

Many students join the dialogue groups expecting to build coalitions. Sometimes this expectation rests mostly on the goals envisioned by facilitators:

As facilitators we have approached these dialogues with the idea of trying to develop more unity, coalitions between Blacks and Latinos. How successful you are has a lot to do with where the student participants are at when the dialogue group starts (cofacilitator, Blacks and Latinos dialogue).

However, the possibility of identifying a common plan at the end of the process depends on the participants and their own political agendas:

The people who were involved in the Black student organization or the Latino student organization were much more politically motivated. They were thinking much more in terms of building coalitions and making things happen on campus whereas students who had not really been involved in those types of organizations were more interested in finding out what the dialogue group was about (cofacilitator, Blacks and Latinos dialogue).

At other times the desire to build alliances rests on the commitments of individuals, and this can be a source of personal conflict:

I was really concerned about how I would be perceived by each of the groups in our first couple of meetings. I knew that although I would identify myself with the heterosexual group, my attitudes and values would be more similar to the other group. I was concerned that this position would land me firmly attached to neither group. This ended up being relatively true. To my group, I probably didn't quite seem like one of them, and as for myself, I dreaded identifying with them because my beliefs were quite different from theirs (student, gays/lesbians/bisexuals and straights dialogue).

Yet a critical issue involves each group's goals and expectations for the dialogue:

The Jewish students came in saying, "I want to sit down and have some good talks and come out of those talks with better understanding of what the issues are" whereas the African American students came in knowing that nothing is going to change in this Black/ Jewish or Black/White conflict without structural societal change, without a reordering of how goods are distributed. The Jewish students in there couldn't give them that. The Black students could give the Jews what they wanted. Both groups came with different expectations, different goals and for that reason this coalition building is not happening; it can't happen until the group with more resources says, "Look, I understand that I have something to give up in order for you to get what you need." Jews might feel very comfortable coming in and talking but when it comes down to giving up resources and access to resources it may be a different story (cofacilitator, Blacks and Jews dialogue).

THE ORGANIZATIONAL STRUCTURE OF DIALOGUE GROUPS: "NUTS AND BOLTS"

The implementation of dialogue groups generally involves four major tasks: determination of the intergroup focus, selection and training of dialogue group facilitators, organization and supervision process, and development of educational resources.

The specific intergroup focus and goals of the dialogue group are determined by a consideration of factors that include the needs and areas of interest of potential participants and the assessment of intergroup relations and climate in various settings (e.g., residence halls, academic units, and the campus at large).[9]

Dialogue groups are facilitated by a two-person cofacilitation team made up of one member of each of the participating groups. For example, a Black and Latino dialogue is cofacilitated by a student of African American descent and one of Latino descent. Ideally, cofacilitation teams are also of different sexes. The facilitators are selected through an application and interview process. The facilitators collectively form a vast pool of experience—"diversity" programmers; residence hall staff; former students in courses examining ethnic identity, intergroup relations, social inequality, and conflict. Facilitators undergo twenty four hours of training in communication, group observation, conflict management, group facilitation, and team-building skills.

Once assigned to a group, facilitators attend planning meetings to develop their respective group's agenda, to work on participant recruitment, and to discuss and evaluate the entire process. They also attend regular supervisory meetings. Such meetings include discussing the preceding dialogue session, discussing the issues that the cofacilitation team is experiencing in the group, and preparing for the next sessions. They serve as an opportunity for ongoing consultation and feedback.

Facilitators also have access to a manual that includes readings about gender, race, ethnicity, class, religion, sexual orientation, and so on; multicultural and group process exercises; group facilitation tips and techniques; campus resources;

and finally, a session-by-session content-process outline to assist them with the planning of each session.

THE DIALOGUE GROUP PROCESS AND CONTENT:
A MODEL OUTLINE

The dialogue group process is structured according to a developmental approach to group work (Stanford 1977). Most dialogues meet for five to seven sessions for about two hours each. Each group is usually formed by fourteen to eighteen participants. In the first two sessions, the goal is to create an atmosphere conducive to dialogue and a constructive confrontation of misinformation and conflict. In session one, students discuss their hopes and fears and list their goals and expectations. They also identify the important ground rules that will help in working through the fears and fulfilling some of the expectations. A norm of active listening is established here with some practice exercises. In session two, students examine ways in which their group memberships affect each other's lives. Students are typically put in identity groups along race, ethnic, gender, or other lines to address specific questions. They continue this discussion in a fishbowl discussion.[10] The combination of these two activities—discussions in identity groups and fishbowl—allow for both intra- and intergroup dialogue. At the same time, it encourages students to explore their group identity. A specific goal of the second session is to identify some of the differences and conflicts that the groups may have with each other.

As part of identifying the dynamics defining the intergroup relationship, in the third session, students critically examine the messages they carry about each other through an exercise on stereotypes. Students analyze the consequences of these messages and the ways in which these are perpetuated in society.[11]

The fourth and fifth sessions are geared toward exploring the connections between students' feelings, attitudes, and behaviors and the institutional and structural forces that influence their relationship with members of the other group. Ideally, students begin to recognize their roles as perpetrators and as victims of discrimination. Students are involved in discussing topics that directly impact upon the intergroup relationship. For example, in an interracial-ethnic dialogue, the topics range from racial discrimination to reverse discrimination to affirmative action to monoculturalism. In a dialogue between men and women, possible topics include reproductive rights, rape culture, affirmative action, sexual harassment, and comparable worth. As students explore these topics, they further examine the impact of group identity on their values and positions.

Finally, sessions six and seven are devoted to building alliances and coming to closure. The alliance-building exercise allows students specifically to exchange information about the impact of group membership on their behaviors, attitudes, and positions along different issues.[12] It also allows students to specify possible actions that members of the other group can take to facilitate partnerships and constructive intergroup relations. The final activity of the dialogue group helps the group to come to closure practically and emotionally. Students brainstorm actions they can take at different levels and settings toward improving the intergroup relationship. The closing exercise is usually an affirmation exercise that validates the students' learning from and about each other during the seven-session period.

THE SPECIFIC CHALLENGES FACING THE DIALOGUE GROUPS

In addressing students' lack of opportunity for substantial interaction and learning, the dialogue groups face several challenges: promoting dialogue rather than debate, exploring the possibility of constructive conflict, examining the multiple layers of identity, and linking micro- and macrolevels of analyses.

Facilitating Dialogue, Not Debate

The concept of dialogue has emerged as a particular discussion format that is radically different from other forms, especially debate. Although both dialogue and debate involve similar communication processes—that is, hearing and understanding the "other"—the goals are different. For example, in a debate the presenters are expected to counter each other's assertions with arguments that attack the other's viewpoints and establish a perception of dominance over the other. David Bohm and F. David Peat (1987: 82–83) summarize the outcomes of such a process: "At best this may produce agreement or compromise, but it does not give rise to anything creative. Moreover, when anything of fundamental significance is involved, then positions tend to be rigidly non-negotiable and talk degenerates either into a confrontation in which there is no solution, or into a polite avoidance of the issues. Both these outcomes are extremely harmful, for they prevent the free play of thought and communication and therefore impede creativity."[13] In dialoguing, however, the goal is to understand and accept the group differences that may exist; it involves working on an ongoing process that validates and uses these differences constructively. It allows for the creative possibility of collaborative, "win-win" solutions to intergroup conflicts.

As can be expected, the process of learning to dialogue is not easy. Students are more used to "win-lose" than "win-win" modes of communication; that is, a "shark mentality" prevails. In fact, one of the major struggles that cofacilitation teams face early on is creating at atmosphere conducive to dialogue, rather than debate. The notion and practice of active listening, though new to most students before joining the group, is a skill quickly identified as critical for facilitating successful dialogue:

I really don't think I could have truly achieved the learning that I did in any other form than the dialogue group—at least not as readily as I did. Being in an atmosphere where active listening was stressed as well as trying to incorporate the reality of cultural dif-

ferences into conversing really took away some of the stumbling blocks that might have
been there in a different situation (student, Whites and People of Color dialogue).

One important aspect of active listening involves the ability to empathize with
others. More specifically, the personalization of issues helps in this ability:

One woman had the courage to admit that she had been confused about her feelings for
a long time. . . . This was the first time that she ever admitted this to anyone, and as she
began to unwind the story of how she first began to feel "different," I began to cry, and
I wasn't the only one. The pain and confusion that this woman felt really touched me,
and I truly empathized with her . . . but I think what touched me the most was the amount
of support [she received] from everyone (student, gays/lesbians/bisexuals and straights
dialogue).

Confronting Conflict Constructively

Students' fear of conflict discourages them from exploring and learning from
each other's differences. In dialogue groups they are provided an opportunity to
learn that conflict is unavoidable and that constructive conflict is possible; the
conflict is acknowledged, validated, and made overt:

I think that the conflict shows that you've really pushed over the fear of offending someone.
It is necessary to generate the conflict so people can feel comfortable talking with each
other. I think if there's one thing that these dialogue groups push towards and really do
a good job with is the idea that conflict is okay and it's okay to disagree as long as you
are open and can discuss it with people different from yourself rather than keeping these
feelings bottled up inside and not getting real answers from people who would know
(cofacilitator, Christians and Jews dialogue).

A key ingredient for constructive confrontation of conflict is safety. In their
evaluations, students emphasize the importance of creating a safe environment
that allows an honest expression of feelings, especially anger. For them, this
plays a crucial role in helping identify conflicts and facilitates the dialogue
process.

Examining the Multiple Layers of Identity

There is an ongoing challenge in exploring the different levels of students'
identities. For the most part, students are familiar with the concept of individual
identity: Who am I? is a preoccupation in their lives. In the dialogues, the notion
of group identity is emphasized. The extent to which students identify themselves
as part of groups tends to depend on their relative positions in the many dominant-
subordinate intergroup relationships. Students learn about the experiences of
being a member of the other group and examine their own group identities and
experiences. The challenge, however, is even greater than just examining the

dynamics of individual and group identities. As some statements cited earlier illustrate, there is yet another layer that students attempt to explore: relational identity. It challenges students to recognize the reciprocal impact they have on each other's identities. This involves not only a process of empathy about each other's experiences but an understanding of the social forces affecting their particular relationship and the society at large.

Linking the Micro- and Macrolevels of Analysis

The final challenge is to have the students link microlevel analysis of individual differences to a macrolevel analysis of group differences, commonalities, and cultures. A monocultural conceptualization of differences is individual and idiosyncratic; that is, differences between the "other" and "me" are particular only to "the two of us." On the other hand, multiculturalism strives to emphasize an analysis of group and cultural differences that impact on individual differences. A macrolevel analysis would also challenge students to recognize the social structural conditions that contribute to injustice, conflict, and oppression, as well as to their perceptions of the other groups and the value system informing their views of the world.

THE DILEMMAS IN DIALOGUE GROUP WORK

After three years of dialogue groups in which the number of groups has almost doubled annually, we are still learning about this pedagogy, new to the University of Michigan campus and nationwide.[14] We now discuss the major dilemmas of this type of work—defining the primary intergroup focus, the limits and possibilities of using a peer education model, the educational role of cultural minorities, and the need to confront misinformation or lack of information about dominant-subordinate groups and the relationship between them.

The selection of a specific intergroup focus imposes a primary group identity on the students. Dialogue groups generally involve self-identified members of two groups, such as African American and Whites, men and women. However, from a particular group composition other individual and group identities emerge; for example, a male and female dialogue comprised of students of diverse ethnic/racial backgrounds and sexual orientations is likely to confront other oppressions in addition to sexism. It, therefore, creates an interplay of issues that may change the specific focus of the dialogue. In some groups, students have suggested "renaming" the group to correctly reflect the actual foci of the group and the tensions that occurred around the central issues. For example, a very ethnically and racially diverse Whites and people of color dialogue group included people of various national origins and diverse cultural experiences. It soon redefined itself as a multicultural dialogue and focused on broader issues (e.g., First and Third World dialectics, language, culture, ethnicity, biracialism) than those anticipated by the facilitators and the process-content outline designed for that group. Similarly, a Blacks and Whites dialogue group comprised of several Caucasians who were also Jewish soon became a Blacks, Whites, and Jews dialogue that focused on issues of race and ethnicity in a predominantly White, Anglo, and Christian society.

Another factor that impacts the way in which an intergroup focus is actually negotiated is the prevalence of an "African American-White paradigm" for defining other intergroup conflicts. This framework usually acts as "the" reference for student participants when addressing issues of race and ethnicity. It renders invisible the experience of students who are not members of these two groups. The facilitators often need to redirect discussion to broaden students' frame of reference to include other groups and intergroup conflicts as well as enable other voices to be heard. At the same time, they need to encourage students to acknowledge the impact of the African American-White conflict on their lives, given the legacy of slavery and history of racial discrimination toward African Americans in the United States. For instance, a Whites and People of Color dialogue is likely to turn into an African Americans and Whites dialogue despite the presence of other students of color. Similarly, an African Americans and Jews dialogue is likely to struggle back and forth between being an African Americans and Whites and/or an African Americans and Jews dialogue.

The primary group focus is also a dilemma in that it forces students to examine their identity in terms of membership in only one group instead of allowing for a multiple group identity. As a Black male student earlier commented, the roles changed as they spoke of sexism, rather than racism. These two dilemmas jointly contribute to a struggle between focusing on the given intergroup focus and allowing for broader examination of issues. For example, facilitators and participants struggle between discussing sexism as it impacts all women and men and issues that are more specific to subgroupings, for example, African American women, African American men, White women, White men, lesbians, gay men, Latinas, Latinos, differently abled people, working-class people.

The emphasis on peer education is a dilemma in two respects. First is the necessity to validate students' experience and promote acceptance and at the same time encourage challenging of views and opinions that are inaccurate or offensive to others. An emphasis on acceptance of students' individual experiences should, therefore, not preclude questioning each other's interpretive framework. An important consideration here is the emphasis on dialogue, co-learning, and different ways of knowing and relating.

Second is the role of facilitators as peer educators. On college campuses, peer education is considered a potentially effective method of intervention, for example, in alcohol awareness, sexual assault prevention, and peer counseling. The dilemma emerges from the essential difference between dialogue groups and the other forms of peer education; rather than a single information-sharing session, dialogues have a content-process agenda for a five- to seven-week period that the facilitators are expected to follow. Therefore, the facilitators are put in a much more demanding and complex role. They are trained to serve as group facilitators. Group facilitation and cofacilitation are difficult tasks, and when the facilitators are also accustomed to the teacher-student hierarchy, it requires substantial training and supervision of the facilitators to develop skills, experience, and clarity about their role as peers in the dialogue.

Another important dilemma that we are confronted with is the role of "minority" students in the dialogue. Oftentimes they feel put in an educational role, informing and teaching other students in the dialogue. There are some new possibilities that are opened as a result. The sense of peerness described above and the possibility of "minority" group members, long silenced, being able to have a voice in the learning process are all benefits in accordance with our pedagogical approach. The dilemma is in the fine line between exploitation and empowerment.

Last, we have identified as a dilemma the need to recognize that both dominant and subordinate group members are misinformed. This lack of knowledge, however, operates differently for each group. For dominant group members, the ignorance lies in their knowledge about other groups and their own group; monoculturalism is indeed myopic, glorifying one group by denigrating the others. These biases permeate the relationship between dominant and subordinate group members both at the macrolevel and at the microlevel. Subordinated group members also suffer the consequences of monoculturalism. Although, in a dominant-subordinate relationship, the knowledge about the dominant group is pervasive, this knowledge may be based on the systematic misinformation that monoculturalism and discrimination produce. In general, cultural minorities know much about the dominant group, less than desired about their own group, and very little about other minority groups.

The dilemmas have challenged us in many ways, primarily in examining our educational framework. A newer definition of education has emerged through the dialogue groups; it involves a multicultural process that considers not only knowing about members of other groups but also knowing about one's own group(s) and knowing how to relate to, and actually relating to, members of other groups. It focuses on a synthesis of different levels of knowing and understanding: the intellectual and the experiential, the inside- and outside-classroom experiences, "me," my group and "they," the "other" group, the individual and the institutional, and the learner and the educator. A critical ingredient in this broader definition of multicultural education is the examination of the intergroup dynamics in a sociopolitical context. These various syntheses bring about a sense of relational identity. This identity emphasizes the dynamic relationship between the groups, the impact that "my" identities and position in society have on the "other's" identities and position and vice versa. It also examines the similar and different impacts of the socio-econo-political context on the identity of each group and the relationships among groups. The outcome is in the ability to recognize and work with the tensions of the interconnections among the "us" collectivity. In other words, this education values the opportunity to bridge connections among students as people, without denying the realities of power and privilege that set them apart and shape the student-student relationship at different levels.

The issues and processes addressed in the dialogue groups are difficult and are not easily resolvable as long as the lack of adequate structures and processes for intergroup interactions in the college community maintains the invisible, but psychologically real, walls that separate different groups. To be maximally beneficial, such changes in interaction processes need concurrently to challenge the institutional structure, content, and process. The dialogue groups provide a process and structure in which discourse about intergroup relations is examined and challenged in vivo, that is, in terms of real people experiencing real issues.

NOTES

We wish to acknowledge the students, facilitators, and colleagues with whom we have worked closely in continuing our understanding of the dialogue groups. We especially appreciate our discussions with John Diamond, Pat Gurin, Andrea Monroe-Fowler, Luis Sfeir-Younis, David Schoem, and Gen Stewart. We also thank Mark Chesler, John Diamond, Jane Mildred, and the editors for their helpful comments in reviewing the paper. Thanks also to our families for their patience and support.

1. The dialogue groups are part of a larger undergraduate initiative on Intergroup Relations and Conflict at the University of Michigan, Ann Arbor. The program, now in its third year of existence, is housed in the Pilot Program—a living-learning community for first- and second-year undergraduates that has long valued diversity and proactively explored racial and social conflict.

2. *New York Times*, May 18, 1991, 1.

3. M. Morganthau et al., "Race on Campus: Failing the Test?" *Newsweek*. May 6, 1991, 27.

4. The quotes cited in this paper are from students' and facilitators' papers and evaluations of their dialogue group experiences.

5. Student participant, Whites and People of Color dialogue.

6. Cofacilitator, Blacks and Jews dialogue group.

7. Cofacilitator, Blacks and Latinos dialogue.

8. Student participant, gays and straight dialogue.

9. Dialogue groups connected to courses provide an experience-based educational activity for students studying intergroup relations topics. For an example, see Chapter 5 in this volume. In other instances, dialogues are organized outside the classroom to manage specific intergroup conflicts and/or to explore the possibility of coalition work.

10. For a detailed description of this exercise, see Part Eight.

11. We often use "stereotypes" exercises similar to the one described by Katz 1978.

12. For a detailed description of this exercise, see Part Eight.

13. D. Bohm and F. D. Peat, 1987. "Transforming the Culture Through Dialogue," *Utne Reader* (March-April 1991).

14. In the 1988–1989 academic year, there was a total of eight dialogue groups initiated. Through 1990–1991, we have had a total of fifty groups, with 650 undergraduates participating.

21

Combating Homophobia Through Education

Billie L. Edwards, Patricia Myers, and Jim Toy

This chapter describes, analyzes, and evaluates educational programs on sexual orientation offered by the Lesbian-Gay Male Programs Office (LGMPO) to students, staff, and faculty at the University of Michigan and in neighboring communities and colleges. The authors are two white lesbians and an Asian American gay man who have been affiliated with the LGMPO for a combined total of thirty-five years, many of which have been spent developing and implementing the educational programs. We hope this chapter will encourage other institutions of higher learning to establish similar programs on sexual orientation and will be helpful to existing speaker's bureaus.

Most universities are a microcosm of our larger society, reflecting and recreating its values, attitudes, and behaviors. While it is accurate to say that the LGMPO was founded during a more liberal campus climate than we experience in the 1990s, one cannot overemphasize the past and present strength of homophobia. By its attitude, the university strives to keep invisible the lesbian and gay men's communities; by its silence attempts to render us powerless, thereby promoting a climate that chills our attempts to make the university environment more humane and welcoming; and it stifles our efforts to end discrimination and harassment.

If lesbians, gay men, and bisexual people did not experience discrimination, verbal harassment, and violent physical attack, the need for the Lesbian-Gay Male Programs Office and its services might not exist (Ager 1984; Goleman 1990; Greer 1986; Herek 1989; Kim 1988; Miessner 1989; National Gay and Lesbian Task Force 1987; Secor 1990; Vance 1990). But homophobia, a complex attitude of ignorance, fear, and hatred of homosexuality, is expressed through psychological and physical assaults that many lesbians and gay men survive every day (D'Augelli and Rose 1990; DeCecco 1985; Goldberg 1982; Lance

1987; Morin 1974; Serdahely and Ziemba 1985; Wells and Franken 1987; Young 1990).[1] In 1970 a group of lesbians and gay men on campus organized a student group, the Gay Liberation Front (GLF), to combat homophobia and its expression at the University of Michigan. Building upon the political achievements of women and African American students, members of GLF founded the Lesbian-Gay Male Programs Office in 1971.

THE LESBIAN-GAY MALE PROGRAMS OFFICE

Since the creation of the LGMPO, our staff has promoted an open and supportive environment at the university to help people experience their sexual orientation as a positive aspect of their identity. Toward this end, the LGMPO provides education about the concerns of lesbians, gay men, and bisexual people to predominantly heterosexual audiences; advocacy for the human and civil rights of lesbians, gay men, and bisexual people; crisis intervention and short- and long-term counseling for individuals, couples, and groups; and consultation and networking for clinical, political, social, and support groups.[2] The LGMPO also provides information, referrals, and liaison services to members of the university and the surrounding community. We are available to the students, staff, and faculty at the University of Michigan, and, as our resources permit, to members of southeastern Michigan communities who are in need of our services. In fact, we act as a clearinghouse and referral network to agencies and organizations serving lesbians and gay men nationwide.

Approximately 10 percent of the general population identifies as predominantly homosexual, according to generally accepted estimates. We suggest this sizable minority group is both similar to and different from other minority groups. We believe, with Howard University professor James Tinney (1983: 1), that "minority" is "a political category representing those persons in the human family, who for reasons other than some bio-physical difference, are negated and denied and discriminated against and oppressed." Similarly, Oliva Espín, in *Lesbian Psychologies* (1987: 39), compares the development of a positive homosexual identity with other forms of minority identity development; all involve a "process that must be undertaken by people who must embrace negative or stigmatized identities."

However, lesbians and gay men are different from other minority groups in several important ways. The familial support and understanding often essential in counteracting negative social messages directed toward people in ethnic, religious, or racial minorities are often not available to lesbians and gay men. Minority families generally help their children transform these messages by affirming the children's difference, validating their experiences, and teaching them coping skills, all of which are critical to the development of a positive self-identity. Lesbians and gay men are not raised in gay-affirming households. When families are told (and not all lesbians and gay men reveal this aspect of their identity to family members), time is needed for loved ones to come to grips with this new reality. The additional pain of seeing family members hurt by one's homosexual identification increases the isolation lesbians, gay men, and bisexual people experience. It is not uncommon for this process of gaining family support to take years, if it occurs at all. The very real possibility of losing one's family prevents many from taking the risk of self-disclosure.[3]

The choice of revealing one's minority status also distinguishes homosexual people from many of the social categories of people based on color or culture. In most circumstances, lesbians and gay men can "pass" for heterosexual unless they choose to divulge information about their sexuality or life-style. Thus, concealment of one's homosexuality can serve as a refuge that others, particularly most people of color, lack. However, choosing to remain invisible brings its own stresses. Being forced to compromise one's integrity by misinterpretation, withholding information, or manipulating language to hide one's sexual identity and intimate relationships often results in self-hatred, alienation, suicidal depression, substance abuse, and physiological impairment. In addition, we believe that invisibility, often necessary for survival in a homophobic society, is the greatest obstacle to obtaining human and civil rights for lesbians and gay men because it allows the actual numbers of gay people to be underestimated and many of the stereotypes of lesbians and gay men to remain unchallenged. Education can chip away at the ignorance, fear, and emotional distancing that permit homophobic individuals and institutions to continue to believe that lesbians and gay men are few in number, psychologically maladjusted, emotionally unstable, or defined solely by their sexual acts.

Like heterosexual people, lesbians and gay men are raised within a heterosexual social construct. As such, we are taught the same prejudices and oppressive behaviors as the dominant culture. In other words, white lesbians and gay men are racist (Bulkin, Pratt, and Smith 1984; Frye 1983: 128–51; Goldsby 1990; Hyder 1990; Rich 1979b; Rich 1986). Gay men are sexist (Larkin and Morse 1989; Frye 1983: 110–27; Harris 1989). Socioeconomic status and its impact on human lives are often ignored or dismissed as irrelevant by middle- and upper-class lesbians and gay men (Chrystos 1990; Fuller 1990; Lo et al. 1990; Lorde 1990; Smith et al. 1990). In response to this reality, the LGMPO has historically made a strong commitment to go beyond supportive rhetoric: we implement anti-racist, pro-feminist, and anti-classist strategies in all the LGMPO's endeavors.

The Lesbian-Gay Male Programs Office has, since its inception, held the belief that education is the most effective way to combat homophobia and work for systemic change within the University of Michigan (Smith 1990). Shortly after the LGMPO was established, the Educational Outreach Program (EOP) was formed to make educational presentations on lesbian and gay men's concerns, including homophobia and heterosexism.[4]

THE EDUCATIONAL OUTREACH PROGRAM

The primary goal of the EOP is to combat individual and institutional homophobia. We believe homophobia, an expression of sexism and other forms of oppression, is the primary "weapon" used to enforce heterosexuality and rigid gender roles (Pharr 1988). Our presentations provide an opportunity to render lesbians and gay men temporarily visible to our audiences. We believe this visibility helps confront and dispel fears of homosexuality. To demonstrate and generate support for the issues of lesbians, gay men, and bisexual people, we emphasize both the individuality and common humanity of lesbians and gay men. In addition, facilitators, as lesbians and gay men, provide positive models for the heterosexual and homosexual people in the audiences.

We believe that information about, and exposure to, lesbians, gay men, and bisexual people encourage attitudinal shifts that help create an environment in which all human beings can thrive. Raising the consciousness of audiences is of primary importance to the EOP. We believe that an intellectual grasp of the issues is only one objective of effective presentations. Equally important is the emotional component that encourages identification, clarification, and alteration of audience attitudes, values, and behaviors (Combs 1972; Fischer 1981; Raths, Harmin, and Simon 1966; Shapiro 1986; Weinstein and Fantini 1970; Young 1990: 155). We accomplish this goal by helping the audience identify and clarify their feelings about lesbians, gay men, and bisexual people. The presentations address misconceptions about sexual orientation, including stereotypes regarding occupations, parenting, relationships, gender identification, health, sexual behavior, and physical appearance. By helping audience members recognize and express their values and attitudes about homosexuality through exercises and discussion, we enable many to reach greater clarity, and an openness to change becomes possible.

Our presentations include specific information about individual and institutional prejudice, discrimination, harassment, and violence. We also outline the connections between various forms of oppression, while acknowledging specific experiences of particular stigmatized groups such as women, people of color, Jewish people, and working-class people. A major focus of our presentation encourages the audience to discriminate among facts, stereotypes, and generalizations when considering lesbians, gay men, or bisexual people. The facilitators utilize specific strategies to address ignorance and combat homophobia, taking into consideration the various roles and responsibilities of audience members, for example, residence hall staff, graduate student teaching assistants, campus security officers, personnel representatives, university administrators, counselors, physicians, and athletic trainers. Strategies may include lectures, brainstorming, values-clarification exercises, role playing, vignettes, handouts, and discussions.

The LGMPO and EOP have evolved over many years. We have strengthened our commitment to address the intersections of race, class, and gender oppression, both in our presentations and within the Lesbian-Gay Male Programs Office itself. The LGMPO's commitment to racial inclusivity is strongly reflected in the EOP's presentations. Lesbians and gay men of color, who face dual and sometimes triple oppression, are fundamental to our work.[5] We are aware that different races and cultures respond to homosexuality differently, and we seek opportunities to reach out to ethnic and racial minorities to combat homophobia within these communities (Hooks 1988; Moraga and Anzaldúa 1983: 107–65; Smith 1983: 145–213; Smith and Gomez 1990). We believe it is essential for people of color in the audience to hear and experience gay people of color. When addressed by other people of color, minority people are less able to deny the existence of lesbians and gay men within their own communities. At the same time, white heterosexual and homosexual people are able to hear more about the experiences of racism and the intersections of oppression based on sex, race, and sexuality.

The Educational Outreach Program has been an effective mechanism for social change both for the workshop participants and for the facilitators. Since 1988 the LGMPO-EOP has presented workshops to more than 12,275 students, staff, and faculty at the University of Michigan.[6] EOP presentations have been made in biology, English literature, Medical School, Nursing School, psychology, social work, sociology, and Women's Studies classes to undergraduate, graduate, and professional students. Increasingly, workshops to address homophobia have been requested by university offices, including the custodial staff, Information and Technology Division, Office of Student Orientation, Sexual Assault Prevention and Awareness Center, and other campus offices that provide support and advocacy services to students, staff, and faculty. Many agencies and institutions beyond the university make use of our programs as well, including other colleges, youth groups, service organizations, and health providers. Educational Outreach Program presentations have led to greater sensitivity to homosexuality and homophobia as demonstrated in workshop evaluations and in discussions following the presentations. The evaluations consistently demonstrate the effectiveness of these workshops in reducing overt homophobia arising from a lack of exposure to lesbians and gay men. Most workshop participants gain a greater understanding of the issues facing lesbians and gay men.

In addition to the benefits for the audience and society that result from EOP presentations, the EOP also plays a critical role in the lives of the EOP facilitators. Internalized homophobia and the resulting shame and self-hatred experienced by many lesbians and gay men at some point in their gay identity development can be confronted in the dynamics of an EOP presentation (Kaufman 1985; Fossum and Mason 1986; Margolies, Becker, and Jackson-Brewer 1987; Padesky 1989; Pharr 1988; Pheterson 1986). EOP facilitators, as invited guests and "experts," challenge the social messages to conceal, disguise, discredit, or disavow their homosexuality, and this challenge creates a powerful self-affirmation. EOP facilitators receive extensive training, and learning to make presentations to potentially hostile audiences while remaining calm, friendly, and articulate empowers the EOP facilitators in other aspects of their lives as well.

An Educational Outreach Program Presentation

The presentation format is consistent with the educational and experiential goals of the EOP. At the beginning of the two-hour workshop, participants are introduced to the LGMPO through a brief description of its history, services, and functions. This information is followed by one or two participatory exercises (depending on time constraints) that engage audience members, intellectually and emotionally, with the concepts and issues surrounding homosexuality, homophobia, and heterosexism. Coming-out stories comprise the next portion of the presentation. Each of the four EOP facilitators spends approximately four minutes sharing an aspect of his or her life with the audience members, thus providing a window through which participants can glimpse the individual realities of two lesbians and two gay men. Facilitators then use the remaining half of the program to respond to audience questions. Finally, each EOP program concludes with evaluations and handouts describing the LGMPO's services, bibliographies, and common questions. Depending on the particular needs of a given audience, facilitators choose from a range of exercises, including guided fantasies, brainstorming, values clarifications, and other activities designed for use in large and small groups. However, the two primary exercises consistently utilized in the EOP presentations are The Line and Take a Stand.

The Line Exercise

The Line exercise was adapted from an antiracism workshop attended by one of the authors.[7] The room is divided by an imaginary line that designates "majority" and "minority" sides. A list of statements that name oppressed minority groups is read by the facilitator. Participants are invited to take the risk of crossing the imaginary line and facing the majority side each time they identify themselves with a category announced by the facilitator. For example, a lesbian first crosses the line as a woman. She may also cross as a person of color, a person who is chronically ill, a person from a blue-collar family, and finally, a lesbian.

We engage audiences in this activity to help them move toward an empathic understanding of the daily life experiences of lesbians, gay men, and bisexual people. The exercise helps participants to understand the connections among oppressions by emphasizing the stigma or privilege attached to social categories, be they obvious or invisible. This society, dominated by white, heterosexual, middle- to upper-class men, often condemns and stigmatizes individuals and groups of people, inhibiting them from disclosing denigrated aspects of their identity. Unlike race and sex, disability, class, ethnicity, religious affiliation, and sexual orientation are sometimes mutable and often invisible, but no less significant than characteristics more visible. Risking disclosure of these characteristics to peers attending the LGMPO workshop engenders anxiety similar in some ways to that of revealing one's homosexuality in a homophobic context.

Moreover, The Line exercise challenges the simplistic reduction of people to their sexual orientation by demonstrating that we all may belong to more than one stigmatized group. The experience of deciding whether to cross the line makes clear possible similarities in experiences of oppression. Great anxiety and stress may result from identifying oneself as a member of a stigmatized group, with consequent risk to one's familial relationships, friendships, employment, quality of health care, educational standing, and opportunities for social and economic advancement. It is difficult for many facilitators to request that participants engage in an activity that may conjure up the embarrassment, shame, guilt, hurt, sadness, envy, and anger felt by people who belong to social categories that are stigmatized, condemned, viewed as threats to the social order, and treated with disdain, rejection, verbal harassment, discrimination, and physical violence. However, this exercise also provides an opportunity to experience our uniqueness and commonalities and to feel pride in the courage required to share these aspects of our lives with our peers. Sharing the pride and the pain of minority membership, in combination, creates opportunities for the personal empowerment of all involved. Workshop participants often mention a new awareness of their own privilege or oppression in the discussion that follows the exercise. Participants also speak of their new understanding of the stress and anxiety that lesbians, gay men, and bisexual people face as they decide whether to "come out" in a particular social context.

Take a Stand Exercise

Take a Stand, a values clarification exercise, focuses less on stigma and privilege and more on issues of human sexuality.[8] Behind the participants, the facilitator marks off a continuum along a wall by taping in the middle of the wall a sign reading, "Neutral—You Can't Stand Here," at one end a sign reading, "Comfortable," and at the other end a sign reading "Uncomfortable." As statements are read, participants are asked to place themselves along this continuum according to their emotional response to the trigger statement. The more comfortable or in agreement they are with a particular statement, the farther away from the center and closer to the "Comfortable" sign they move. Likewise, people who feel uncomfortable or disagree with the particular statement move away from the center in the direction of the "Uncomfortable" sign. Participants redistribute themselves as the next statement is read. Audience attitudes can be assessed using trigger statements or phrases such as "cohabitating heterosexual couples," "homosexuality is a phase," "Sex with the 'right person' can change your sexual orientation," "legalizing consensual sex laws," and "an openly gay public school teacher." The facilitator may wish to ask the participants to share why they are standing where they are, but doesn't allow debate among the participants. The facilitator chooses approximately ten statements, depending on the size of the audience, members' backgrounds, age, educational level, special interests, and so on. A discussion is then facilitated that explores audience members' reactions to participating in the exercise and encourages them to ask questions regarding civil rights, sexual behavior, familial relationships, and religious beliefs, among other topics. The discussion that follows the exercise is often lively and engaging.

Reactions to this exercise vary according to sex, race, age of participants, and their relationships to one another. In academic settings, entry-level students are often less verbal and find the exercise and discussion most threatening, particularly if they do not know one another. We think this has more to do with the developmental issue of needing peer approval and being new to university norms than with having little to say about the issues. We have found that older undergraduate and graduate students who are more acclimated to university life and more secure within themselves are far more likely to engage in deeper discussions. When this exercise is presented to staff, faculty, or an outside agency where participants are older, the discussion often takes on a different and more sensitive tenor.

This exercise provides an opportunity to talk about subjects that are often taboo or seldom mentioned. Participants frequently report anxiety in addressing some of the issues, but are also appreciative of the opportunity to discuss human sexuality. The trigger statements and phrases often reflect heterosexual people's negative or hostile beliefs. Reading the statements and remaining neutral to participants' comments and reactions are sometimes difficult and painful for the facilitator. Conversely, it can be a positive experience for facilitators to see and hear that not all heterosexual people hold negative attitudes and values toward them. Each time a facilitator leads this exercise is an opportunity to grow stronger and more empowered.

Coming-Out Stories

The next part of the program, the coming-out stories, focuses on facilitator self-disclosure to the audience. "Coming out" is an abbreviation for "coming out of the closet," a phrase popularized in the 1970s to describe the lifelong process of understanding and revealing one's non-heterosexuality to oneself and others.[9] Facilitators briefly describe a stage of their coming-out process, which may include the circumstances under which they came to terms with their own homosexuality; their everyday interactions with other lesbians, gay men, and heterosexual people; or how this aspect of their identity impacts their family life, personal development, and career choices. At this point in the program participants are invited not only to glimpse the personal lives of four individual gay people, but to gain a sense of their emotional lives as well. The stories of some are painful, outlining a journey of isolation, fear, and alienation. For others, humor is woven into the individual stories because situations viewed in retrospect are often funny and demonstrate that we, too, can laugh at ourselves. Through the personal sharing audience members are moved to see lesbians, gay men, and bisexual people as individuals, distinct from each other, and transcendent of stereotypes. This part of the program often has the most impact on participants because in their eyes we change from "others" to human beings. The coming-out story of each of the facilitators is unique. Yet the stories resemble one another in their disclosure of the struggle to come to terms with one's orientation and whether and how to share this information in the variety of social settings that we move in throughout our lives.

For many audiences, this is the first opportunity to interact with an openly gay person and consequently the first chance to hear an individual's story about coming to acknowledge and accept his or her sexual orientation. Moreover, the openly gay facilitators at EOP presentations serve as positive role models for the lesbians, gay men, and bisexual people in an audience: those who may be struggling with their own sexual orientation; those who contemplate revealing their sexual orientation to friends, colleagues, or family members; or those who are seeking validation. The need for positive gay role models may be especially acute for lesbians and gay men of color in a racist and homophobic culture. For the facilitators, telling their coming-out stories is therapeutic in the sense of "enhancing self-esteem" by renegotiating "personal perceptions of stigma"; thus, disclosure is "a way of soliciting support" and "sharing the emotional burden" of being a lesbian or a gay man (Miall, cited in Cain 1991: 69). The LGMPO-EOP regards the telling of these stories as an essential component of the workshops.

Question-and-Answer Session

The second half of the EOP program allows time for participants to ask questions of the facilitators. This is often the most fruitful portion of the workshop. By this stage of the presentation the participants have experienced the stress of self-disclosing to their peers, made visible their attitudes and beliefs about homosexuality, and listened to the personal stories of lesbians, gay men, and bisexual people.[10] Much has been stirred up, and more often than not, the audience has many questions to ask the facilitators. High school students tend to wonder more about dating within the lesbian or gay men's communities, norms in relationships, or interactions with parents. Undergraduate students, depending on age and year in school, may be more interested in peer relationships in residence halls and classrooms or in plans following college. University staff often ask how being gay might affect job choices, working relationships, and family formation. Most audiences are interested in religious issues, AIDS (acquired immunodeficiency syndrome), harassment, discrimination, and violence. EOP presentations encourage discussions of a range of personal values including religious, moral, familial, sexual, or political beliefs and judgments.

Facilitators frequently elaborate on the connections among homophobia, sexism, and racism. Audience members often have a basic understanding of oppression, and facilitators can then discuss the commonalities and distinctions between homophobia and other forms of individual and institutional oppression. The more receptive an audience, the more likely the question and answer portion of the program will be a lively discussion. When this happens, participants and facilitators alike experience emotional connection and intellectual growth. It is during these kinds of presentations that participants feel the most enriched and empowered.

CONCLUSION

The Educational Outreach Program of the Lesbian-Gay Male Programs Office has been evolving since 1971. Education is a process, and through our presentations we invite audience members to join us for a moment in time to explore another way of being in the world. In this chapter, we have sketched our history and discussed our workshop format, goals, and content. We have illuminated the experiences of facilitators and participants as they engage in a workshop on homophobia and sexual orientation.

In this country we hear time-sanctioned sentiments: "We, the people . . . government of the people, by the people, for the people." The "people" to whom the Declaration of Independence and the Gettysburg Address refer were and continue to be white heterosexual men of property. Small wonder, then, that these "people" strive to retain the control they wield over the lives of all the people. Small wonder, then, that children learn early such pejorative labels as "nigger," "bitch," "lezzie," or "fag," used as catchall terms of contempt and derision. Small wonder, then, that from our infancy we the people are taught to esteem and obey the privileged "people" whose values inform our daily existence and sustain our oppression. Small wonder, indeed.

But we choose to shape a greater wonder. We believe that attempts to gain and retain power, acceptance, and self-esteem at the expense of others are nothing more and nothing less than matters of choice. But we also believe that attempts to build a campus environment, city, and world where diversity and equality are accepted and celebrated are a matter of choice: a choice that the Lesbian-Gay Male Programs Office has made and implements through its hiring practices, its Educational Outreach Program presentations, and all its other programs and activities. A world in which mutual support and sharing are more valued than power and material goods is the world we have chosen to help create: a world for all its people.

NOTES

We wish to acknowledge the help in writing this chapter from Ronald Wheeler, Jr., J. D.

1. We are using this definition of homophobia throughout this chapter. Other scholars and activists choose to use different words to describe this collection of attitudes and behaviors: for example, homonegativism, homosexism, antihomosexual, homoerotophobia, homosexphobia.

2. Our preferred phrase for talking about gay people as a group is "lesbians, gay men, and bisexual people." It is our belief that the popular phrase "lesbians and gays" reinforces lesbian invisibility in a sexist content by equating gay with men. We use the

term *gay* inclusively to describe both lesbian women and gay men. Similarly, *homosexual*, while overly clinical, is used to describe both women and men.

3. For more information on coming out to family members and responses to a child or sibling's coming out, you may wish to consult the following: Borhek 1983; Clark 1978; Fairchild and Hayward 1979; Griffin et al. 1986; Rafkin 1987. On the experiences of lesbian and gay male parents, including coming out to children, please see the following: Alpert 1988; Gay Fathers of Toronto 1981; Hanscombe and Forster 1982; Pollack and Vaughn 1987; Rafkin 1989; Schulenburg 1985.

4. For information on other gay speakers' bureaus, see the following: Diffloth 1987; The Gay and Lesbian Speakers Bureau of Boston 1984; Maran 1990.

5. On the experiences of African American lesbians and gay men: Beam 1986; Cornwell 1983; Lorde 1985; Smith 1983. On Asian American lesbians and gay men: Kim 1987; Lo, Aguilar-San Juan, and Ching Black 1990; Woo 1983. On the perspectives of Latina/o lesbians and gay men: Anzaldúa 1990; Herdt 1989; Moraga 1983; Ramos 1987. For discussions of Jewish lesbians and gay men: Beck 1982; Newman 1988; Rich 1986; Zahava 1990. Native American lesbians and gay men write about their experiences in the following: Brant 1984; Roscoe 1988.

6. The EOP made seventy-one presentations to approximately 4,253 people in 1988, sixty-five presentations to 3,894 people in 1989, and eighty-one presentations to 4,128 people in 1990.

7. The Line exercise was introduced to one of the authors at the Unlearning Racism Workshop, developed and facilitated by Ricky Sherover-Marcuse, Ph.D., at the University of Michigan, 1987.

8. Take a Stand exercise has been developed and expanded over the years for our own purposes. We regret not being able to supply information on the original version of this exercise, but it has been an important piece of the LGMPO-EOP presentations since the LGMPO began in 1971.

9. For collections of coming-out stories, an important part of lesbian and gay men's culture making, see the following: Adair and Adair 1978; Alyson 1980; Fricke 1981; Hall Carpenter Archives, *Inventing Ourselves*, 1989, *Walking After Midnight*, 1989; Heron 1983; Holmes 1988; Reid 1976; Stanley and Wolfe 1989.

10. In recent years, our facilitating teams have also included people raised by lesbian and gay male parents.

22

FAIRteach: Faculty Development on Issues of Racism and Diversity

Linda Frankel

What spurs university faculty members to take on the issues of racism and diversity in the classroom, and how can this motivation be harnessed to challenge the institutional status quo? These questions lie at the heart of a faculty development project—FAIRteach—initiated in the late 1980s by a small, interdisciplinary group of faculty members at the University of Michigan. The group received $100,000 from the university administration to carry out a project to improve teaching around issues of racism and diversity on campus.[1]

HISTORY AND CONTEXT

The group and its project grew out of a larger organization formed to address racial tensions on campus. In the mid-1980s a wave of racial incidents at the University of Michigan, along with other campuses, sparked protest by students against the institutional barriers and culture that prevent minority students from obtaining the same quality of educational experience as their white peers. The university's president responded by drafting a document that voiced commitment to supporting diversity on campus and sketched some of the institutional changes, including funding, that were needed to achieve this goal (Duderstadt 1988).[2]

Some faculty members were catalyzed, too, not only by the overt manifestations of racism on campus, but also through the everyday classroom experiences that underscored for them the difficulties and the promises of creating an equitable and diverse educational environment. Numerous efforts were launched to improve the curriculum on issues of race and diversity. For example, a group of faculty members worked to design and implement an undergraduate course specifically focused on the historical and contemporary roots of racism. Others developed and successfully pursued the adoption in the College of Literature,

Science, and the Arts of an undergraduate course requirement on racism and other issues of diversity and inequality.

Within this context in 1987 a multidisciplinary group of white faculty members at the University of Michigan formed Faculty Against Institutional Racism (FAIR) out of concern over the lack of systematic and coordinated efforts to address racism at all institutional levels of the university. Members felt strongly that the majority white faculty must take responsibility for creating awareness of institutional racism, initiating change, and monitoring the university's progress toward eliminating inequities. These white faculty members wanted to support their less numerous minority colleagues who, they acknowledged, assumed an unfair burden in speaking to these issues and dealing with the institutional and personal consequences. By assuming a more organized presence and consulting with other groups on campus—minority faculty and students and other faculty groups—members hoped to legitimate and emphasize the importance of work to eliminate racism on campus.

FAIRteach formed as a subgroup of the larger FAIR organization to focus attention on the critical domain of classroom teaching. Group members recognized that faculty members on university campuses are not generally encouraged to share their pedagogical anxieties or expertise. Good teaching in general remains something of a mystique, occasionally recognized by an annual teaching award, but rarely dissected or transmitted. Furthermore, the constraints of the status hierarchy at a major research university and the institutional and disciplinary rewards that are involved ensure that most tenure-track faculty will necessarily focus more of their attention on research.

Yet group members strongly felt that teaching and mentoring are at the heart of undergraduate experience and professional training. The values and institutional culture of the university are communicated and reinforced most forcefully in the domain of classroom teaching and related advisory activities. Good teaching takes on special meaning and presents additional challenges when traditional content and methods are challenged by new scholarship and new participants in the academic arena. Group members asked, How could the faculty act responsibly to create a learning atmosphere that allowed all students to thrive and develop respect for one another? These were the concerns that FAIRteach formed to address and that motivated the development of a teaching project. The group aimed to explore the dimensions of pedagogy and curriculum that facilitate or hinder the emergence of a culturally diverse teaching and learning environment.

Faculty development is not a new concept. In fact, faculty development seminars, conferences, regional networks, and workshops have been the linchpin of scores of curriculum-change projects initiated over the last fifteen years (Andersen 1988a; Schuster and VanDyne 1985; Spanier, Bloom, and Boroviak 1984). These projects fall into three distinctive patterns: the top-down model; the piggyback model; and the bottom-up model. The first aims for university-wide change in basic courses flowing from an administrative directive; the second targets interdisciplinary courses or programs that Women's Studies or administrative groups hope to influence; the third develops internal or regional resources through peer collaboration (Schuster and VanDyne 1985: 92–96).

The FAIR teaching group fits the bottom-up model in several respects. It was initiated by faculty members seeking to discover, connect, make visible, and expand the internal resources and expertise needed to transform teaching across the university. Also, it was organized outside the framework of existing institutional structures—departments, programs, schools, and colleges. These features continue to present both opportunities and constraints for the group's work as it moves from self-education toward outreach to the wider university community.

Although FAIRteach has met since 1987, funding for the project was released only in the spring of 1989. It took two years of lobbying and negotiation on the part of group members and supportive colleagues to arrange for funding. Part of the difficulty lay in the unsanctioned form of the group—cutting across the usual units of accountability—coupled with the lack of internal clarity within the administration over responsibility for diversity goals. Who would oversee the project? How would it be managed? How would progress toward specific goals be assessed? These were issues that had to be resolved before the project received administrative support. Thus, the start-up for the project was rather protracted.

From the beginning, two related purposes have driven the group's activities. On one hand, group members have devoted a great deal of time to self-education and to systematizing and analyzing pedagogical experience and expertise gleaned from group members, fellow colleagues, and the literature. On the other hand, the larger goal has been to reach out to a wider constituency through workshops and through the collection, development, and dissemination of concrete resources. These activities are not contradictory, and ultimately they reinforce each other. Yet, in the face of constraints of time, resources, and institutional climate, there can also be some concern about the appropriate balance between one focus and the other. The small but diverse nature of the group, the delay in obtaining institutional support and funding, and the perceived need for carefulness and caution in approaching colleagues who aren't accustomed to reflecting on their classroom behavior are three factors that have affected the balance of the activities of FAIRteach.

PROJECT RATIONALE AND GOALS

Soon after it formed, the FAIR teaching subgroup submitted a proposal to receive university funds to carry out a faculty development project.[3] Our proposal outlined a three-year project aimed at upgrading the faculty's ability proactively to confront institutionalized bias and promote diversity in the classroom and other instructional settings. We based our proposal on four assumptions. First, we argued that a proactive, rather than a reactive, stance is needed to ameliorate racial/ethnic intolerance and discrimination on campus. Rather than waiting for racial incidents to occur, faculty members must create a climate that actively undercuts the deleterious effects of racism and promotes a community that is both tolerant and knowledgeable about diversity.

This idea is linked to our second assumption: pedagogy and classroom culture are at the heart of university culture. Thus we concluded that major initiatives to confront and counter racism must occur in this arena. To support this claim we pointed to a number of features of classroom organization and teaching strategies that needed to be addressed in order to overcome the exclusion, invisibility, or discrimination that whole groups of students encounter. Among these we included recruitment of students so as to avoid/overcome classes or disciplines that are populated by members of one racial group; techniques of classroom organization that overcome, without intrusion or embarrassment, racial self-segregation in seating patterns; assignments and assistance that encourage students of different racial groups to work together collaboratively and effectively; assignments that utilize the resources of all students in a positive and respectful manner; instructional efforts that examine the impact of race in the development, status, or application of knowledge in a discipline or topic area; instructional procedures that improve minority students' opportunities for academic success, without remedial or punitive stigma.

Third, we asserted that while we believe that most faculty want to teach well and do not want to promote intolerance in their classrooms, we also must acknowledge that, for the most part, they are unprepared to take a proactive stance toward diversity in their teaching. Our project aimed to fill some of the collective gaps in our knowledge and skills.

Finally, we felt that any progress toward retooling faculty to incorporate pedagogical and curricular innovations pertinent to multicultural issues must be accompanied by efforts to implement broad structural changes that would legitimate and institutionalize this work.

We proposed to address these concerns through a number of interrelated activities: identifying barriers and generating resources for multicultural teaching; piloting a series of informative and problem-solving workshops for faculty; broadening our network to encompass more disciplines and schools through support and consultation; and continuing to work toward necessary institutional change.

As part of this work we thought it would be important to develop mechanisms for faculty self-exploration as well as for self- and peer evaluation. We also proposed to adapt or create pedagogical and content-related resources for the classroom that faculty members could use to help students explore their values and assumptions, to explore the micro- and macrolevels of institutional bias, and to examine the structures of the various disciplines in relation to multicultural concerns.

PARTICIPATION AND GOVERNANCE

By drawing on the interest of those who already had some awareness and knowledge of the relationship of pedagogy to multicultural concerns, FAIR's teaching group provided a forum and a support network for those who had been puzzling over and working on these teaching issues either alone or with a few like-minded colleagues in their own fields. However, the group wanted to reach across departments and disciplines to broaden the pool of ideas, resources, and skills available to improve classroom teaching around issues of racism and diversity. The goal was to build a nucleus of support and legitimation for these concerns as a basis for increasing the awareness and skills of colleagues and thus affecting the institutional climate.

About twenty faculty members from a variety of disciplines, including sociology, public health, social work, music, mathematics, architecture and urban planning, African American studies, the undergraduate writing program, Women's Studies, and education, initially joined these discussions. Participation has been heavily weighted toward the social sciences and the humanities, where the manifest content of the disciplines is more apparently congruent with a focus on multicultural concerns. Over the first four years the group has existed, participation has fluctuated during different stages of activity, with an active core of about ten to twelve members. The majority of the membership has been white, although a few faculty of color have become active members and others have consulted with the group. Other aspects of diversity are better represented in the mix of gender, age, and status. The membership of the group cuts across the status hierarchy of the university, encompassing senior faculty, lecturers, program coordinators, and other academic support staff.

Since there is no built-in institutional context for sharing concerns about teaching, the group had to overcome discomfort over exposing problems and revealing uncertainty or lack of control. The relatively small size of the group made it easier to establish the trust needed to do this. It also helped that several members had experience and expertise in community organizing, intergroup relations, conflict resolution, and feminist organizational practice. In addition, high-status males (full professors) in the group participated alongside others in self-disclosure. Like other settings in the university community, however, the group has not been immune to differences in self-presentation, communication styles, or prerogatives that relate to gender and positions of status. Some of these differences have been reflected in varying degrees of interest or investment in process issues.

Nevertheless, the group has worked hard to maintain openness and inclusiveness in its participation and decision making. Considerable effort has gone into monitoring and assessing the group's own process. Frustration over the need to get things done has also pushed the group to reevaluate how members can work together most effectively. Particularly after the FAIRteach project was funded, the group spent a lot of time working out how to preserve the informal, open, collaborative nature of the project while at the same time ensuring productivity and accountability.

This was accomplished by setting up a two- or three-person steering committee, rotated every three months or so, to assist a paid coordinator in setting the agenda for meetings and pinpointing the tasks and decisions that emerge from the ongoing activities. A policy board—comprised of one long-term member (female professor), an inactive founding member now attending law school (retired male professor), and the director of the Center for African and African-American Studies (black male professor)—chosen by the participants, oversees the long-range financial interests of the funded project.

The group has tried to put into practice the cooperative, democratic values it hopes to encourage in the broader arenas of the classroom, the university, and society. Many group sessions and steering committee meetings were devoted to developing a consensus model for decision making. Guidelines were drawn up to ensure that everyone's ideas are taken into consideration, particularly for any products—written pieces or workshops—that represent the work of FAIRteach as a whole. Despite the emphasis on trust in the group, the volatile aspects of working to improve intergroup relations on campus mandate that individual participants feel that they have the right to express their distance from any product or activity with which they do not fully agree. So far this has not been necessary, but sensitivity to this issue remains.

For a long time the group was sustained on the basis of strictly volunteer labor. With the availability of university funding for FAIRteach's teaching improvement project, it has been possible in some cases to pay members to work on tasks such as workshops, concept papers, and collection of materials and data. The biggest portion of the funding supports the position of coordinator (half-time during the fall and winter terms; full-time during the spring and summer terms). The coordinator writes and distributes detailed minutes of FAIRteach meetings to members and a network of interested people across the university; works with the steering committee, individual members, and workshop teams to prepare agendas, materials, or publicity; organizes and develops the resource file, which contains memos produced by group members, articles, exercises, data about minority students' experiences, and other information on multicultural teaching efforts across campus and at other universities; participates in workshop development and preparation; and tries to keep the many facets of the group's efforts moving along in some reasonably organized fashion.

Nevertheless, much of the activity and oversight needed to keep things going is still provided by members who choose to expend time and energy outside the bounds of their regular academic responsibilities without extra compensation. This has been a strain on the core of active members, particularly because they are also involved individually in other related endeavors both in their departments and in university-wide contexts. This aspect of the grass-roots level of the organization has sometimes been problematic. Although funding has helped, the lack of an institutional base has meant that office space, telephone, secretarial services, computer, and the usual accoutrements of university life have had to be scrounged or obtained through the limited time and resources of group members.

SELF-EDUCATION

FAIRteach began with a flood of questions participants brought to the group. How can we get more content relevant to diversity into the curriculum, syllabi, and classroom activities? How do we encourage faculty and administrators to think of multicultural teaching as a serious endeavor? How can we influence the reward system to acknowledge successful efforts in this area? Can we identify different teaching/learning styles and incorporate these in a way that promotes the best education for all students? How do we overcome inertia, mistrust, and fear on the part of colleagues and students?

Although we envisioned being able to offer workshops to interested faculty across the university, we also felt the need to extend our own process of discovery and to educate ourselves about the problems that multicultural teaching should address. Awaiting the outcome of the funding decision, the group continued its initial efforts toward self-education as a basis for sharing elements of this process and any expertise we developed along the way with our colleagues.

We needed time to draw together or generate the resources necessary for our outreach goals. Therefore, we began by organizing a workshop for ourselves in the form of a day-long event and continuing meetings. Members of the group prepared memos on various topics, led discussions to clarify problems and brainstorm actions, and shared classroom designs, assignments, and experiences. Among the topics explored were the problems of teaching well in a university context that devalues teaching; methods for increasing cross-cultural sensitivity among students; course content that reflects racial bias or, contrastingly, challenges racism; the relevance of racial issues to disciplines; authoritative versus student control of the learning process; power issues in the classroom; faculty-student interactions in and out of the classroom; standards of academic performance; classroom assignments and materials; and teaching/learning styles.

Discussion and memo writing helped to pinpoint areas that needed clarification and expansion. We asked some of our colleagues and group members who had expertise in intergroup relations, in teaching about gender, race, and class, and in using small group and cooperative learning techniques and other skills relevant to fashioning a more multiculturally oriented classroom to share their knowledge with us. In addition, we collected examples of planning and evaluation tools; articles on feminist pedagogy; learning exercises for small group and cooperative work; and materials on integrating gender, race, and class into the curriculum.

As we tried to probe and systematize some of the ideas generated in our discussions, members produced a more detailed series of memos on "naming the issues" that focused more particularly on faculty-student relations in the classroom and in advising situations; power in the classroom; identifying the dimensions of racism in the classroom; and learning exercises and activities relating to these issues. Singly, in pairs, or in small groups, members took responsibility for laying out the different dimensions of classroom and institutional culture that either hinder or promote awareness of multicultural concerns.

These memos and think pieces formed the basis of extensive discussion, were then revised and reworked, and ultimately paved the way for workshop design and development of resources to help colleagues understand and address these issues in their own teaching.

WORKSHOPS AND RELATED OUTREACH

Although FAIRteach's project proposal outlined overall goals and strategies, it did not specify concrete action plans. The number, location, recruiting mechanisms, length, and format of workshops, for example, all had to be worked out. Extensive discussions were held about what kind of approach to take in the workshops, particularly in relation to the nature of the audience in different settings. FAIRteach participants expected various forms of resistance among colleagues—either in acknowledging that problems existed, in addressing the root causes, or in seriously considering alternatives to familiar teaching habits.

The first issue was, Whom should we try to reach? We agreed that there were probably different levels of awareness and support for these endeavors among the faculty. We identified three broad groups: those who are highly aware of the problems and very open to new ideas; those who are somewhat neutral, either unaware of the extent of the problem or unsure about how to change; and those who deny the existence of the problem and are generally hostile to imposition on their authority or ''freedom'' as teachers. Feelings varied on when and how to approach these different types. We felt that we needed to try out our ideas on identifiably sympathetic colleagues so that we could assess the value of the material we presented to those most likely to use it. Yet we also felt that we must reach into more conventional departments and units where change was most needed. Some felt that we could circumvent the issue by modifying the components of workshop design for different audiences. This, in fact, became an important dimension of workshop organization. As we began to develop workshops for specific groups of faculty, the teams of leaders worked closely with representatives from these units to tailor the activities, format, and other features of the presentation to the needs and interests of each group.

There was also discussion about how participants should be recruited—as individuals, by departments, or by larger units such as schools. Should administrative sanction be sought—a letter from a chair or dean requiring or encouraging faculty to attend? Would this lend legitimacy or feel like coercion? Again, although general issues could be debated, decisions had to be made about each specific case.

In reality, choice of workshop location, although guided by the concerns mentioned above, often comes from the institutional contacts of FAIRteach members, willingness of various units to participate, and response by FAIRteach to requests for a workshop. The first workshop FAIRteach conducted was a follow-up to a prior exploratory session held for faculty from the School of Education by three FAIRteach members in that school. For the second workshop,

FAIRteach worked with the staff of the Center for Research on Teaching and Learning to recruit a group of interested faculty from across campus. In the third case, FAIRteach received a request from the School of Public Health to conduct a workshop on ways to teach about racism and diversity using health-related data and statistics. This grew out of a schoolwide investigation and report on problems relating to racism produced by a committee on which two FAIRteach members in the School of Public Health served.

A second issue that arises is, Who should "lead" the workshop, that is, who should most visibly be in charge, and how should the leadership team relate to one another? This design dimension also varies by case. In some cases it is more appropriate for outsiders to lead the workshop to prevent the workshop ideas from being too closely associated with colleagues who were already perceived to represent particular views. In other cases it might be valuable for a high-status person, either in the unit or not, to play a significant role to encourage or validate participation. However, FAIRteach also feels that it is important that the leadership team, to the best extent possible, include both males and females and faculty from different racial/ethnic groups. An important aspect of the workshop experience is witnessing the cooperative interaction of the workshop team as a modeling device that faculty can apply to multicultural teaching in the classroom.

Third, what format should we use? In FAIRteach workshops the goal has not been to deliver a prepackaged formula for classroom behavior, but rather to engage participants in a process of discovery that is catalyzed and enriched by the resources and perspectives the FAIRteach group can bring to bear on the issues. An important feature of all of the workshops has been an opportunity for participants to work in small groups on specific problem areas illustrated by descriptive vignettes. FAIRteach members have collected and distilled data from a variety of sources on students' experiences and concerns over lack of attention to diversity in the classroom and in faculty advising situations. From this data FAIRteach constructed scenarios that illustrated facets of teaching interactions in which multicultural concerns surfaced, including course assignments and informal, out-of-class contacts; conflict between students in the classroom; and student reactions to course content and materials. Workshop participants receive guiding questions to facilitate brainstorming on these problems. The results are then reported in the larger grouping, where further advice can be shared. Other components of the workshops have included demonstrations/exercises on managing and rethinking classroom conflict; self-assessment exercises on multicultural teaching; and mini-lectures based on conceptual frameworks for moving from monoculturalism to multiculturalism in the university. The basic notion of workshop design is to demonstrate or engage participants in a variety of techniques that can be adapted for classroom use, such as get-acquainted exercises, role plays, small group problem solving using vignettes, large and small group facilitation.

Feedback from initial workshops was encouraging. Participants' evaluations have been used to determine the effectiveness of the materials and to identify areas that need to be explored further. One such need that emerged in the Center for Research on Learning and Teaching (CRLT) workshop was more material on how to deal with classroom conflict. In order to extend its efforts, FAIRteach hopes to develop protocols for working with a wider variety of departments and units that wish to develop workshops and materials tailored to their own specific needs. Of particular concern is how to address multicultural issues in the sciences. FAIRteach is trying to find ways to raise these concerns in situations where large lectures are the norm or where the manifest content of the discipline has not been open to viewing knowledge in socially grounded contexts. FAIRteach's activities also extend beyond the scope of workshop design and implementation. Group members are working with some computer consultants to construct a computer simulation game on institutional racism and with a colleague from the Center for Research on Learning and Teaching to produce an interactive computer/video program utilizing some of the vignettes and other materials developed by FAIRteach.

At the same time, participants continue to refine and clarify the conceptual components of teaching for and about diversity. For example, one group member is developing a working paper articulating the relationship between anti-racist and multicultural teaching. This has been the basis of extensive discussion in the group addressing such questions as, What is encompassed by each term? What are the shared or contrasting features of each? Are these two approaches mutually reinforcing, or are there important distinctions between the two? Differing understandings and emphases with regard to these visions have implications for course content and class organization that need to be spelled out. Another domain of critical importance that the group intends to address and translate into workshop design is how different manifestations and dimensions of power operate in the classroom. Being able to identify these dimensions and illustrate their impact on different groups of students may help faculty members to empower students to learn more effectively and actively. Group members are also interested in envisioning and identifying the components of multicultural thinking in contrast to other modes of thought. This, too, would assist faculty in guiding students to deeper understanding of different forms of knowledge and helping them to see alternatives in the ways they approach intellectual and social issues.

CONCLUSION

None of these issues is simple, nor are the routes to pedagogical transformation straightforward. At this writing it is too early to assess the overall impact of FAIRteach's faculty development activities. It is clear that the group has served an important function as a sounding board for pedagogical concerns surrounding diversity. It has given participants support and motivation for developing a deeper understanding of the issues and sharing the skills needed to bring this awareness and expertise to an expanding network of colleagues. More telling, however, will be the extent to which the dialogue and increasing knowledge about multicultural teaching that the group has fostered become an integral feature of campus culture and institutional goals. This remains an open question and one that depends not only on the continuation of these grass-roots efforts but also on the way in which this work can be incorporated into officially supported channels.

NOTES

1. I was a founding member and the initial coordinator of the FAIRteach project. At the end of 1990 I left the University of Michigan. The role of coordinator was assumed by someone new to the group who also has a position in the teaching assistant training program.

2. An excellent discussion of institutional racism and the structural constraints on change in the university can be found in Chesler and Crowfoot (1990).

3. In this section I have summarized, condensed, and in some cases drawn directly from the language of the FAIRteach proposal entitled, "Proposal to Improve Undergraduate Teaching Around Issues of Racial Diversity." FAIRteach members collectively generated the ideas that a small group, myself included, shaped into the final proposal.

23

Constructing a Teaching Assistant Training Program with a Multicultural Emphasis

David Schoem

This chapter examines approaches for training teachers to be more aware of issues of multiculturalism and diversity. The specific case examined here looks at training for graduate student teaching assistants or, TAs, as they are commonly called. By thinking about how to educate teachers, one is forced to consider carefully what is meant by multicultural teaching in terms of content, process, and approach, what place multicultural teaching has in the overall enterprise of pedagogy, and what personal and intellectual issues one must consider in order to become an effective teacher in this area.[1]

In recent years increased attention has been given to training graduate students as teachers. I have overseen the development and initial implementation of a program that each year trains about three hundred graduate students who are first-time teachers. Although the training itself is not a new enterprise, the fact that it is a coordinated and required college-wide effort is new.

The institutionalization and requirement of TA training have come in response to a variety of pressures, including renewed interest in undergraduate education and concern for the performance and English language skills of foreign-born TAs (Boyer 1987; Briggs and Hofer 1991). The establishment of centralized control of such training allows for greater consistency in quality and content across academic departments. TA training in prior years had been largely idiosyncratic, the quality and intensity depending in any given year upon the good intentions of a particular faculty member or department chair.

IDENTIFYING TEACHER TRAINERS FOR
MULTICULTURAL TEACHING: QUALIFICATIONS AND
ISSUES OF STATUS

Coming at a time of increased attention and interest in diversity and multiculturalism on campus, a universitywide mandate was instituted by the University of Michigan in an attempt to achieve far-reaching changes in all aspects of diversity. With this mandate officially and publicly announced, politically it became possible, even expected, for training in multicultural teaching to be a part of the TA training program. However, even an institutional commitment did not in every case necessarily translate into departmental support or individual TA support either for the notion of a required teacher training program or for multicultural teaching as a part of the training. Furthermore, when we started to develop the TA training program, it was not clear to us exactly what we or others had in mind by "diversity training" or how we might best accomplish it.

Given that our initial planning period and start-up time were less than three months, we were required to organize and make decisions on short notice. The lecturers, chosen as the staff for the training program on the basis of their commitment and excellence as teachers, had low status within the hierarchy of the professoriate. These lecturers, who had been hired to develop, implement, and teach the TA training program, although sympathetic, were also not experienced in the area of multicultural teaching. Clearly, training academics to teach is not a career path in the academic world; training academics in multicultural teaching is most certainly not what anyone is typically credentialed or rewarded highly for doing.

I soon discovered that a second group, those most experienced in the specific area of training about multiculturalism, had even lower status in the academic world—workshop leaders from student services staff, graduate students, and lecturers. Not surprisingly, these people were, for the most part, people of color.

Issues of academic status were not insignificant considerations for this training. To develop a new program on teacher training in a university whose prestige was built on research without the direct involvement of respected faculty, that is, senior professors, only lent credence to the relative unimportance of the endeavor. An even stronger case could be made for the lack of credibility attributed to multicultural teaching. Nevertheless, I invited some of the most experienced people on campus, regardless of rank or status, to sit with the team of lecturers for the TA training program to think through approaches for training on multicultural teaching and diversity. I decided that what was most important was expertise and experience and that prior even to thinking about campus politics, we needed to know what it was we wanted to teach and how best to go about doing it (Palmer 1983). As part of this process we also interviewed several others, including some ranking faculty, who were knowledgeable in this area but were not able to meet with us as part of an intensive planning effort.

We discovered that the challenging task we had imagined would be even more difficult than we had expected.

RESISTANCE TO TEACHER TRAINING AND TO MULTICULTURAL TEACHER TRAINING

Our TA training class is for one credit, meets for eighteen contact hours, is graded satisfactory/unsatisfactory, and is required of all first-time TAs in the College of Literature, Science, and the Arts. It was initially organized with a large lecture followed by small sections.

Since the first semester of training we have reorganized our class so that we now meet exclusively in small sections (fifteen students), place greater emphasis on classroom observation, and balance the centralized approach to the training with options and incentives for discipline-specific training within departments. The course itself, in addition to training in diversity, emphasizes active student participation in learning, critical thinking, and collaborative or group learning opportunities (Myers 1986); offers instruction on labs, lecturing, discussion sections, and testing and grading; and makes extensive use of micro-teaching, an analysis of one's teaching with the help of videotaping (McKeachie 1986).

We initially faced great resistance from individual TAs to the required status of the course and concern from a number of departments that such training took away too much time from graduate study. Although the TA union strongly supported the notion of teacher training, the fact that we offered TAs one free credit instead of direct monetary compensation for the training did not sit well with our first group of graduate students.

The intense resistance we thus faced to our initial training on diversity was set within a context of overall resistance to the course itself. However, we responded to constructive critiques of our training generally and to the training on multicultural teaching specifically and made numerous changes in the course content and pedagogy (Banks 1991). We also discovered that there was greater acceptance of the overall training when it was viewed as an integral part, albeit still not a central part, of graduate training, that is, that teaching "mattered" in one's graduate education. Similarly, we found greater acceptance of training in multicultural teaching when it was viewed as an integral part of the overall teacher training and not as an "addition to" that training. For instance, there was greater acceptance when issues of multicultural teaching were integrated throughout the entire training as opposed to one special session on that topic. Over a relatively short period of time, about two years, we had made significant changes, including changes in the expectations of TAs and their departments, such that our training program received very satisfactory ratings on TA evaluations for both the overall teacher training course and for training on multicultural teaching.

PLANNING TRAINING FOR MULTICULTURAL TEACHING

Among the planning group for the multicultural training, there was immediate debate and disagreement about the substantive focus of the training, about teaching strategies, and about time constraints and pedagogical issues. We identified several potential topics for training, but disagreed on whether to focus on any or all of the following: self-exploration of issues of diversity and racism, classroom dynamics, dissemination of information on university rules and regulations on sexual harassment, and review of course content and readings.

We also discussed and disagreed about the teaching strategy for training TAs in this area. Some argued strongly for an approach that emphasized direct confrontations of TAs' values and assumptions about race and diversity; others preferred an approach that accepted TAs' existing thinking about race and diversity issues as a legitimate starting point for discussion and moved along from there. Still others suggested that we offer a variety of approaches, giving TAs the opportunity to choose from among them. Finally, we discussed at length whether diversity training could be successfully accomplished in one three-hour session or needed to be woven into the entire course.

The argument for self-exploration states that unless individual TAs develop an understanding of their own attitudes on racism, sexism, and intergroup relations, they will be unable adequately to conceptualize themselves as teachers or their classrooms as places in which multicultural teaching can flourish. While one can prepare teachers in specific content areas and for the most standard classroom situations, this perspective argues that without critical self-reflection they will not be able to adapt to the numerous unforeseen circumstances, conflicts, and opportunities to infuse multiculturalism in the teaching. The self-reflective teacher, it is argued, could respond with greater insight to situations such as a student unknowingly making a racist comment, some students feeling excluded from class discussion because of communication styles, or other students complaining that their lab partner, from a different racial background, is causing their grades to suffer.

The argument for focusing instruction on rules and regulations states that this approach is best suited for a short time frame. If, in fact, one has only very limited time to conduct such training, it is best to emphasize specific behavioral changes upon which one can have a direct and immediate influence. In this case, we had been told by the TA union leadership that a concern of theirs was the not uncommon practice among male TAs of dating undergraduate female students in their classes (Hall and Sandler 1982). The university had long had informal guidelines about, and admonishments against, such behavior and had more recently begun attempting to put in writing some specific language discussing this problem. It was argued that one tangible effect of this approach would be that male TAs would no longer take advantage of their power status in the classroom to initiate unequal and compromising relationships with their female students.

Some argued that we emphasize course content as the focus of our diversity training. Ostensibly removed from personal feelings, the topic could be addressed without defensiveness and would at least raise awareness of this debate in intellectual circles. It was thought that such an approach might also result in actual curricular changes by the action of some TAs to introduce materials traditionally excluded from courses in their departments.

Finally, some argued that the most practical emphasis would be to focus on classroom dynamics. Supporters of this approach stated that the training program should expose TAs to a variety of classroom situations that could lead to conflicts. They argued that reviewing case studies based on actual incidents would both help them to understand issues of race and diversity as they relate to classroom dynamics and also give them a chance to practice, in a protected atmosphere, alternative educational responses to such situations. As a result, they would be better prepared for actual conflicts that might arise.

In the end we decided to experiment with all of these approaches in our first training sessions. Depending upon the inclination of particular staff members, one or more of these approaches were attempted with different sections of the TAs. We were to learn a considerable amount from this first attempt.

RETHINKING AND REDESIGNING THE TRAINING PROGRAM

As stated, our first attempt did not go well. Although there were a few sessions that were well received by TAs in some departments, there were many others that left participants disgruntled, accusatory, and angry. A discussion with one department, the only case in which the TAs in attendance were all White and male, was heated and angry, dotted with slurs and patronizing comments to the female facilitator during attempts to elicit personal introspection about experiences with racism and sexual harassment. They had made it clear to the facilitator prior to the discussion that they saw no need for training in multicultural teaching. Another discussion ended in a shouting match among our own TA trainers over their very different approaches to conducting the training.

Our reaction to these sessions was to back off from the value-confrontational approach and the attempt to elicit personal reflection. We decided, at least in the short time frame available, that discussion of professional behavioral change and course content were the areas to emphasize. In this type of setting any attempt to address "personal" beliefs was more likely to be perceived defensively as an accusation of racism, sexism, or homophobia than as a constructive exercise in self-reflection. On the other hand, the focus on behavioral and intellectual issues allowed a greater opportunity for an initial opening of the discussion of multicultural teaching precisely because there was less suspicion or defensiveness related to finger pointing. However, we recognized quickly, as we had suspected, the futility of a one-shot workshop to deal with issues of diversity. Not only were we stymied in accomplishing our goals in a single three-hour required session, but the students themselves were very cynical about a single moment of "diversity time." By structuring only one discussion, ironically we sent a message that this was not a particularly serious part of teaching and that our intention was merely to make a political statement in a contentious climate.

In preparation for the next semester we decided to rethink carefully the entire course in terms of how we might address issues of diversity in every class meeting in addition to devoting one entire session to diversity (Butler 1989; Schoem 1991; Schuster and Van Dyne 1983). This was not a difficult task, just one that took some reconceptualizing. For instance, we already emphasized attention to individual learning styles in the classroom to sensitize new teachers to the effectiveness of various teaching approaches as opposed to a single teaching style that might be effective only for students with a corresponding learning style. Our TAs had always accepted and appreciated this emphasis. Now, however, we considered how we could assist TAs to make linkages between the different learning styles of individuals and different patterns of discussion and learning styles in various racial and ethnic groups and by gender. We asked TAs to take note of which students they called on to participate in class discussions to see if there was any differentiation that could be attributed to race or gender. We also asked TAs to think about how they used office hours and whether such one-on-one contacts were equally valuable for both their male and female students and across different racial and ethnic groups.

We looked at the content of problem sets and exam questions for their accessibility and incorporation of all groups. We offered actual examples of students who had reported instructors' statements about the expected success of students based on their skin color or their family name as listed on the class roster. We advised TAs not to succumb to a common problem of falling back on jokes about women, lesbians, gay men, and others, ostensibly to "break the ice" on the first day of class. We used vignettes, again from reports of actual classroom situations, to illustrate potential conflicts and problems related to classroom dynamics involving students from diverse backgrounds. As part of our microteaching session (videotaping of TAs), we examined how much time TAs spend with each student in answering questions, which students are called on most frequently, and which students are challenged most to think critically.

By the fourth time we offered the TA training course, a year and one-half after the first attempt, we had made yet another change in our approach to diversity training. Realizing that our course could serve as only a very limited introduction to these issues, we created a variety of optional opportunities for TAs. We utilized our Friday Forum, a bimonthly discussion on topical teaching issues, to focus attention on the classroom experience of students from different racial/ethnic and economic backgrounds. We offered special advanced workshops for TAs who wanted to pursue topics in greater depth, and we organized panel discussions on diversity training, addressing issues such as intergroup relations, race relations, and gender issues.

Finally, we also established highly successful incentive grants to departments to encourage their development of discipline-based teacher training including instruction on diversity. With our funding and staff resources, several departments that had not previously offered training on diversity organized well-attended programs and discussions for their faculty and TAs. Other departments experimented with other training opportunities such as classroom observation and mentoring by experienced teaching assistants.

Underlying these alternative approaches to training for multicultural teaching is the fact that it takes time. Our training program faced severe limitations in this respect because the time allotted for the entire TA training course was inadequate. Given this constraint, we concluded that our goals for teacher training, including multicultural training, must be precisely defined.

Perhaps our most important contribution is that our TA training program places the topic of multiculturalism on the teaching agenda for our new TAs. It gives them questions and issues to consider as they begin to teach. By addressing this topic throughout the course, we model our view that multicultural teaching can be woven into every aspect of one's course and ought not be thought of as an adjunct to core learning. The college-wide course allows TAs to participate in cross-disciplinary discussions with their peers while the departmental workshops provide the opportunity for application of specific disciplinary content. Optional programs, such as the advanced workshops and Friday Forum, allow TAs to follow up in specific areas as they grapple more fully with the complex issues that multicultural teaching entails.

TAs learn to expand their definition of good teaching so that it incorporates an awareness of multiculturalism, including issues such as the instructor's personal relations with individual students, classroom dynamics, attention to learning styles, course content, grading, and developing assignments and exams. As the TAs go on to teach throughout their graduate student years, they take with them from this course a definition of good teaching that includes multiculturalism and a set of different questions and issues to continue to explore in their classrooms.

NOTE

1. I wish to acknowledge the following people for thinking with me about the issues of multiculturalism as applied to TA Training: Catherine Bach, Susan Carlton, Mark Chesler, Cathy Cohen, Begona Garcia, Lorraine Gutiérrez, Bronwen Gates, Anne Harrington, Laurie Lytel, Patricia Myers, Peter Olsen, Luis Sfeir-Younis.

Part VI

Roundtable Discussion: The Insiders' Critique of Multicultural Teaching

ROUNDTABLE PARTICIPANTS

T. Alexander Aleinikoff, Law

Bunyan Bryant, Natural Resources

Mark A. Chesler, Sociology

Billie L. Edwards, Lesbian–Gay Male Programs Office

Thomas J. Gerschick, Sociology

Christina José, Women's Studies

Edith A. Lewis, Social Work

Eliana Moya-Raggio, Latino Studies and Residential College

Patricia Myers, Women's Studies

Robert M. Ortega, Psychology

David Schoem, Sociology

Kristine Siefert, Social Work and Public Health

Luis F. Sfeir-Younis, Pilot Program and Sociology

Ralph D. Story, English and Comprehensive Studies Program

Ximena Zúñiga, Education and Project on Intergroup Relations and Conflict

Teaching is a strength all of our authors bring to this book; they all have considerable experience as teachers. But writing about teaching is not an exercise with which most are familiar. Thus, in the process of writing about teaching for this book, new insights, intellectual challenges, and personal dilemmas became evident for most involved.

Early in the project we invited our authors to join us for an open-ended discussion about their teaching and about their writing about their teaching. The value of our coming together in this way was immediately evident. We covered considerable ground on substantive issues about multicultural teaching and about our chapters for this book. But what stood out was the collective support represented in the room for our attempts at multicultural teaching. This came in marked contrast to the sense of isolation and vulnerability that many experienced, whether having tenured positions or not, in their home departments.

After a second meeting, we decided to invite the authors to a more structured, yet free-flowing, roundtable discussion that we would transcribe for a chapter of the book. We asked the authors in advance of the discussion to consider a number of questions. First, we were interested in comparing our authors' definitions of multiculturalism and multicultural teaching. We wanted to know what they meant when they talked about multicultural teaching. Importantly, we wanted to discuss what was lacking in our paradigm(s) of multicultural teaching. It was our desire to have the authors present and debate their critique of multiculturalism and multicultural teaching. We expected these topics to lead to some discussion of issues such as academic freedom, charges of political correctness, and a comparison of multicultural teaching and anti-racist teaching. Finally, as a result of our prior roundtables, we anticipated that there would be considerable sharing of practical teaching strategies and concerns as well as further discussion of the risks and rewards of doing multicultural teaching.

The lively conversation that follows raises more issues and questions than it answers. It represents multiple perspectives and definitions of multiculturalism and multicultural teaching as part of the effort to reach a deeper understanding of the term. In part, the differences expressed reflect the different ways of knowing that may very well constitute multiculturalism; in part, the differences represent an exploration of ideas and issues that are still unfolding and not fully developed with regard to this term.

In fact, we believe that it is precisely the unfolding of ideas and issues with an unusually high degree of openness and candor that provides the richness of this chapter. For the participants this is not an attempt to make a final statement on the topic. To them, this discussion about multicultural teaching is a piece of what they expect to be a long-term exploration of ideas, issues, and practices. To share thoughts and feelings about one's teaching—multicultural teaching—with a sizable group of colleagues represents a unique and stimulating moment in what has been a largely isolated and unrewarded process.

We recognize that the path to knowledge is rarely straight and direct; thus we believe that by presenting here some of the twists and turns of the conversation we help give the reader a closer, more personal view of the authors' thinking on the topic. Clearly, the participants bring different approaches to the interactive process of the discussion, but those multiple discussion styles also represent a core component of our understanding of multiculturalism. We have organized

Part Six according to five substantive themes and edited the transcript of the discussion to conform with those themes. The five themes are:

1. Multiculturalism: Whose Culture, Whose Definition?
2. Multicultural Thinking: Ways of Knowing
3. Multiculturalism and Social Justice
4. Multicultural Discourse
5. In the Classroom: Final Thoughts on Multicultural Teaching

MULTICULTURALISM: WHOSE CULTURE, WHOSE DEFINITION?

Definitions and interpretations of the term *multiculturalism* abound. The focus of the authors' concern, however, has as much to do with the issue of power as it does with definition. Which cultural groups are in positions of power to determine the definition of multiculturalism? Who will decide how expansive or narrow the definition should be? How will it be determined how inclusive or exclusive the definition will be?

In the wider national debate, there has been concern expressed that the history and culture of Whites, or European Americans, will be excluded from the discussion, that is, that multiculturalism is an attempt to bring attention exclusively to people of color whose histories and cultures have been largely ignored in the United States. But our authors speak only for a broadening and expanding of knowledge, not the diminution of Whites or elimination of study of Western culture. Interestingly, they report that White students are confused about their own identity in the class discussions of culture. White students have assumed there is but one culture, but in discussions about multiculturalism, they wonder aloud, What is my culture?

Individual authors argue that lesbians, gay men, and bisexuals represent cultural groups and therefore should rightly be included in the definition of multiculturalism. But, they point out, heterosexuals, as a matter of course, do not include them as part of multiculturalism, even in this roundtable discussion. Similarly, what is the place of gender in the discussion? Can the definition of multiculturalism extend beyond ethnicity so that women's concerns, for instance, can be included? Some of the authors argue strongly for including issues of social class in the discussion of multiculturalism as well.

There is discussion about maintaining a balance between the particular and the general, about giving recognition to specific groups, yet not letting the pendulum swing too far to the point of nationalism. While one author speaks for a human culture, others worry about generalizing or glossing over the particulars of distinct cultures to such an extent that multiculturalism overemphasizes commonality and homogeneity. The authors find that students are more ready to accept other groups once they have had an opportunity to learn about their own.

THE DIALOGUE:

Edwards: If we were to expand what multicultural means beyond just ethnicity and color, it seems to me that people who are not of color could find a way to fit into the dialogue and not feel blamed. Can we think about how we can make this term be more inclusive of all of us as having some culture? If this cannot be done, can we at least find a way that we can really talk without people feeling they're being attacked? Because when I raise issues about heterosexism or homophobia, I'm talking about reality, I'm talking about some very rigid social structures that prevent me and you from interacting as human beings. So I get really excited about the idea of finding a way to broaden this perspective, especially with this kind of group.

Gerschick: Multicultural education must include (1) moving away from thinking about culture only in terms of ethnicity, (2) validation of concerns, which speaks directly to Billie's [Edwards] point, and (3) recognition of contributions of all peoples.

Aleinikoff: Another aspect of culture that seems to be missing in our discussion so far is class culture. It is now common to be aware of racial and gender issues and to notice occasionally heterosexism, but the issue of class discrimination is absent. My sense is that the role of class should be a part of any full-fledged multicultural teaching.

Moya-Raggio: Multiculturalism is not any elimination but is rather an expansion of knowledge. It's a broadening of courses and information, not a narrowing or a competition of one view versus the other. I think there has been some mistake in interpreting multicultural teaching as meaning the elimination of Western culture or that we are not going to focus on Western culture.

José: Multicultural teaching means students will learn about their own culture, too. Many times white students will say, Do we, as white students, have ethnicity? Learning about your own culture is very important. Once you know about your culture, you are more able to accept it and also more able to accept other cultures.

Sfeir-Younis: Most students from dominant groups talk about the one culture, American culture. It is very difficult to suggest that there are other cultures that have validity and a history. It is very hard for the mainstream to accept the idea of other cultures within the United States. In my personal experience the American white male student feels, on one hand, that we're all part of one culture, but on the other hand, as individual whites, they don't have a culture. It suggests the idea of a culture-less culture.

Myers: What I'm afraid happens as a result of what Luis [Sfeir-Younis] is reporting is that people turn to generalizations, saying, for example, Blacks are like this, in the same way that Native Americans are like this, and the specificity of our experiences smashes together. When that happens, from what perspective can we critique?

Moya-Raggio: And I think that is a very real concern on the part of the students, too. They hear these generalizations, and when they are taught that Latinos, for instance, are a heterogeneous group with all the diversity that exists among all of the subgroups, it is incredibly difficult for them to understand.

Aleinikoff: At the same time, we need to resist going to the other extreme— essentialism—in our multicultural teaching. We must take note of the overlaps and intersections of the various groups.

Bryant: Perhaps we ought to think in terms of a ''human culture'' that we transcend, much as we are discussing with regard to multiculturalism. I worry that people get so locked in wanting to learn about their own culture that they end up either not respecting or even trying to dominate some other cultures. There are a lot of positives in multiculturalism, but there are potential negatives, too, like the dangers of nationalism, and we need to be very mindful of these negatives as we travel down this road.

Edwards: As I look around the table and I listen and we talk about teaching, we speak of a way of being, and I have been waiting to hear the words *sexual orientation*. And they haven't come up. I'm also aware that it is very difficult to continue to raise that issue. At the same time it's difficult to trust that others will raise the issue. Unless you raise it, I'm still at the point of not believing that sexual orientation will be woven into the tapestry of education. When you talk about multiculturalism, where does that lead? I have a culture, but it's not usually thought of in terms of fitting into a discussion on multiculturalism. So, one of the things that happens to us is that we're struggling to define where we, lesbians and gay men, fit and how we can be a part of the conversation and dialogue.

MULTICULTURAL THINKING: WAYS OF KNOWING

The authors all understand multiculturalism to represent a broadening of thinking, information, and knowledge, bringing new perspectives to join the old. No one speaks of eliminating ideas or narrowing perspectives. But the authors do view multiculturalism as going well beyond the mere awareness and celebration of difference.

There is discussion here of multiculturalism as increasing our ways of knowing, as enabling us to reread texts we have understood to have a particular meaning and uncovering new meanings and perspectives that we could not previously see. But there is some disagreement about whether that actually indicates new ways of knowing or, rather, just the broadening of what we previously have been taught or permitted to know.

One of the authors speaks of a multicultural quality of mind that reaches beyond notions of critical thinking. He describes this quality of mind as the ability to understand truth or reality from different points of view.

THE DIALOGUE:

Bryant: I define multiculturalism as a critique of White Western culture. It is a way of putting forth some alternative cultural paradigms for discourse. After my teaching became more multiculturally oriented, students began to get a different point of view with respect to (1) what other cultures were like and (2) how we could begin to look at both similarities and differences among a variety of cultures as compared with White Western culture. Multicultural education is not only a critique of White Western culture, but it broadens our thinking and our knowledge base.

Myers: My concern is that with multiculturalism we might lose those broadening perspectives. If we lose our ability to distinguish our cultures through an all-encompassing multicultural view, how can we differentiate our perspectives in order to separate out my understanding from your understanding?

Sfeir-Younis: To me, multiculturalism is a way of thinking, a way of approaching reality. It is a quality of mind that enables people to create and participate actively in a diverse society. Multicultural teaching transcends critical thinking. It helps students to see their reality from other points of view and to welcome other views and other cultures that are different from theirs. What we are doing in multicultural teaching is trying to create learning conditions and develop a special body of knowledge that fosters a multicultural quality of mind.

Moya-Raggio: I truly think that Luis [Sfeir-Younis] has interpreted my thoughts. I am going to be a little bit personal. Women's literature has been absent from the literature courses on Latin America for a long time. When I used to read women's literature, I read it simply in my home. Suddenly I discovered that the same books that I had read before needed to be read again with different eyes, with a different focus, from a different perspective, not only from a feminist perspective. In a way I engaged in a reassessment of knowledge that I had already acquired but I had acquired in a very different way.

Aleinikoff: I agree that multicultural teaching, in the way we usually think about it, is an epistemological idea—concerned with ways of knowing. But, contrasted with anti-racist teaching or anti-domination teaching, which is more concerned with issues of power and hierarchy, it seems to me that multicultural teaching is not just about different ways of knowing, but also about recognizing the ways in which our current worldview hides things from our sight. I'll give an example from my discipline, constitutional law. If one studies the framers and the document, it is clear that the original Constitution protected slavery. When you communicate this to white students who've grown up in the dominant culture, it can be eye-opening news to them; yet they can "see it"—once it's pointed out—without changing their "way of knowing." What I mean is that other things can be "known" or learned within existing ways of knowing.

MULTICULTURALISM AND SOCIAL JUSTICE

The authors note and challenge their own apparent sentimentalizing about the good of multiculturalism. Is multiculturalism by definition tied to some notion of social justice, or is that association simply wishful thinking?

As noted earlier, there is strong feeling that any understanding of multiculturalism must be tied to discussion of issues of power and equity, that cultural awareness, for instance, represents a very limited definition of the term. As such, some authors very directly link multiculturalism to notions of change in social and economic structures and argue that there may be greater commonality across ethnic lines, but within socioeconomic classes, than within ethnic groups. Finally, there is the admonishment to be patient, to remember that change comes about slowly.

THE DIALOGUE:

Schoem: From listening to our discussion today, I wonder whether when we define multiculturalism, we are implicitly attempting to define a just multicultural society, particularly when we include issues such as class. Couldn't there be a multicultural society that is unjust and that maintains rigid class divisions, for instance? Couldn't a multicultural society turn out to have features that we don't necessarily feel positive about? Are we perhaps merging two issues—justice and multiculturalism? What we may want is a just and progressive society that is multicultural, but, in fact, that ideal is more than this term *multicultural* really represents. Perhaps this term is not really adequate for what people here are intending or hoping for.

Bryant: It seems to me that two of the key issues are justice and equity. I don't want to be a part of multicultural teaching or part of a multicultural society if it's going to maintain oppression or inequity.

Sfeir-Younis: I think it is crucial that within diversity we recognize the issue of power.

Bryant: One reason the existing pluralistic society doesn't work is the unequal distribution of power. Some people have more power than other people. As I think about multiculturalism, I think we need to talk about it not only in terms of understanding different cultures, but also in terms of what we do after we understand. The question for me is, How do we begin to change power relations and incorporate cooperation and nonviolence within the context of multicultural education? Somehow we need to talk about a world citizenship based upon egalitarianism.

José: When you really have to give up power and move along the lines of what David [Schoem] was saying about justice, there is much more in common between a poor White, poor Black, poor Latino, and any other ethnic group—the poor share a tremendous culture between them—than between a middle-class White and a poor White or a middle-class Latino and an upper-class Latino.

Story: I think you've got to see this as a very, very long-term struggle. In 1968, people were raising the same kinds of issues we're discussing here. Maybe we're flailing away at this too much, wondering whether or not we're doing the right thing. Inevitably we will address justice; inevitably we will address equity. I think we broke stride back in the seventies, and I think we're just starting all over again, and it's going to take a long period of time. It's never easy. We're not trying to set the world on fire immediately. It's just going to take some time. Multiculturalism is certainly better than being myopic and monocultural.

MULTICULTURAL DISCOURSE

This discussion serves more as an example of the difficulties and complexities of multicultural discourse than as any guide to conducting multicultural discussions. It demonstrates that we must be attentive not only to multicultural content, but to the different communication styles that exist across ethnic groups and gender. How, in fact, do we talk to one another in a multicultural classroom, in a multicultural society?

The authors again speak of the importance of power as a key to how we live and communicate in a multicultural society. The dominance of one communication style over another or one form of group process over the next is related to one group's social and political domination over the other. Traditionally, some argue, that has meant styles of White discourse having dominance over styles of discourse of people of color and men controlling the form, style, and processes of communication over women's preferences.

The authors express disagreement over the language of the debate, even as it is discussed in terms of form rather than substance. Some prefer the term *multiculturalism* to *anti-racism* because multiculturalism sounds more positive and less discomforting. But others, while their desire is not to cause discomfort, do not wish to eschew a particular language choice because of its potential to make some feel uncomfortable. Rather, they argue the importance of recognizing that both monocultural societies and multicultural societies that exclude certain groups create hurt and discomfort for some people on a daily and systemic basis.

Finally, the authors discuss the risks and rewards of doing multicultural teaching within a monocultural university. As part of that discussion, they talk about privilege and status by professional rank within the university and the impact that academic status and security have for open, free, and multicultural discourse, particularly when certain groups are underrepresented in positions of higher status. Nevertheless, these participants are not willing to be silenced or censored by virtue of either their status or their commitment to multicultural teaching.

THE DIALOGUE (in three sections):

Section One:

Bryant: As we talk about the differences between anti-racist teaching and multicultural teaching, what comes to mind about anti-racist teaching is something very negative. Even the word *"racist"* is very scary to a lot of people. There's that threat that students will be labeled racists. Nobody likes to be labeled as a racist; it makes people feel uncomfortable. I think multiculturalism comes across as being more positive than anti-racism.

Siefert: I agree. From my own disciplinary framework it's the difference between primary and secondary prevention. Primary prevention is health promotion and specific protection against disorders of known cause while secondary prevention is treating something or intervening when a problem is already present. It seems to me that multicultural teaching is really trying to promote and protect rather than treating a problem.

Myers: I agree that multiculturalism has a much more positive sound, but the fact is that I live in a world that is made uncomfortable by my speaking as a lesbian and as a working-class woman. When I have to teach out of that particular spot, at the same time that I'm challenging contexts as they exist, I can work to create other contexts, but for me it has to be a simultaneous thing.

Section Two:

Schoem: The first time we came together a few months ago, people expressed a strong sense of feeling vulnerable and marginalized, and there was a lengthy discussion about the risk and pain of doing this kind of teaching. Although there wasn't much talk about rewards, it was clear that people were still choosing to continue to do this kind of teaching in spite of the risks. In light of the current attention being given to "political correctness," we thought it would be worthwhile to explore these issues further.

Chesler: To me the question of risks and rewards makes good sense once and only if you develop the analytical frame about what is a multicultural organization. Then you can ask whether it is even possible to do this kind of teaching in this type of organization. I question whether it is possible to do multicultural teaching in a monocultural university.

Bryant: When I leave here and think about trying to enhance multicultural education, I'll be shaky, because my school is a White male monoculture. So while I feel very good about this conversation, there are some things I just can't deal with in my school. When you're in this kind of institution, you definitely need a support base.

Moya-Raggio: I think that is easier when you have a position that is protected, because if you are a woman or if you are a lecturer, then it is even more difficult. To do this teaching becomes risking practically your life because of the way in which you are attacked internally or externally or because of the way you are not considered for certain things.

Myers: All of these strikes are against me as a graduate student.

Edwards: From my perspective we are carving out a space where we can talk, and there are not many opportunities for this to happen. And the conservative right, who are having a very strong reaction, are doing what they always do, which is to attempt to silence me by using the red herring of "political correctness." My conflict, how I react emotionally to them, is to want to say to them you can't use offensive language and be responsible and humane human beings. I want to speak and be heard. There has to be some way to go through this and stand steady because there is going to be a lot of reaction to what we're attempting to do—trying to create a new way of doing things and a new way of being with each other. That's very threatening.

But I'm not willing to quit, even though it's sometimes very painful. There are still many people who are comfortable and don't want to think about other views. I do what I do because it's right for me. It's right, and I can't imagine not doing it, even though there's a cost, personally, and sometimes a very high one. But every time I see a mental light bulb go on or every time I know that somehow another human being is able to experience the world in a more expanded way, I feel very positive.

Section Three:

Story: I want to respond to what Mark [Chesler] said earlier. I think that what has to take place in the multiculturalism debate is point, counterpoint, substantiation, support for your position. You have to demonstrate through example, through illustration, through history, through the discourse that this is a monocultural institution, that the kind of education these young students have received has been myopic, has been monocultural. I think you have to have some weapons at your disposal to defend multiculturalism. Some of the young people we have in our classes are going to say, "What do you mean? What are you talking about?" I don't think they're going to sit down or cease and desist based on your saying, "How can you even think that?" They're going to say, "Well, I do think that!"

Edwards: You have just illustrated an issue of concern for me, the presumption that the only way to dialogue and talk about this is in the White male model. The point-counterpoint model is linear and has a language of its own that we must use to speak and converse in. But there are other styles of communicating that are just as valid that students need to be exposed to so we can honor who we are, especially as women.

Siefert: I think that's a pertinent observation—I felt uncomfortable when I came in. First of all, the conversation started with men, all men, and then finally a couple of the women spoke out. And then I felt really bad hearing the response that gay women have had to be the ones to raise the issue of sexual orientation, and I thought to myself that if that happened in my class, I would really feel guilty.

Story: I wasn't suggesting this as a model for the way that the discourse should proceed every day. But I know that in my situation, even when I taught African American literature at a predominantly white institution, I've had people who just wanted to challenge me constantly, all the time, every day, and typically the discourse has been more like that than it's been participatory or cooperative.

Aleinikoff: Related to this discussion, I have found that techniques for hearing people out and helping them feel comfortable may be as important a component as what we're teaching them in class.

Myers: I have to disagree about the issue of comfort. I'm not sure how much my teaching makes people comfortable. I try to create a safe space, and I try to make it possible for people to speak to each other across the gulfs in their experience. But I also know that in critiquing power relationships there is a discomfort, and sometimes my goal is to make people as uncomfortable as I possibly can, short of their leaving the room. So if there was agreement that we should try to make people comfortable, then I guess that's a critique that I have.

Edwards: I would just like to dovetail with what Patti [Myers] is saying. If we wait for people to be comfortable, lesbians, gay men, and bisexuals will never be included, because the majority of the university community, particularly students, are very uncomfortable with concerns about sexual orientation. I think part of what this is about is how we manage these conflicts, how we create an environment where we make room for the anxious, because anxiety is part of that awareness that develops. For instance, there have been moments where I have been anxious at this table.

IN THE CLASSROOM: FINAL THOUGHTS ON
MULTICULTURAL TEACHING

Questions remain for our authors. Is the purpose of multiculturalism to work toward a unified vision, distilled from many cultural perspectives, for any given question? Or is it to give a set of possible explanations from many different cultural perspectives? Or is it to identify a single, correct answer from a single, distinct culture after having evaluated the alternative responses from many different cultural perspectives? In fact, those choices may be too sharply drawn.

It may very well be that multiculturalism represents a unified vision, but it is one with multiple avenues of understanding and explanation.

Our authors wonder about students' ability to link learning and practice. On issues that are as personally and socially connected as those of multiculturalism, should the teacher's role be to reinforce those connections or to help students make a distinction between knowledge and behavior? Similarly, our authors argue that it is not necessarily the teacher's background or skin color or even the course content that makes for a multicultural classroom; rather, it is how the teacher approaches learning, whether the teacher incorporates a multicultural quality of mind, and whether the teacher has developed multiple ways of knowing and seeing.

The authors speak, too, of the different learning environment associated with multicultural teaching. They speak of welcoming ideas and perspectives into the classroom that represent a broadening from what has been traditional thinking and practice. They speak, too, of welcoming individuals who have traditionally been absent from the classroom and from intellectual inquiry and scholarship.

Finally, the authors talk about the need for collegial support and of the value of coming together to talk about their work in multicultural teaching. To do so represents the beginnings of creating a different university culture, one that is more open and more collaborative and places an emphasis on teaching and learning. In substance and in process, it is a step toward a multicultural university community.

THE DIALOGUE:

Aleinikoff: The question I have not yet resolved in my own mind is, Does multicultural teaching hope to produce a new, better truth, or does it hope to produce multiple truths? What I mean is, if we have different perspectives, and we all talk, should we end the discussion roughly agreeing on one story or account; or should we leave all believing different accounts—conceding that the discussion has enriched us—and say that all those "truths" are equal? The other way to think about this question is, Would a multicultural history book have different chapters written by different cultures on the same events, or would it present a unified story that was based on the perspectives of the different groups?

José: One of the things that I struggle with all the time teaching multiculturally is the big gap between learning the concepts of what a different culture can be and actually acting on your prejudice. But I don't see that connection taking place in my students' lives. I see in my classes people being so happy about learning all these new things, and it's wonderful, but when it comes to sharing the power, and it's going to be between you and me, people say, "No way."

Moya-Raggio: I want to add that even in courses in which some faculty might not imagine the opportunity for multicultural teaching, it does exist. When I teach language, for instance, a subject that some view merely as the acquisition of skills, I include an understanding of Latin American culture. Some students have problems as I attempt to engage them in the reading of the culture, but I view such problems as educational challenges—even multicultural ones.

Ortega: In my courses, too, I attempt to help students think about what culture means, about the cultural context of the material they are studying.

Sfeir-Younis: Even if a course is not dealing with problems of ethnic groups and even if there are not any people of color in the classroom, it's still possible to teach multicultural issues. But I would add that it is likely to be a much greater and richer experience if there is also diversity in the course content and readings and also among the teacher and students.

Moya-Raggio: I would like to follow up Luis's [Sfeir-Younis] point that sometimes when you teach, it's not the color of your skin that makes a difference in the classroom, but rather what you have to say and where you are coming from—how you read the culture. It's how you read culture that makes an impact, that makes a difference in your classes and your students.

Gerschick: Multicultural teaching has to be an ongoing process. Some of our efforts at multiculturalism are one shot deals; they're very sporadic; we do something nice, but the ramifications and the lasting effects are questionable.

Siefert: I hadn't really thought about multicultural teaching until I was contacted by this group. There just isn't much discussion of it in the academy. It was such a pleasure to find people who were doing this same thing. One thing that I liked about Luis's [Sfeir-Younis] definition was the comment about welcoming different groups because that's something that I see as a really integral part of the kind of teaching I'm trying to do. It's a kind of appreciation and a welcoming of different people, and there isn't much talk about that.

Gerschick: It's really nice to be here because just as we talk about isolation and some of the risks and the costs associated with these issues, it's also nice to know that there are people in this university and elsewhere who are doing this work. It's nice to get together to just talk—it gives me energy in much the same way we've been talking about the light bulb illuminating for the first time and the fuse giving us energy to continue generating this kind of light.

Edwards: This opportunity doesn't happen very often for me. It's really validating for me to hear others speak. This, for me, makes me stronger and more comfortable.

Part VII

Questions and Responses on Multicultural Teaching and Conflict in the Classroom

The editors and authors found that one of the most enriching aspects of collaborating on this book was our ability to share with each other our methods of handling the recurring and potentially difficult aspects of multicultural teaching. Through our discussions, we found that many of us had experienced the same types of challenges in the classroom and had found some unique ways of managing them.

This chapter is a compilation of the responses of selected authors to fifteen questions posed by the editors.[1] While certainly not exhaustive, these questions do address some of the struggles faced by faculty attempting to consider the impact of race, ethnicity, sexual orientation, gender, and class in the courses we teach, as these are reflected in ourselves, our students, and course content and design.

The first group of questions (1 through 8) address broader pedagogical issues for the planning of a course, such as course design, classroom dynamics, and evaluation. The second group of questions (9 through 15) are of a problem-solving nature that the teacher must respond to in the classroom. Each question is followed by responses from three of the authors or editors. This chapter is presented in the hope that others facing similar questions will find some new ways of thinking through these issues.

1. How do you create an open, comfortable, and challenging multicultural classroom environment? What do you do to encourage students to discuss openly their fears about dealing with racism and differences? How do you help students feel comfortable with sharing views and experiences that may offend other students in the class? What kind of ground rules do you establish in the class?

During the first session I generally hand out and discuss some version of the ground rules developed by Lynn Weber Cannon of Memphis State University's Center for Research on Women (Cannon 1990a). I spend a lot of time talking about the importance of agreeing on how we are going to achieve our learning goals, in addition to giving an overview of the content of the course. I present myself as someone who, while having expertise in certain areas, is striving to view material in new ways. I emphasize the necessity for each student to take responsibility for her or his own learning as well as that of the group as a whole. Depending on the time constraints, I also plan a small group activity for the first or second session. I first ask students to spend about ten minutes writing a paragraph on how they identify themselves—for example, as a Jewish, White, middle-class woman and mother—and what aspects of their identity are most salient in various contexts. The class then divides into small groups to discuss these paragraphs. I also do the writing exercise and join one of the groups. We then reassemble in the larger group to discuss issues of appearances, self-identity, self-disclosure, trust, diversity, and commonalities. This helps to cut down some of the unstated assumptions students make about one another. It also brings to the fore differences that are masked behind apparent homogeneity.

I explicitly acknowledge that dealing with some of the issues we will be addressing will not be easy, that at times they will feel "too close to home," and that they will probably make us feel uncomfortable and as if we want "to run away." I stress the value of conflict even when it may make us uncomfortable. I also make explicit that I am committed to facilitating a process where we can work through some of these issues and that both the content and the process of the course are very important to me and subject to ongoing examination. Then I proceed to facilitate an icebreaker activity that will help students get to know each other's names and share aspects of themselves that will give participants a better sense of where people are coming from. I facilitate a Hopes, Fears (Concerns), and Expectations exercise. I ask students to jot down on index cards two hopes, two fears, two expectations. I usually ask them to indicate at the bottom of the card their race/ethnicity and gender. As participants share their hopes, fears, and expectations with the rest of the class, I write these on newsprint. If the class is not skewed along racial/ethnic lines, I jot down these in separate newsprints; that is, I create different listings for White students and students of color. If I notice that people are having a hard time owning their hopes or fears, I usually collect the cards and proceed to read them aloud while one of the students jots them down. This is a very powerful exercise in that it usually sends a clear message about how prevalent the issue of safety is, regardless of students' race/ethnicity or gender. This usually comes as a surprise to most students, especially to White students. Students indicate that they are afraid of being attacked, of offending others, of conflict, of being insensitive to others, of being perceived as racist, sexist, or homophobic; in the same vein, most students express similar hopes regardless of their racial/ethnic and gender background—

they hope to be listened to, to be able to challenge themselves and others, to help others understand their views, to learn about people who are different from themselves, and to deal with conflict constructively. I spend at least ten to fifteen minutes processing what comes up in this activity and then stress the need for having some norms like "I statements," "active listening," "respect for others' opinions," and "conflict is OK."

At the start of the class I express my personal and intellectual enthusiasm for the anticipated discussion and learning that will take place throughout the semester. I try to empower students by making them aware that what they have to say is important and I, the teacher, can't wait to begin the semester precisely because I want to hear their voices as participants in the discussion.

I also play a simple name game whereby all of the students must remember all of their classmates' names in order. It's a good icebreaker, it's not threatening, and students have an experience of laughing together.

I also directly address issues of potential conflict and say that conflict is likely to occur and that I expect the class to learn from conflict. We discuss and read about the different communication styles, and I set as ground rules that students listen to one another, show respect for each other, and approach class with a mind-set that is critical yet open to new and opposing ideas. Most importantly, I try to give students a sense that we have an entire semester to work on these issues, that we have all made a commitment to stay together for the duration, and that the intensity of our discussions can proceed as slowly or as quickly as is appropriate.

2. What do you do to help students integrate theoretical material with their personal experience? What kind of assignments do you give? What kind of activities do you plan for the classroom?

We need to acknowledge that the notion of integrating personal experience with theoretical/analytical material is new for most students (and faculty members); students, for the most part, are not encouraged to examine their "personal troubles," in C. Wright Mills's words, in the context of larger sociopolitical structures and modes of thinking, but rather to separate thought from feeling, theory from experience, and subject from object. In addition, we need to keep in mind that some students will feel more comfortable writing or talking about their personal experiences or perhaps integrating the two and, more specifically, that students' ability to share openly in journal assignments, self-reflection papers, or classroom discussions vary along race/ethnicity and gender lines.

I usually structure one experiential activity every other session during the term; I do this to stimulate students' individual growth and group development. For example, I encourage students to examine and value their individual experiences and those of their classmates by looking at different dimensions—their feelings, behaviors, and values; to explore how their personal biographies and their membership in different cultural groups (e.g., race/ethnicity, gender, social class, sexual orientation, religion) influence their worldviews and behaviors; to develop as a group through activities that promote personal sharing and through small group activities where they can learn from, and challenge, each other; last, to examine what unfolds in the classroom as a way of understanding intragroup and intergroup relations. I specifically ask students to look at the patterns of interaction, conflicts, and norms that emerge as source data; I also ask them to pay attention not only to what is said but to what is not said so we can become aware of issues of inclusion and exclusion in our midst. At the end of the activity, we spend time "processing" what emerged before making connections with readings or larger societal structures.

I try to vary the types of readings on specific topics so that they reflect different styles of communicating and interpreting evidence and analysis. I use novels, autobiographies, and oral histories along with materials from the social sciences and history. In discussion we try to use the more theoretically oriented pieces to frame the questions we ask of the more subjective materials, including the experiences students bring to class. I have also planned assignments to move outward from self-exploration. For example, I sometimes ask students to keep journals that integrate their reflections on the issues with critical assessment of reading assignments. A midterm assignment might be to write a critical essay comparing two autobiographies written by women of different races and classes or to conduct an oral history with a person of a race, class, or gender different from that of the student. This gives students a chance to apply some of the concepts we have been exploring—gender, race, class—in a more systematic way. Finally, the group projects and papers presented at the end of the term require that students look at a topic from a comprehensive perspective, incorporating the whole range of patterns of social differentiation we have been exploring.

In discussion I relate theoretical questions to students' personal experience, to their group experience in society, or to related campus issues. I try to help students take a view of themselves as active players in the real world of intergroup relations and see themselves in the scholarly material, that is, to ensure that they realize that the theory is about them and their lives.

I also ask students to respond to theoretical questions in their analytical journals. Since much of the work in these journals is of a personal, reflective nature, the assignment of theoretical questions results in students' moving easily between the two and increasingly to an integration of the personal and the theoretical.

3. How do you help students learn from classroom dynamics that directly result from the class composition?

First of all, I always encourage students to pay attention to issues of group composition; I facilitate a wide range of exercises to help students examine the makeup of the class—"who is there" and "who is not there"—and to become increasingly aware of people's multiple identities (visible and invisible) using, for example, the Line exercise; the Multiple-Role exercise; identity groups along gender, race/ethnic lines; and the Alliance Building exercise.[2] I invite students to explore the impact of the class composition on the way individuals, subgroups and the class as a whole deals with issues, manages conflict and works together. I also encourage students to examine the patterns of interactions that surface from time to time as we deal with specific topics or confront issues of conflict.

I always incorporate many opportunities for group evaluation, self-evaluation, and feedback into my courses. We explore the different dimensions of group process such as participation, power, cooperation, and task orientation. We usually reserve the last few minutes of class for comments and reflection on process issues. Sometimes course materials on particular topics raise questions about class dynamics; that is, readings or discussion of materials pertaining to gender or race provokes debates that heighten or highlight tensions in class. We then discuss these parallels. If unresolved feelings or unanswered questions remain, we sometimes devote a whole class session to the issues, often reading additional articles that might help us to get to the root of our differences/conflicts. Not infrequently, students will approach me individually or collectively outside the classroom to discuss concerns over classroom dynamics. It is sometimes easier to get a handle on how students perceive classroom dynamics by speaking with them more informally outside class. This kind of communication is sometimes less threatening and involves less risk of self-exposure. Therefore, it is a good prelude to discussion in the larger group. After we try to lay out the issues, I encourage these students to present their concerns to the class as a whole. Then we brainstorm about ways to remedy the situation. We try to differentiate between taking individual responsibility for acting on new information versus singling out or blaming individuals. If skewed patterns of participation or other issues of classroom dynamics remain hidden, I often point these out to students as matters for reflection and discussion.

I have tried some of the following techniques in the courses I teach. First, I simply make a process comment on the discussion in terms of who is taking what stand on an issue and comment on what patterns are emerging. It is usually a comment to invite more discussion, not a definite opinion as such. Students are welcome to share their observations also.

Second, I pause in the ongoing discussion and do a process check with the students. How are they feeling about the discussion? Are there any observations that students would like to share? What are students' comfort levels? This can also be done as a round, with students' always having the option to pass. What often happens is that students who are active in the discussion are the only ones who will make a comment on the process, and part of my goal in pausing is to allow those whose voice is not being heard to contribute.

Third, a technique I have found very effective is to incorporate the dynamics that I observe as a learning tool for the students in a journal assignment. This is especially feasible in one course that I teach because the students are required to write a weekly reflection journal, and I usually provide guidelines for them. Often, I design the journal guidelines with a few considerations in mind: (1) the lecture topics and issues, (2) important points relevant to these issues that were either not stressed in lecture or simply not covered, (3) what transpires in discussion, and (4) questions that can set the stage for the following week's topics/ issues. The students know ahead of time that if they don't receive a journal assignment in class, they are to pick it up from my office the next day or so. In this way, I have time to reflect upon the discussion and use it as a learning tool. I usually make a point of asking students to observe classroom dynamics and process (what's going on both among the class members and inside themselves) as the concept of group identity becomes clearer to them.

4. What are the arguments for and against the individual instructor's recruiting more balanced class composition? How do you do it?

I pay a lot of attention to issues of class composition, given that my approach to multicultural teaching emphasizes an intergroup relations focus. I strongly believe that students will benefit more from a diverse class composition. I actively recruit students from diverse backgrounds to provide opportunities for intragroup (e.g., women only, men only, White only, and people of color only) and intergroup dialogue (e.g., between men and women and between white students and students of color). I do so by preparing and mailing fliers to different academic and student services units and student organizations, posting messages in computer conferences, and asking friends to pass the word. This process can be time-consuming but is worth it.

I think that there are some situations where homogeneous groupings are appropriate, whether by gender or race. However, the worst scenario, particularly in classes that focus explicitly on issues of diversity, is a gross racial imbalance, for example, one student of color in a classroom of white students and white teacher. Actually, a large gender imbalance—one or two men in a group of women—tends to work all right because, at least in my experience, the male students who have enough motivation to learn about Women's Studies have experienced being in the minority and have accepted different norms and learned ways to participate comfortably. With only one or two males present, they can discuss the issues as individuals without dominating the conversation as a group. (I encourage male students to take classes on family and gender because relatively few see these topics as relevant to themselves.) Students of color also have plenty of experience being in the minority and develop their own responses. But particularly in classes that include race as part of the manifest content, it benefits both students of color and White students to have a more balanced composition. I have not tried to do any recruiting along these lines but would do so in the future.

For a small class with an enrollment under twenty-five, the active recruitment of students prevents a block of students with high registration priority from filling all the seats in a class for which they have only marginal interest. It allows the teacher to have, on the whole, a class of students with an interest in the topic who are prepared to do serious work. The downside of recruiting students is that it is time-consuming for the teacher. I recruit students by preparing fliers, speaking in classes, and asking friends to spread information about the course by word of mouth. If I find that all of the student interest seems to be coming from a particular group, I will adjust my recruiting effort to attract a wider group of students, but I do not turn people away because of their background.

5. How can an instructor encourage students to say what they think without supporting "racist" views?

One of the multicultural ground rules states that individuals are likely to bring their isms into the classroom and are not to be held responsible for the racist/sexist/classist views they have learned over time. They are to be held responsible, however, for not further transmitting these ideas once new information has been shared with members of the class.

When racist views are presented, we do not attack the messenger. Instead we explore the content of the views, how they might have originated, and what is available to counter the view.

I think we have to distinguish between those remarks that are blatantly provocative—that is, the student knows perfectly well the implications of his or her views and states them in such a way as to pose a challenge—and those that are more naive or whose consequences are unanticipated and unexplored. In the first case, both the affect and the content of the remark must be addressed, calmly but firmly. Other students' challenges to the offensive statements should be supported in a way that focuses on acknowledging the pain caused while trying to cast the issue in terms amenable to rational discourse. In the second case, the student should be supported for his or her honesty and encouraged to explore the source of the ideas and possible alternatives to them. The teacher should model and foster the idea that learning is an ongoing, self-reflective process and that emotional content and intellectual work are not always in sync with one another; in fact, much can be learned from using this interface as a source of data about how we understand ourselves and others. Also, as much as possible, ideas should become the common property of the group so that they can be critically examined without criticizing individuals.

I think the idea here is to let the fizz out. Often, I use the example of a champagne bottle that has been very agitated, and the cork has not been removed. What results is simply an "eruption," with the champagne spilling all over the place. But if the fizz is let out, the champagne can be managed and allowed not to spill.

By the end of the first class meeting, we have already established some basic ground rules and made it clear that offensive, volatile comments may come up from time to time. In going over the ground rules, I also spell out as much as possible, and whenever I can, the way I would like to approach some "violations" of the rules. With that background, when a student does make an offensive "racist" comment or expresses a "racist" view, there are a couple of ways that I go.

One approach is to ask the student to clarify herself or himself simply because I do not want to assume that I know what may be underlying the comment. Of course, I have my own intuitions or theories, but I try to have the student probe the comment. Following the original comment or responses to the probing, I also ask other class members to share their views on the specific comment. Do they agree? Disagree? How do they feel about the comment?

Another approach I have used to simply to "own" my gut reaction and explain it. Emphasis is on how the comment/view affected me personally. I would also invite the student to share or own his or her feelings and engage in dialogue about the comment. Also I have sometimes said that I have often heard such comments and I say how I have reacted or responded. In this way the comment is not individualized to one student, but it is noted that such misinformation and ignorance do exist around us.

Another approach is to probe the student by asking for introspection about how a person of color or a group of persons of color might react upon hearing this view expressed. I think it is also important to approach the student on a one-to-one basis and give some feedback on the comment and my feelings about it.

A strategy that I have not used but may also be effective is to emphasize the courage it may have taken for the student to express that view because others may see it as a racist comment and the consequences could be threatening to have such a view expressed publicly.

6. Do you use your own race, ethnicity, gender, or other relevant social characteristics to personalize issues or to represent another point of view or experience in the discussion? How do you do this?

My pedagogical style is to be a learner as well as a teacher. As such, I also sometimes share the misinformation I was raised with as a way of eliciting discussion on the topic. I realize that I am the first professor who is a woman of color whom many of my students have encountered in their years of education. Students generally have stereotypes about who I am that must be dispelled, and I use personal experiences to do this. For example, often students are genuinely surprised to find that my position at the university does not exempt me from racist treatment in retail stores, banks, or public services in the community in which I live and teach. In my opinion, carefully and selectively balancing the theoretical with the practical helps students to make these linkages in their own thinking and subsequent practice.

I see myself as a facilitator, resource person, teacher, learner, and counselor. As such, I play different roles in the classroom, including participating in group activities. I do use my experiences as a woman, as a person of color, as a person from the Third World, and so on to illustrate the impact of the isms in our lives as well as complex interpersonal and intergroup dynamics. I tend to do more of this early in the term as a way of making it OK for students to look at themselves more openly, to examine the ways they may impact upon other people or other people may impact upon them, and to reflect upon the ways in which their cultural upbringing has influenced their values and behaviors. I also do it to model, for example, a process for sharing and conversing about internalized racism, sexism, homophobia, classism, ethnocentrism. However, my level of active participation in exercises and/or self-disclosure varies depending on the size of the class. I do more of this in classes comprised of twenty students or so than in larger classes (thirty to forty students). Not only is it easier for me to be a participant in a class of small size, but I feel that there is less opportunity for misunderstanding and stereotyping because there is more air space to talk about how students are hearing what is being said by the various constituencies in the class. As a woman I'm aware that some of my comments may sound "out of line" to the men in the class, so I prefer making them when I know that we have space to talk about the impact upon us of my comments and other people's comments.

I have done this to the greatest extent in regard to gender, parenting roles, and social class. Particularly when we discuss work and family issues, my own experience as a parent provides some useful materials that few students have considered except as the children of working parents. Reflections on my personal growth as a participant in feminist activities and scholarship also add some dimension to the more theoretically or historically distanced material in courses on gender, race, and class. Lately, I have tried to bring in other components of my identity that I previously took for granted or that had seemed tangential to the discussion, namely, being a Jewish, White person. As I have reshaped my courses to incorporate greater attention to race and ethnicity, I find that my own engagement with these concerns can provide useful stimuli for engaging students in a similar process.

7. What do you do to empower "underrepresented voices" in the class-room? Do you encourage "identity" or "constituency groups"?

We consider it to be of great importance that in our course all voices enter into the discussion and that none is isolated or remains silent. To facilitate across-the-board participation, we use several approaches: attempts to limit or tone down those individuals or groups that frequently try to monopolize class discussion; solicitation of viewpoints alternative to those that are normally more dominant; and assessment of the nonverbal behavior of nonparticipating students or groups and consultations with them outside class to encourage articulation of their perspectives in subsequent classes. While we make an effort to encourage "underrepresented voices" to speak up in class, we also appreciate that some students prefer to listen primarily (while remaining silent), and therefore we refrain from coercing any one person or group to talk in class. Occasionally, we have asked a student whose voice may be underrepresented for permission to share with the class a section of his or her written assignment containing different experiences, viewpoints, or interpretation.

The following example illustrates one way we have responded to a particular class situation. One year an unusually large and articulate group in our class was composed of lesbian women who often dominated class discussion to the extent that heterosexual women felt uncomfortable talking about their marital status, family situations, and reproductive health concerns. We encouraged several members of the latter group to bring up their discomfort in class and to make a plea for more balanced discussions. The lesbian women became cognizant of what had happened, explained that most of their classes lacked the safety to speak up about homosexuality, and became more inclined to engage in dialogues with students of different sexual orientations.

I encourage subgroupings within the larger classes to give all voices a chance to be heard. This is a delicate balancing act, to be sure. Anytime I incorporate these activities, however, I am careful also to build in time to acknowledge all students' responses to the constituency groups, including the one of which they have been a part.

I ensure that such voices are represented in the course syllabus and in assigned readings. I organize fishbowl exercises, which allow all voices to speak and require students to listen carefully.

One term I experimented with an optional class hour in which students met by their own ethnic group, self-determined. Although I had some hesitation about doing this, which I expressed to students, I offered the option on an experimental basis for as few or as many meetings as they desired. The students, as it turned out, found this meeting time one of the highlights of the course. They were able to bring issues of the large group back to these small groups for discussion and debriefing and then bring back new insights and perspectives to enrich the large group. At the same time that these small discussion groups brought students from separate groups closer together, they did nothing to inhibit the cross-group interaction and cross-group discussion from occurring.

8. How do you assess student learning and evaluate your teaching throughout the semester?

Through the journal I get plenty of information on the progress of the class. Students go over points that create confusion or ask questions about those points.

Many times the questions are posed in a direct manner; other times they are presented in a more convoluted way. I always answer and try to be as forthright as possible. The journals constitute an ongoing dialogue over the semester; students are able to say things they would not feel comfortable bringing to class discussions, for example, deep-seated fear in relation to "the other"—whether about race or social/economic class. When a point raised in the journals is relevant to all the class, I bring it to class discussion and expand on it with background information if necessary. The other way in which information is gathered throughout the semester is through informal conversation at office hours.

I have learned to do ongoing assessments of the classes I teach in two ways. First, formal, written evaluations are done at two points in the semester, at midterm and at the end of the class. Second, weekly or biweekly session evaluations are held at the end of class periods, by doing "rounds" so that each class member gets a chance to express his or her perception of the process and the content of the session. When we have been discussing a potentially difficult subject, I might directly ask students to speak about one way the session has been difficult and stimulating for them. In this way, we keep the acknowledgment of conflict within the session and give students a chance to process it, rather than having to find other ways to process it outside the classroom.

I gather substantial information in order to stay in touch with what goes on with the class as a whole, as well as with individual students, and to introduce changes as needed. I also do it to convey the notion that we all should take responsibility for what goes in the class and that learning is also about process. First of all, in the first session students in my classes complete a personal information sheet that asks about their background, goals for the class, hopes and fears, style of participation in groups, and so on. This information gives me a better sense of the composition of the class and some insight into where the students are coming from and what they are looking for. Second, I try to include an evaluation/feedback activity at the end of each session throughout the term for about ten minutes to get a sense of how the session went and to facilitate group building and group responsibility; when this is not possible, I ask students to jot down evaluative/feedback comments five minutes before the session ends every other week or so. I usually share with them what comes up in the following session and ask for specific suggestions as needed. I say, "Write one or two pluses about today's session, one or two minuses, and one or two things you would change." Third, I usually structure a midterm written evaluation, especially when I haven't been able to gather feedback on an ongoing basis. In some instances, I schedule conferences with every student in the class halfway through the semester to get a better sense of how the class is working for him or her. Last, I always do a final written evaluation in addition to the one administered by the college.

9. What do you do when a student in class discussion makes an explicitly racist or sexist remark? For example, a student may say: "Women are

simply not as capable in math and science as men. Those fields just weren't meant for women" or "Blacks are admitted to this university only because of affirmative action policies."

First of all we spend time at the beginning of the course creating an atmosphere of safety and comfort to facilitate free expression of attitudes and diversity of opinions. Given that this kind of atmosphere can be achieved, we can count on one or several students in the class to respond when a classmate makes an explicitly racist or sexist remark. Neither of the two illustrative cases of student remarks described in the question is likely to go unnoticed or would fail to evoke a detailed and serious response. Our role is likely to be that of moderator to assure that all those who wish to speak have a chance to do so and to ask questions related to the background, origin, and basis of the racist or sexist statement. In the event that the racist or sexist position is supported by others in the class or meets with silence, our tendency would be to probe the intent of, and supporting evidence for, the statement, in order to stimulate further discussion and then to state a counterposition, if no one else in the class had done so.

We consider it important that the proponents of racist or sexist feelings be listened to as well as confronted, for several reasons. First, their attitudes represent those of a sizable segment in our society—individuals we encounter frequently and whose viewpoints will confront us over and over again. All of us need experience in sorting out differences in values and perspectives so that we can learn better to understand, communicate, and defend what we ourselves stand for. Second, for the sake of diversity it is important that even racist and sexist positions not be banned from class discussions, so as to forestall inhibition of stating minority and controversial opinions in subsequent classes, thus limiting openness and receptivity of the class to a range of perspectives and also curtailing the opportunities for learning from each other. Finally, racism and sexism are so deeply entrenched in all aspects of our culture that it is likely that all of us, consciously or subconsciously, carry within ourselves traces of racism and sexism. This realization would urge each of us to question our identity and the origins of our values and beliefs and to engage in a process of learning about ourselves by learning from each other.

It's clear to me that teachers need to be aware of what research has been done and what books are available in order to handle these questions comfortably; I would have to say, however, that if you aren't prepared to respond to students with information and can't point the student in a scholarly direction, a path that encompasses an enlightening journey and a destination, then questions of this sort are troublesome. *You have to be very well read to deal with multicultural issues and concerns.* To be honest, I haven't had to answer questions of this sort often.

This is a point where I have found that sharing my personal experiences helps clarify reality for the students. I will often bring in cases or biographical illustrations to suggest alternative ways of thinking about these issues. I have found so often that people's reliance on the isms is based on misinformation and can be countered with the provision of more accurate data. This does not always work, of course, but I learned long ago as a beginning practitioner that people must be open to changing their inappropriate cognitions for other changes to occur. I cannot force it and no longer take responsibility for its occurrence or non-occurrence.

10. What do you do when a student asks a question with apparent racist implications? For example, a student may say, "But isn't it true that the West has been superior economically and intellectually to African nations and that most Westerners are White and most Africans are Black?"

I interpret this as an issue of misinformation and attempt to initiate a dialogue, which can be entered into by the entire class, to offset the misinformation with more accurate data. This can be done by examining the distorted pictures we have been given to explain an individual's status in our society and world and by thinking about ways these distortions affect the very questions we are able to ask about different populations. For example, if we are taught to define individuals in terms of their problems or pathologies, it is difficult for us to build interventions on the strengths that have sustained them. In terms of the specific case raised in this question, I would help the class brainstorm contributions by African peoples, pointing out, for example, that the first institutions of scholarship in the world were in Timbuktu.

I would first ask for evidence for what the student has inferred to be factual information. Second, I would talk about causal relationships in reference to her or his question and what appears to lie behind the question. Finally, depending on my knowledge of the particular student and her or his probable intentions, I would draw out the student in private conference or in the classroom to probe the implications of the statement.

I would invite the student to elaborate more on his or her claim. What kind of evidence does he or she have to support that line of thought? I would then invite the student and the class to explore both the validity and the political implications of the claim. I would probably also say something like, "A lot of people think that way, in fact, a lot of people, particularly people of European descent, think that one of the reasons Third World countries are underdeveloped is that the majority of their population is non-white so there is no way they can catch up with the modern world." Then I would challenge the students to examine critically their sources of information, as well as the consequences of a claim of that sort, and to draw parallels and comparisons with other situations.

11. What do you do when there is a racial conflict in the classroom between students of different racial/ethnic backgrounds? For example, student A

may say, "I really think that your position [referring to an African American student's comment supporting affirmative action] implies that it is OK to lower admission standards so minority students can come to this university." Student B may respond, "I think you [speaking to a white student] are being racist, and I resent that."

Intervene as soon as it is helpful to do so. Help both students verify to what degree the "message intended" by A was heard by B. Help clarify the message to the degree needed. If it seems helpful, state that conflictual statements are often generated by feelings such as anger, hurt, guilt, depression, and worthlessness.

Help both students explore their feelings to the degree that it seems helpful. If it seems helpful, state that the conflict cannot always be resolved, but that it can usually be addressed in a positive way, so that the parties to the conflict can, at a minimum, "continue to coexist."

Throughout the intervention, engage other class members to the degree possible. "Debrief" the interventions: "How do you, students A and B, feel about what we've tried to do?" "Other people, what are your feelings about this?" "How might we address similar situations in the future, if they arise?"

Continue to stress the importance of addressing "diversity" concerns in every way possible.

I firmly believe that conflict is a part of everyday life and, as such, is unavoidable. This is particularly true when dealing with sensitive topics like racism, sexism, classism, or sexual orientation. Given this belief, I raise the probability of conflict within the classroom in the first class session and then use the multicultural ground rules as a basis for our collective behavior when these conflicts occur.

On how to handle specific instances, I can only state that this depends on who is involved in the actual conflict. Sometimes I ask the students to take center stage in the class and dialogue with each other for five minutes, each stating his or her points in a nonabusive manner. We then discuss these points as a class. When I sense a power imbalance between the actors in the conflict, I may intervene and offer the conflict as a question to be discussed by the entire class. In rare instances, I will use the conflict to develop an exercise or incorporate an existing exercise to allow the entire class to participate in examining the conflict. In even rarer circumstances, I will let the class immediately join in participating and managing the conflict, as was done in the earlier T-group experiences. This last approach requires very skillful group management skills, however, and is not one I recommend as a first step.

I try to channel the discussion into a more constructive dialogue that can illuminate larger issues. I give each of the students time to express her or his concerns, both in the classroom and privately during office hours if necessary. I try to mobilize the rest of the class, not to take sides, but to become negotiators who can help the students recognize the boundaries and sticking points of their disagreement. If I feel the conflict is getting out of hand, I sometimes assign articles that can help the students put things into more useful context. One example is Audre Lorde's piece on "The Uses of Anger" (1987), which helps white students to understand better the sources and significance of the frustration and anger expressed by Blacks. I also would not hesitate to consult with colleagues who have more experience in intergroup relations to give me advice or, if necessary, to lead the class through conflict resolution exercises.

12. What do you do when you, the teacher, make a racist remark (e.g., you are presenting statistical information about drug addiction in an urban environment and equate poverty with being Black)?

I believe that education is a process. Whether I am in the role of educator or learner, I seek to further my own growth and development. I don't think I have all the knowledge or the only answer, therefore I seek feedback and invite dialogue. When I make a racist remark, and I have, I acknowledge my error and strive to learn from the experience. The way that I acknowledge my mistake has a direct bearing on how each of us can learn and broaden our understanding of the complexities and subtleties of what racism is and how each of us contributes to its manifestation.

When I am called on a racist remark (usually not of the type outlined in this question, as I, as an African American, am particularly sensitive to such remarks), I admit my own faulty learning and participate in an examination of the assumptions contributing to my own misinformation. That's the role of the teacher-learner and the way I can continue to learn from my teaching experience. One of my colleagues has called these "teachable moments," and I like the label.

If the remark is pointed out by my students and if I agree that I have made a racist remark or a statement with racist overtones, I acknowledge as such what I have said. I attempt to use the experience to be instructive of the need for ongoing learning and reflection about such issues as racism. If I realized on my own what I had said, I would also acknowledge the comment for what it was and try to let it be an instructive moment for students. If I did not agree with students who took my remarks to be racist, then I would acknowledge their concern, but explain why I disagreed or why I thought they had misinterpreted or misunderstood my remarks.

13. What do you do when a student challenges what you've said as being biased, suggesting that you are discriminating against Whites? For example, a student may say: "You are wrong. You are just saying that to protect the Blacks. The truth is that Blacks are more likely to assault White women."

The first thing I do is to try to understand where the student is coming from. What is the underlying pain, what is making him or her feel uncomfortable? I have had this actual incident occur. What I did was to find out what the student's "hurt" was. This particular student felt that all rape victims he knew had been raped by Black males, so what we did in class was to bring in "facts" and talk statistics; we brought historical documents to see the roots of the assumption that Black males are more likely to rape. As a class we also talked about how we are all more likely to understand experiences that we have had, so it is easier for me as a Latino woman to be more understanding of experiences that African Americans or other minority groups have had. This makes it look as if I am in favor of a particular group, and finally we turn it around for the White person to see herself or himself.

In my teaching experience, gender bias has been the more frequent charge. Male students want to read and discuss more material about men—whether Black, White, or another ethnic group. When we read about or discuss gender relations, which, of course, includes men, they assume that the material is about women if it takes the experience of women as central to the story. I would imagine that the same might hold true regarding that material on race that takes the Black experience as central. I try to deal with this by presenting a notion of how history, social science, or literature can be constructed from different perspectives and by showing that some perspectives have been marginalized. I include pieces written from contrasting viewpoints on a particular topic such as slavery. It is difficult for some White students and some males to recognize that certain accounts or analyses contain a particular standpoint—White and/or male—one that addresses some questions while omitting other sources of knowledge and experience. In some cases, however, students are legitimately asking for material that breaks down the categories of White or male and reexamines the diverse experience of these groups in more complex, historically constructive ways. If we haven't been able to cover this adequately in class, I would give students the chance to address these topics in their final group projects or papers.

I would first explore the student's intellectual argument and factual information apart from his challenging my motives. But I would also then explore the student's personal challenge to try to understand why the student had made such a charge. I would reaffirm my commitment to be unbiased in the classroom and in intellectual discourse. I would also let the student know that while I am open to challenges from students, I expect there to be some evidence to support whatever charges are made and that it is not sufficient to bring such a challenge on the basis of my suggesting an idea or presenting a fact that differed from what the student had grown up believing.

14. What do you do when there is only one member of an identified minority group in the class? For example, a student, speaking to the only Jewish student in class, may say, "Well, what do Jewish people think about affirmative action?"

One approach is for the teacher to answer the question, instead of the student who has been targeted as being from the ethnic group. Another approach is make the question an issue for the entire class. Finally, the teacher might choose to raise the issue generally (or confront the individual questioner) by pointing out that this question was asked specifically of the Jewish student, not others, and use this as an opportunity for a discussion of group process and intercultural communication.

In terms of this particular situation, I'd try to intervene with: "It's not really fair to ask this student to speak for all Jewish people. What do the readings and films suggest about the potential reactions to affirmative action based on a number of characteristics, including cultural and religious affiliations?" I think, in practice, it is possible to intervene in such situations without blaming the individual who has made the "mistake." Sometimes humor can help.

In the future I would make a concerted effort to recruit more minority students. Otherwise, especially in a class that addresses issues of particular concern to the minority person, I would try to offer a variety of materials and viewpoints and avoid forcing the student to become a spokesperson for his or her community. On the other hand, I would try to encourage the student to contribute ideas and expertise on whatever aspects of the discussion interested her or him. I would try to set a tone in the classroom that encouraged the group to listen to each other, including the minority student, respectfully, but not deferentially. Also, I would actively support this student if she or he did want to challenge an individual or the group or raise an issue that the student felt should be addressed.

15. What do you do when the men in the class dominate discussion, using a "debate" format in which the only goal is to "win" the discussion? For example, a male student with the loudest voice may interrupt: "That is ridiculous, Jennifer. Don't you know the history of the Civil War and the role that Lincoln played? I can't believe you said that."

I stress active listening in my classes. I usually incorporate one or two active listening exercises at the beginning of a course that attends to multicultural issues. As we process what happens for people during the exercise, I also ask them to reflect upon the ways in which they think their gender, race or ethnicity, and the communication patterns in their family of origin have a bearing on their communication styles. I do this to model other ways of communicating and to establish some connections between our individual communication styles and our membership in different social groups. Students are always surprised by how hard it is for many of us just to sit and listen to someone else talking without interjecting comments or asking questions and to see for themselves how their family of origin and their respective gender/race/ethnicity plays into their communication styles. So when the discussion turns into a debate format, it is easy then for me to point, for example, to gender (or racial) dynamics in the class's communication patterns or simply to state that "this seems more like a competition for who is right rather than an opportunity for learning about each other's ideas." In some instances, I've asked the most talkative people to sit back and listen and to share later what they learned by taking that role with the class. In most instances students, particularly male students, really appreciate what they learn through listening even when they had strongly resisted the idea to begin with.

I would talk with students about the purpose of class discussion, that it is for intellectual inquiry and analysis, not for winning points in a debate, convincing others of one's point of view, or silencing classmates with different opinions. In some cases, the discussion can be structured so that no interruptions are permitted. I do this as part of the fishbowl discussion. There I act as the monitor to ensure that students speak without interruption. It's always possible to be selective in calling upon people to speak and to limit the speaking time of those who are dominant. In those situations it is important to talk to students individually so that one group can become more aware of their verbal dominance and the other group can feel empowered and supported to speak up more in class. If there are clear discussion patterns along gender lines, then it might be more useful to focus on issues of gender, rather than on the behavior of the individual. As a time-limited instructional exercise, discussion could be structured so that the women in the class are allotted the approximate time for discussion that the male students have been utilizing and vice versa. It will be eye-opening to all to see the roles reversed: for men to have to listen and for women to have unimpeded access to participation in the class discussion.

I use a combination of strategies ranging from subtle cues to direct confrontation, depending on the intransigence of the situation. In larger groups I try to monitor the discussion to prevent students from interrupting others. I also intervene when the exchange becomes focused on a debate between two individuals. At various points I synthesize what has been said and help the students to lay out the various positions and the gaps in our inquiry. Sometimes I break up the class into smaller groupings and separate the more domineering students into their own group. I think the fact that I am a woman and a figure of authority gives support to the women students. Often, they will raise the issue of male dominance in the classroom and force the group to come up with strategies for creating a more cooperative classroom environment.

NOTES

1. The following authors contributed to parts of this chapter: Irene Butter, Linda Frankel, Christina José, Ann E. Larimore, Edith A. Lewis, Patricia Myers, Eliana Moya-

Raggio, Biren A. Nagda, David Schoem, Kristine Siefert, Sharon E. Sutton, Jim Toy, and Ximena Zúñiga.

2. For examples of exercises mentioned in Part Seven, see Part Eight.

Part VIII

Classroom and Workshop Exercises

One of the outcomes of our continuing discussions as this book evolved was our ability to exchange exercises with each other. Following are several examples of our collective workshop and classroom work. Many individuals contributed to this resource section. In some cases, variations in content from some of the same basic exercises emerged from many sources. We have attempted to acknowledge the original designers of an exercise, when known, in each case.

The section is divided into three parts. Introductory and icebreaker exercises can be used in various classroom or workshop settings where race, gender, sexual orientation, class, and ethnicity are going to be addressed. These exercises are designed to sensitize participants to their own personal characteristics as well as those of others.

The exercises focusing on issues of prejudice, discrimination, and alliance building use many spatial, as well as verbal, configurations. Many of these exercises have been adapted for use with a wide variety of populations and are increasingly used in community workshops and seminars as well.

Many of the awareness exercises are especially designed for use in the classroom. The guided fantasies, however, are also particularly suitable for workshop use. Many of the chapter authors have discussed their use within the contexts of their chapters. As with all of the other exercises, each is presented here with an introduction about its appropriate use, directions for completing the exercise, and process comments.

A word of caution is important, however, to those who are using these exercises for the first time. While the contributors have attempted to provide detailed introductory and process instructions with the exercises, a range of responses is possible from workshop or classroom participants, and these cannot always be anticipated by the facilitator. We recommend that new users pay particular attention to their own feelings of discomfort about the incorporation of a particular exercise in their work, as well as the potential discomfort levels of participants. Only in addressing these dynamics over time will facilitators become adept in choosing the appropriate exercise for the target group.

LIST OF EXERCISES

A. GROUP PROCESS AND ICEBREAKER EXERCISES

A1. Active Listening Exercise

A2. Multiple Roles and Multiple Choice Exercise

B. EXERCISES ADDRESSING ISSUES OF PREJUDICE, DISCRIMINATION, AND ALLIANCE BUILDING

B1. Concentric Circles Exercise

B2. Alliance Group Exercise

B3. Exploring Values and Value Clarification

B4. The Line Exercise

C. AWARENESS EXERCISES

C1. Identity Group Exercise

C2. Take a Stand Exercise

C3. Exploring Family Histories

C4. Exploring One's Group Background: The Fishbowl Exercise

C5. Ethnographic Charting

C6. "How Ethnic Am I?" Exercise

C7. Guided Fantasies: Exploring Issues of Homophobia and Heterosexism

A. GROUP PROCESS AND ICEBREAKER EXERCISES
A1. Active Listening Exercise

Biren A. Nagda and Ximena Zúñiga

Introduction. This exercise is designed to help participants practice active listening skills and understand the factors that contribute to effective communication. It is also useful for helping participants become aware of their own communication styles in interpersonal and group situations.

Directions. Select a topic or question relevant to course goals. This exercise lends itself to a variety of formats. One option is to ask participants to break into pairs. Each member of the pair will alternate as the listener and speaker. Alternatively, the facilitator can structure triads. In this case, each person in a triad will take the role of listener, speaker, and observer. All three roles are described below.[1]

The speaker's role is to talk for a limited amount of time without interruption on a given topic or question (e.g., three to five minutes, depending on the time available). It is important for participants to keep in mind to speak with the intention of being understood. This may be done by sending one's message in "small packages" and paying attention to the words and tone used so that they are congruent.

The listener's role is active listener, that is, hearing and receiving the message with understanding. Participants should keep in mind that they are to try to listen without judging and allow the speaker to send the full message before reacting. They should also try to note both the verbal and nonverbal communication that the speaker is sending, that is, facial expressions, tone of voice, and body language, and their effect on how the message is received. After the speaker is done, the listener should paraphrase to the speaker what he or she has heard. Paraphrasing includes both repeating what one has heard in his or her own words and saying what one "felt" as the speaker was talking. The listener is encouraged to make the link between the two. The listener may also ask questions of clarification before "reflecting back" what was heard.

The observer's role is to observe alertly and give feedback once the speaker and listener have completed their interaction. Feedback should be specific to the actual observed behavior and not directed at the personalities of the speaker and/ or the listener, and it should be given in a timely fashion. One should recognize the needs of both the speaker and the listener if some change in behavior is expected; the feedback should be requested rather than imposed upon the receiver. The observer can give feedback to the listener on his or her paraphrasing, to the speaker on his or her clarity in communicating, and to both on the components of their interaction (e.g., body language, affect, and so on) that facilitated or hindered effective communication.

The following are examples of questions:

1. What is the predominant style of communication in the participants' families?
2. How do participants communicate in large groups? In small groups?
3. How do participants communicate when they are the only person of a certain background or identity in a group?
4. What communication style prevails when participants are in a group with only members of their own group?
5. How do participants know when they are not listened to? How do participants feel when they are not listened to ?
6. How do participants know when they are not listening to someone else? How do participants feel that they are not listening to someone else?

Process Comments. In the debriefing following the exercise, some questions that can be asked are: How did each participant feel in the different roles? Which roles come naturally? Which roles require more work? What are some reasons for this? What did they notice about the others' body language, affect, and what was said? What similarities and differences did they notice about each other's styles? What worked to help effective communication, and what hindered it?

In addition to the issues that come up from these questions, it is important to emphasize the verbal and nonverbal communication patterns, how affect may be culturally bound, the situational context of the interaction, the differences in styles as a function of the power differences in the situation, and so on. The facilitator may also make some comments about different communication styles depending on one's group membership(s).

A2. Multiple Roles and Multiple Choice Exercise

Ximena Zúñiga and Patricia Myers

Introduction. These exercises are designed to acquaint participants with each other and explore commonalities and differences among group members.[2] The Multiple Roles exercise provides the opportunity for participants to identify and discuss aspects of their social background, interpersonal styles, and roles they usually play in a group. The Multiple Choice exercise allows participants to identify and discuss their core beliefs or values about a particular topic or issue. Both may facilitate discussion about participants' fears and expectations about a topic, course, or workshop.

Directions. Facilitators should choose categories from the following list or develop their own list. Target statements are written on the board and read aloud. The responses are posted on newsprint around the room (e.g., the four corners of the room, with the middle for "other" or "none of the above"). The number of responses to a question may vary depending on the size of the group. For certain questions, the number of responses may not match the full set. If so, a blank sheet of newsprint can be left for that response.

After a target statement has been read aloud, students choose the response that is closest to their behavior/role, demographic characteristic, or belief. They discuss their choice with fellow "response members," meeting under the appropriate newsprint response sheet. After about five minutes, the signs are removed and students are asked to choose another response to the next target statement. To explore and discuss five categories or concepts, the facilitators should expect to spend approximately an hour.

Following are examples of categories and responses for the Multiple Roles exercise. Modifications can be made to meet the needs of a particular course or workshop, in this case, a workshop to train dialogue group facilitators.[3]

In my family I am the
- only child.
- oldest child.
- middle child.
- youngest child.

I grew up in the
- Midwest.
- East.
- South.
- West.
- Not in the United States.

In a group I tend to

• talk a lot.

• take a leadership role.

• mostly listen.

• make sure group members get along.

• be a risk taker.

In this class I am concerned that I will

• be perceived as inexperienced.

• say something offensive.

• talk too much.

• feel silenced.

I usually handle conflict by

• avoiding, running away.

• accommodating, giving in.

• compromising, meeting others halfway.

• competing, fighting to win.

• collaborating, working with others to create alternative solutions.

I am taking this class

• to develop new skills.

• to fulfill a requirement.

• to gain a better understanding of multicultural issues.

• to meet people of diverse backgrounds.

• because I needed the credit.

Following are examples of categories and responses for the Multiple Choice exercise. Modifications can be made to fit a workshop or course dealing with a particular issue or topic, in this case the Lesbian Studies class.[4]

I believe feminism means

• the liberation of both men's and women's lives.

• the focus on women as an oppressed class.

• too many radical changes.

• a narrow movement that ignores such characteristics as race, age, class, and/ or sexual orientation.

• none of the above.

I took this course to

• meet other lesbians.

• learn about lesbians.

• earn needed credit.

• have an interesting class.

• none of the above.

I believe that a lesbian is

• a woman who dislikes men.

• a woman who has sex with other women.

• a woman who loves other women.

• a woman who identifies with other women.

• none of the above.

My biggest concern about this class is

• I won't be able to participate comfortably.

• my opinion and views won't be respected.

• it will be too much work.

• my identification as a lesbian/ heterosexual/gay man/bisexual will be questioned.

Process Comments. Emphasize at the beginning and throughout the exercise that there are no right or wrong answers. It is important to keep this exercise moving until all the categories are covered. Allow fifteen to twenty minutes at the end for debriefing. You may consider the following questions: How did you feel? Did you have a chance to meet everyone? What did you learn about yourself and others? What did you notice about the composition of the group? Did you observe any patterns along race, ethnic, or gender lines? The instructor may wish to share some of his or her observations (e.g., that most people are talkers or are conflict avoiders or are afraid of offending others), particularly as they may affect classroom dynamics.

B. EXERCISES ADDRESSING ISSUES OF PREJUDICE, DISCRIMINATION, AND ALLIANCE BUILDING
B1. Concentric Circles Exercise
Patricia Myers and Ximena Zúñiga

Introduction. The Concentric Circles exercise is designed to give group members a chance to have a one-on-one interaction with each other.[5] This exercise is effective because it gives people the chance to express their feelings and experiences on issues that are relevant to the group. Ideally this exercise should be run with about fourteen participants, although it can be done with larger and smaller numbers. The questions used in the exercise depend largely on the focus or goals of the workshop and can thus be modified accordingly.

Directions. Situate people in two concentric circles, facing one another. They can all be sitting or standing. Allow about six minutes in total to address each question. People in the inner circle answer the first question by speaking to the person facing them in the outer circle (three minutes); then the person in the outer circle answers. The facilitator calls time after three minutes, so that each person gets equal time to talk.

After everyone answers the first question, the facilitator instructs people in the inner circle to move one seat to the right. Everyone should be facing a new partner. The facilitator asks the second question, giving each person three minutes to answer, then has the inner (or outer) circle move one space again so that they face a new partner for the next question. The facilitator repeats this until all questions are answered and then asks the participants to come together in a large group (or two to three smaller groups) for a general discussion on the thoughts, observations, and feelings that came up during the exercise.

The following are possible topics and questions:

1. Talk about a time you felt different from the people around you. How did you feel about it?

2. What were your first experiences of gender? What did you learn (from parents, neighbors, childhood friends, school, and so on) about what it meant to be a girl? About what it meant to be a boy? What were some of your first experiences of sexism?

3. What did you learn about what it meant to be a member of your racial group? What did you first learn about people of color? About white people? When did you realize

that people of different races/ethnicities were treated differently? What were some of your initial experiences with racism? How did the significant adults in your life help to interpret those experiences?

4. When did you first notice lesbians and gay men? What were your first experiences with homophobia or heterosexism?

5. How have these early messages affected you as an adult (particularly in terms of your identity, education, aspirations, opportunities, living situation, partner, choice of friends, and so on?

6. Describe to your partner a time when you were a target of stereotyping, discrimination, or harassment. How did you feel about it?

7. Describe an incident in which you were perceived as being prejudiced (i.e., racist, sexist, anti-Semitic). How did you feel about it? What was your response to the person who spoke with you about it?

8. How are you challenging the racism, sexism, and homophobia that you experience now? How effective do you think your resistance is? What can you do to become more effective?

Process Comments. The processing of this exercise should focus on how the participants felt as they responded to the questions. Having talked about the trigger questions, they will have likely done some personal reflection. Ask participants which questions were particularly easy or difficult to answer, which questions were the most interesting, and what things they learned about themselves from conversations with other participants. It may also be helpful to have participants share specific experiences they've had that relate to the issues raised. Linkages to the larger issues may be discussed if time permits. Allow at least twenty minutes for debriefing. The entire exercise should take about forty-five to sixty minutes.

B2. Alliance Group Exercise

Ximena Zúñiga, Biren A. Nagda, Andrea Monroe-Fowler,
and Gen Stewart

Introduction. The Alliance Group exercise is designed to help participants identify differences and potential areas of conflict between groups.[6] It provides the opportunity to discuss issues underlying existing conflicts and to begin identifying ways of building bridges between groups. One group's responses may be difficult for another group to hear, but it is important that the concerns of both groups are heard in order to open up the lines of communication among those involved.

Directions. Divide the large group into two alliance or identity groups.[7] These groups are based on ethnic, racial, gender, class, sexual orientation, religious, or other distinctions that exist within the large group. Each group answers the questions (forty minutes), records the responses on newsprint, and reports back to the larger group.

The following are possible statement completions:

1. When your group is trying to learn about my group (race/ethnic, gender, class, and so on), statements or questions such as _____ are difficult/uncomfortable/ offensive for my group to hear from members of your group.

2. My group will be hesitant to discuss our experiences with _____ (e.g., sexism, racism, anti-Semitism, and/or heterosexism) with the other group if they say things like _____. (Be specific and be able to explain briefly why you don't like such statements.)

3. I, as a _____ (member of a racial/ethnic, gender, class, religious, and so on group), feel

   _____ when I hear a member of your group say,

   _____ or when I see a member of your group doing _____ (action). I interpret it as your group's saying _____ about my group.

4. The other group can do _____ to demonstrate that they are committed to working with my group to combat _____ (e.g., a specific form of ism) on campus. (Be specific. For example, what can one group do to convince the other that they understand and respect their concerns and/or struggles? What can one group do to support the other's efforts to work with them?)

5. When my group is trying to learn about your group (race/ethnic, gender, class, and so on), statements or questions such as _____ are difficult and uncomfortable for my group to ask members of your group.

6. What can my group do to be supportive of the group that is trying to work with me?

If time permits:

7. What actions or statements interfere with building alliances or coalitions with the other group?

Process Comments. During this exercise it is important for participants to be very specific. Group behaviors that are problematic should be stated explicitly so that everyone knows exactly what is blocking or interfering in the relationship between the groups. Both groups should have an opportunity to share responses to each question without interruption. Stress the importance of active listening and respect for the opinions of others so that all viewpoints and feelings can be heard and understood. You should allow at least forty-five minutes for reporting and debriefing.

B3. Exploring Values and Value Clarification
Kristine Siefert and Irene Butter

Introduction. The journals will help students clarify their own values and attitudes about gender, race, ethnicity, and health as they confront controversial topics. In our society many of our opinions about these topics are based on hearsay or on fears and suspicions absorbed from a number of undefined sources.

By reading and discussion, students will be confronting their present ideas and will be able to accumulate ammunition to defend themselves in arguments and conflicts. Thus, when a student states a value position and someone asks, "What is it based on?" the student will have the knowledge and the processing of that knowledge for backup and substantiation.

Directions. The journals should be in a separate notebook or folder to be handed in three times during the term. The journal for Module I should not exceed fourteen pages (one page per concept); the journal for Module II should not exceed three pages (one page per concept), and the journal for Module III should not exceed fifteen pages (one page per concept).

The following are concepts (core concepts are marked by an asterisk) for each module:

Module I	Module II	Module III
*racism	occupational segregation	*feminism
*sexism	*hierarchy	*ethnic pride
*homophobia	*affirmative action	*gay rights
*inequality	equal opportunity	*diversity
autonomy	comparable worth	advocacy
*choice		empowerment
accountability		*genocide

The following are questions to be addressed in process journals.
Questions for Module I:

1. Define the meaning of these twelve core concepts in your own terms.
2. Define the additional concepts listed under Module I in your own terms.
3. How do you feel about each concept and why? The purpose is to examine ideas and your present values. What was the origin of your values, and are you still influenced by the origin?
4. Have you had any past experiences with these concepts? How have these concepts affected your life in the past and present?

Questions for Module II:

1. Define the additional concepts listed under Module II.
2. Answer Questions 3 and 4 listed under Module I for the three new concepts.

Questions for Module III:

1. Define the additional concepts listed under Module III.
2. Answer Questions 3 and 4 listed under Module I for the new concepts.
3. Redefine the twelve core concepts you defined for Module I, referring to illustrative readings, lectures, and class discussions. What changes have occurred in your defi-

nitions of these core concepts? Describe in detail the changes that have occurred in your attitudes and feelings during this semester about these concepts.

4. How can these concepts and any changes you perceive be applied to promote social justice? Please give an example of how you could attempt to bring about justice at the individual, institutional/community, or national level.

B4. The Line Exercise
Patricia Myers and the Lesbian-Gay Male Programs Office

Introduction. The purpose is to help participants think about the social categories that often divide individuals and the differing experiences each person brings to the job, classroom, relationship with colleagues, friends, lovers, and family and to this workshop. Categories have been chosen in which one group is often "targeted" for differential treatment or oppressed in some way.[8]

Directions. You need a fairly large space that can be divided in half by an imaginary line. At the beginning, everybody begins on the majority side, for example, the left half of the room. As a category is read, people move to the minority side (e.g., the right side) if they identify with that target category and face the majority side. The facilitator may wish to encourage honesty and risk taking.

The following are target categories:

- Women
- People with a disability or chronic illness
- People who are over fifty
- People with one or more parents without a college degree
- People for whom English is not a native language
- People who grew up in a rural area
- People who are Jewish
- Lesbians, gay men, and bisexual people
- People who've been told they are fat

- People who are under eighteen years of age
- Single parents or children of single parents
- People whose parents work in blue-collar jobs or low-status jobs
- People who are immigrants or children of immigrants
- People who grew up in a religious minority
- People of color
- People who haven't yet crossed the line (optional)

Discussion Questions. Did you like or dislike the exercise? How did people feel when they crossed the line? Were any of the categories confusing? Did everybody cross the line at least once? If not, how did it feel to stay on the majority side throughout the exercise? Did you learn anything new about yourself or the other participants? Any final comments or questions?

C. AWARENESS EXERCISES
C1. Identity Group Exercise
Ximena Zúñiga and Biren A. Nagda

Introduction. This exercise is designed to help participants grapple with issues of individual and group identity in the safety of a constituency group (e.g., people of color, white, Jewish, African American, Latino/a, Asian American).[9] It allows participants to explore some of the rewards and penalties of being a member of a particular group. It can also provide an opportunity for participants to begin to see specific areas of conflict between the groups and explore avenues for coalition building. Identity groups are defined here as the groups that individuals belong to (or identify with) by virtue of their race, ethnic background, gender, socioeconomic class, sexual orientation, and so on.

Directions. Have group members meet in their own "identity" groups to discuss the questions listed below. Each group should select a facilitator, a reporter, and a note taker. The answers may be written on newsprint and shared with the group as a whole upon regrouping. The most likely identity groups would be white people and people of color; other possibilities may surface depending on the size and composition of the group.

- What are the advantages and disadvantages of being a person of color/white person, man/woman, white woman/woman of color?
- What things about the other group make me angry/nervous/scared/uncomfortable?
- What makes it difficult to talk to members of the other group about our differences?

Process Comments. This exercise is very powerful and elicits a lot of emotion and the exchange of much new information. Therefore, it is important prior to the exercise that the group as a whole has developed some trust and feeling that the environment is "safe." Make sure to allow about thirty minutes of processing time after each identity group has reported back. Reporting back can be done in one of two ways. Each group can simply report back to the large group, or the fishbowl format can be used.[10] The advantage of the large group is that it takes less time and allows for more open discussion immediately following the identity group. The advantage of the fishbowl format is that it allows a "safe" environment for each group to report what took place in their identity group discussion. This exercise (along with the debriefing) will likely take no more than ninety minutes to complete: thirty minutes for the identity group discussion, thirty minutes for reporting to the large group, and thirty minutes for debriefing.

C2. Take a Stand Exercise
The Lesbian-Gay Male Programs Office, University of Michigan

Introduction. The Take a Stand exercise is designed to clarify values, leading to increased discussion on controversial issues. Many of the statements are purposely ambiguous to allow for individual interpretation and decision making about the particular issue at hand. The exercise is called Take a Stand because it involves risk taking; it also provides a good opportunity for participants to gain insight about others' viewpoints and perspectives on particular issues.

Directions. On the wall behind the participants, the facilitator marks off a continuum by taping a sign in the middle of the wall reading "Neutral—You Can't Stand Here," a sign at one end reading "Comfortable," and a sign at the other end reading "Uncomfortable." As statements are read, participants are asked to place themselves along this continuum based on an emotional response. The more comfortable they are with a particular statement, the farther from the center toward the "Comfortable" sign they move. Participants redistribute themselves as the next statement is read. The facilitator may wish to ask the participants to explain why they are standing where they are, but debate should not be encouraged among the participants. This exercise is intended simply to share information among the participants and with the facilitator. The facilitator should choose approximately ten statements, depending upon the size of the audience, their backgrounds, age, educational level, special interests, and so on. A minimum of ten minutes should be expected for this exercise, depending on amount of discussion.

Racism trigger statements:

- Affirmative action
- "Passing"
- Reverse discrimination
- White guilt
- Busing as a means of forced integration
- All of my friends are white
- I am not racist
- I make an effort to read works written by and about people of color
- Some scientific researchers have traced the origin of AIDS to the African continent
- Minority student lounges
- Long-term interracial relationships
- Mulatto
- Events for people of color only
- I am primarily attracted to members of my same ethnic/racial group
- Increasing numbers of minority faculty and students at this institution could lead to a decrease in academic standards

Sexuality trigger statements:

- Premarital sex
- Pornography
- Monogamy
- Erotica
- Promiscuity
- Masturbation

- Oral-genital sex
- Anal-genital sex
- I'd consider an abortion
- Free condom distribution
- Sex toys

- Sadomasochism
- Committed non-monogamous
  relationships
- Mutual masturbation
- Prostitution

Sexual orientation trigger statements:

- Dyke
- Faggot
- Homosexuality is a choice
- A lesbian or gay man makes a pass at
  you
- Homosexuality is an illness
- Use of student funds to support lesbian/
  gay men's student groups
- I have felt emotionally attracted to
  members of the same sex

- My roommate comes out to me
- Two men kissing on the street
- Civil rights for gay people
- Queer
- Openly gay teachers in public schools
- Lifetime commitment to a relationship
- A lesbian high school student takes
  same-sex date to prom
- Artificial insemination for lesbians to
  become parents

Process Comments. In processing this exercise, you should talk about the feelings of participants in different situations—for example, being in the most uncomfortable position or being in the minority on a given statement or being in the minority on a particular question. It can also be helpful to recognize where particular groups stand on different statements.

C3. Exploring Family Histories
K. Scott Wong

Introduction. The goal of this writing assignment is to convey to the reader a good sense of what it has been like for someone to grow up as an Asian American or to enter American society as an immigrant from Asia.[11] That someone could be the student herself or himself, a friend of the student, a member of the student's family, the student's whole family, an acquaintance, or even a total stranger who agrees to being interviewed. The student's initial reaction may be, "But why should the experience of growing up as an Asian American be any different from anybody else's?" For some Asian Americans, life, indeed, has not been any different, but for a good many there are experiences that may set them apart. The student's job is to discover (1) those features in the protagonist's life that have been similar to most people's and (2) those aspects that may be quite different.

Directions to the Student. Whether you write about yourself or others, the key is to go beyond the obvious. Ask about the life events that the subject remembers most clearly—occurrences that made a distinct impression. Then ask why those memories affect how the subject dealt with later experiences. In short, the writer is looking for keys that explain why a person became who he or she is today. You should also ask about people who strongly influenced the subject (yourself or your interviewee) in either positive or negative ways. Also consider periods in the life of the person you are writing about. People's lives can often be seen in stages, rather than simply as a series of events. Keeping this in mind may help you conceptualize and organize your paper. Most important, I want you to enjoy doing this assignment. The goal is not merely to write a good paper but to learn something about yourself or your interviewee that leads you to a new understanding about our lives in America.

C4. Exploring One's Group Background: The Fishbowl Exercise

David Schoem, Ximena Zúñiga, and Biren A. Nagda

Introduction. This exercise is designed to help participants begin the process of self-reflection as well as listening to and understanding the experiences of the "other" group.[12] It also helps participants identify areas of commonality and difference among groups as well as potential sources of conflict and coalition. This exercise gives participants a chance to reflect on their experiences and share aspects about themselves with members of their own group and the other group.

Directions. In a fishbowl exercise, each group takes turns sitting in an inner circle (facing each other) while the rest of the class sits around them in an outer circle. Each group has twenty to thirty minutes to discuss a set of questions among themselves. Participants can do this in a round—one by one—or as group discussion. People in the outer circle may be given the opportunity to ask clarifying questions at end of the allotted time for about ten minutes. Groups switch until every group has had a chance to be in the inner circle. Ask participants to divide into identity groups to talk about some of the questions listed below when it is their turn to be part of the inner circle or fishbowl.

The topics can be very general, such as:

1. Describe yourself as a Black/Latino(a)/American Indian/Asian American/Jew/White/ man/woman.
2. Discuss your identity as a Black/Latino(a)/American Indian/Asian American/Jew/ White/man/woman.

The questions can be more specific, such as:

1. What was it like for you to grow up _____(e.g., American Indian/Asian American/ White, Jewish, African American, Latino) in your hometown, to attend the schools

you did? What did you learn about what it meant to be a member of your racial/ethnic group?

2. When did you realize that people of different races/ethnicities were treated differently?

3. What were some of your initial experiences with racism/anti-Semitism/ethnocentrism? How did your parents, teachers, and community leaders help you interpret those experiences?

4. Why did you choose to attend this university? How similar or different is this environment from where you grew up?

The questions may also be targeted toward gender and sexual orientation issues while still addressing issues of race and ethnicity:

1. When did you first learn about sex roles and what it means to be raised as a boy or a girl? What were your first experiences with sexism?

2. What are some of the advantages and disadvantages of being a man or a woman?

3. What is it like to be a woman or a man on this college campus?

4. What is it like to be a woman or a man in this class?

5. How did you find out that you were heterosexual, bisexual, or homosexual?

6. When did you first notice lesbians and gay men? What were your first experiences with homophobia or heterosexism? How did your parents, teachers, and community leaders help you interpret those experiences?

7. How was it for you to come to this university? How similar or different is this environment from where you grew up?

Process Comments. Allow thirty minutes for discussion of commonalities and differences and areas of conflict. It is important to follow the process of this exercise closely. Interruptions or a lack of active listening from the outside group can result in the exercise being ineffective. It is also important to note that the questions that are asked of the inside group should be for clarification purposes only and not to challenge members' experiences. It should be emphasized that the primary purpose of the exercise is to listen and understand the experience of the "other" group and not to challenge or question its validity. Subsequent discussions should be scheduled for in-depth and more probing follow-up.

C5. Ethnographic Charting

Edith A. Lewis

Directions.

1. Develop a chart of the ethnic origins for at least three generations of your family, using your generation (i.e., you and any siblings) as the base generation. In your chart, both maternal and paternal generations should be represented, with their ethnic groups of origin identified. See M. McGoldrick and R. Gerson, *Genograms in Family*

Assessment, Chapter 2 (New York: Norton, 1985) for examples of symbols utilized in genograms.

2. Identify the immigration (or migration) patterns for the members on the chart, including the year of entry into the United States.

3. List five values held by one member of each generation in your chart, including yourself. There should be a minimum of fifteen values listed. (Note: Items 2 and 3 may be summarized in a brief paper (no more than three pages) and submitted with the chart.)

Follow-up Questions.

1. Are the values you identified for each family member (including yourself) consistent with the class readings for that ethnic group? Specifically list how they are similar and/or different, referencing course citations or your own. Are your values identical to those in the two generations preceding you or different in some way? Explain. (Note: If your ethnic group is not represented among those discussed in class, choose at least two articles on this group for discussion in your final paper. Please see the instructor if you need assistance in locating readings.)

2. Are any of the norms you identify also shared by any other ethnic group of color discussed in class? Which ones and how? (Note: If you are a student of color, pick a group other than your own ethnic group of origin.)

3. What is your analysis of the impact of race, ethnicity, gender, and class on your ethnic group(s) of origin, given the projected demographic trends of the twenty-first century? How will the population of color you discussed in item 2 be affected by these changes? How must current social welfare policies change given the realities of the twenty-first century?

C6. "How Ethnic Am I?" Exercise
Edith A. Lewis

Introduction. This exercise is designed for participants of all ethnic backgrounds to look at how important their ethnic background is to their identity. It also allows for comparisons with other populations, particularly populations of color. The exercise promotes not only European American self-reflection, but the necessity for populations of color to examine experiences that are similar across ethnic groups as well as unique to their own particular group.

Directions. Answer all of the following questions, using all appropriate sources of information at your disposal.

1. What is (are) my ethnic group background(s)?

2. Name at least five of the values for at least one member of my parental, grandparental, and great-grandparental generations.

3. To what extent are these values consistent with any literature I'm aware of regarding my ethnic background?

4. What are the five values I hold most dearly?

5. Are these ordered the same or differently from those identified in question 3 given my knowledge of the literature of people from my ethnic background?

6. How did social, historical, or political forces shape the experiences of my family and the ordering of their values? How do these same forces shape my identified values?

7. Do I perceive these values to be more like or unlike the families of color I encounter in my life?

8. What differences are there between the social, political, and historical forces currently influencing my life and those influencing the persons of color with whom I work?

Process Comments. This exercise can be used as a class assignment (including family interviews and student research on the history and status of particular groups) or modified to serve as a class/workshop dialogue among participants. After they have answered the above questions, ask participants to talk about how it felt to be categorized by group affiliation. Encourage individuals to discuss whether they view themselves more as part of their ethnic group(s) or racial group(s). Has the exercise modified their perception of the importance of their ethnic group background? What parallels do they see between their own background and other ethnic groups (particularly ethnic groups of color)? Of what importance is question 8 in influencing the participant's worldview?

C7. Guided Fantasies: Exploring Issues of Homophobia and Heterosexism
Guided Fantasy: Reversing Sexual Orientation

The Lesbian-Gay Male Programs Office, University of Michigan, Ann Arbor

Introduction. The purpose of this exercise is to help people think about heterosexual privileges and the impact of homophobia on individual lives. Make sure to read the entire fantasy slowly in order to give ample time for experiencing the relaxation and altered reality. The entire exercise should take about ten to fifteen minutes. Turn off the lights in the room in order to minimize self-consciousness.[13]

Directions to the Participants. The guided fantasy encourages increased understanding of how heterosexist our society is by helping you to envision a lesbian/gay world where heterosexuals are the minority. First I will read brief instructions to help you relax, and then we'll begin to imagine an altered reality.

Relaxation Script:
Get as comfortable as you can so that you feel relaxed. Close your eyes, listen to my voice, and focus on what I am saying. Take three deep breaths. Breathe in. Exhale. Breathe in. Exhale. And again breathe in. Breathe out. Relax. Focus on your relaxed breathing.

Guided Fantasy Script:
Reflect on the last time you spent an evening or afternoon with someone very

special—a lover, a girlfriend, or a boyfriend. Remember all the special things you did. Maybe you went for a walk through campus or in the park. Maybe you went to the movies. You might have gone to the mall to do some shopping. Remember holding hands, putting your arm around your special friend. Maybe you kissed this person while you walked or were at the movies. Picture yourself being very close to this person and how you felt about that closeness. Remember all the different things you did that afternoon or evening. Think about the people you ran into while you were out together—old friends, coworkers, acquaintances. Remember how it felt for you to be seen with this special person, how other people reacted to the two of you holding hands, or the smiles you might have gotten if you kissed. Take a minute and remember those things from that afternoon or evening together. Now, imagine that the world is different. Imagine that the "norm" is homosexuality. The vast majority of the people on the face of the earth are gay. Heterosexuality is illegal and considered sick. Imagine that afternoon or evening you spent with your special friend. How would things have been different? What would you have done differently? What couldn't you have done? Go back over everything that you and your special friend did together the last time you spent together, but in a world that says, "No, you can't do that!" How would your coworkers react? What about the people you might have run into at the mall or the movies? How could you possibly explain your behavior to the people who care about you? Take a minute and reflect on these feelings as you begin to return to this room.

Discussion Questions. How was this exercise for you? Did anybody have trouble imagining this change? Was it easier for other people? Why do you suppose it was easier for some to imagine than for others? What portions of the fantasy were particularly significant? Did you learn anything about your society? How did it feel to be with the person you love in this different world? How do you feel about your friend? About yourself? About the world?

Guided Fantasy: Secrets

Billie L. Edwards

Introduction. This exercise is designed to develop understanding and empathy for the experiences of lesbians and gay men. The focus is on each individual's unique experience with some secret held in privacy that has a connotation of stigma or shame to it. The discussion questions attempt to draw participants into a dialogue of their experience of doing the exercise while, at the same time, helping them to see the similarities between their experience during the exercise and the day-to-day experiences of lesbians and gay men. It is critical to read slowly, allowing sufficient time after each statement or question for participants to be guided rather than rushed through the exercise. Vocal tone is important; it is most effective to read slowly and gently.

Directions to the Participants. The exercise that we're going to participate in is a guided imagery. I'm going to ask you to take a risk, and that is to go inside yourself and get in touch with a part of your life experience that may be uncomfortable for you to remember. I would like you to participate in this exercise as fully as you will allow yourself. When we finish this exercise, I'm not going to ask you to reveal to anyone in this room what your secret is. So sit back in your chair, remove everything from your lap, and get comfortable. Close your eyes.

Relaxation Script:

Get as comfortable as you can so that you feel relaxed. Close your eyes, listen to my voice, and focus on what I am saying. Take three deep breaths. Breathe in. Exhale. Breathe in. Exhale. And again breathe in. Breathe out. Relax. Focus on your relaxed breathing.

Guided Fantasy Script:

Everyone has experienced having a secret. I want you to go inside yourself and pick a secret. If you have more than one, choose one that you feel particularly protective of, that you have not shared with many people, if anyone. Perhaps you would risk choosing a secret that you feel shame or embarrassment about. (Allow enough time for them to experience their secret fully). I want you to imagine getting up tomorrow morning. When you get up, you go through your regular morning ritual. As you go by the mirror in the bathroom, you notice that there's something on your forehead. Something that symbolizes your secret so that everyone will know what it is. As you look closely at the symbol in the mirror, you discover that it won't come off. You become aware that it can be seen from a distance. What do you feel? Do you attempt to rub it off? When you leave the bathroom to get dressed, you notice that the same symbol is woven into the fabric of every garment you have. Into every article of clothing. What do you do? How do you feel?

You have a very busy schedule for tomorrow, and you cannot avoid going out of your home. What does it feel like, knowing that you're going to go out into the world, whether it's to your classes, out into the residence halls where the residents will see you, to work, to a doctor's appointment, to see your parents, to teach classes, and so on? What kind of meetings do you have scheduled? You have no option—you must go. What is it like when you walk out your front door? When you walk down the hallway? Are you wondering what people think? Are they staring? Are you wondering if they know?

For those of you who are students or instructors, you go into your first class. You notice that people are looking at you. You encounter people in your class with whom you have spent time or shared conversations. Do they react any differently to you? And if they do, what do you feel?

For those of you who are not students, but who work, how does it feel to enter your workplace with your secret marked on your forehead and your clothes? How do you feel about encountering your boss? Lunch with coworkers? That presentation? For whatever reason, you have scheduled a lunch with some of your friends. What do you feel as you sit down at the table, and they all notice?

Do they ask you? Or do they all pretend that they don't notice? How is that for you? This happens to you throughout the day, but finally you have an opportunity to go home. You walk through your door, and you lean against the door with a sigh of relief that you've made it through the day. And as you reflect on the day, remember your experiences. What surfaces as the most significant experience? What do you feel now that you are at home?

You've made a social engagement for the evening, one that you cannot get out of. What do you do? Are you anxious? Would you like to get out of it? Do you suddenly find yourself getting ill? You get ready to go out one more time. Do you take a deep breath before you go out? Do you say anything to yourself about what the evening's encounters are going to be like? You make it through the evening, and you come home for the last time, knowing that you do not have to go out again. Are you tired? Do you want to talk to someone? And if you were to tell someone what it is like going through the experience, what would you want to tell them? How would you want them to be with you as you talked? What would you need from them? Would you want anything from them or for them to be a certain way with you? As you're lying in bed, you find that you're absolutely exhausted. Do you tell yourself that it was no big deal? Are you flooded with feelings? Are you fortunate enough to have friends to whom it doesn't matter, or are you alone with your secret and your feelings of exposure? (Allow time for participants to reflect on their experiences and internally to reflect on these questions.)

As you're ready, slowly come back to this room and into this time. And when you feel that you're here, open your eyes.

Discussion Questions. Now that you are back in this time and space, I would like to spend a few minutes talking about your experience in participating in this exercise. I am not asking you to share your secret, but to risk sharing your experience. Did you learn anything about yourself or about the experience of being vulnerable that perhaps you didn't already know? Did you get a clearer sense of what you wanted from your friends? Did you get a better idea about what you need from someone in order to be able to talk to him or her? As you reflect on this experience, do you have a better understanding of what it might be like to be a lesbian or a gay man? Do you have a clearer sense of what they might need from you in order to talk to you about their life as a lesbian or gay man? I hope this exercise will continue to prove useful to each of you in the future as you interact with members of the lesbian and gay male communities.

NOTES

1. From Patricia Bidol, ''Interactive Communication,'' in *Alternative Conflict Management Approaches*, ed. Bidol et al. (Ann Arbor: University of Michigan, Environmental Conflict Project, 1986).

2. Both versions have been adapted from Beth Reed, ''Multiple Roles Exercise,''

Women's Studies 350, *Women and the Community: Instructor's Manual* (Ann Arbor: Women's Studies Program, University of Michigan, 1986).

3. Refer to Chapter 20.

4. Refer to Chapter 11.

5. Adapted from Harvey Reed, Office of Minority Affairs, University of Michigan, Ann Arbor, 1989. It should be noted that the notion of "concentric circles" is used by human relations trainers in various fields to deal with a wide range of topics or issues. See Katz, 1978: 38, for an icebreaker version of concentric circles.

6. A version of this exercise was introduced to Andrea Monroe-Fowler and Genevieve Stewart at the Confronting Racism workshop facilitated by Tony Harris at the University of Michigan, winter 1990.

7. Please refer to the Identity Group Exercise in this chapter.

8. A version of this exercise was introduced to Patricia Myers at the Unlearning Racism workshop, developed and facilitated by Ricky Sherover-Marcuse, Ph.D., at the University of Michigan in the fall of 1987. It was re-created from memory and widely redistributed on the University of Michigan campus through the Lesbian-Gay Male Programs Office, Educational Outreach Program by Billie Edwards, Jim Toy and Ronald Wheeler, Jr.

9. Several colleagues have contributed to developing the many versions of this exercise: John Diamond, Steve Derringer, Genevieve Stewart, and Mark Chesler, University of Michigan, Ann Arbor.

10. See Exploring One's Group Background: The Fishbowl Exercise in this chapter.

11. It should be noted that these papers are not intended to be taken as scholarly endeavors or personal memoirs. The main objective is to allow the student to explore his or her (or an interviewee's) experiences and feelings about being Asian in America or, in the case of non-Asian students, to reach understanding of the Asian American experience through direct contact with an Asian American. Rather than pieces of professional scholarship, these papers should be seen as preliminary steps in understanding and articulating a particular facet of American culture.

12. The notion of using fishbowls to explore issues of ethnic identity was suggested to D. Schoem by James Crowfoot, University of Michigan.

13. For examples of guided fantasies attending to race, see Katz, 1978: 102; for examples attending to gender, see Theodora Wells, "Woman—Which Includes Man, Of Course," in *Issues in Feminism: An Introduction to Women's Studies*, ed. Sheila Ruth (Mountain View, CA: Mayfield, 1990), 141–42.

Selected Bibliography

BOOKS

Abercrombie, M.L.J. 1970. *Aims and Techniques of Group Teaching*. London: Society for Research into Higher Education Ltd.

Achebe, Chinua. 1959. *Things Fall Apart*. Greenwich, CT: Fawcett.

ACSA Task Force on the Status of Women in Architecture Schools. 1990. *Status of Faculty Women in Architecture Schools: Survey Results and Recommendations*. Washington, DC: ACSA Press.

Acuña, Rodolfo. 1972. *Occupied America: The Chicano's Struggle Toward Liberation*. San Francisco: Canfield Press.

Adair, Nancy, and Casey Adair. 1978. *Word Is Out: Stories of Some of Our Lives*. New York: Delta.

Alba, Richard, ed. 1988. *Ethnicity and Race in the U.S.A.: Toward the Twenty-First Century*. New York: Routledge.

Albrecht, Lisa, and Rose Brewer, eds. 1990. *Bridges of Power: Women's Multicultural Alliances*. Philadelphia: New Society.

Alpert, Harriet. 1988. *We Are Everywhere: Writings by and About Lesbian Parents*. Freedom, CA: Crossing Press.

Alyson, Sasha, ed. 1980. *Young, Gay and Proud!* Boston: Alyson.

Andersen, Margaret L. 1988. *Thinking About Women: Sociological and Feminist Perspectives*. New York: Macmillan.

Andersen, Margaret L., and Patricia Hill Collins. 1992. *Race, Class, and Gender: An Anthology*. Belmont, CA: Wadsworth.

Angelou, Maya. 1970. *I Know Why the Caged Bird Sings*. New York: Random House.

Anzaldúa, Gloria. 1987. *Borderlands-La Frontera; The New Mestiza*. San Francisco: Spinsters/Aunt Lute.

Anzaldúa, Gloria, ed. 1990. *Making Face, Making Soul-Hacienda Caras: Creative and Critical Perspectives by Women of Color*. San Francisco: Aunt Lute Foundation Books.

Arendt, H. 1958. *The Human Condition*. Chicago: University of Chicago Press.

Arnow, Harriette. 1954. *The Dollmaker*. New York: Macmillan.

Auvine, Brian, et al. 1978. *A Manual for Group Facilitators*. Madison, WI: Center for Conflict Resolution.

Bach, Richard. 1977. *Illusions*. New York: Delacorte Press.

Baetz, Ruth. 1988. *Lesbian Crossroads*. Tallahassee, FL: Naiad Press.

Baker, Gwendolyn C. 1983. *Planning and Organizing for Multicultural Instruction*. Reading, MA: Addison-Wesley.

Banks, James A. 1988. *Multiethnic Education: Theory and Practice*. Boston: Allyn & Bacon.

Banks, James A., and C. A. Banks, eds. 1989. *Multicultural Education*. Boston: Allyn & Bacon.

Basso, Keith. 1979. *Portraits of "The Whiteman": Linguistic Play and Cultural Symbols Among the Western Apache*. New York: Cambridge University Press.

Beam, Joseph. 1986. *In the Life: A Black Gay Anthology*. Boston: Alyson.

Beck, Evelyn T., ed. 1982. *Nice Jewish Girls: A Lesbian Anthology*. Trumansburg, NY: Crossing Press.

Belenky, M. F., B. M. Clinchy, N. R. Goldberger, and J. M. Tarule. 1986. *Women's Way of Knowing*. New York: Basic Books.

Bellah, R. M., R. Madsen, W. M. Swidler, and S. M. Tipton. 1985. *Habits of the Heart: Individualism and Commitment in American Life*. New York: Harper & Row.

Bennett, William. 1984. *To Reclaim a Legacy: A Report on the Humanities in Higher Education*. Washington, DC: National Endowment for the Humanities.

Bernal, M. 1987. *Black Athena: The Afroasiatic Roots of Classical Civilization*. New Brunswick, NJ: Rutgers U. Press.

Billingsley, A. 1968. *Black Families in White America*. Englewood Cliffs, NJ: Prentice-Hall.

Bloom, Allan. 1987. *The Closing of the American Mind*. New York: Simon & Schuster.

Borhek, Mary. 1983. *Coming Out to Parents: A Two-Way Survival Guide for Lesbians and Gay Men and Their Parents*. New York: Pilgrim Press.

Boyd-Franklin, N. 1990. *Black Families in Therapy: A Multisystems Approach*. New York: Guilford.

Boyer, Ernest. 1987. *College*. New York: Harper & Row.

Brandt, Godfrey. 1986. *The Realization of Anti-Racist Teaching*. London: Falmer Press.

Brant, Beth, ed. 1984. *A Gathering of Spirit: Writing and Art by North American Indian Women*. Montpelier, VT: Sinister Wisdom.

Brown, Cherie. 1984. *The Art of Coalition Building*. New York: American Jewish Committee.

Bryant, B. 1989. *Social Change, Energy, and Land Ethics*. Ann Arbor, MI: Prakken.

Bulkin, Elly, M. B. Pratt, and B. Smith. 1984. *Yours in Struggle: Three Feminist Perspectives on Anti-Semitism and Racism*. Ithaca, NY: Firebrand Books.

Bunch, Charlotte. 1987. *Passionate Politics: Feminist Theory in Action*. New York: St. Martin's Press.

Bunch, Charlotte, and Sandra Pollack, eds. 1983. *Learning Our Ways: Essays in Feminist Education*. Trumansburg, NY: Crossing Press.

Butler, Johnella, and John Walter, eds. 1991. *Transforming the Curriculum: Ethnic Studies and Women's Studies*. Albany, NY: State University of New York Press.

Campbell, Bebe Moore. 1990. *Sweet Summer: Growing Up With and Without My Dad*. New York: Ballantine Books.

Cannon, Lynn Weber 1990a. *All Our Ways of Being: Taking on the Challenge of Diversity in the College Classroom*. Memphis, TN: Memphis State University, Center for Research on Women.

————. 1990b. *Curriculum Transformation: Personal and Political*. Memphis, TN: Memphis State University, Center for Research on Women.

Chávez, John. 1984. *The Lost Land: The Chicano Image of the Southwest*. Albuquerque: University of New Mexico Press.

Childress, Alice. 1986. *Like One of the Family: Conversations from a Domestic's Life*. Boston: Beacon Press.

Cisneros, Sandra. 1991. *The House on Mango Street*. New York: Vintage Books.

Clark, Don. 1978. *Loving Someone Gay*. New York: Signet.

Cohen, Steven. 1988. *American Assimilation or Jewish Revival*. Bloomington, IN: Indiana University Press.

Collins, P.H., and M. Anderson, eds. 1987. *Toward an Inclusive Sociology: Race, Class, and Gender in the Sociology Curriculum*. Washington, DC: American Sociological Association.

Cornwell, Anita. 1983. *Black Lesbian in White America*. Tallahassee, FL: Naiad Press.

Council on Education for Public Health. 1986. *Criteria for Accreditation of Graduate Schools of Public Health*. Washington, DC: Council on Education for Public Health.

Council on Social Work Education. 1979. *Curriculum Policy for the Master's Degree and Baccalaureate Degree Programs in Social Work Education*. Washington, DC: Council on Social Work Education.

Cruikshank, Margaret, ed. 1982. *Lesbian Studies: Present and Future*. New York: Feminist Press.

Culley, M., and C. Portuges, eds. 1985. *Gendered Subjects: The Dynamics of Feminist Teaching*. Boston: Routledge & Kegan Paul.

Daniels, Roger. 1962. *The Politics of Prejudice: The Anti-Japanese Movement in California and the Struggle for Japanese Exclusion*. Berkeley, CA: University of California Press.

Darty, Trudy, and S. Potter, eds. 1984. *Women-Identified Women*. Palo Alto, CA: Mayfield.

Davis, Angela. 1981. *Women, Race, and Class*. New York: Random House.

DeCecco, John, ed. 1985. *Baiters, Bashers, and Bigots: Homophobia in American Society*. New York: Harrington Press.

Deloria, Vine. 1970. *We Talk, You Listen*. New York: Macmillan.

D'Emilio, John, and Estelle Freedman. 1988. *Intimate Matters: A History of Sexuality in America*. New York: Harper & Row.

Devore, W., and F. Schlesinger. 1987. *Ethnic-Sensitive Social Work Practice*. 2d ed. New York: Guilford.

DeVos, George, and L. Romanucci-Ross, eds. 1975. *Ethnic Identity*. New York: Mayfield.

Diffloth, Natalie, ed. 1987. *Workshops on Homophobia and Homosexuality on College Campuses*. New York: National Lesbian and Gay Resource Center (Fund for Human Dignity).

Dill, Bonnie T., and Maxine B. Zinn. 1990. *Race and Gender: Re-visioning Social*

    Relations. Memphis, TN: Memphis State University, Center for Research on
        Women.
Dix, L. S., ed. 1987. *Minorities: Their Underrepresentation and Career Differentials in
        Science and Engineering*. Washington, DC: National Academy Press.
D'Souza, Dinesh. 1991. *Illiberal Education*. New York: The Free Press.
Duberman, Martin, Martha Vicinus, and George Chauncey, eds. 1989. *Hidden from
        History: Reclaiming the Gay and Lesbian Past*. New York: New American Library.
Du Bois, W.E.B. 1972. *Black Reconstruction in America: 1860–1880*. New York:
        Atheneum.
Durr, Virginia. 1985. *Outside the Magic Circle: The Autobiography of Virginia Foster
        Durr*. New York: Simon & Schuster.
Faderman, Lillian. 1981. *Surpassing the Love of Men*. New York: Morrow.
Fairchild, Betty, and Nancy Hayward. 1979. *Now That You Know: What Every Parent
        Should Know About Homosexuality*. New York: Harcourt.
Fawcett, James T., and Benjamin V. Carino, eds. 1987. *Pacific Bridges: The New
        Immigration from Asia and the Pacific Islands*. New York: Center for Migration
        Studies.
Feagin, J., and C. Feagin. 1986. *Discrimination American Style: Institutional Racism
        and Sexism*. Englewood Cliffs, NJ: Prentice-Hall.
Fossum, M., and M. Mason. 1986. *Facing Shame: Families in Recovery*. New York:
        Norton.
Foster, Jeannette. 1975. *Sex Variant in Literature*. Baltimore: Diana Press.
Foucault, Michel. 1988. *Politics, Philosophy, Culture*. New York: Routledge.
Freedman, Estelle, Barbara Gelpi, Susan Johnson, and Kathleen Weston, eds. 1985. *The
        Lesbian Issue: Essays from Signs: Journal of Women in Culture and Society*.
        Chicago: University of Chicago Press.
Freire, P. 1972. *Pedagogy of the Oppressed*. New York: Seabury Press.
———. 1981. *Education for Critical Consciousness*. New York: Continuum.
———. 1985. *The Politics of Education: Culture, Power, and Liberation*. South Hadley,
        MA: Bergin & Garvey.
Fricke, Aaron. 1981. *Reflections of a Rock Lobster: A Story About Growing Up Gay*.
        Boston: Alyson.
Frye, Marilyn. 1983. *The Politics of Reality*. Trumansburg, NY: Crossing Press.
Gay Fathers of Toronto. 1981. *Gay Fathers: Some of Their Stories, Experience, and
        Advice*. Toronto: Gay Fathers of Toronto.
Giddings, P. 1984. *When and Where I Enter: The Impact of Black Women on Race and
        Sex in America*. New York: Morrow.
Gillespie, Sheena, Robert Singleton and Robert Becker, eds. 1986. *The Writer's Craft:
        A Process Reader*. New York: Scott, Foresman and Company.
Glazer, Nathan, and D. P. Moynihan. 1975. *Ethnicity*. Cambridge: Harvard University
        Press.
Goffman, E. 1963. *Stigma: Notes on the Management of Spoiled Identity*. Englewood
        Cliffs, NJ: Prentice-Hall.
Goldsmid, Charles A., and Everett Wilson, 1980. *Passing on Sociology*. Washington,
        DC: American Sociological Association.
Green, J., ed. 1982. *Cultural Awareness in the Human Services*. Englewood Cliffs, NJ:
        Prentice-Hall.

Griffin, Carolyn, Marian Wirth and Arthur Wirth. 1986. *Beyond Acceptance: Parents of Lesbians and Gays Talk About Their Experience*. New Jersey: Prentice-Hall.

Gutiérrez, Lorraine. 1989. *Ethnic Consciousness, Consciousness Raising, and the Empowerment Process of Latinos*. Ph.D. Diss., University of Michigan. Ann Arbor, MI: University Microfilms.

Gwaltney, John Langston. 1981. *Drylongso: A Self-Portrait of Black America*. New York: Vintage Books/Random House.

Hairston, Maxine. 1982. *A Contemporary Rhetoric*. Boston: Houghton Mifflin.

Hall Carpenter Archives, eds. 1989a. *Inventing Ourselves: Lesbian Life Stories*. London: Routledge.

————, eds. 1989b. *Walking After Midnight: Gay Men's Life Stories*. London: Routledge.

Hall, R., and B. Sandler. 1982. *The Classroom Climate: A Chilly One for Women?* Washington, DC: Association of American Colleges Project on the Status and Education of Women.

Hanscombe, Gillian, and Jackie Forster. 1982. *Rocking the Cradle, Lesbian Mothers: A Challenge in Family Living*. Boston: Alyson Publications.

Harrington, M. 1984. *The New American Poverty*. New York: Viking Penguin.

Heger, H. 1980. *The Men with the Pink Triangle*. Boston: Alyson.

Herdt, Gilbert. 1989. *Gay and Lesbian Youth*. New York: Haworth Press.

Hernandez, Hilda. 1989. *Multicultural Education: A Teacher's Guide to Content and Process*. Columbus, OH: Merrill.

Heron, Ann, ed. 1983. *One Teenager in Ten: Testimonies by Gay and Lesbian Youth*. New York: Warner.

Higginbotham, Elizabeth. 1988. *Integrating All Women into the Curriculum*. Memphis, TN: Memphis State University, Center for Research on Women.

Ho, M. K. 1987. *Family Therapy with Ethnic Minorities*. Beverly Hills, CA: Sage.

Holmes, Sarah. 1988. *Testimonies: A Collection of Lesbian Coming Out Stories*. Boston: Alyson.

Horton, Myles. 1991. *The Long Haul: An Autobiography*. New York: Anchor Books, Doubleday.

Hull, Gloria, Patricia Scott, and Barbara Smith, eds. 1982. *All the Women Are White, All the Blacks Are Men, But Some of Us Are Brave: Black Women's Studies*. New York: Feminist Press.

Jay, Karla, and Joanne Glasgow, eds. 1990. *Lesbian Texts and Contexts: Radical Revisions*. New York: New York University Press.

Johnston, J. and Kleinsmith, L. 1987. *Computers in Higher Education: Computer-Based Tutorials in Introductory Biology*. Ann Arbor: University of Michigan, Institute for Social Research.

Kanter, Rosabeth Moss. 1977. *Men and Women of the Corporation*. New York: Basic Books.

Katz, Judith. 1978. *White Awareness: Handbook of Anti-racist Training*. Norman: University of Oklahoma Press.

Kaufman, G. 1985. *Shame: The Power of Caring*. Cambridge, Mass: Schenkman.

Keefe, Susan, and A. Padilla. 1987. *Chicano Ethnicity*. Albuquerque: University of New Mexico Press.

Kehoe, Monica, ed. 1986. *Historical, Literary and Erotic Aspects of Lesbianism*. New York: Harrington Press.

Kingston, Maxine Hong. 1976. *The Woman Warrior: Memoirs of a Girlhood Among Ghosts*. New York: Knopf.

Kitano, Harry, and R. Daniels. 1988. *Asian Americans*. Englewood Cliffs, NJ: Prentice-Hall.

Kochman, Thomas. 1981. *Black and White Styles in Conflict*. Chicago: University of Chicago Press.

Kogon, E. 1973. *The Theory and Practice of Hell*. New York: Berkeley.

Krieger, Susan. 1983. *The Mirror Dance: Identity in a Women's Community*. Philadelphia: Temple University Press.

Kriesberg, L. 1973. *The Sociology of Social Conflicts*. Englewood Cliffs, NJ: Prentice-Hall.

Lappé, F. M. 1989. *Rediscovering America's Values*. New York: Ballantine Books.

Leicester, Mal. 1989. *Multicultural Education: From Theory to Practice*. Windsor, England: Nfer-Nelson.

Lorde, Audre. 1984. *Sister Outsider*. Trumansburg, NY: Crossing Press.

———. 1985. *I Am Your Sister: Black Women Organizing Across Sexualities*. Latham, NY: Kitchen Table-Women of Color Press.

Marquez, Gabriel García. 1970. *One Hundred Years of Solitude*. New York: Harper & Row.

Marshall, Paule. 1981. *Browngirl, Brownstones*. New York: Feminist Press.

May, Rollo. 1972. *Power and Innocence: A Search for Sources of Violence*. New York: Norton.

McGoldrick, Monica, and R. Gerson. 1985. *Genograms in Family Assessment*. New York: Norton.

McGoldrick, M., J. Pearce, and J. Giordano, eds. 1982. *Ethnicity and Family Therapy*. New York: Guilford.

McKeachie, W. J. 1986. *Teaching Tips*. Lexington, MA: Heath.

Mead, Margaret. 1963. *Sex and Temperament in Three Primitive Societies*. New York: W. Morrow.

Menchú, Rigoberta. 1984. *I, Rigoberta Menchú: An Indian Woman in Guatemala*. London: Verso.

Miller, Stuart C. 1969. *The Unwelcome Immigrant: The American Image of the Chinese, 1785–1882*. Berkeley: University of California Press.

Minnich, Elizabeth, Jean O'Barr, and Rachel Rosenfeld, eds. 1988. *Reconstructing the Academy: Women's Education and Women's Studies*. Chicago: University of Chicago Press.

Montagu, Ashley. 1968. *The Natural Superiority of Women*. New York: Macmillan.

Moody, Anne. 1968. *Coming of Age in Mississippi*. New York: Dial Press.

Moore, Joan, and Harry Pachon. 1985. *Hispanics in the United States*. Englewood Cliffs, NJ: Prentice-Hall.

Moraga, Cherríe. 1983. *Loving in the War Years*. Boston: South End Press.

Moraga, Cherríe, and Gloria Anzaldúa, eds. 1983. *This Bridge Called My Back: Writing by Radical Women of Color*. New York: Kitchen Table-Women of Color Press.

Morrison, Toni. 1972. *The Bluest Eye*. New York: Washington Square Press.

———. 1974. *Sula*. New York: Knopf.

———. 1978. *Song of Solomon*. New York: New American Library.

———. 1981. *Tar Baby*. New York: Knopf.

———. 1987. *Beloved*. New York: Knopf.

Myers, C. 1986. *Structuring Classes to Promote Critical Thought, Teaching Students to Think Critically*. San Francisco: Jossey-Bass.

National Assessment of Educational Progress (NAEP). 1988. *The Science Report Card: Elements of Risk and Recovery; Trends and Achievement Based on the 1986 National Assessment*. Princeton, NJ: Educational Testing Service.

National Gay and Lesbian Task Force. 1987. *Anti-Gay Violence, Victimization and Defamation in 1987*. U.S.: National Gay and Lesbian Task Force.

Naylor, Gloria. 1983. *The Women of Brewster Place*. New York: Penguin Books.

Newman, Leslea. 1988. *Letter to Harvey Milk: Short Stories*. Ithaca, NY: Firebrand Books.

Newman, William. 1973. *American Pluralism*. New York: Harper & Row.

Nyquist, Jody D., Robert Abbot, Donald Wulff, and Jo Sprague. 1991. *Preparing the Professoriate of Tomorrow to Teach*. Dubuque, IA: Kendall/Hunt.

Ogbu, John. 1978. *Minority Education and Caste*. New York: Academic Press.

Oliver, R. 1981. *The Making of an Architect 1881–1981*. New York: Rizzoli International.

Palen, J. J. and B. London, eds. 1984. *Gentrification, Displacement, and Neighborhood Revitalization*. Albany: SUNY Press.

Palmer, P. J. 1983. *To Know as We Are Known: A Spirituality of Education*. San Francisco: Harper & Row.

Parmeter, Sara-Hope, and Irene Reti, eds. 1988. *The Lesbian in Front of the Classroom: Writings by Lesbian Teachers*. Santa Cruz, NM: McNaughton & Gunn.

Phalen, Shane. 1989. *Identity Politics: Lesbian Feminism and the Limits of Community*. Philadelphia: Temple U. Press.

Pharr, Suzanne. 1988. *Homophobia: A Weapon of Sexism*. Iverness, CA: Chardon Press.

Plant, R. 1986. *The Pink Triangle*. New York: Holt, Rinehart, & Winston.

Pollack, Sandra, and Jeanne Vaughn, eds. 1987. *Politics of the Heart: A Lesbian Parenting Anthology*. Ithaca, NY: Firebrand Press.

Purpel, D. E. 1989. *The Moral and Spiritual Crisis in Education: A Curriculum for Justice and Compassion in Education*. Granby, MA: Bergin & Garvey.

Rafkin, Louise, ed. 1987. *Different Daughters: A Book by Mothers of Lesbians*. Pittsburgh: Cleis Press.

———. 1989. *Different Mothers: Sons and Daughters of Lesbians Talk About Their Lives*. Pittsburgh: Cleis Press.

Ramos, Juanita, ed. 1987. *Compañeras: Latina Lesbians*. New York: Latina Lesbian History Project.

Ramsey, Patricia G., Edwina B. Vold, and Leslie R. Williams. 1989. *Multicultural Education: A Source Book*. New York: Garland.

Ransby, Barbara. 1990. *Racism in Education*. Ann Arbor, MI: Ella Baker/Nelson Mandela Center for Anti-Racist Education.

Raths, Louis, M. Harmin, and S. Simon. 1966. *Values and Teaching*. Columbus, Ohio: Merrill.

Reed, B., and C. Garvin, eds. 1983. *Groupwork with Women/Groupwork with Men: An Overview of Gender Issues in Social Groupwork Practice*. New York: Haworth Press.

Reed, Ishmael. 1967. *Freelance Pallbearers*. Garden City, NY: Doubleday.

———. 1972. *Mumbo Jumbo*. Garden City, NY: Doubleday.

———. 1978. *Shrovetide in Old New Orleans*. New York: Doubleday.

Reid, John. 1976. *The Best Little Boy in the World*. New York: Ballantine Books.

Rich, Adrienne. 1979. *On Lies, Secrets, and Silence*. New York: Norton.

————. 1986. *Blood, Bread, and Poetry: Selected Prose 1979–1985*. London: Virago Press.

Richards, Dell. 1990. *Lesbian Lists: A Look at Lesbian Culture, History and Personalities*. Boston: Slyson.

Rollins, Judith. 1985. *Between Women: Domestics and Their Employers*. Philadelphia: Temple University Press.

Roscoe, Will, ed. 1988. *Living in the Spirit: A Gay American Indian Anthology*. New York: St. Martin's Press.

Samuda, Ronald, John Berry, and Michel Laferriere, eds. 1984. *Multiculturalism in Canada*. Boston: Allyn & Bacon.

Schoem, David. 1989. *Ethnic Survival in America: An Ethnography of a Jewish Afternoon School*. Atlanta: Scholars Press.

————, ed. 1991. *Inside Separate Worlds: Life Stories of Young Blacks, Jews, and Latinos*. Ann Arbor: University of Michigan Press.

Schon, D. A. 1987. *Educating the Reflective Practitioner*. San Francisco: Jossey-Bass.

Schulenburg, Joy. 1985. *Gay Parenting: A Complete Guide for Gay Men and Lesbians with Children*. New York: Anchor Books.

Schuster, Marilyn, and Susan Van Dyne, eds. 1985. *Women's Place in the Academy: Transforming the Liberal Arts Curriculum*. Totowa, NJ: Rowman & Allanheld.

Simonson, Rick, and S. Walker, eds. 1988. *The Graywolf Annual Five: Multicultural Literacy*. St. Paul, MN: Graywolf Press.

Smith, Barbara, ed. 1983. *Home Girls: A Black Feminist Anthology*. Latham, NY: Kitchen Table-Women of Color Press.

Sollors, Werner. 1986. *Beyond Ethnicity: Consent and Descent in American Culture*. New York: Oxford University Press.

Spanier, Bonnie, Alexander Bloom, and Darlene Boroviak, eds. 1984. *Toward a Balanced Curriculum: A Sourcebook for Initiating Gender Integration Projects*. Cambridge, MA: Schenkman.

Spradley, J. P., and David McCurdy. 1972. *The Cultural Experience: Ethnography in Complex Society*. Chicago: Science Research Associates.

Stack, G. 1974. *All Our Kin*. New York: Harper & Row.

Stanford, G. 1977. *Developing Effective Classroom Groups*. New York: Hart.

Stanley, Julia, and Susan Wolfe. 1989. *The Coming Out Stories*. Freedom, CA: Crossing Press.

Steinberg, Stephen. 1981. *The Ethnic Myth: Race, Ethnicity, and Class in America*. Boston: Beacon Press.

Takaki, Ronald. 1979. *Iron Cages: Race and Culture in Nineteenth-Century America*. Seattle: University of Washington Press.

————, ed. 1987. *From Different Shores: Perspectives on Race and Ethnicity in America*. New York: Oxford University Press.

Tannen, Deborah. 1990. *You Just Don't Understand: Women and Men in Conversation*. New York: Morrow.

Task Force on Racial and Cultural Concerns. 1990. *Year-End Report of Problems Identified and Actions Recommended*. Ann Arbor: University of Michigan, School of Public Health.

Tiedt, Pamela L., and Iris M. Tiedt. 1979. *Multicultural Teaching: A Handbook of Activities, Information, and Resources*. Boston: Allyn & Bacon.

Troyna, Barry. 1987. *Racial Inequality in Education*. London: Tavistock.

Tuan, Y. F. 1989. *Morality and Imagination: Paradoxes of Progress*. Madison: University of Wisconsin Press.

United States Task Force on Women, Minorities, and the Handicapped in Science and Technology. 1989. *Changing America: The New Face of Science and Engineering*. Washington, DC: Task Force of Women, Minorities, and the Handicapped in Science and Technology.

Valdéz, Luis, and Stan Steiner, eds. 1972. *Axtlan: An Anthology of Mexican American Literature*. New York: Knopf.

Verma, Gajendra, ed. 1989. *Education for All: A Landmark in Pluralism*. New York: Falmer Press.

Veroff, Joseph, Douvan, Elizabeth, and R. Kulka. 1981. *The Inner American*. New York: Basic Books.

Walker, Alice. 1983. *The Color Purple*. New York: Pocket Books/Washington Square Press.

Washington, Joseph, ed. 1984. *Jews in Black Perspectives* Cranbury, NJ: Associated University Presses.

Wehr, Paul. 1979. *Conflict Regulation*. Boulder, CO: Westview Press.

Weiler, K. 1988. *Women Teaching for Change*. South Hadley, MA: Bergin & Garvey.

Weinstein, Gerald, and Mario Fantini. 1970. *Toward Humanistic Education: A Curriculum of Affect*. New York: Praeger.

White, L. 1949. *The Science of Culture: The Study of Man and Civilization to the Fall of Rome*. New York: American Books, Stratford Press.

Wilson, W. J. 1987. *The Truly Disadvantaged: The Inner City, the Underclass, and Public Policy*. Chicago: University of Chicago Press.

Wolf, Deborah. 1979. *The Lesbian Community*. Berkeley: University of California Press.

Women's Issues Commission of the Michigan Student Assembly. 1991. *Gender and Academic Climate at the University of Michigan: Student Voices*. Ann Arbor: Michigan Student Assembly.

Yezierska, Anzia. 1925. *Bread Givers*. New York: Braziller.

Young, Iris M. 1990. *Justice and the Politics of Difference*. Princeton, NJ: Princeton University Press.

Zahava, I. 1990. *Speaking for Ourselves: Short Stories by Jewish Lesbians*. Trumansburg, NY: Crossing Press.

ARTICLES

Ager, Susan. 1984. The Silent Minority. *Detroit Free Press*. April 29, 8.

Aleinikoff, T. Alexander. 1991. A Case for Race-Consciousness. *Columbia Law Review* 91 (5): 1060–1125.

Allen, Walter. 1978. The Search for Applicable Theories of Black Family Life. *Journal of Marriage and the Family* 40 (1): 117–29.

Andersen, M. 1987. Denying Difference: The Continuing Basis for Exclusion in the Classroom. Keynote address at the Third Annual Workshop on Women in the Curriculum, sponsored by the Center for Research on Women at Memphis State University.

———. 1988a. Changing the Curriculum in Higher Education. In *Reconstructing the*

Academy: Women's Education and Women's Studies, ed. E. Minnich et al., 36–
    68. Chicago: University of Chicago Press.

————. 1988b. Moving Our Minds: Studying Women of Color and Reconstructing
    Sociology. *Teaching Sociology* 16: 123–32.

Anderson, Beverly. 1990. Minorities and Mathematics: The New Frontier and Challenge
    of the Nineties. *Making Mathematics Work for Minorities*. Washington, DC:
    Mathematical Sciences Education Board, National Research Council.

Ann Arbor News Editorial Board. 1990. Gay Counseling: Regent Fails to Understand
    Concept. *Ann Arbor News*, July 24.

Aptheker, Bettina. 1981. Strong Is What We Make Each Other: Racism Within Women's
    Studies. *Women's Studies Quarterly* 9 (4): 13–16.

Arthur, Herman. 1983. The Japan Gap. *American Educator*. Summer.

Bacca Zinn, Maxine. 1990. The Costs of Exclusionary Practices in Women's Studies.
    In *Making Face, Making Soul, Hacienda Caras: Creative and Critical Perspec-
    tives by Women of Color*, ed. Gloria Anzaldúa, 29–41. San Francisco: Aunt Lute
    Books.

Baker, Deane. 1990. Viewpoint: Counseling for Gays at U-M. *Ann Arbor News*, July
    27, A11.

Banks, James A. 1991. Teaching Assistants and Cultural Diversity. In *Preparing the
    Professiorate of Tomorrow to Teach*, ed. J. D. Nyquist, 65–72. Dubuque, IA:
    Kendall/Hunt.

Barale, Michèle Aina. 1989. The Lesbian Academic: Negotiating New Boundaries. In
    Loving Boldly: Issues Facing Lesbians, ed. Esther Rothblum and Ellen Cole, 183–
    94. New York: Harrington Park Press.

Beauchamp, Bill, and Bonnie Wheeler. 1988. From Achilles to the Heel: Teaching
    Masculinity. *Women's Studies Quarterly* 16 (3–4): 100–111.

Beck, Evelyn Torton. 1981. Self-Disclosure and the Commitment to Social Change.
    Unpublished Manuscript.

Beckman, Charlene. 1989. Effects of Computer Graphics Use on Student Understanding
    of Calculus Concepts. *Dissertation Abstracts International* 50: 5–B.

Berkeide, C., and M. Segal. 1985. Teaching About Sex and Gender: A Decade of
    Experience. *Teaching Sociology* 16: 123–32.

Billson, Janet M. 1986. The College Classroom as a Small Group: Some Implications
    for Teaching and Learning. *Teaching Sociology* 14: 143–51.

Braverman, Scott. 1990. Telling (Hi)stories: Rethinking the Lesbian and Gay Historical
    Imagination. *OUT/LOOK* 2(4): 68–74.

Briggs, Sarah, and Barbara Hofer. 1991. Undergraduate Perceptions of ITA Effectiveness.
    In *Preparing the Professoriate of Tomorrow to Teach*, ed. J. D. Nyquist. Du-
    buque, IA: Kendall/Hunt.

Bronski, Michael. 1990. Outing: The Power of the Closet. *Gay Community News* 17(45):
    8–9.

Bulkin, Elly. 1980. Heterosexism and Women's Studies. *Radical Teacher* 6(3): 25–31.

Butler, Johnella. 1989. Transforming the Curriculum: Teaching About Women of Color.
    In *Multicultural Education*, ed. J. Banks and C. A. Banks, 145–63. Boston: Allyn
    & Bacon.

Butler, Johnella, and Betty Schmitz. 1989. Different Voices: A Model for Integrating
    Women of Color into Undergraduate American Literature and History Courses.
    Radical Teacher 37: 4–9.

Butter, I., E. Carpenter, B. J. Kay, and R. Simmons. 1987. Hierarchies in the Health Labor Force. *International Journal of Health Services* 17: 133–49.

Cain, Roy. 1979. Stigma Management and Gay Identity Development. *Social Work* 36(1): 67–73.

Carby, Hazel V. 1989. The Cannon: Civil War and Reconstruction. *Michigan Quarterly Review* 28(1): 35–43.

Carl, Iris M. 1989. Mathematics Education Today: What Are We Doing and Where Are We Going? In *Making Mathematics Work for Minorities*, 1–5. Washington, DC: Mathematical Sciences Education Board, National Research Council.

Cass, V. 1979. Homosexual Identity Formation: A Theoretical Model. *Journal of Homosexuality* 4: 219–35.

Chan, C. 1989. Issues of Identity Development Among Asian American Lesbians and Gay Men. *Journal of Counseling and Development* 68(1): 16–20.

Chapman, Diana. 1987. Exit 10: An Allegory. In *Heterosexuality*, ed. Gillian Hanscombe and Martin Humphries, 104–14. London: GMP.

Chasteen, Ed. 1987. Balancing the Cognitive and the Affective in Teaching Race Relations. *Teaching Sociology* 15: 80–81.

Chau, K. L. 1991. Social Work with Ethnic Minorities: Practice Issues and Potentials. *Journal of Multicultural Social Work* 1(1): 23–29.

Chesler, Mark, and James Crowfoot. 1990. Racism on Campus. In *Ethics and Higher Education*, ed. W. May, 195–230. New York: Macmillan.

Chesler, Mark, and Ximena Zúñiga. 1991. Dealing with Prejudice and Conflict in the Classroom: The Pink Triangle Exercise. *Teaching Sociology* 19(2): 173–81.

Chrystos. 1990. Headaches and Ruminations: Class in Lesbian/Gay Communities. *Gay Community News* 17(29): 9.

Clarke, Cheryl. 1983. Lesbianism: An Act of Resistance. In *This Bridge Called My Back: Writings by Radical Women of Color*, ed. Cherríe Moraga and Gloria Anzaldúa, 128–37. Kitchen Table: Women of Color Press.

Clarke, Kim. July 20, 1990. Sexually Confused Need 'Neutral' Office, Regent Says. *Ann Arbor News*, 1.

Clarke, Kim, and Judson Branam. 1990. U-M Can't Probe Complaints Against Regent. *Ann Arbor News*, August 7.

Coleman, E. 1982. Developmental Stages of the Coming-Out Process. *American Behavioral Scientist* 25: 469–82.

Collins, James W., and Richard J. David. 1990. Effects of Traditional Risk Factors on Infant Birthweight Among Blacks and Whites In Chicago. *American Journal of Public Health* 80: 679–81.

Collins, Patricia H. 1986. Getting Off to a Good Start: The First Class in Black Family Studies. *Teaching Sociology* 14: 193–95.

———. 1989. Toward a New Vision: Race, Class, and Gender as Categories of Analysis and Connection. *Integrating Race and Gender into the College Curriculum*. Memphis, TN: Memphis State University, Center for Research on Women.

Combs, Arthur. 1972. Humanistic Goals of Education. In *Educational Accountability: Beyond Behavioral Objectives*. Washington, DC: Association for Supervision and Curriculum Development.

Cook, Blanche W. 1979. The Historical Denial of Lesbianism. *Radical History Review* 20: 60–65.

Crenshaw, Kimberle W. 1989. Forward: Toward a Race-Conscious Pedagogy in Legal
    Education. *National Black Law Journal* 11(1): 1–14.
Cruikshank, Margaret. 1982. Lesbians in the Academic World: The Personal/Political
    Experience. In *Lesbian Studies: Present and Future*, ed. Margaret Cruikshank,
    3–21. New York: Feminist Press.
Crumpacker, Laurie, and Eleanor Vander Haegen. 1987. Pedagogy and Prejudice: Strat-
    egies for Confronting Homophobia in the Classroom. *Women's Studies Quarterly*
    15(3–4): 65–73.
D'Augelli, Anthony, and Melissa Rose. 1990. Homophobia in a University Community:
    Attitudes and Experiences of Heterosexual Freshmen. *Journal of College Student
    Development* 31: 484–91.
Davis, B. G. 1990. Diversity and Complexity in the Classroom: Considerations of Race,
    Ethnicity, and Gender. In *Tools for Teaching*. Berkeley: University of California,
    Office of Educational Development.
Davis, L. E., ed. 1981a. Ethnicity in Social Groupwork Practice. *Social Work with Groups*
    (special issue) 7(3).
———. 1981b. Racial Issues in the Training of Group Workers. *Journal for Specialists
    in Group Work*, 17, 155–60.
Delpit, L. D. 1988. The Silence of Dialogue: Power and Pedagogy in Educating Other
    People's Children. *Harvard Educational Review* 58(3): 280–98.
D'Emilio, John. 1987. Homosexual Professors Owe It to Their Students to 'Come Out.'
    Chronicle of Higher Education, A52.
Duderstadt, James. 1988. The *Michigan Mandate*: A *Strategic Linking of Academic
    Excellence and Social Diversity*. Ann Arbor: University of Michigan.
Dukes, Richard, and Gay Victoria. 1989. The Effects of Gender, Status, and Effective
    Teaching on the Evaluation of College Instruction. *Teaching Sociology* 17: 447–
    57.
Epstein, Steven. 1987. Gay Politics, Ethnic Identity: The Limits of Social Construction-
    ism. *Socialist Review* 17: 9–54.
Escoffier, Jeffrey. 1990. Inside the Ivory Closet: The Challenges Facing Lesbian and
    Gay Studies. *OUT/LOOK* 3(2): 40–48.
Espín, Oliva. 1987. Issues of Identity in the Psychology of Latina Lesbians. In *Lesbian
    Psychologies: Explorations and Challenges*, ed. Boston Lesbian Psychologies
    Collective, 35–55. Chicago: University of Illinois Press.
Fischer, Bernice. 1981. What Is Feminist Pedagogy? *Radical Teacher* 18: 22–24.
Flores, Juan, and George Yudice. 1990. Living Border/Buscando America: Languages
    of Latino Self-Formation. *Social Text* 24: 57–84.
Folsom, Jack. 1983. Teaching About Sexism and Language in a Traditional Setting.
    Women's Studies Quarterly 11(1): 12–15.
Fuller, Charles H. 1990. When the Shoes Don't Fit: Class and Race in the Workplace.
    Gay Community News 17(29): 6.
The Gay and Lesbian Speakers Bureau of Boston. 1984. *The Gay and Lesbian Speakers
    Bureau Manual*. Boston: The Gay and Lesbian Speakers Bureau of Boston.
Giroux, Henry. 1985. Introduction. In *The Politics of Education*. Paulo Friere. South
    Hadley, MA: Bergin & Garvey.
Goldberg, R. 1982. Attitude Change Among College Students Toward Homosexuality.
    Journal of American College Health 30: 260–68.
Goldenberg, E. Paul. 1988. Mathematics, Metaphors, and Human Factors: Mathematical,

Technical, and Pedagogical Challenges in the Educational Use of Graphical Representation of Function. *Journal of Mathematical Behavior* 7: 2.

Goldsby, Jackie. 1990. What It Means to Be Colored Me. *OUT/LOOK* 3(1): 8–17.

Goleman, Daniel. 1990. Studies Discover Clues to the Roots of Homophobia. *New York Times*, July 10, B1.

Gómez-Pēna, Guillermo. 1989. The Multicultural Paradigm: An Open Letter to the National Arts Community. *High Performance* 12: 18–27.

Gondolf, E. 1985. Teaching About Utopian Societies: An Experiential Approach to Sociological Learning. *Teaching Sociology* 12(2): 229–41.

Greer, William. 1986. Violence Against Homosexuals Rising, Groups Seeking Wider Protection Say. *New York Times*, November 23: L36.

Gutiérrez, L. M., and R. M. Ortega. 1991. Developing Methods to Empower Latinos: The Importance of Groups. *Social Work with Groups* 14(2): 23–43.

Hamlin, John, and Susan Janssen. 1987. Active Learning in Large Introductory Sociology Classes. *Teaching Sociology* 15: 45–54.

Harris, Craig. 1989. Weaving the Future of Black Gender Politics. *Gay Community News* 17(19): 7.

Hayes-Bautista, David, and J. Chapa. 1987. Latino Terminology. *American Journal of Public Health* 77(1): 61–68.

Henley, N., M. Hamilton, and B. Thorne. 1985. Womanspeak and Manspeak: Sex Differences and Sexism in Communication, Verbal and Nonverbal. In *Beyond Sex Roles*, ed. Alice Sargent. St. Paul, MN: West.

Herek, Gregory. 1989. Hate Crimes Against Lesbians and Gay Men. *American Psychologist* 44(6): 948–55.

Hilliard, Asa G. III. 1990. Changing Attitudes. In *Making Mathematics Work for Minorities*, 69–80. Washington, DC: Mathematical Sciences Education Board, National Research Council.

Hooks, Bell. 1988. Reflections on Homophobia and Black Communities. *OUT/LOOK* 1(2): 22–25.

Horney, Karen. 1987. Conflict Between the Sexes. In *Final Lectures*, ed. Karen Horney. New York: Norton.

Hyder, Happy. 1990. Racism: Lesbian Artists Have Their Say. *OUT/LOOK* 2(4): 38–43.

Jackson, J. S., W. R. McCullough, and G. Gurin. 1988. Family, Socialization Environment, and Identity Development in Black Americans. In *Black Families*, ed. H. McAdoo, 54–76. Newbury Park, CA: Sage.

Jenkins, Mercilee. 1990. Teaching the New Majority: Guidelines for Cross-Cultural Communication Between Students and Faculty. *Feminist Teacher* 5(1): 8–14.

Kampf, Louis, and Dick Ohmann. 1983. Men in Women's Studies. *Women's Studies Quarterly* 9(1): 9–11.

Katz, Judith. 1988. Facing the Challenge of Diversity and Multiculturalism. (Working Paper #13). University of Michigan, Program on Conflict Management Alternatives.

Kim, James. 1988. Are Homosexuals Facing an Ever More Hostile World? *New York Times*, July 3.

Kim, Willyce. 1987. Willyce: Shy Woman, Bold Poet. In *A Lesbian Photo Album: The Lives of Seven Lesbian Feminists*, ed. Cathy Cade. Oakland, CA: Waterwomen Books, pp. 21–36.

Kirchstein, R. L. 1991. Research on Women's Health. *American Journal of Public Health* 81: 291–93.

Kleinsmith, L. J. 1987. A Computer-Based Biology Study Center: Preliminary Assessment of Impact. *Academic Computing* 2: 32–33, 49–50.

Klepfisz, Irena. 1982. Anti-Semitism in the Lesbian/Feminist Movement. In *Nice Jewish Girls: A Lesbian Anthology*, ed. Evelyn Torton Beck, 45–51. Trumansburg, NY: Crossing Press.

Kotch, Jonathan. 1991. Low Birthweight and Maternity Care for All. *Journal of Public Health Policy* 7: 156–60.

Kramer, L., and G. Martin. 1988. Mainstreaming Gender: Some Thoughts for Non-Specialists. *Teaching Sociology* 16: 133–40.

Kramer, Michael. 1985. Blacks and Jews: How Wide the Rift. *New York*. February 4: 26–33.

Krieger, Nancy. 1990. Racial and Gender Discrimination: Risk Factors for High Blood Pressure. *Social Science and Medicine* 30(2): 1273–81.

Krupnick, C. Spring. 1990. Women and Men in the Classroom: Inequality and Its Remedies. In *On Teaching and Learning*, 19–23. Cambridge, MA: Harvard-Danforth Center for Teaching and Learning.

Lance, L. 1987. The Effects of Interaction with Gay Persons on Attitudes Toward Homosexuality. *Human Relations* 40(6): 329–36.

Larkin, Joan, and Carl Morse. 1989. Not Separate, But Distinct. *Poets and Writers Magazine*, 17(2): 31–40 Mar/Apr.

Lathrop, Julia. 1919. Income and Infant Mortality. *American Journal of Public Health* 9: 270–74.

Lautmann, R. 1981. The Pink Triangle: The Persecution of Homosexual Males in Concentration Camps in Nazi Germany. *Journal of Homosexuality* 6(1–2): 141–60.

Leinhardt, Gaea, and Orit Zaslavsky, and Mary K. Stein. 1990. Functions, Graphs, and Graphing: Tasks, Learning and Teaching. *Review of Educational Research* 60: 1.

Lo, Jo, Karin Aguilar-San Juan and Jacquelyn Ching Black. 1990. Asian Cultures, Sexuality and Class: Sorting It All Out. *Gay Community News* 17(27): 7.

Loiacano, D. 1989. Gay Identity Issues Among Black Americans: Racism, Homophobia, and the Need for Validation. *Journal of Counseling and Development* 68(1): 21–25.

Lorde, Audre. 1981. An Open Letter to Mary Daly. In *This Bridge Called My Back*, ed. C. Moraga and G. Anzaldúa, 94–97. Watertown, MA: Persephone Press.

———. 1987. The Uses of Anger. *Women's Studies Quarterly* 9(3): 7–10.

———. 1990. Unused Privilege Is a Weapon in the Hand of Our Enemies. *Gay Community News* 17(27): 5.

Lowney, Kathleen. 1989. Victimization of Women: Trying to Link Community and Coursework. *Feminist Teacher* 4(2–3): 33–38.

Maher, Frances. 1984. Appropriate Teaching Methods for Integrating Women. In *Toward A Balanced Curriculum*, eds. Bonnie Spanier, Alexander Bloom and Darlene Boroviak. Cambridge, MA: Schenkman Publishing Co.

Malcolm, S. M. 1981. Women and Minorities in Science and Technology. *Science* 214:137.

Maran, Meredith. 1990. Ten for Bravery, Zero for Common Sense: Confessions of a Speaker's Bureau Speaker. *OUT/LOOK* 2(3): 68–73.

Margolies, Liz, Martha Becker and Karla Jackson-Brewer. 1987. Internalized Homophobia: Identifying and Treating the Oppressor Within. In *Lesbian Psychologies: Explorations and Challenges*, ed. Boston Lesbian Psychologies Collective, 229–41. Chicago: University of Illinois Press.

McBay, Shirley M. 1990. Minority Success in the Mathematics Pipeline: A National Concern. In *Making Mathematics Work for Minorities*. Compendium of papers prepared for regional workshops, Mathematics Sciences Education Board.

McDavid, Alex. 1988. Feminism for Men: 101 Educating Men in Women's Studies. *Feminist Teacher* 3(3): 25–33.

McIntosh, Peggy. 1988. White Privilege and Male Privilege: A Personal Account of Coming to See Correspondences Through Work in Women's Studies. Wellesley, MA: Wellesley College Center for Research on Women.

———. 1989. White Privilege: Unpacking the Invisible Knapsack. In *Peace and Freedom*. London: Women's International League for Peace and Freedom.

———. 1991. Interactive Phases of Curricular and Personal Revision with Regard to Race. In *Transforming the Curriculum: Ethnic Studies and Women's Studies*, ed. Johnella Butler and John Walter. Albany, NY: SUNY Press.

McKinney, K. 1985. Ethical Issues and Dilemmas in the Teaching of the Sociology of Human Sexuality. *Quarterly Journal of Ideology* 9: 23–27.

McLeod, Keith. 1984. Multiculturalism and Multicultural Education: Policy and Practice. In *Multiculturalism in Canada*, ed. Ronald Samuda, John Berry, and Michel Laferriere. Boston: Allyn & Bacon.

Miessner, Joseph. 1989. Anti-Gay Violence on the Rise in Ann Arbor. *Campus Report: Monthly Journal of MSA* 7:2.

Minnich, Elizabeth K. 1991. Discussing Diversity. *Liberal Education* 77(1): 2–7.

Morales, Iris. 1974. Voices of Anger and Protest. In *Puerto Rico and Puerto Ricans: Studies in History and Society*, ed. Adalbeto López and James Petras. Cambridge, MA: Schenkman.

Morin, W. S. 1974. Educational Programs as a Means of Changing Attitudes Toward Gay People. *Homosexual Counseling Journal* 1(4): 160–65.

National Association of Scholars. 1988. *Is the Curriculum Biased? A Statement of the National Association of Scholars*. Princeton, NJ: National Association of Scholars.

Newton, Esther. 1987. Academe's Homophobia: It Damages Careers and Ruins Lives. *Chronicle of Higher Education*, 33(26): 104.

Nilsen, Alleen Pace. 1972. Sexism in English: A Feminist View. *Female Studies* 4.

Orozco, C. 1983. Culture: Responsibility in Teaching. Paper presented at the 14th Annual Conference of the Rocky Mountain Educational Research Association. Tucson, Arizona. November 2–5.

Orwell, George. 1953. Shooting an Elephant. In *A Collection of Essays*. New York: Harcourt Brace Jovanovich.

Padesky, Christine. 1989. Attaining and Maintaining Positive Lesbian Self-Identity: A Cognitive Therapy Approach. In *Loving Boldly: Issues Facing Lesbians*, ed. Esther Rothblum and Ellen Cole, 145–56. New York: Harrington Park Press.

Painter, Nell Irwin. 1984. Who Speaks for the South? *Southern Exposure* 7(6): 92–93.

Pease, Bob. 1990. Challenging Domination in Social Work Education. Paper presented at the 25th International Conference of Schools of Social Work, Lima, Peru, August 16–20.

Pence, Ellen. 1982. Racism—A White Issue. In *All the Women Are White, All the Blacks*

Are Men, But Some of Us Are Brave: Black Women's Studies, eds. Gloria T. Hull, Patricia Bell Scott and Barbara Smith, 45–47. New York: Feminist Press.

Pheterson, Gail. 1986. Alliances Between Women: Overcoming Internalized Oppression and Internalized Domination. *Signs: Journal of Women in Culture and Society* 12(1): 146–60.

Pruitt, A. S. 1984. G*POP and the Federal Role in the Graduate Education of Minorities. *Journal of Negro Education* 53:106–13.

Pruitt, A. S., and P. D. Isaac. 1985. Discrimination in Recruitment, Admission, and Retention of Minority Graduate Students. *Journal of Negro Education* 54: 526–36.

Ravitch, Diane. 1990. Multiculturalism: E Pluribus Unum. *The American Scholar* 59: 337–54.

Rich, Adrienne. 1979a. Toward a Woman-Centered University. In *On Lies, Secrets, and Silences*. New York: Norton.

———. 1979b. Disloyal to Civilization: Feminism, Racism, Gynephobia. In *Lies, Secrets, and Silences*. New York: Norton.

———. 1980. Compulsory Heterosexuality and Lesbian Existence. *Signs* 5(4): 631–60.

Robledo, S. Jhoanna. 1990. Gay Activists: Baker Must Quit Over Comments. *Ann Arbor News*, August 1, A1, 7.

Rothenberg, Paula. 1988. Integrating the Study of Race, Gender, and Class: Some Preliminary Observations. *Feminist Teacher* 3(3): 37–42.

Ryan, Maureen. 1989. Classrooms and Contexts: The Challenge of Feminist Pedagogy. *Feminist Teacher* 4(2): 40.

Sanderson, Chela. 1990. Feminism and Racism: A Report on the National Women's Studies Association Conference. In *Making Face/Making Soul*, ed. G. Anzaldúa. San Francisco: Aunt Lute Foundation Books.

Sayer, Dorothy. 1986. Are Women Human? In *The Writer's Craft: A Process Reader*, ed. Sheena Gillespie, Robert Singleton and Robert Becker. New York: Scott, Foresman.

Schneidewind, Nancy. 1990. Feminist Values: Guidelines for Teaching Methodology in Women's Studies. In *Politics of Education: Essays from Radical Teachers*, ed. Susan O'Malley, Robert Rosen, and Leonard Vogt. Albany, NY: SUNY Press.

Schoem, David. 1991. College Students Need Thoughtful, In-Depth Study of Race Relations. *Chronicle of Higher Education*, April 3, A48.

Schoem, David, and Marshall Stevenson. 1990. Teaching Ethnic Identity and Intergroup Relations: The Case of Blacks and Jews. *Teachers College Record* 91(4): 579–94.

Schuster, M. R., and S. R. Van Dyne. 1983. Feminist Transformation of the Curriculum. Wellesley, MA: Wellesley College Center for Research on Women.

Secor, John. 1990. Officials Worry About Rise in Hate Crimes at Colleges. *Ann Arbor News*, July 11, A4.

Serdahely, William, and Georgia Ziemba. 1985. Changing Homophobic Attitudes Through Sexuality Education. In *Bashers, Baiters, and Bigots, Homophobia in American Society*, ed. John DeCecco, 109–17. New York: Harrington Park Press.

Shapiro, Amy H. 1991. Creating a Conversation: Teaching All Women in the Feminist Classroom. *National Women's Studies Association Journal* 3(1): 70–80.

Shapiro, Stewart. 1986. Survey of Basic Instructional Value in Humanistic Education. *Journal of Humanistic Education and Development* 24(4): 144–58.

Short, Thomas. 1988. "Diversity" and "Breaking the Disciplines": Two New Assaults on the Curriculum. *Academic Questions* 1(3): 6–29.

Sleeter, Christine, and Carl Grant. 1987. An Analysis of Multicultural Education in the United States. *Harvard Educational Review* 57(4): 421–44.

Smith, Barbara. 1982. Racism and Women's Studies. In *All the Women Are White, All the Blacks Are Men, But Some of Us Are Brave: Black Women's Studies*, ed. Barbara Smith, 48–51. New York: Feminist Press.

Smith, Barbara, and Jewelle Gomez. 1990. Taking the Home out of Homophobia. *OUT/LOOK* 8: 32–37.

Smith, Beverly et al. 1990. It Feels Like Exile, After Exile. *Gay Community News* 17(28): 5–6.

Smith, Daryl. 1990. Embracing Diversity as a Central Campus Goal. *Academe* Nov/Dec 76(6): 29–33.

Spelman, Vicky. 1982. Combatting the Marginalization of Black Women in the Class Room. *Women's Studies Quarterly* 10(2): 15–16.

Staples, R. 1984. Racial Ideology and Intellectual Racism: Blacks in Academia. *Black Scholar* 15(2): 2–17.

Stein, Arlene. 1989. All Dressed Up, But No Place to Go? Style Wars and the New Lesbianism. *OUT/LOOK* 1(4): 34–41.

Stimpson, Catherine R. 1991. New "Politically Correct" Metaphors Insult History and Our Campuses. *Chronicle of Higher Education*, May 29, A40.

Suzuki, Bob H. 1977. Education and the Socialization of Asian Americans: A Revisionist Analysis of the Model Minority Thesis. *Amerasia Journal* 4(2): 23–51.

Takaki, R. 1989. An Educated and Culturally Literate Person Must Study America's Multi-Cultural Reality. *Chronicle of Higher Education* March 8, B1–2.

Tannen, Deborah. 1991. Teachers' Classroom Strategies Should Recognize That Men and Women Use Language Differently. *Chronicle of Higher Education*, June 19, B1–3.

This Week in Japan (A Syndicated Program). 1987. *Cable News Network*. August 8.

Thomas, W. I. 1931. The Relation of Research to Social Process. In *Essays on Research in the Social Sciences*. Washington, DC: The Brookings Institute, 186–197.

Thurgood, Delores H. and Joann M. Weinman. 1990. Summary Report 1989, Doctorate Recipients From United States Universities. Washington, DC: National Academy Press.

Tinney, James. 1983. Interconnections. *Interracial Books for Children Bulletin* 14(3–4): 1–5.

Toth, Susan Allen. 1986. Dating. In *The Writer's Craft: A Process Reader*, ed. Sheena Gillespie, Robert Singleton and Robert Becker. New York: Scott, Foresman.

Turoff, M. 1975. The Future of Computer Conferencing: An Interview with Murray Turoff. *The Futurist* Vol. 9(3): 182–195.

Vallee, J., R. Johansen and K. Spangler. 1975. The Computer Conference: An Altered State of Communication? *The Futurist* 9(3): 116–121.

Vance, Noelle. 1990. From Slurs to Threats: Harassment Takes Many Forms at "U." *Michigan Daily*, April 18, 1–2.

Vandewater, Elizabeth, and Abigail Stewart. 1991. *Report on Introductory Course Survey for the WING Curriculum Committee*. Ann Arbor: University of Michigan.

Wells, J., and M. Franken. 1987. University Students' Knowledge About and Attitudes

Toward Homosexuality. *Journal of Humanistic Education and Development* 26(2): 81–95.

Wells, Theodora. 1976. Woman—Which Includes Man, Of Course: An Experience in Awareness. In *Female Psychology: The Emerging Self*, ed. Sue Cox, 340. Chicago: Science Research Associates.

Woo, Merle. 1983. Letter to Ma. In *This Bridge Called My Back: Writings by Radical Women of Color*, ed. Cherrie Moraga and Gloria Anzaldúa, 140–47. New York: Kitchen Table: Women of Color Press.

Yankauer, Alfred. 1990. What Infant Mortality Tells Us. *American Journal of Public Health* 80: 653–54.

Zimmerman, Bonnie. 1985. What Has Never Been: An Overview of Lesbian Feminist Literary Criticism. In *The New Feminist Criticism: Essays on Women, Literature, and Theory*, ed. Elaine Showalter, 200–24. New York: Pantheon Books.

Index

About the Contributors

T. ALEXANDER ALEINIKOFF received his B. A. from Swarthmore College and his J. D. degree from the Yale Law School. He is a Professor of Law at the University of Michigan and currently teaches a course on Race and the Law.

MARTHA ALIAGA earned a doctorate from the University of Michigan and is a Lecturer in the Comprehensive Studies Program at the university. She currently teaches mathematics courses within the program.

BUNYAN BRYANT has his major faculty appointment in the School of Natural Resources at the University of Michigan; however, he also works with the Urban Technological and Environmental Planning Program and the Center for Afro-American and African Studies.

IRENE BUTTER is a Professor of Public Health Policy and Administration at the School of Public Health, University of Michigan. She currently does research in the areas of maternal and child health and gender differentiation in the health work force.

MARK A. CHESLER is a Professor of Sociology at the University of Michigan and a core member of the Program for Conflict Management Alternatives. His areas of specialization include the study of conflict and social change and race and gender equity/inequity in organizations.

ELIZABETH DOUVAN is a Professor of Psychology and Program Director of the Survey Research Center at the University of Michigan. She teaches in the

Psychology Department and the Women's Studies Program at the University of Michigan.

BILLIE L. EDWARDS received her M. A. in Clinical Humanist Psychology from the Center for Humanistic Studies in Detroit. She serves as Co-coordinator of the Lesbian-Gay Male Programs Office at the University of Michigan.

LINDA FRANKEL received her doctorate in sociology from Harvard. Recently she has been a scholar-in-residence in Women's Studies at the University of North Carolina at Chapel Hill and is a consultant on curricular innovation. At Michigan she was a faculty member in the Residential College, taught in Women's Studies, and served as the first coordinator of FAIRteach. She co-authored (with Pauline Bart) *The Student Sociologist's Handbook*.

THOMAS J. GERSCHICK, a doctoral student in sociology at the University of Michigan, has taught extensively within the university and serves as Coordinator for Undergraduate Programs in the Department of Sociology.

LORRAINE GUTIÉRREZ is an Assistant Professor in the School of Social Work at the University of Washington. She has written several articles on issues of the empowerment of women and people of color.

CHRISTINA JOSÉ is an Assistant Professor in the School of Education at Eastern Michigan University and has taught in the Psychology Department there and in the Women's Studies Program at the University of Michigan.

LEWIS J. KLEINSMITH is the Arthur P. Thurnau Professor of Biology at the University of Michigan. He is a Guggenheim Fellow and a member of the American Society for Cell Biology, the American Society of Biological Chemists, and the Society for Development Biology.

ANN E. LARIMORE is a Professor of Geography and Women's Studies at the University of Michigan. As a founding faculty member of the Residential College, she has been teaching in alternative modes for twenty-five years.

EDITH A. LEWIS received her M.S.W. from the University of Minnesota and her Ph.D. in Social Welfare from the University of Wisconsin-Madison. She is currently an Associate Professor of Social Work and holds an adjunct position in the Women's Studies Program at the University of Michigan. She is also a core faculty member of the Program for Conflict Management Alternatives at the university.

ANDREA MONROE-FOWLER received her M.A. in Educational Leadership from Eastern Michigan University. She is currently the Diversity Programs Coordinator in the Office of Minority Affairs at the University of Michigan.

ELIANA MOYA-RAGGIO directs the Intensive Spanish Program in the Residential College. Originally from Chile, she studies and researches the culture, history, and literature of Latin America, especially of women from the Southern Cone.

PATRICIA MYERS is a doctoral student in the American Culture Program and a Graduate Certificate student in the Women's Studies Program at the University of Michigan. Her work examines the intersections of gender, sexuality, and race.

BIREN A. NAGDA is a doctoral student in the joint program in Social Work and Organizational Psychology and is a Fellow and Research Associate in the Program on Intergroup Relations and Conflict and the Pilot Program.

ROBERT M. ORTEGA is an Assistant Professor of Social Work at the University of Michigan. He specializes in group intervention research and Latino populations.

DAVID SCHOEM received his M.Ed. from Harvard and his Ph.D. from the University of California-Berkeley and is currently Assistant Dean for Undergraduate Education in the College of Literature, Science, and the Arts at the University of Michigan. He is also a lecturer in Sociology and a core faculty member in the Program for Conflict Management Alternatives. His most recent publication is *Inside Separate Worlds: Life Stories of Young Blacks, Jews, and Latinos*.

LUIS F. SFEIR-YOUNIS received his doctorate in sociology from the University of Michigan. He teaches courses in Intergroup Relations and Conflict in the Pilot Program at the university.

KRISTINE SIEFERT received her M.S.W. from the University of Michigan and her Ph.D. and M.P.H. from the University of Minnesota. She is Associate Professor of Social Work at the University of Michigan, where she also teaches in the School of Public Health.

GEN STEWART received her Master of Public Health degree from the University of Michigan in 1989. She works as a health education coordinator at the University of Michigan Health Service.

RALPH D. STORY is Associate Director for Administration of the Comprehensive Studies Program at the University of Michigan. His poetry and articles have appeared in *Confrontation: A Journal of Third World Literature*, *CLA Journal*, *The Journal of Popular Literature*, *Black American Literature Forum*, and *The Black Scholar*.

SHARON E. SUTTON, an Associate Professor of Architecture at the University of Michigan, is also coordinator of the Urban Network, a national program that involves elementary and middle school children, teachers, and parents in learning about, and improving, their neighborhoods.

JIM TOY received his M.S.W. from the University of Michigan and is Co-coordinator of the Lesbian-Gay Male Programs Office at the university. He has served as trainer and coordinator of programs on social justice and the rights of lesbians and gay men.

JOSEPH VEROFF is a Professor of Psychology and Research Scientist in the Survey Research Center at the University of Michigan. He is also a Fellow in the American Psychological Association and the American Psychological Society.

K. SCOTT WONG is currently an Assistant Professor in the History Department of Williams College in Williamstown, Massachusetts. He recently received his doctorate in history from the University of Michigan and taught at the University of California, Santa Barbara, as a Dissertation Fellow.

XIMENA ZÚÑIGA received her Magister in Education from the Universidad Catolica de Chile and her Ph.D. in Education from the University of Michigan. She is project director of the Intergroup Relations and Conflict Program at the University of Michigan and has also taught in the Pilot Program, Residential College, and Women's Studies Program.